Jackie

This is [illegible]

to pass [illegible]

a gift from your parents.

So Enjoy.

P.S. Thank you for passing

Snapshots - A Life Revisited

to Dr. Rudy! (your doctor)

Always

James Hayes

SNAPSHOTS II

Navigating the University Years

FRANK MARAJ

Order this book online at www.trafford.com
or email orders@trafford.com

Most Trafford titles are also available at major online book retailers.

© Copyright 2011 Frank Maraj.
All rights reserved. No part of this publication may be reproduced, stored in a retrieval system, or transmitted, in any form or by any means, electronic, mechanical, photocopying, recording, or otherwise, without the written prior permission of the author.

Editor and Co-author: Diana Maraj
Cover Design: Ron Hines and Dany Michaud

Printed in the United States of America.

ISBN: 978-1-4269-5322-4 (sc)
ISBN: 978-1-4269-5321-7 (hc)
ISBN: 978-1-4269-5323-1 (e)

Library of Congress Control Number: 2011902482

Trafford rev. 02/15/2011

 www.trafford.com

North America & international
toll-free: 1 888 232 4444 (USA & Canada)
phone: 250 383 6864 ♦ fax: 812 355 4082

Dedication

*Once again,
with love, I dedicate this book to my three children,
Trevor, Lee-Anne, and Dee-Dee,
my grandchildren, Jayden and Jasmine,
and to the memory of Ma.*

You are <u>still</u> my inspiration.

Acknowledgements

To all of my students—thank you for your continued inspiration.

To the many who have encouraged and even insisted that a sequel to Snapshots I be written; here is hoping that this project meets with your approval. My sincere thanks for your encouragement.

To *all* of my friends and family—I thank you for your abiding and valued support.

For transcribing my difficult handwriting into printed text, I deeply thank you:

Ravyn Bedard	Brittany Hayes	Ron Hines
Susan DeGagne	Lee-Anne Hines	Missy Woolsey
Kasey Hawrylak		

Thanks to my colleagues, and there are many, especially Tracy Treflin, for lending me support and expertise. How often have you rescued me?

To that long distance voice that has critiqued so much for so long. Special thanks,

Dee-Dee Maraj

Special thanks to my daughter, Lee-Anne, who helped out with her special talents and valued expertise. I still know your worth.

This work would not have been complete without my family. Thank you ever so much Ma and Pa, Clive, Dolly, Boysie, Paula, Pinky, Kay, Basdaye, Suresh and Kalie. You may not know it, but each one of you, in your own, unique way, has enriched my life.

With Gratitude

Diana

Once again…

*Thank you, Diana, my loving wife.
I appreciate your unwavering devotion to this project.*

*After completing the first book,
I was not sure we were up for the challenge of a second one.
Thank you for working alongside me in <u>this</u> project also.
Once again, you transformed my draft into a completed work.
Your dedication and spirit continues to enrich <u>our</u> work always.*

*Love,
Frank*

Author's Note

Did everything in *this* work occur exactly as recorded? I have once again attempted to capture "life as it happened." I may have taken certain liberties and at times I might have unwittingly dramatized certain incidents to make the story interesting.

Not all the stories are in chronological order, yet I have attempted to give some logical order to the time of the occurrences. In some instances, fictitious names have been used.

If at any time throughout this project I have appeared unduly critical, then once more, I ask for your understanding. It is not my intention to offend anyone.

Above all, I hope this work is a good read.

PART I

Into Another World

1
Immigration

"Mr. Maraj, do you understand?"

An awkward silence ensued. Mentally and physically exhausted from the day's travel, I was unable to process the words just spoken by the immigration officer.

Over the last few days I had travelled from New York to Toronto visiting with family and friends; I had no real occasion to feel homesick or lonely. Landing at the airport in the Lakehead however, I was suddenly overcome with emotion. Trinidad, my native country, seemed millions of miles away. My head was spinning; my mind unfocused, I responded, "No, Sir, I am not sure I understand you."

"Mr. Maraj, let me inform you plainly. You are here in Canada on a student visa. This means that you are not allowed to work during the academic school year. That is the law. If you work, you would be violating the law. If you break the law and you are caught-*and you will be caught*-you will be *deported*-sent back to Trinidad."

Shivers ran up and down my spine; the mere idea that I could be deported brought with it images of shame and horror. To be deported meant that one had committed some unholy act and had brought shame and degradation, not only to oneself, but also to the country from which one came. The very idea of deportation threatened my inner peace.

It was painfully ironic that the customs officer should warn me against working during the school year, because it was precisely my *aim* to work during the school year. *How else was I to survive? I simply had to work, I must...*

My mind reeled; everything became a blur. Once more I heard the voice of the officer, "Now, Mr. Maraj, do you understand me?"

I reacted automatically and instinctively to this voice of authority. "Yes, Sir, I do." I barely managed to get the words out when satisfied, the officer stamped my passport.

The inscription on my passport now read: "Summer Employment authorized April 20, 1968."

That single entry stunned me and dashed my hopes for achieving success in Canada.

Short minutes ago, I had been so optimistic. I recalled being at peace just as the plane was about to land. I remembered thinking, "Canada, here I come." I felt that nothing could stop me from achieving my goals.

In a few short minutes, despair had set in; I knew that the officer was merely performing his duty. An air of professionalism was stamped in his every syllable. His uniform and badge spoke decidedly. There was no mistaking his message: *if I were to work I would be deported*.

I wondered, *Does this officer intend to make it his personal mission to keep tabs on me?* I realized that that was just my paranoia taking over my mind. All the same, I wondered, *Did he have to be so officious, so pointed? Could he not have simply smiled and said,* "Welcome, Frank Maraj."

Already I had misgivings. I found myself asking, *"Canada, should I have come?*

2

Registration and Accommodation: What a Reality....

Still at the airport, I made my way to the baggage area. After claiming my large but inexpensive suitcase, which was now somewhat damaged, I headed for the arrival lounge. I briefly surveyed the area hoping to find a representative from the university. I had been led to believe that someone from there would be on hand to greet me. I saw no one fitting that description. No eyes but mine scanned the room; no eyes but mine looked anxiously and beseechingly around. Meanwhile, the other passengers had all but disappeared and I was alone.

Sometimes being alone is a good thing; this was not one of those times. I felt keenly the absence of a single solitary welcoming face. I felt empty and somewhat abandoned. I parked myself on an orange coloured sofa with aluminum legs; it reminded me of Trinidad and I was happy to see something familiar. The sofa was near the exit area and it was there that I awaited the arrival of the university representative. As I looked around I thought to myself, "*Why is everyone so preoccupied? Where is that laidback attitude that characterized the people at Piarco airport back home?*"

One thing was perfectly clear: I was no longer in Trinidad. Yet, I still had this desire for someone, for *anyone* to say welcome. How could I think otherwise? "*Well,*" I reasoned, "*if there is no one here to greet me, then I may as well greet myself.*" I did just that.

"*So this is Canada. Welcome Frank Maraj.*" Although the greeting took place in my mind only, it made me feel better.

Just then a cab driver entered the area. It appeared that he was looking for a particular passenger. He paced the floor restlessly for a few moments but then decided to leave.

When he noticed me seated and alone, he paused.

"Say, you need a ride?"

"No thanks."

"Where are you going? Maybe I can give you a lift, seeing I don't have a fare. How about it, happy to offer you a ride?"

"Sorry, I am waiting for a representative from Lakehead University to pick me up. But, I do appreciate the offer."

"The university is on my way. You sure? No trouble at all."

He was so friendly; he deserved to be properly acknowledged. I stood up, walked over to him and shook his hand. As we shook hands, I introduced myself, "I am Frank Maraj."

"So glad to meet you Frank. I am Lewis. I work for Roach's Taxi. Where are you from?"

"Trinidad."

"Trinidad? Man you are a long way from home. Good luck."

He turned around to leave. He was at the exit door when he returned and affirmed, "Frank, excuse my manners. Welcome to Canada, and a big welcome to the Lakehead."

Then Lewis was gone. Once again I sat down overcome with emotion at this unexpected turn of events; was it not just a moment ago that I was bemoaning the fact that something was missing since I landed in Canada? And then, this cabdriver shows up from nowhere and not only *says* welcome but makes me *feel* welcome.

Some time elapsed and a young man entered the airport. He was holding a sign above his head. It read: "Frank Maraj."

Yes, that's me, Frank Maraj, not Frankie Boodram. Yes, I must remember that now and forever I am Frank Maraj. I made my way over to where the young man was standing and identified myself.

"I am Frank Maraj."

"Good. Come along."

There were two of them. Neither one of them seemed to notice that I was struggling with two heavy suitcases and a small briefcase. They chatted amicably to one another as they made their way to the parking lot some distance away. The driver got in and closed his door. The other stood at the side of the car near the open door, awaiting me. I was still some good distance away. No offer was made to relieve me of any part of my burden. When I reached the car, the young man kindly folded the front seat forward so that I could squeeze myself and my three pieces of luggage into the back seat of the compact two-door Volkswagen. I had not completely adjusted myself and my luggage when the car sped off.

I wondered why there had been no attempt at an introduction. I let that thought go for the moment.

We travelled but briefly on a divided highway. Soon we came to a main street where many businesses occupied both sides. Then the driver made a left turn at a set of lights and occupied the right side of the road. I was about to scream, *You are on the wrong side of the road*, when I realized that all the other vehicles ahead of us were on the same side. This was my first real introduction to North American driving. I admit that this was a little disconcerting for me having just arrived from that part of the world where it is customary to drive on the left. When I visited England, there was no need for adjustments for there too, drivers drove on the left.

Suddenly my luggage became dislodged as we encountered a rough patch on the road. The three pieces showed no regard for my person as they bounced liberally around me and pounded me repeatedly. When I took the time to look at the road, I was horrified to discover that we were travelling on gravel. I could not believe that I would encounter a gravel road en route to a university in Canada. I was shocked. My companions in the front seat carried on as if nothing had happened. The two of them were totally oblivious to me and to my plight. For all I knew, they had forgotten that I even existed.

I wanted to yell, *Hello, I am here, talk to me!*

I remained quiet. They continued their friendly discourse.

After a while I decided to make the first move. I asked, "Are we headed to the university? Perhaps we could stop for a coffee?" I had hoped that they would understand the significance of my gesture and begin to interact with me. Alas, it was not to be. They responded to my request quite dismissively.

"Sorry, no time for that. We'll be there soon."

I held my peace as the two continued their exclusive discourse. I was not offended by their action; I was simply disappointed. I did not understand this culture. I decided that it was futile to attempt to communicate with them. *What a curious way to begin a new life in a new country.*

Soon we arrived at the university and I was deposited at the entrance of a building. As I reached in to grab my three pieces of luggage, I was informed that they would be back in two hours to pick me up. With that brief assurance, I made my way to admissions.

Signs were posted directing students to the registration area. It was extremely crowded and soon I was lost in a sea of people. Students were lined up everywhere and I felt totally out of place lugging my huge arsenal of belongings.

I decided to step out and blaze my own trail. My efforts were rewarded when I found an information centre. I waited in line to speak to the young lady who appeared quite accommodating. After a while the line became shorter. Finally, it was my turn. My face was full of hopeful expectation. When she looked up and saw me she smiled. There was not a single hint of the officiousness that had plagued my first encounter with Canadian authority. An air of natural accommodation accompanied her speech.

"How may I help you?

At last, a beacon of hope.

I showed her my university documents and my three pieces of luggage. She looked at me and my luggage for a moment and responded, "Mr. Maraj, I could hang on to your suitcases until you complete registration."

I was more than a little relieved and grateful for her offer of assistance with respect to my cumbersome luggage. The greater, and for me, more pressing problem of registering remained unsolved. I thanked her for her offer and then queried, "But, how do I register? What do I do? Where do I go? There are so many lines. Which one do I join?"

The young lady must have been quite accustomed to such panic for she was completely unflappable. She responded with calm assurance. "Mr. Maraj, these lines are not long at all. Two weeks ago you should have seen the lines. They were huge. Now let's see. You are in the Arts programme and the line you want is there—the sign that reads: First Year Arts Programme. Start there and you will be fine."

Her calm manner found its way directly into my blood. Instantly, I was relieved. I felt that now I had a means to navigate my way through the sea of registration. I charted my course and soon took my proper place in line. When I reached the front of the line, I faced the further challenge of filling out multiple forms, asking and answering questions. The ordeal seemed endless. At last I was finished; I had registered.

That was just step one, however. The next task proved to be even more taxing. I was directed to the finance office. While waiting in another long line, I had the additional burden of fighting fatigue. Real physical collapse felt only moments away.

Finally, I came face to face with the clerk. I handed her my documents. She quickly perused my course selection and flatly declared, "That will be five hundred and fifty dollars." She looked at me and then added, "In Canadian funds."

Mustering up all my courage, I spoke as though I was unshaken. "Yes, yes of course."

My voice did not betray the magnitude of my terror. I was completely traumatized. My total finances amounted to just less than six hundred dollars Canadian. If I were to give her the full amount, I would have less than fifty dollars to see me through for the balance of the year. I saw my dreams crumble.

I thought that I had planned out this first year so very carefully before I embarked on my journey to Canada. I had counted on having the ability to work while going to school to see me through financially.

My thoughts immediately returned to the immigration officer and his stern warning: *If you work you will be breaking the law and if you break the law you will be in violation...and you will be deported.* I shivered at the mere thought of deportation. I wondered: *Was this it? Does my road end here? Is this financial dragon unconquerable?* Fear washed over me. The voice of the clerk brought me back to the present.

"Sir, that will be five hundred and fifty dollars," she repeated.

I searched for my voice.

"But I don't have all…" The words were thick and seemed to stick to the roof of my mouth. My voice must have betrayed my desperation for the clerk sensed my need for compromise.

"Sir, you can make alternative arrangements."

Had I just been granted a reprieve or was this merely a postponement of the inevitable? The only thing that I knew for sure was that for that one fleeting moment, hope was alive.

I jumped with gratitude at the lifeline that had just been thrown my way. Words of thanks gushed from my lips. "Thank you, Miss. Thank you so very…" I never even got to finish my sentence before she interrupted with, "But not here."

"Where?" I inquired hastily.

She wasted no time in pointing out a distant location. "That line over there."

My eyes followed her hand gesture. I don't know if it was my extreme fatigue that blurred my focus or if that new line really was the longest one that I had encountered that day. All I could do was stare dumbly at it. I showed no sign of moving.

"Sir, you do have to move along. There are many others waiting."

Once more, I made my way to the end of one more line. My one consolation was that I was not carrying my three pieces of luggage. Fatigue was still plaguing me however and I was desperate for rest. At some point, I lost complete track of time and drifted off while still standing in line. Imagine my surprise when I opened my eyes and found myself next in line to receive help. The clerk's voice brought me out of my reverie and once again I was face to face with my financial reality. The young woman, however, was not an obstacle to be overcome; she was my lifeline.

She asked me some questions about my finances. After some brief calculations, she concluded that I could pay two hundred and fifty dollars now, then after the first semester, I would pay the remaining balance.

So that was it. I had a one semester reprieve. I simply nodded my head in agreement. I was too tired to express anything remotely resembling joy. The clerk then indicated that I must now proceed to the Alma Mater Society and pay my social fees.

Social fees? What are social fees? I wondered.

This piece of information was both confusing and devastating.

Nevertheless, I dragged my reluctant body to the end of the next new line. Although it too was extremely long, it seemed to move along at a very reasonable pace and in no time at all I was at the front of the line. I soon discovered why this line seemed so efficient. At this office you accomplished one thing only: the payment of the fee. No discussion. No negotiation.

When I discovered that the cost of the fee was fifty dollars, I weakened. The brief confidence that had been restored regarding the viability of my financial state here in Canada, was depleting rapidly. My mind quickly started to determine the amount of money I would have left for general living expenses. It took only a few seconds to realize that I would not have enough money to support me for the rest of the year. Regardless of these facts, the fees had to be paid. I paid.

Just as I turned away from paying the fees, I overheard one student say to another student that his rent had cost fifty dollars, and that he had not yet purchased the books for his courses. The student's words were a harbinger of doom.

BOOKS.

I still had to purchase my books! Any remaining bravado and confidence was shed. I tried desperately to hoard my remaining two hundred dollars. That was all that I had left; it was upon that two hundred dollars that my future rested. I decided to defer book purchasing for another day. All I wanted to do now was sleep. That was what I needed most. My financial battle had been forcefully waged. While not yet a victor, I settled for a truce. I determined that a retreat was in order; this battle could be resumed another day.

I headed back to the entrance to await my two new "friends." They were there waiting for me. Too tired to talk, I forced a smile of acknowledgement and climbed into the back of the vehicle. No sooner had I sat down, when the driver inquired, "Where are your suitcases?"

I had forgotten them; more evidence of my fatigue. I don't know how I was able to muster up enough strength to return to the admissions desk and retrieve the suitcases, but I did. After loading them beside me, I once again resumed my all too familiar cramped position in the back seat of that tiny Volkswagen.

"Where to?" asked the driver after I was settled.

"What do you mean?"

"Don't you know?"

"No."

"You have to tell us the address of your destination."

"I don't know. I thought you knew where I was staying."

The two looked at each other in bewilderment. It was now obvious that they had no idea that I had no accommodation and no place to go.

They both left the car and together went into the university. I decided to content myself with just sitting in the back seat, resting my head on my luggage. Soon they emerged waving a sheet of paper at me. On the paper was a list of addresses of possible accommodations.

We left the parking lot with a new mission. The two boys were optimistic. They began with the address closest to the university. No vacancy. Each and every other address on the list was visited with the same results. No vacancy. It was getting late and the boys advised me that they would begin the search again the next day. For tonight I would have to go to a motel.

My heart sank. *How was I to tell them that I didn't have money for a motel room?* I still had to purchase my books and who knows what else. I swallowed my pride and explained my predicament.

"You mean you cannot afford a motel room for the night?"

They turned away from me and talked in a low tone. I knew that they were discussing my situation. Occasionally their voices became animated. I overheard a word here and there "*for crying out loud*" and "*what kind of cheapskate is he*" and understood that they were frustrated by my plight. I felt that my dignity had been assaulted and I needed to address the young men directly.

"You need not struggle on my account. You have done so much for me already and I am so grateful. I am so tired. Would you take me to a motel please?"

They both turned and looked at me—confused. No one uttered a word. We drove off. We pulled up to a modest motel. No vacancy. Visits to two other motels had the same results.

We soon discovered that there was a special event happening in town and every available venue had already been booked.

In frustration, one of the boys yelled, "What are we supposed to do with him now?"

My heart sank. I prepared to come out of the car right there. My pride had been compromised once again. As I reached out to grab my luggage, the other young man turned to me and said, "I have an idea. Trust me; it will work."

We drove off. Voices ceased; the radio began playing a familiar piece: Eddy Arnold's, *Make the World Go Away*.

My sentiments exactly. Take this burden off my shoulders.

We drove to Fort William to the residence of the Catholic priests. I was confused. *What are they thinking?*

By now it was really late. I needed sleep. I prayed that this was the last trip of the night. Both boys got out of the car. Soon one returned and motioned for me to follow. I grabbed my bags. This time, my companion grabbed a suitcase. I was grateful for this small gesture of assistance. Once inside I was introduced to Father Lacey who greeted me warmly and explained, "Frank you can spend the night here, no problem. I have to be at the church early in the morning. I won't be here but Jim and Tommy will come and get you. Good luck. I'll show you to your room."

So those were their names, Jim and Tommy. Good to know.

Jim told me he would be back to get me by 9:00 am the next day. Soon I was all alone in a comfortable room and an inviting bed.

It had been a long day.

I must have been more tired than I realized because I barely had time to reflect on whether or not I had made the right decision in coming to Canada. The thought would have to await further examination. My bed beckoned.

What a curious destiny that brought me once again into the presence of a Catholic priest at whose home I would spend my very first night in Canada.

****

The next morning Jim and Tom arrived bright and early. Gone was the fatigue that we each endured the previous night. Replacing it was a renewed spirit of optimism. This was the day I was to find my new home in Canada. The task, however, proved far from simple. For hours we scoured the addresses reasonably close to the university. None yielded a positive outcome. We eventually had to expand our search to include areas that would require me to take a bus to get to and from school.

Tom tried his best to put a positive spin on this new reality. "Many students have to take the bus. Sometimes, the rent is cheaper the further you live from the university. We'll do our best to find you a place that is on a direct bus route. Okay?"

I nodded and smiled trying my best to mask the foreboding welling up inside. *How far would I have to travel? Would I have more expenses?* I banished those feelings and struggled to regain the optimism with which we had begun our day.

We visited four addresses without any success. Jim began to show frustration. Tom remained calm. Tom's calm focus proved to be a further inspiration for me as things became increasingly bleak. Most of the addresses had been available only hours before. No one could understand why there were suddenly none available. Tom decided to look down the list to areas that were the farthest from campus. His face lit up when he recognized one particular address.

He called out to Jim, "Let's go here. I am almost certain that it is still available and I know the family. I think Frank will fit in with them perfectly."

Jim voiced his agreement. "You know, Tom, I think you're right. Frank may have to take two buses, but it could work out very well. Let's get moving before somebody else snaps it up."

Instantly the car and its three occupants sped away on a new course. No one spoke as we snaked our way along a road which wound itself around the lake. Finally we arrived at the Hodder Avenue address where Tom exited the car alone. He knocked on the door. A lady answered. They spoke for a few minutes then Tom returned and invited us to come into the house.

Introductions were made. Tom started, "Frank, this is Mrs. Cloutier."

"Hello, Frank."

"Hello, Mrs. Cloutier."

"So, you are far away from home, from Trinidad."

"Yes."

"Do you come from a large family, by chance?"

"Yes, I have six sisters and three brothers."

"Well, you should feel right at home here. We are a large family too. Come, I will show you your room."

It was a reasonably sized room with twin beds. One was already claimed by another tenant. Mrs. Cloutier then asked, "Well, Frank, what do you think?"

The idea of sharing a room with a complete stranger startled me and caused me a moment's hesitation. Mrs. Cloutier's forthright manner and disarming personality invited my trust.

"Thank you Mrs. Cloutier, I love the room, but can I afford it?"

"Oh, yes, you can," she quipped. She told me the price which seemed steep but then added quickly that it also included my meals. I accepted.

Jim and Tom smiled. I could see that they were both relieved and genuinely pleased at the outcome. I recognized just how arduous a task they had undertaken on my behalf and I thanked them both.

Jim headed for the car. Tom stayed back. He had an intensity about him that I had not before noticed.

"Frank, you will be fine, here?"

"Yes."

"Frank, I wish to apologize for our behaviour yesterday. Jim and I meant no offence."

"Thank you, Tom. No offence taken. You found me a place to stay last night. I owe you a special thanks."

"May I ask you a personal question?"

"Yes."

"You said you could not afford a motel, yesterday…" An awkward silence ensued. Tom continued hesitantly but with a most respectful tone, "Well, Jim and I thought that people like you, you know, *Asians*, are academically strong and financially independent…"

"And you are wondering about my inability to pay for a motel. Let's put it this way. I am from Trinidad, a small country off the coast of South America. My roots are very humble. I am trying to make a go …. '

"We certainly made a mistake. We misjudged you. Sorry, Frank."

His candour gave me the courage to ask a question that had been plaguing me since last night. "Tom, may I ask you a question?"

"Certainly."

"What prompted you to take me to Father Lacey?"

"Let's say Father rescued me when I was headed in the wrong direction in life. I owe him so much. It is like he saved me from a kind of hell. Frank, are you Catholic?"

"I was born and raised a Hindu but I was educated in the Catholic school system. I even taught in the Catholic system for several years. While I have never officially converted, I do try to understand the dictates of Jesus."

Wow. So much information. What prompted me to say all that? What will Tom think now?

"Frank, I too am not a Catholic although I know that is what Father wants. But I am not sure about that. Yet, I fear that if I do not become a member of the faith I shall disappoint him. Anyway, I knew that Father would want to help me help you, and that is the reason I brought you to his place. Besides, even though I did not know you, I felt in that late hour last night that you needed, shall we say, a hand?"

"How perceptive you are Tom. Perhaps…"

Jim blew the horn of the car and Tom was gone. My thought remained unspoken. Perhaps it was what was meant to be. Tom's mission with me was completed. Gone, too, was some measure of my *'aloneness.'* Some part of Tom's story resonated in me. *Have we not struggled along similar paths?*

I headed back inside. I looked at Mrs. Cloutier. There was something about her that seemed to suggest that at last I had found my new Canadian home.

3

My First Sunday

Sunday finally arrived. All week long the Cloutier family had been bragging about Sunday and what a special treat Sunday dinner was going to be.

After having spent a week in this home, I had become accustomed to the household and bus routines.

To Canadian meals, on the other hand, I had not yet become accustomed. Since I did not eat either pork or beef Mrs. Cloutier was constantly searching for inventive ways to substitute lamb or chicken for me. She was certainly up to the challenge. Every day her gourmet expertise rose to the occasion and every day, my dietary needs were expertly accommodated. A good dash of Tabasco sauce was often all that was required to boost the flavor level to satisfy my Trinidadian palate.

On Friday Mr. Cloutier announced that Sunday had been confirmed as his day off and that he *would* be preparing supper.

One of the children excitedly quipped, "We can't wait. We love it when you cook your feast."

Everyone else added their positive comments, and I too began anticipating Sunday.

In Trinidad Sunday was a special day too. Ma and the girls would spend the whole morning preparing a veritable feast for lunch. A variety of Chinese and West Indian dishes would ultimately end up on the table tempting us with their intoxicating aromas. The more I reminisced, the more I longed to experience the great feast promised by Mr. Cloutier.

On Saturday I had gone for a walk. I wanted to explore and to familiarize myself with the surrounding area. I found a grocery store and went inside. I was looking for any products reminiscent of the Caribbean, particularly my part of the Caribbean—Trinidad. I discovered no such items. My eyes scanned the produce section looking for the fruits that I had enjoyed as a boy. There were none. No Mangoes. No Chennet. No plums. Nothing looked familiar, and a wave of homesickness threatened to wash over me. But, as soon as I spotted the bananas and oranges, that feeling vanished.

I purchased an orange and went outside to enjoy my treat. My taste buds could hardly wait for me to bite into it and reward them with a huge burst of familiar flavours. I bit in. My taste buds were disappointed; the flavor was most foreign. I realized right then that if I were to enjoy Canadian fruit, it was going to require a great deal of adjustment on my part. (And just maybe a sprinkling of salt and hot pepper.)

Putting aside my disappointment, I went back into the store and walked down the aisle which had various jams on display. I read every label on every jar. There was raspberry, strawberry, peach, marmalade and even blueberry jam. I saw no label announcing guava jam. Guava jam had been my all time favourite jam in Trinidad. When I asked the grocer, he informed me that he had never even heard of guava jam.

That feeling of homesickness that I had managed to avoid earlier, cascaded down on me. Determined to escape it, once again I paced up and down every aisle in the store hoping to find something, anything to remind me of Trinidad. I found nothing. I decided to retreat to the Cloutiers' and indulge myself in my homesickness.

Sunday dawned and I was energized. Today at last was the feast of which Mr. Cloutier spoke and I, for one, could not wait. After a modest breakfast, Barry, the oldest of the four children, asked if I would accompany him on a hike around Boulevard Lake; how could I refuse?

We headed off to the lake. What a beautiful sight! The rocks bordering the river looked as if they had been guided there deliberately by some unknown hand. The total effect was breathtaking. And it was just minutes from home. I took comfort in knowing that I could enjoy this view any time I wanted and feel renewed.

Barry and the gang, having grown up here, seemed oblivious to its charm. They began running and jumping over the rocks. I was content to merely take in the sights. The boys kept glancing at me and I sensed that they expected me to follow in their footsteps. I did not think that I was up to the task.

Barry's comments led me to believe that he thought that I was some kind of natural athlete and that I had slowed my pace to accommodate them. Nothing could have been further from the truth. My slightness of build might have given me an athletic appearance but I was far from athletic. My years of teaching and tutoring left me seriously impoverished in the athletic department. In fact, if the truth be told, I was having the utmost difficulty negotiating the many stones and boulders along the banks.

No matter how hard I tried, I fell behind my adventurous companions. Each step seemed exponentially more tedious than the one before. The teenagers seemed to float over the rocks. I, on the other hand, had to make a conscious decision with each and every step. *Do I jump over the rock and step into the mud or do I risk slipping off a wet rock?* Every step felt like an exam. The beaches of Trinidad were sandy and smooth—nothing like this rugged terrain. Because the guys thought that I was being deliberately slow on their account, they continued to urge one another to 'pick up the pace' to accommodate me. Their consideration threatened to be my ruination. I thought I was going to die from exhaustion. Some time later the ordeal ended and I was spared the humiliation of collapse. I made a mental note to avoid such family outings.

We returned to the house. Although it was now past noon, there was a noticeable absence of activity in the kitchen. *Was I missing something?*

Then Mrs. Cloutier explained, "Frank, we take it easy on Sundays. If you are hungry, have some toast and jam. But don't eat too much. You don't want to be filled up for supper. It will be early today. You are in for a special treat."

Assured by her words, I observed her caution and had only a light snack. By mid-afternoon I was famished. From time to time I would inspect the kitchen; still no activity. *What was I missing? Aha! They are ordering supper in. That's it. I bet it is Chinese food. I love Chinese.*

Confident that I had solved the problem, I determined to be patient. Contentment would follow in about an hour or so when we all would be feasting.

Then the thought hit me, *Could I wait that long?* I decided that I needed a distraction. I went to my room to study. I felt that I could now get some studies done because I had reconciled the apparent contradiction of an inactive kitchen with a pending feast.

Alone in my room, I was unable to settle down to my studies as I had intended. My mind drifted to Trinidad and a melancholy seized me. Today, being Sunday, I would have been engaged in some pleasant activity with my friends but I would always endeavour to make it home for Sunday dinner.

Even though I was hundreds of miles away from home, I was not about to forget my island. I knew that I was here for just a period of time. *Yes, I was simply on loan to Canada for a few years. No, I must not think in terms of years, rather I must think months. That will make it much easier to bear the sadness. I anticipate that soon I will be back in Trinidad once again.* There, my spirits were lifted and I began to focus on my studies.

Some time later, I returned to the living room and discovered that there was still no evidence of any action in the kitchen. This confirmed my theory that supper was being ordered in.

It was past 4:00 before Mrs. Cloutier made her way to the dining room to begin setting the table. Sunday style. Everything from the main course plate to the cups and saucers matched. *Yes, supper was on the way.*

Then came the official announcement. *Dinner's ready.* Everyone scrambled to the table.

But, where was supper?

There was nothing but the dishes on the table. And there was no food on the kitchen counters or in the oven.

Then Mr. Cloutier entered the dining room. He was carrying an enormous silver platter that had an equally impressive silver cover over it—hiding the contents and thus adding to the already escalating anticipation.

I was already envisioning the lavish Chinese dish simmering beneath the cover. I was ready to indulge my appetite and I was quite prepared to treat myself to a most generous serving.

I glanced over at Mr. Cloutier. He was smiling as he placed the platter at the head of the table and took his seat. No one was permitted to have anything until Mr. Cloutier offered up the meal. The children were full of praise for their father. They knew exactly what to expect and they were primed. "Isn't this gorgeous? Oh thank you, Pop. We love it, just love it."

Then with the grace and style befitting a monarch, Mr. Cloutier removed the cover to reveal a platter full of… **corn**. There was nothing on that platter but boiled corn.

I screamed silently, *What was this? Some cruel joke? Where was the rest of the supper?*

I must compose myself. Perhaps I am overreacting. This is just an appetizer; the main course is yet to come. I just have to be patient.

By now everyone had passed their plates to the head of the table and had been served. All were heartily engaging with their corn. Mr. Cloutier urged me to pass my plate. I obliged. I was just going through the motions.

I didn't really want the corn. I wanted the main course. I took one piece when it was offered just to be polite. It was lovely and I said as much when I was asked how I liked it. My response seemed to please the family. By now, everyone was having seconds and thirds. When asked, I declined any further helpings. I did not want to fill up on corn. I chose to patiently await *supper*.

There was but one cob of corn remaining on the platter. Mr. Cloutier offered it to me.

"Frank, have the last one. We don't have any more."

"I am okay for now," I responded still wondering when the main course would be delivered.

Mr. Cloutier looked at me as he smiled and bit into the last piece.

The children then began to remove the plates. Barry reached out for my plate and said, "Sure hope you love apple pie and ice cream."

What is he saying? You can't have apple pie and ice cream before supper? Something is wrong here.

Finally everything began to make sense. Barry's words jolted me out of my confusion. The naked truth washed over me; supper was over. The boiled corn *was* the long awaited treat and I had had precious little of it.

Sadness settled in my spirit. A deepening disappointment engulfed my mind and I was unable to claim my share of the magnificent dessert as quickly as the others. I had a really difficult time truly understanding that there was no more supper to come. The pie really was delicious but it did little to assuage my disappointment. Soon, dessert too was finished and we were ushered from the table. Mr. and Mrs. Cloutier and I retired to the living room while the children took care of dishes.

After the dishes were done the rest of the family joined us in the living room. They were still raving about the excellent supper. I could not share in their contented chatter for I was starving. I needed something to eat—something of substance. So consumed was I by my hunger that I could not focus on their conversation.

"Please excuse me, Mr. and Mrs. Cloutier, I think that I would like to go for a walk. I shouldn't be too long. I would like to check out the neighbourhood."

"Good idea, Frank," Mr. Cloutier responded. "Do you want me to come with you?"

"No, Dad, I will go with Frank. You relax," interrupted Barry.

"I want to come too," added another voice. "Mom and Dad, you stay. The rest of us will go with Frank. Right, Frank? You want us to come?"

No, you cannot come with me, was my silent response. But I had to think quickly, "Would you, this one time, let me go by myself? It is so good for all of you to be together."

"But, Frank, we want to be with you. We don't want you to be all alone. You might become sad, and... "

Mrs. Cloutier came to my rescue. "Let Frank be. The walk will be good for him."

"Thank you, everyone. I just want you to know that you all have done so much to make feel at home."

I quickly left. I walked north on Hodder Avenue. If my memory served me correctly, there was a restaurant not too far away. Within minutes I was standing in front of the restaurant. It was open. I entered. No sooner had I seated myself at an empty table when a waitress appeared and handed me a menu. Pleased that I did not have to wait, I quickly scanned the menu. One dish stood out immediately—*Hot Chicken Sandwich.*

I could picture it already: spicy hot chicken, roasted and succulent, surrounded by a bed of colourful vegetables. Yes, that was it. It would more than make up for the earlier disappointment. I ordered. I hoped it would not take too long to prepare.

While waiting for my meal to arrive, I took a moment to check out the restaurant. There were not many customers. The jukebox filled the room with music as a few teenagers sipped their floats or drank coffee.

In almost no time, the young waitress returned to my table and placed before me a plate containing two slices of white bread. In between the bread was some sort of meat. A small clump of mashed potatoes hovered near the bread. All were saturated with a thick brown liquid. No aroma accompanied the meal. As hungry as I was I did not rush to satisfy my appetite. I took my fork hesitantly. I managed to extract a small serving and put it in my mouth. It tasted as bland as it looked. I could not bring myself to eat it. I stared disappointedly at my plate.

The waitress came by and asked, "Sir, how is everything?"

"Miss, I think there has been some mistake in my order?"

"What mistake, Sir?"

"I ordered *hot* chicken. This is not the hot chicken I ordered."

"Sir, this *is* hot chicken," she affirmed. "Is there a problem?"

Not wishing to make a fuss over my first restaurant meal in Canada, I stammered, "N..no problem."

Yet, there was a problem; I was still so very hungry. Furthermore, I was completely unable to appease my appetite. The day, which had begun with such promise, met with disappointment at every turn. If ever there was one single moment in my life that marked how much I missed my family, this moment would be it. A thought that came immediately to my mind, *Yo go cry blood*. That Trinidadian expression captured completely the depth of the despair I felt at that moment.

The waitress smiled as she placed the bill on the table completely oblivious to my state of mind. I looked blankly at the bill; I knew I had to pay it. If I had been able to enjoy even one small portion of the meal, it would have taken some of the sting out of the situation. I could ill afford the meal in the first place. To now be required to pay for something from which I derived no benefit, pained me to the core. Nevertheless, I paid the bill and even left a little something for the waitress. She would never suspect that I was a miserable soul missing my family, missing my familiar cuisine, and missing my culture on that very first Sunday in Canada.

Reflections

That night I was unable to sleep. Recollections of the past week, my very first week in Canada, occupied my mind. Foremost, I realized that I was now a minority in a sea of white. I did, however, notice a very few students, who were like myself. I took a secret comfort from their presence. Seeing them made me feel less alone. I never anticipated that I would ever live in an exclusively white Canadian community. Nor did I ever think that my very first home in Canada would be white. The realization that that was exactly what was happening to me suddenly scared me.

Living thousands of miles away from home, surrounded by strangers and feeling desperately alone at times consumed me. I lay on my bed wallowing in my own sadness. A part of me was ready to return home and reclaim my former life. I was truly shocked at how much I missed the staff and students of St. Charles' High School. I questioned why I gave up such a good, comfortable life.

Then I remembered. A moment of clarity illuminated my dark world. I had come to Canada to become a qualified teacher at a respected Canadian university. I felt that my despondency would be temporary.

For now I cry; tomorrow I try.

4
A Chance Meeting

It happened only a few days after classes started at the university.

I was still classified as a novice when it came to taking public transportation. The bus that I caught at the university did not go to my home on Hodder Avenue in the Current River area. Its route terminated in front of the Prince Arthur Hotel in downtown Port Arthur. Students needing further transportation either to Current River or Fort William had to ask for a transfer ticket and make their way to the appropriate bus. I had to pay particular attention to make sure that I boarded the right bus. That is how I came to be standing outside the Prince Arthur Hotel in downtown Port Arthur and that is how I met Dot.

I watched as all the buses came and parked. I couldn't find the piece of paper on which I had written the correct information for my bus. I boarded a bus with some degree of hesitation and asked the lady standing near me if this was the bus headed for Hodder Avenue in Current River.

To my great relief she answered in the affirmative and added, "I live on Hodder Avenue too. What is the number of your house?"

When I told her, she explained that she lived a little further on down the street. She told me that I had nothing to worry about because she would tell me when my stop was coming up. Her friendly tone and assuring words relieved my anxiety. We chatted amicably for several minutes when I just happened to glance out the window and see the number of my house flash past. I had missed my stop. I immediately jumped up from my seat, said a hasty good-bye to the helpful lady, and got off when the bus stopped. I remembered my manners just as I was descending the steps and managed a quick wave in her direction. She did not return my wave and I noticed that she seemed quite perplexed at my conduct. Her eyes were open wide in stunned amazement.

I knew that I had passed my stop so I backtracked until I came to the correct number. Well, the number may have been right but the neighbourhood was all wrong. I was standing in front of a gas station. *Where was my house?* It seemed to have vanished into thin air. As I looked about, I noticed that the street was lined with businesses, not homes. The situation was quite perplexing. I was uncertain as to my next move. I decided to walk into the gas station. I felt totally stupid.

A young attendant greeted me and asked, "May I help you?"

Without thinking, I blurted out, "Yes. I am supposed to be living here… at this address."

"This is a gas station. You could not be living here. One of us is crazy and it ain't me. Are you sure you aren't living over there in that home?"

He pointed in a northerly direction as he stepped outside, "I am sure that is the place you *belong* in."

At that moment the phone rang. The attendant shook his head as he went in to answer the phone. I waited for him to return but he did not. I guess he was finished with me.

His strange remarks left me even more perplexed than before. As I stood there trying to figure where I was, a taxi stopped to let off a passenger.

I approached the driver and asked, "Can you help me?"

"What can I do for you?"

I told him the number I was seeking.

"Then you are at the correct address. It's right here."

"But I am supposed to be living at this number, and this is not my house. This is not where I live."

"What exactly is your address?"

I fumbled through my pockets and pulled out a wrinkled piece of paper. "Here it is."

"Well, there is your mistake. You are on Cumberland Street, not Hodder Avenue."

"What do you mean? How can that be?"

"Easy. Newcomers make this kind of mistake all the time. Cumberland Street ends where Hodder Avenue begins. It's one long street. Got it?"

"You are saying that I am not yet on Hodder, correct?"

"Yes, you got it."

Finally, I understood what had happened. I had panicked and got off too quickly. My thoughts went straight to the lady from the bus. *I wonder what she must think of me.* I felt so embarrassed.

Then the driver continued, "All you have to do is go back there to the bus stop and grab the next bus. It will pass right in front of your address. Easy."

"Thanks so much."

"What the heck," he began, then he motioned to the door. "Get in."

"How much is the…..?"

"It's on me, buddy, now hop in."

He opened the front door of the taxi and I entered. We had not travelled very far when I noticed the building to which the young gas station attendant referred. I asked the driver, "Could you tell me what that building is over there?"

"Hey, buddy. You don't want to go there, believe me. That's the Lakehead Psychiatric Hospital—otherwise known as the nut house. You and me never want to go there. Got it?"

I understood the cabbie. I took no offence at his remark and knew that he had intended none. My mind went to the young gas station attendant and his cutting remarks. *Had he meant to be offensive or merely sarcastic?* Perhaps I will never know.

There was only one thing of which I was certain. Thanks to the kindness of a complete stranger, I had been treated to my very first *complimentary* cab ride in Canada and to my second delightful encounter with the Roach's Taxi line of cabs.

Some days elapsed.

Then one day as I headed down the street, I happened upon a stereo and TV store. There, right on display in the front window was the largest coloured television set that I had ever seen. I *had* to go in.

While standing mesmerized in front of the television, a woman's voice interrupted my reverie.

"Sorry to bother you. Are you the person that I..."

I turned around. It was the lady from the bus! I was so happy to see her. This was my chance to make things right. "Yes, I remember you. I am so glad to finally see you again. I am Frank Maraj."

"And I am Dorothy Jensen," she returned. "Dot, for short. I can't tell you how happy I am to see you. That day on the bus... I was so worried..."

"I am sorry I caused you to worry."

"I told my family about you. Never mind all that. What are you doing right now? Are you headed home?"

"Yes, I am. And you?"

"As a matter of fact, I am heading home also. Shall we take the bus together?"

"Absolutely."

Together we boarded the bus. As the rush hour was over, we were able to sit together. Dot and I chatted with ease. Before we knew it, we were nearing my stop. Just as I was getting up from my seat, Dot asked, "Frank, I hope I am not too late asking you. Are you free for Thanksgiving? Could you come and have Thanksgiving dinner with us? It will be a simple affair."

"I would love to come."

"Great. Here is my address and phone number. See, I don't live far from you."

She had the address and phone number already written down on attractive stationery. *Did Dot have that all written up and waiting in her purse hoping to meet me?* She exuded such genuine kindness and warmth. She was forthright without being forward. I took to her instantly. The next stop was mine. As I alighted from the bus I wondered, *Was this lady destined to be my very first Canadian friend?* I looked at her once more and waved. I had been invited for Thanksgiving supper. I could hardly wait to meet Dot's family.

5
Thanksgiving

Thanksgiving weekend had finally arrived and I was excited. My landlady understood that I would not be having supper with her family but was happy that I had been invited out. Actually, it was my very first invitation since my arrival in Canada.

Now, it was time. I began to walk towards the Jensens'.

The air felt cool and crisp; much cooler than I had anticipated for such a bright and sunny day. I soon came to realize that I had not worn enough clothing to keep me warm in this weather. Funny thing about sunshine–it fools you. I see sunshine and I think the weather is warm. I couldn't get used to the idea that it could be very cold in spite of a brightly shining sun.

The nearer I came to the house, the more nervous I became. I did not know what to expect. I worried that my presence at Dot's home might create a problem. I worried that my not eating beef or pork had proven a hardship for my hostess.

I knocked on the front door. I waited. No answer. I knocked again. Still no answer. I could hear voices. *Why was no one coming to the door? Did I have the wrong number? No.* I checked several times. This was the correct address. Before I could knock a third time, a smiling Dot opened the door.

The living room was full of bodies. All were handsomely dressed in their Sunday best. All were smiling and chatting. Some had plates full to overflowing. Others were about to fill their plates. Some were sitting, while others were standing enjoying a beverage. Dot closed the door.

Then I noticed. No one had shoes on except for me. *Where were all the shoes?* I soon came to realize that I had already committed my first social *faux pas* of the day. I came to the front door. Everyone else had come through the side door entrance. I was very embarrassed by my mistake. I had inconvenienced more than one person by my action. I then realized that is why it took so long to answer the door. People were crushed for space in the living room and had set up chairs in front of the front entrance. Quickly, I removed my shoes lest I appear even more insensitive. The lush carpet completely embraced my feet. I do not recall experiencing anything so soft and plush in my life. I had some degree of difficulty maintaining my balance as Dot helped me manoeuver between the various pieces of furniture and bodies that were between us and her kitchen.

As we made our way through the throng of people, Dot announced, "Everyone, this is Frank Maraj."

"Hello, Frank."

"You will get to know each one gradually," Dot assured. "Come. Let's get you something to eat."

A veritable smorgasbord awaited in the kitchen.

Dot directed, "Frank, here is the turkey; here is the dark meat, and here is the white meat. And gravy. You'll just have to have it. And the veggies are there."

White meat, dark meat? What's that? And gravy, I did not see any gravy. There were so many dishes. Then Dot urged, "Help yourself, Frank," pointing to the cutlery.

Everything was so very elegant. I was so very nervous. This feast was fit for royalty. *What was I doing here? How could I presume to belong?* In spite of my misgivings, I reached out and claimed a plate and a knife and fork as Dot had directed. These were no ordinary dishes; they appeared to be tinted with gold. I filled my plate with food and returned to the living room. Someone had kindly set a chair out for me. *How does one eat when there is no table to rest one's food?* I looked around for cues. Everyone else seemed completely at ease balancing their plates on their laps and eating. Trying to mimic their actions, I sat down and carefully rested my plate on my lap. My knees started to shake. I fought hard to compose them. I examined the distance my hand would have to travel carrying a loaded fork from my knees to my mouth. The distance was intimidating. I was not as accomplished as I would have liked in the art of dining with knife and fork. I had mastered the basics only, and that was when a steady firm surface such as a table was available. I was now being required to use these utensils while balancing a plate on my nervous knees. *The child in me asked, Was I mad? What made me think that I could fit in?* I still had so much to learn.

I looked around. Smiles greeted me from every quarter. I knew that I wasn't being judged by anyone but I felt very self-conscious. Friendly eyes they were to be sure… but eyes all the same. Relief followed my first successful attempt at eating a piece of white meat. The taste was most strange to this Trinidadian palate and I thought that a few drops of Tabasco sauce would improve the flavor. (Sorry, Dot.) But, there was no such condiment in view and I was too embarrassed to ask. Next, I tried the 'gravy' thinking that perhaps it would give the meat a lift. It didn't. The gravy was unlike any I had tasted before. It looked wonderful. It was rich and brown. But, again, it lacked the element of spice. I realized that perhaps it was going to take some time to adjust my palate to Canadian cuisine. I gave up trying to eat any more of the meat and concentrated my efforts on the salads and vegetables. Their flavours were universally safe. Then Dot introduced me to a favourite Canadian dessert: cherry pie and ice cream. I am not ashamed to admit that I returned to the dessert tray several times and sampled several other delightful offerings. When Dot's husband Ray, invited me to try a piece of his favourite cheesecake, I willingly obliged. My shyness and nervousness seemed to have evaporated. Ice cream has that effect on me.

Even though I was not able to enjoy the turkey, I certainly appreciated and enjoyed the many other dishes. I understood why everyone raved about the marvelous supper. But, for me, there was something even more fascinating and more profoundly interesting than the food. It was the people gathered in the home; it was the loving family who opened their home to me, a veritable stranger. And, most of all, it was Dot. Dot with her beautiful bright eyes and loving expression. Dot, with her open heart, made me feel welcome. Dot's mom, Mrs. Vester, also made me feel at home. Dot and Ray's three children expressed a keen interest in learning about Trinidad and about me. It was not long before we were all just chatting. The children were not shy about asking all kinds of questions and I took great satisfaction in answering. I began to relax and started to feel a sense of identification that I could not explain. All I knew for sure was that this family made me feel good.

At one point, Dot's mother gently pulled me aside and whispered, "Frank, I don't live very far. I'm just around the corner on Dacre Street. Come see us soon. The twins would love it; so would Billy. It's been so nice to meet you!"

Mrs. Vester's invitation signaled acceptance. Ray reinforced this sense when he remarked, "Frank, it was good to meet you. How do you feel about sports? I am a sports enthusiast and I have my retreat in the basement. How would you like to see it?"

I followed this gentle man downstairs. The first thing that caught my eye was his giant television set. I had never seen a screen so large.

"You like football, Frank?"

"Do I like football? I grew up with football."

"If I'm not mistaken, there's a game on right now. Let's take a look. I'm anxious to see the score."

I was mesmerized by the stunning coloured images on the giant screen. Ray sat on the sofa and directed me to a comfortable armchair.

Ray was excited. His team was winning. "Isn't this just great football, Frank?"

What football, Ray? That is not football. It is nothing like football. Everything about it is wrong. Football players don't dress like that. No contact is allowed. You can't pick up the ball like that with your hands. And the ball... it's not even round. This isn't football. My protests were made silently and only to myself. Actually, I was anxious to watch a game of football on this huge coloured TV set. This would be my first ever game on TV. To Ray I merely commented, "Are you going to put the football game on? What channel is it on?"

"What do mean Frank? This is football. It's on now. This *is* the football game."

"Ray, excuse me please, but this game is not football. It has to be something else."

We sat in awkward silence for a moment. Suddenly, Ray's hearty laugh broke the silence and a broad smile lit up his face.

"Frank, you must be talking about soccer. You call it football in Trinidad, right? Well, here, football is a little different game. Sorry it's not the game you were expecting. Maybe we should head upstairs, okay?"

Upstairs everyone was waiting, wondering what had happened to the two of us. Dot's mom was about to leave and was anxious to say her farewells. As she did so, she reiterated her previous invitation. As I prepared to leave, by the *side* door, Ray, too, extended an invitation for a return visit. Dot overheard Ray's remarks and added, "Frank, Ray must like you. He doesn't give out such invites very often. He means it. And I want you to come and see us too. We loved having you."

As I walked home, I was reminded of one of my life dreams. I remembered wanting to expand my horizons and experience life in another country. And, here I was… in Canada, doing just that—experiencing another culture. I recognized that if I were to be successful here, I would need to adapt to and absorb some of the aspects of Canadian life. I learned that Canadians are open and accepting too. They want to learn about me, and my country, and my culture, just as I wanted to understand them, and their country, and their culture. I did not have to choose between two life styles. I was not torn. I did not have to abandon all that had made me, me; I was not being asked to give up my identity. I was simply being required to open myself up to new experiences, new ways of being in the world. I rationalized that some day these experiences in Canada would serve me well in some capacity after I returned to Trinidad.

Little did I know that Destiny had other plans. For now I was happy and excited. Had I not just found my first Canadian friends?

6
Bleak November

Frank McG and I shared a room at the Cloutiers'. We were two Franks sharing the same accommodations. We could not have been more different. The only thing we truly had in common was our first name. Frank McG was extremely social; he hardly missed an event at the university. I, on the other hand, avoided social functions. I avoided them, not because I was antisocial, but because I suffered financial woes.

Frank loved to go out. He was forever inviting me to go with him. But, I had to refuse his invitations. I could not afford to be foolish with even one penny. Most of the time, Frank McG took my rejections in good stride. Today, things were different. Today he seemed so very serious and concerned as he approached me. He told me about a dance happening there on the week-end and he wanted me to go out and meet *girls*.

Frank McG did not know my situation. There was so much to consider. So many expenses were attached to attending any extra activities. First, there was the cost of the dance itself. Then, I had to consider the cost of transportation to get to the university. Add to that the need to appear social and have some type of beverage. There was just no way that I should even be thinking of such frivolities. I would literally have to spend my last penny if I agreed to go to the dance. This reality sickened me; I really wanted to go. I wanted to lose myself for once and do something impetuous and fun. But, the reality was that I just couldn't. Not if I had hopes of surviving for another month. I found it difficult to speak. I had no words to express to Frank how bleak my situation was. My pride wouldn't let me confide in him. I didn't want to set myself apart even further.

All these thoughts were swirling around in my head and I was just about to respond when Frank spoke. There was a slight hint of irritability and an edge in his voice, "Frank, have I in some way offended you? Have I wronged you or something?"

"Of course not, Frank. Never."

"Now say you'll go out to the dance. It'll be fun."

How could I say no? He felt that he had wronged me somehow. Because I couldn't tell him the truth, I agreed to go. I even managed a slight smile as I confirmed, "I will go to the dance."

"Great. You won't regret it! We should leave here around 8:00." And with that, he was gone.

I was alone with my grim reality.

*****

That evening we arrived early at the university and it wasn't long before Frank McG wandered off in search of new friends. Soon the band began to play. Well, *play* might not be the correct term to use to describe what was happening. The term play, when applied to music, implies that there is tangible evidence of structure and rhythm. I found no such evidence. I thought that the members of the band were still tuning their instruments and warming up their voices. Voices screeched. Instruments blared. Bodies moved on the dance floor. *What were they doing? Were they dancing? It couldn't be.* They too, looked like they were tuning up their bodies; warming up for the main event.

In truth, it was I who was very much out of touch with the music of the day and the whole university scene. My mind was still wedded to the more classic style of dance—the waltz. Defined structure and smooth, graceful movement were prerequisites. Sadly, it became apparent that I was the one who was out of step. I did not know how to abandon my preconceptions of what dancing should be. I did not feel comfortable adopting this more liberal expression of the body where everyone seemed to be dancing alone, in isolation. Each body swayed to its own internalization of the music.

Frank ambled by and offered this encouragement, "Hey, Frank, join in! There are many beautiful girls here tonight. Go on, get dancing."

I knew that he was right. I should make some sort of effort to join in the festivities. But, my heart just wasn't in it. I almost had myself talked into getting up to dance, when the band stopped playing; they were taking their first break. I promised myself that I would make an attempt when the band resumed playing.

Just then, three girls approached me. I recognized one of them, Kathy, from my English class. "Frank, I want you to meet my friends," she enthused. "Come join us. We have a table nearby. Come on."

I wanted to join them. But then again I did not. I was torn between my desire to be with friends and my need to regroup my thoughts and regain my courage in the face of this all female cast. I allowed myself to be led to their table. Once seated and introductions completed, Kathy noticed that I was cold and offered this solution, "Frank, you need a drink. That'll warm you up. What would you like? It's my treat."

I was taken aback by her offer. *A young lady offering to buy me a drink? That's not how it's done.* I simply stated, "This round is on me." I paid for everyone's drinks.

Only I knew the true cost of that gesture.

But, I could not allow the young lady to pay for my drink. That was not how I was raised. I would face the consequences of my actions tomorrow. I just hoped that I had enough money to get me home tonight. We chatted amicably over our drinks. A most vigorous outburst of voice and music signaled the band's return. Excitedly, the girls urged that we all hit the dance floor. One of the girls playfully encouraged, "Come, Frank. Show us your Trinidadian moves."

Trinidadian moves? Who, me? Wrong person. I was definitely the wrong person to represent Trinidad in any kind of dance event. Dancing was not part of my repertoire growing up so I knew very little. What little I did know came from what I observed in movies.

Kathy urged, "Frank, come join me," I was evasive with my response.

"Excuse me for a moment. I shan't be long."

I made it look as if I was headed for the bathroom. But, I wasn't. There was no way for me to remain at the dance. I thought that I could hide my despair but old memories rendered me unfit for socializing. I could keep up the pretext of a carefree exterior no longer. My troubled heart led my feet away from the dancers. I walked down a set of stairs leading to the cafeteria. The cafeteria was empty—just like me. I found a seat near a window and sat down. I emptied my pockets. My wallet yielded a single one dollar bill and some loose change—enough to get me back to Current River tonight and a few trips back and forth to the university the following week. The thought that loomed in the back of my head ever since I paid for that round of drinks made its way to the fore. *Was this the end of the road for me?*

I had not been a student in the country long enough to understand the unspoken traditions of Canadian university students. It was generally understood that students, whether male or female, shared expenses when going out. Each understood the other's predicament; no one was self-sufficient; they understood their mutual interdependence. Even when I learned of this reality later on in my university life, I still found it a difficult practice to observe since I had been schooled from a very young age that the male paid for the female when they were out together socially.

Sitting alone in the cafeteria I had time for regrets. *I wished that I had not felt obliged to pay for that round of refreshments. Yet, I did it. It was done. There was no going back.* In the greater scheme of things, the amount spent was minute compared to the amount I needed to get me through November's dark reality. I had no money for rent, and no money for my outstanding tuition fees.

Again my brother's words reverberated: *Frank, if you ever need help, don't send home. Who go help you?*

Those words, coupled with the words of the immigration officer caused my heart to despair. *Mr. Maraj, you are not to work until spring. If you work, and you are found out, you will be deported. You understand?*

I despaired, not just because I found myself in financial difficulty. That difficulty in and of itself had been faced many times before and I had always managed to find a way to overcome it. No, my despair came from the fact that I was threatened with deportation if I broke the rules. All my life, the one constant that had upheld me in challenging situations, was my desire and my ability to work. I still had the *desire* to work, but the officer's words challenged my *ability* to work. In essence, the officer had chopped off my feet.

Still, I clung to hope. There had to be some way out of this dilemma. I stared out the window into the vast darkness seemingly transfixed—praying for an answer; hoping for a sign.

How many times before had I reflected on the Eternal One? Once again I found myself reaching out to the Great Almighty.

Lord, how many times have I sought your counsel?
Once again I seek your help. I know not what to do.
I am desperate...

Prayerfully confiding in the God that I could not see eased my desperation; a sense of calm gently invaded my soul.

The sound of footsteps jolted me back to reality.

The footsteps belonged to the manager of the cafeteria and he was headed my way. I did not want to see him—I was busy drowning in an ocean of self pity and was not ready for conversation.

Go away, I urged in silence.

Neither the footsteps nor the man went away. Soon he stood beside me. I knew I had to meet his gaze. Reluctantly and perhaps even rebelliously, I turned to face him. My eyes demanded: *Go away. Leave me alone.*

He did not know how to read my eyes. He did not smile. He did not make small talk. He simply looked at me. It seemed like an eternity had passed before he broke the silence, "You look lost. What has you feeling so down? Why aren't you out there having fun with the rest of the university crowd?"

Without a moment's reflection or the slightest hesitation, I blurted out, "Mister, I don't have a dime. I have no rent money and I have no way to pay my school fees. I have no one in my life that I can turn to for help. And worse, I am not *allowed* to work. I have no way out."

Even I was shocked by such full disclosure; it was so unlike me to be that open about my personal situation. I could not explain my conduct. *How could I have spoken that way to a complete stranger? Was it because he was a complete stranger that I felt that I had nothing to lose by being perfectly and nakedly honest?*

He looked at me in silence. He then asked, "Do you mean you are literally broke? You know no one? You cannot pay your fees?"

"Yes."

"And you are not allowed to work?"

"That's correct."

I described my situation in detail and was shocked by my candid disclosures.

"I've never known anyone like that. When someone here is down and out, it's not like your situation. I thought I knew what hardship was. Yours is another dimension. You really need help."

I was quiet.

He was pensive as he paced back and forth. I got the sense that he truly wanted to help me in some way.

He told me that his name was Steve.

Once the awkward introductions were over, Steve told me that he may have an idea about how to help. He asked me to come to see him Monday morning around 9:00.

I agreed.

"Then so be it. I will see what can be done. Now go back upstairs and have fun."

And with that, he was gone. Only moments ago I was bordering on despair. Then Steve entered my life. He made no promises; offered no help. Yet, I sensed a promise.

7
Life at the Cafeteria

After classes the next day, I hurried to the cafeteria. (I had met with Steve and the Dean of Students earlier. Together they found a way to help me.) Steve awaited me, eager to show me around and introduce me to the rest of the staff. He then outlined my duties. My job consisted of collecting the dishes, loading them on a large trolley, wheeling the trolley to the kitchen, and finally unloading the dirty dishes. The task seemed simple enough and I was anxious to start.

It was suppertime. The cafeteria was filling up. As I made my way through the noisy room, trolley at hand, I saw several familiar faces; they were the faces of students from some of my classes. Without meaning to, I suddenly became self-conscious and awkward. As I reached out to collect the dirty dishes, the feelings intensified. I was forced to examine myself. *Why was I reacting that way? Did my years in Trinidad working as a teacher make me feel a sense of entitlement? Did I feel that the cafeteria job was somehow beneath me? Had my mind adopted a certain mentality because of my exposure to my own culture where most men were not required to work in kitchens while there was a mother and sisters to do that work?* I pondered the irony inherent in this reversal of fortune. The very tasks that I had never performed while in Trinidad, were the very tasks that were proving to be my salvation here in Canada. I who had never done the dishes nor cooked was now in the very midst of dirty dishes. My thoughts must have transported me elsewhere and I was unaware that Steve was at my side. It was only when he asked me how I was doing that I was jolted back to my present tasks. Only slightly embarrassed by my *apparent* lack of work ethic, I took the hint. Immediately I resumed my duties; soon I was buried in my work. When the work day ended, I caught the bus to downtown Port Arthur.

The bus was full of students traveling to the downtown area. Very few made the transfer to the bus to Current River. Virtually alone at that late hour I had time to reflect on the day's events. I refused to entertain any negative thoughts regarding the nature of the work. I decided to adopt a spirit of gratitude for the work at the cafeteria. That spirit gave me peace.

Some days later I witnessed a behavior that left me disquieted and filled with questions.

One evening as I was leaving the students' lounge to make my way to work, I noticed some students seated on the sofas engaging in conversation. In those days, smoking was allowed in the university and many students were habitual smokers. Ash trays were not hard to find so I could not understand the many cigarette burns that dotted the arms of the sofas. It was that day that I first witnessed a flagrant act of desecration.

One of the students took his cigarette and butted it out on the sofa. His buddy did the same. Not content with one burn mark, they each continued to pierce the sofa as if to mark their territory. Their acts put me in mind of dogs urinating on trees to mark their territory. They showed such callous disregard for the furniture. I was baffled by their action. As I continued my way to work, I observed that another student had ground out his cigarette butt in the mashed potatoes that remained on his plate. As I looked around I observed that so many meals—plate after plate—hardly touched—were set aside simply discarded. I was aghast at the sheer volume of waste and I wanted so much to say, *Please, please, do you not see the terrible waste? Do you not know that there are so many who would give a limb for the crumbs from your plate?*

To witness such waste made me sad. And as the days progressed I became increasingly troubled. I had never expected to find such waste here in Canada. I had always imagined Canadians through the eyes of an idealist. I had envisioned Canada and its people to be sensitive and progressive. To find myself working amidst such wastefulness was beyond my imaginings. I knew poverty; I understood what it was like to be hungry and poor. These thoughts swirled in my head and caused me to silently protest the actions of the students. If they had seen what I had seen and if they had known what I knew, I do not believe that they would have acted in the same manner. These students were but innocent miscreants. I had to think of them in that way; to think otherwise would invite trouble in my soul. All the same, I found it a great challenge to confront such waste each and every day.

One evening as I was getting ready to leave the cafeteria Steve asked me to stay awhile. He told me that the kitchen staff was happy to have me working with them. He too was happy that things were working out. Then he asked me how I was doing because he had noticed that I seemed to be troubled and solitary. He wanted to know if anything was troubling me.

This was the second time Steve had asked me such a question and like before I found myself blurting out my concerns.

"Steve, I'm finding it extremely trying working here at the cafeteria."

"Why, what do you mean, Frank? Did anyone give you trouble? I want to know. I will..."

"No, no Steve. The problem is me. It is not anyone. It's within me, Steve."

"What is the problem, Frank? You can tell me."

"Steve, I find it difficult to cope with how food is wasted in the cafeteria. We throw away food, Steve – and I am having a difficult time coping with it. I don't ..."

"Wait a minute, Frank. You are saying that you can't stand to see the waste we generate. It bothers you."

"Yes. I don't mean to be critical."

"Frank you are here at university to get an education. This is but one small phase in your life. You have to witness this wasteful behavior for only a few months. I have to live in this *pigsty* every single day. I cannot begin to tell you how revolted I am by the students' apathy. And I cannot do one blessed thing. *This is my profession and I am cursed by it.*"

"Steve, I am so sorry for your situation. I have so much to understand. I would have never thought that you would be so upset."

"I'm not alone, Frank. So many are disgusted and some of them are students. We have many students on campus; only a few act so revoltingly. We tolerate, and we learn to cope. We try to keep things in perspective. Now, can you try and do the same? Come, my friend, and do it with a smile."

I felt so lucky to have a man like Steve as my boss. I came to Canada to get an education. I never thought that working in the cafeteria as a bus boy, would offer up such a challenge to my perspective. Truly I was receiving an education from all quarters of my life. The new perspective that Steve had presented to me was put into action the very next day. I resolved to be tolerant. As a result, I was less unhappy as I surveyed the cafeteria. I did not just see the discarded dishes of food; I had a new focus; I saw those who actually ate returned their dishes to the trolley after eating their meals. I rolled up my sleeves and got to work.

Soon I had wheeled so many dishes into the kitchen that it was difficult for the cleaning staff to keep up. I decided that not only could I help but that I should help. Accordingly, I rolled up my sleeves and dug in and began to wash the dishes. (If only my mother and my sisters could have witnessed that, I doubt that they would believe it otherwise.) The kitchen staff was very appreciative and, as the days went by, I became more and more a true part of the cafeteria staff. Soon I became part of their suppertime ritual; I joined them on crates in the kitchen while grabbing a bite to eat. Someone always thought to prepare something especially for me. Once again I felt spoiled…

8

A Rude Awakening

November brought with it another surprise—snow. It came early on a Saturday morning in the first week of November. Mrs. Cloutier excitedly ushered me to the large living room window to witness the falling snow. The outside world was being transformed. I was stunned by the enormous blanket of white engulfing everything: the pavement, the trees, the cars, the sidewalk, and the steps. It looked so light and fluffy. An irresistible urge seized me and I rushed through the front door and threw myself with reckless abandon upon the piling snow. The primal exhilaration that that action yielded was short lived however; the cold reality registered on my bare feet and my freezing toes begged for protection from my temporary insanity.

How could anything that looked so pure and beautiful inflict such pain? Its beauty camouflaged the true measure of its harm. My light pyjamas were no match for nature's deception. I hurried back inside and sought relief under a long hot shower.

Showers had been a daily ritual in Trinidad. I maintained that early morning ritual here in Canada. One day, not long after that first snowfall, I was running late. I could not forsake my morning shower for it was that shower that prepared me for the day. I used that time to work out my daily schedule and wash away any residual worries. Showers were invigorating; a necessary start for each day. Not wishing to give up that part of my routine, I decided to forfeit the follow up—the towel drying of my hair. I dressed quickly, skipped breakfast, and made a mad dash for the bus stop- my hair still wet. An extreme coldness enveloped my head. Each individual shaft of hair hardened; each strand trying to outdo its neighbour in its ability to stand taller and straighter. It was a most uncomfortable sensation. I reached up to touch my hair. It was a mass of hardness. I thought that pieces would splinter off if I applied too much pressure. I then began to worry that something was wrong with my hair; perhaps I had contracted some strange ailment related to the extreme cold. When the bus arrived, I clambered aboard and found a seat near a heat vent. When hot air began to blast from it, I began to experience a new and even more curious sensation. I felt movement throughout my scalp. I thought that my hair had been invaded by a host of small creatures. *I must be sicker than I thought.* I began to feel frightened. Soon little rivers of moisture began to run down my forehead, and encircle my eyes. The back of my neck and my ears were saturated with moisture. The hair on my head began to loosen and fall limp. I reached up tentatively and touched my head; all my hair still seemed to be intact. I tugged at a strand or two. *Ouch.* Nothing came loose. By the time I arrived at the university, I figured out what had happened; I was not sick. Needless to say, I never took another shower in the winter without drying my head completely before venturing outside.

No matter how warm I was indoors I could not endure the outside cold. I could not understand how Canadians survived the climate. I could not even bear to imagine the next few months. The strong winds blowing off Lake Superior in the month of December intensified the cold. I was chilled to the bone.

But nothing, absolutely nothing could have prepared me for the chill yet to come—a chill completely unrelated to the weather.

9
Professor F

Our English professor gave us a list of topics; we were to chose one and write an essay. I chose mine and was busy working on it when a few of my fellow classmates approached. They knew that I had taught English in Trinidad and asked for my help in getting started. We exchanged ideas and I assisted them in structuring their essays. They each went back to their tasks excited about their newfound focus. I too went back to my writing.

Some days later our essays were due. Some days after that, the marked essays were returned. Some of the students whom I had "coached" were very pleased with their grades. They smiled at me and asked how I had done. Since my essay had not yet been returned, I shrugged hesitantly and remained nervously expectant. The professor returned the rest of the essays. Mine was not among them. Several other students were in the same situation. Then the professor announced, "I would like to see the following students in my office after class." My name was listed among the names of the students he wished to see.

One of my classmates whispered, "Frank, congratulations, you must have aced your essay." I was hopeful that I had done reasonably well, but never did I imagine that I had done so well as to have "aced" the essay.

My heart raced expectantly as I walked down the corridor to the English Languages offices. The door to my professor's office was open; the professor was seated behind his desk. When I walked through the door, he looked up and motioned for me to sit. He did not speak; he did not offer even a hint of a smile. Something was wrong.

Then he spoke, "Mr. Maraj, do you intend to continue with your studies here with us at Lakehead University?"

What type of question was that? What was I to think? I was expecting some kind of recognition, some kind of compliment – not this question.

I responded, "Yes, Mr. F."

"Well, Mr. Maraj, you certainly will have to do a whole lot better if you wish to continue with us."

I felt my world implode.

He continued, "Mr. Maraj, let me comment on your essay and I suggest that you pay careful attention. The marker has underlined your errors in red ink. I read your paper myself and I concur with the marker's evaluation. In fact, I have added to his remarks. My comments are written in blue ink."

He opened the essay and displayed the first page so I could see the many lines underlined in red. On the flip side he wrote in blue – volumes of blue formed a dense landscape on each and every page.

I don't know for sure which emotion ranked higher in degree— humiliation or degradation. Together they catapulted me into a sea of dejection. My soul wanted to leap into the chasm of oblivion never again to resurface.

I didn't know how much more I could take. The professor removed his glasses as he cautioned, "Be warned Mr. Maraj that your essay is substandard. I really do not know what your background in English is, and at this point it is of no consequence. What matters is that you learn to write a proper essay. I expect then, Mr. Maraj, that I shall see a marked improvement in your work. I dare say however, that this is close to ... if truth be told ... hopeless. But then again, one should never underestimate the power of the human will."

Was this really happening? Had those words truly been spoken? I couldn't move. I remained seated as my professor announced that he had an appointment. Sensing the impact that his words had on me, he did not rush me from his office.

"Well Mr. Maraj, I do have to leave. You may stay if you wish. I will leave you to your deliberations. And on your way out, do be sure and close the door."

Then he was gone.

His words had seared my soul. *Where was I to go? What was I to do?* Never had there been a more sobering moment in my life. Completely stripped of any illusion, I faced this new reality.

The fact that my professor had not been unkind in manner or in word made it all the more difficult to dismiss his words. He had been genuine and sincere with his comments. I was left to struggle with my own inner conflict. *Could it be that my English was suspect; that it lacked competence? How could this be so?* Uncertainty and self-doubt plagued me over the next few hours. I could not face my peers who were curious about my final grade. How *could I tell them that I was a failure?*

I had gained a confidence as a teacher in Trinidad. I could not help but now wonder whether I had short-changed my students; that thought was too demoralizing to dwell on for long. Had I been a sub-standard teacher? My *paper* was substandard. Did that make *me* substandard? For a while, I thought that the answer to that question was *yes*. With my spirits crushed, all I could think about was returning home to Trinidad. I began yearning for its everyday comforts: family, friends and warm weather. No longer did I wish to broaden my horizons; no longer did I desire a higher education.

December's chill cut to the bone. My academic hopes were frozen. My mind could not escape the grim reality that I had failed and failed miserably on my first English essay. And now the Christmas holidays were about to begin.

The only positive thought I had through that long night of deliberation was that I would not have to face Mr. F for a while. I was relieved.

With that relief came the dawning of an idea. *If I knew of a student in this situation, what would my advice be?* It soon became clear what I had to do; what I needed to do. I grabbed the essay and headed for the library. I stared at it for a while; finally I forced myself to read. So many red marks scarred the pages; I found it difficult to stay focused on my task. It took everything in me to resist the temptation to just close the essay and blot out the humiliation of the red and blue markings. I read each criticism carefully; I wanted the satisfaction of knowing that I *did* read them. That was the first step in overcoming my humiliation. I then re-read the criticisms. I read them over and over until I could recite them by heart. As I read, I discovered that a great deal of my errors resulted because I lacked proper format and footnoting skills; these were areas I had not studied as a student in Trinidad. I needed to become knowledgeable in these areas if I were to be successful at the university. Immediately I began a reconstruction program: a total reconstruction of the essay. I began my research; first, I secured a book on grammar, then one on proper footnoting. I decided to dedicate all my efforts to improve my condition.

One final step remained; it was of vital importance to my personal sense of dignity. I rewrote the entire paper and submitted it to my professor. Since he was not in the office, I slid it under the door. I did not do this to receive a better mark. (Mind you, had I been offered a better grade I would have welcomed it.) I felt that I had to take responsibility for my mistakes since it was I who had made them; it was left to me to upgrade myself.

That was not the first time that school had proven to be a challenge.

****

When I was a child at elementary school, my teacher openly chastised me for my many failures. While she warned that my English was "very poor," she found my arithmetic skills particularly deficient. She openly criticized my inability to grasp the times tables. She was never without a thick ruler in her hand. She walked up and down the aisles brandishing this extra appendage while loudly reciting some fact from the times tables. The students were expected to repeat the facts back to her in unison. She was a great proponent of rote style learning. Before any math lesson began, we were expected to assume the proper position: we were required to place our hands on the top of our desks palms down. At any given moment she would take a break from her walking routine and strike a desk. The pupil thus chosen had to answer a random multiplication fact. Failure to respond in a timely and correct manner invited the wrath of the teacher. This wrath took the form of blows to the knuckles. (Hence the need to have us sit with our hands palms down on top of our desks.) My knuckles, having received more than their fair share of blows appear to be larger than most. Each time I was singled out to answer a question, I was unable to respond. It appeared that I did not know the answer. Yet, on my own time and away from everyone, I would practise my times tables; I knew the answers; I knew them cold. I could not understand why I would freeze in front of this teacher every time she asked me a simple question; some deep rooted fear prevented me from articulating any form of expression. Because of this, my teacher determined that I was unable to speak proper English. Her corrections numbered in the thousands. Is it any wonder then that my classmates teased me and dubbed me the class *dunce*? It was not unusual to find me in the midst of a mob of chanting classmates; each one delighting in adding to my humiliation. *Frankie stupid, he ugly, he stupid.*

The soul of that ten year old boy was particularly vulnerable to the harpoons of derision; his fractured soul retreated.

I did not like school; no, I *despised* school. On this particular day, when I had failed to respond to her question, my teacher did not strike my knuckles as was her custom. I wished she had. Her attack assumed another dimension.

"Frankie Boodram, stand up!" she barked.

Oh, no, please Teacher, don't make me stand, I begged in shocked silence.

If Teacher says *stand*, you stand.

I stood.

But I could not make my body stand up straight; I was far too nervous and shaky. Since she was making me stand, I felt that I must have done something really, really bad.

She looked me over, scanning me from top to bottom, in a relentless search for complaint. I could feel her eyes inspecting my head. It was only that morning that Ma had doused my head with a generous application of coconut oil; this oil was now oozing from all quarters of my head. How many times had I protested her generous applications but to no avail. Ma insisted that the oil was *healthy*. While it may have been healthy for my scalp, it most certainly was unhealthy for me personally. She could not begin to comprehend how her motherly expression of love and care could be the source of so much pain. My shiny greasy head made me stand out; it was just one more flaw in my already too flawed appearance. Any suggestion of criticism fell on deaf ears, for Ma would not brook anything that remotely resembled a complaint about any teacher. Such was the blind respect given to our teachers by our parents. Some teachers took complete advantage of this fact. My teacher was still staring at my head; abruptly she turned her dagger-like eyes to my shoeless feet; I felt them puncture my open sores.

Please, Teacher, ah begging you, don't shame me in front the class. Please, Teacher, I prayed silently. I wanted to sit, but sitting was not an option.

Then she began to recite her list of complaints against me: "Frankie Boodram, you speak so badly, so very poorly. You never know your times tables. Why do you not know your times tables? Do you want everyone to think you are stupid? Are you stupid? Answer me, why don't you speak?"

How does a mere child in Standard Five answer such a question? I just remained quiet; I did not wish to aggravate my teacher any further. She came closer to me and threatened me with her ruler. My body recoiled instinctively as it braced to receive the intended assault. Then she resumed her verbal assault, "Frankie Boodram, you are stubborn. Worse, you are rude. For your rudeness, I have to punish you. You will have to say aloud, *Holy Mary* five times and pray to Our Holy Mother of God for the removal of your sins.

Teacher, Teacher what sins? I asked silently.

"Now, say your *Holy Marys*. Begin!" she commanded.

I searched desperately to find my voice. Nothing came out. Teacher became more insistent as she drew closer. She raised the ruler. A croak found its way out of my mouth. It was an unrecognizable sound that managed to delight my classmates. Now thoroughly incensed, Teacher continued to launch her attack, "So, you are now making a joke of our Holy Mary in my classroom. Frankie Boodram, how would you like it if I made a joke about your Hindu religion? Come to think of it, you know you are going to hell. Hindus worship cows and they worship idols. That is cause for going to hell. Do you want to go to hell, Frankie?"

"No, Teacher."

"Well, if you want to go to heaven, you have to accept Jesus. Otherwise you are going to hell; yes, straight to hell. Now I will whip that little devil out of you."

The ruler was unleashed; my bruised shoulders bore testimony to my teacher's zeal to rescue me from the road to hell and advance me to the gateway of heaven. I shuddered under the avalanche of blows which seemed to further feed my teacher's anger. *What had I done?*

Holy Mary, Mother of God, help me. Ah don't know what to do. Me teacher is so vex with me. Help, please, I prayed silently.

No angel appeared to take me away. I guess the Catholic god was not available to the Hindus. Then my teacher grabbed my ear and led me to a corner of the classroom visible to all who passed by. I was on display; I knew that soon the teasing would be widespread; the river of derision would soon overflow its banks.

She barked, "Frankie Boodram, kneel down. You *will* obey me. You *will* learn your times tables, and you *will* speak proper English or you *will not speak at all*. Shame on you. Do you hear me? And don't be so stupid."

"Yes, Teacher," I managed. I wanted to die.

My spirit protested her condemnation, *Teacher, teacher Ah ain't stupid. Ah just look stupid.*

I could hardly wait for the day to end. I needed to be away from everything; I needed to be away from prying eyes and jeering looks. It was for that reason I did not go home my usual way. It was for that reason I chose to not go with friends. And it was for that reason I chose the long way home.

From school I took the street that led to the railroad station. Beyond the station and to the right, lay the cemetery; to the left was the open savannah. Expansive fields of farmland lay beyond the savannah. A large avocado tree grew in the very midst of one of these fields. Its branches formed a tower to the sky. It was there, amongst those branches that I wanted to be. With great respect for the sanctity of the tree, I climbed; all the while praying that the tree would pardon my intrusion. Finding a comfortable position I nestled in. My eyes regarded the heavens; at last I found my voice.

So, God, ah have to tell you that ah is troubled, ah confused.
Teacher says ah going to hell because ah is a Hindu.
Ma says if yo bad and yo don' listen to your elders yo go to hell.
Answer me, God. Who is right?

I waited some minutes before continuing.

Well, God, ah make up me mind,
You may not like me choice.
If ah have to choose between me teacher's Christan god
And me mother's Hindu god,
Ah choose Ma's god even if that means
Ah go to hell with Ma,
So be it.

Ma cares and shows love.
She accepts other people's gods.

One day when I went to the Muslim mosque
To pray with me friend Raffi,
Ma found out.
She did not get vex like me teacher.
She said God is in the mosque too.

But she reminded me that ah was a Hindu.

When all the different Christian groups
Come home to preach,
Me ma always listens,

Me ma always shows respect.
In her heart
She feel that God is there
In all the different religions.

God, is me ma right?
Is me teacher right?
Are YOU sending we to hell
Because we born Hindu?
Ah so confused.

And ah don't know how
Me teacher could bark her way to heaven.
Ah see no love in her.
Now God,
Ah want to know from You,
Who would You choose first,
Me teacher, or
Me ma?

I waited. I expected an answer. Well, I *hopefully* expected an answer. When I thought that I could wait no longer, I waited. Then I left.

There was so much I had to learn about the mysterious ways of the Almighty. For now, I was satisfied. I had had my talk with God; I needed to make my way home.

While walking home, I recalled that I hardly spoke in that teacher's classroom. I don't even remember her name. We called her, Teacher. But, I also remembered the dawning of a certain consciousness that was to become part of my psyche even when I was not aware of it. I vowed to myself that I would do something to improve my circumstance. That promise translated into a code of action. I joined the library and read greedily. Over time I filled countless notebooks, writing out words that I did not understand and checking for their meanings. I also quietly embarked on my quest to speak proper English. Many, including both family and friends, disapproved of my efforts and regarded me as an impostor of sorts. In my heart I knew that I would sooner suffer the disparagement of many, than to accept that I was somehow inferior or second class.

Glad was I that I was able to cultivate a sense of dogged determination at such a young age. That resolute will has helped me to improve my standard over the years. And here, at university, once again I realized that it was that type of resolution that I needed to summon if I had any hopes of success. My very first English essay was a miserable failure. That did not mean that I was a failure. My professor had been very blunt in pointing out my errors. Maybe his sharp criticisms were a blessing in disguise.

When the semester resumed, Mr. F never mentioned anything about my essay. I never asked. It was sufficient that I had made that effort to overcome my deficiency. Did I succeed? Suffice it to say that Destiny did deliver me to the office of this same professor, once more, years later.

10

A "Whyte" Christmas

In the late fall I was attempting to hitchhike to the university. I was running late and hoped that if a car picked me up I would arrive sooner than the next bus. It wasn't long before a small car stopped and picked me up. The driver was on her way to work near the university. It took at least fifteen minutes to drive to the university and during that time the lady and I struck up a conversation. I cannot remember her name so I'll refer to her as Mrs. Whyte. When she found out that I was from Trinidad, she immediately shared that her family loved the music of Harry Belafonte. Before she departed, she gave me her phone number and asked that I contact her if ever I needed a ride. On rare occasions I accepted her kind offer.

Then one day shortly before Christmas, I happened to be standing at a bus stop when Mrs. Whyte spotted me. She signaled me to get in her car. Again she drove me to the university. I was happy to see her especially as she extended to me an invitation to spend Christmas at her home with her family. I accepted her invitation gladly; my happiness at being invited out for the holidays kept me warm over the next few days.

Both Mr. and Mrs. Whyte came and picked me up in the late afternoon on Christmas Eve. The weather was bitterly cold. Once inside the car I was introduced to Steve, a student from China. Then we were off to the Whytes' residence somewhere on the Nipigon Highway. The steady fall of gentle snow gave the scene a Christmas card appearance. Trees laden with snow bordered the sides of the highway giving way only intermittently to the occasional house.

Soon we arrived at the Whytes' residence. Theirs was a huge two-storey home. The entrance seemed a bit small for such a large sprawling home. We were hurrying to remove our trappings of winter before entering the living room. It took a little time for each person to remove boots, hats, scarves, mitts and jackets. Since I was at the back of the line, my body was half inside and half outside the door. It was the part that was half outside that caused me the most concern; it was freezing. Again I wondered how people lived in such a brutal climate. Yet, once inside, all thoughts of the cold were banished.

In the living room was an old-fashioned fireplace; it generated so much heat that for a moment I thought I was back in Trinidad. Genuine warmth radiated not only from the fireplace but also from each member of the Whyte family.

Then, my eyes were drawn to their Christmas tree with all its lights and sparkling adornments. That tree took my breath away; I wanted to yell, *so this is a real Christmas tree.*

For a brief second, my mind wandered back to Trinidad but there was no time for nostalgia or sadness for our host family was most attentive. I could see that the finishing touches were being put to the dining room table; a Christmas cheer was served and a welcoming toast was made to all. Then it was time for supper.

The main meal was over and the whole family helped to clear off the table whilst Steve and I were ushered to the living room. That Christmas tree was so inviting. I could hardly avoid staring at it. The flickering lights were mesmerizing. Steve and I chatted and I had the distinct impression that he was accustomed to the finer things in life even before I heard him speak about his life in China.

When the Whytes rejoined us, Mrs. Whyte commented, "So, Frank, I noticed you staring at our tree. Do you like it?"

"I love your Christmas tree. All the glittering silver and gold tinsel. Your beautiful bells and ornaments. They are all so lovely. And your angel on top the tree. It's exquisite!"

"Tell us about your traditions in Trinidad. Do you have a tree?"

Then the children added their comments. They too wanted to hear about Trinidad.

All other chatter ceased and all eyes were on me – expectant.

I felt that I had to say something.

"Well, we don't have a tree like yours and our decorations are a little different."

"How so, Mr. Frank?" asked one of the children.

Then another intervened, "No Christmas tree, Mr. Frank. How awful. How do you have Christmas without a tree? It doesn't seem right. I feel sorry, Frank…"

Mrs. Whyte interrupted, "David, now let Mr. Frank finish his story."

"We do have a kind of a tree…" then I paused.

How could I tell them about the modest twig fashioned into a tree by the loving hands of my mother year after year? A wave of nostalgia flooded through me; nothing matched my childhood image of Ma wrapping the twig with her simple hand-crafted paper ornaments. Each creation was unique and made all the more special because it came from her loving hands; hands that were always occupied in the thankless tasks of day to day life; hands that were never too tired to attempt to make Christmas a special time.

Then I continued, "It is a twig. We bring this twig into the house and dress it up as best as we can. My sisters make decorations from paper and hang it on the branches. We even pretend to have snow..."

"You pretend to have snow," a young David declared in disbelief. "How do you pretend to have snow?"

"Well, that is easy. We buy a can of foam and spray the ends of the twig; then it really looks like snow."

Soon Mr. Whyte announced that we had to put an end to our enjoyable chat as it was time to attend midnight mass. We all climbed into their van and headed for their church which was located back in the Port Arthur area of town.

The church was packed that Christmas Eve and the priest spoke passionately about the meaning of Christmas. He was fervent in his plea for us to reach out to our fellowman; not just to the familiar, but extend our good will to the strangers among us. He noted especially that we should treat the downtrodden with dignity and kindness, not just at Christmas, but all through the year. I was moved by his words. As I looked around the church I saw heads nodding in quiet acquiescence; we all appeared to be of one mind. At the conclusion of the mass, Father shook hands and exchanged Christmas greetings with all who passed by on their way out of the sanctuary. I began to follow my hosts out of the building when my eyes caught sight of an older man standing near the exit. With hands outstretched, he appeared to be begging. As I drew closer, I noticed that his clothes were well-worn and showing signs of age. The man appeared desolate. No one stopped; no one seemed even to notice; it was as if he did not exist. I felt that I had to do something; after all, hadn't Father just preached his homily exhorting us to reach out to the less fortunate.

I turned back around and found Father and told him about the beggar. Father explained that he would look into it. He closed the doors behind me as I left. Only Father and the beggar remained inside. I wondered how Father would help this sorry looking man. I cannot explain why I did what I did next. Overcome by an inexplicable urge, I reentered the church. As I opened the door I saw the priest metamorphose from the humble and godly man who had delivered a moving homily to a raging vindictive individual in total violation of his own pious teachings.

Father's back was to me and he did not see me bear witness to his outrage.

"Get out of the house of God. How many times have I told you not to come here begging anymore? You are a chronic drunk I am sick and tired of telling you the same thing over and over. You are an embarrassment to God and…"

I could bear to hear no more.

I had to get out of that church; I needed to be away from what I believed was a hypocrite. In fact, I had to fight the urge to yell the words, *sanctimonious hypocrite* at Father. I wondered how he could desecrate God's house on this holy night with his behavior. My peace shattered, my spirit broken, I fought hard against the urge to judge this priest. It would be so easy to condemn Father; so easy to pass judgment on him the way he had just passed judgment on another.

Yet, Father may have had many reasons for his actions. For my part, I was at a loss to understand; I wondered how Jesus would have responded to these actions. *Would Jesus weep for this lack of mercy?* Surely on a night like tonight, the Blessed Beatitudes from the Sermon on the Mount deserved to claim our hearts and our actions. I too, had to guard against sitting in judgment of this priest. To do so would be to offend the very spirit of Christ and the Christmas message.

It was Christmas Eve and a beautiful message had been delivered and lost all in one single moment. I did not want that feeling to be the final end to the night.

I needed to do something to restore the spirit that had been wrenched from my heart. As I headed toward the van, I caught sight of the beggar. He was walking away from the church in a state of utter dejection. I bent down to give the appearance that I was tying up my shoelaces. I waited for the man to get closer. As he passed by me, I reached my hand out to him in greeting. As we shook hands, I transferred a quarter from my palm into his and whispered, "I wish that I had more to give. Merry Christmas."

He smiled and I smiled. I turned to cross the street to catch up to the others who were by now piling into the van, when suddenly I slipped and fell. It was a most awkward sight. The slippery road claimed my legs and pulled them in opposite directions. My legs stretched out endlessly in opposition to one another. Trying to avoid further embarrassment, I attempted to pull myself up quickly. I fell again; this time I hit my head. Dizzy from the fall, I again attempted to regain my composure. As I raised my head and struggled to find my footing, I beheld a vision. I caught a mere glimpse of Father descending the stairs of the church; he appeared to be floating with his solid white robes draped around his body guarding against the night's chill. With arms outstretched he appeared to be carrying a coat; yet he himself bore none. Without uttering a word, he draped the coat over the shoulders of the beggar. The beggar stood transfixed: utterly shocked. Like a frozen pillar he remained until Father placed his arm around his shoulders and whispered something to him. Suddenly this frozen statue thawed and moved with childlike joy. Thus infused with spirit I heard these words thunder against the quiet of the night, "Supper tomorrow? Yes, Father."

My heart was filled with absolute joy at that vision. *Was it real or imagined? Does it matter?* The true spirit of Christmas had been restored to a soul that only moments ago had felt such agony.

****

I felt a presence at my side; it was Mr. Whyte.

"Frank, are you okay? You had quite a fall."

Surprised at finding myself still on the ground, I scrambled to get up. Mr. Whyte assisted me in regaining my footing. As he did so he observed, "Frank, you don't have the right shoes. You're wearing dress shoes. No wonder you fell. We'll just have to fix that up and soon."

Soon we were all once more comfortably seated in the van. A gentle snow fell as we headed back to the Whytes'. As I wiped condensation off the window and peered through at the cascading snowflakes I experienced a real serenity. That sight was heavenly. Then the van veered to the right quite unexpectedly. Mr. Whyte quickly regained control and a near accident was averted. Soon the van was filled with his deep baritone voice; we all joined him in singing *Silent Night*. As we pulled in to the yard I marvelled at the magnificent whiteness that silently enveloped this beautiful land; it truly was a silent and holy night.

Once inside, Mrs. Whyte brought out more food: sandwiches and dessert. Mr. White brought a bag; its contents revealed some winter wear including an almost new pair of winter boots. I just looked at him and nodded. Little did he suspect that I could not, would not accept his gift. *How foolish was I?* Later, we were gathered around the fireplace exchanging stories; soon fatigue claimed us, one by one, and we stole away to our beds. As I lay on my bed, I recalled the beggar; in recalling the beggar, I also recalled my hastiness to condemn another.

****

That next day was Christmas day: my very first in Canada and grateful was I to be part of this family. A host of outdoor activities was planned. I particularly enjoyed the snow ball throwing until I inadvertently launched a missile at Mr. Whyte; it struck him in the head. When he fell and showed no signs of movement, I was terrified. After what seemed an eternity, he regained consciousness. Following that close call, we all went inside for dinner. What a relief to see him at the table enjoying his meal. Everyone indulged heartily, both in food and conversation. Then we each sought out a little 'alone' time. I retreated to the living room and sat quietly reflecting on the day's events. I don't know for sure how long I sat there but suddenly I became aware of another presence in the room. It was Mrs. Whyte.

"Mrs. Whyte, I did not see you, sorry."

"No need, Frank. You were lost in thought; a penny for your thoughts."

"Well, my mind drifted back to Trinidad and to my family and friends; I was just thinking of everything and everyone."

"Anything I could do to help, I would be more than happy."

"Mrs. Whyte, you have done so much already. You will never really know how much just being here has helped me. I never knew I would feel like this."

"You mean miss your family? Of course, Frank, you will miss your family. After all, you are hundreds of miles away. Have you ever been away before at Christmastime?"

"No."

"And you wonder why you miss your folks. I would be surprised if any of my children were away and did not miss me. I know that when the time comes, and a child of mine has to be away for Christmas, that child had better miss me, and really miss me, or else." She paused for a moment and then added, "Frank, why don't you phone your mom? Here, use our phone."

"Oh, Mrs. Whyte, she's probably out visiting—thanks. I'll probably do that later on." I quickly changed the subject to a less sensitive topic, "Where is everyone? Are they avoiding us?"

"Well, let me look into it."

As she left to gather up the rest of the family I wondered if Mrs. Whyte suspected that we did not have a phone. I could not tell her that since leaving home I had never even heard the voice of anyone from home. Had my solemn disposition revealed my homesickness?

I could not tell her that the only source of communication available to me was letter writing; each letter took a minimum of two weeks to complete its journey from Port Arthur to Tunapuna. This Christmas, my salvation had been the radio. Through that medium I was able to send a live voice message back home to my family in Trinidad and a few days ago I had done just that. Foreign students from the university had been invited to tape brief messages to their families which would then be forwarded to their homeland and aired on the local radio stations. When I sent my message I tried so very hard to disguise my longing to be home. I just said that I was thinking of everyone, and that I was doing okay. But, I knew that I was not okay. I was extremely sad that I was away from home at Christmas. How does one's voice conceal such feelings?

I could not tell her that I had left my brother alone in Trinidad to manage the family when we both should have been sharing the load. I could not tell her that a millstone of guilt threatened to smother me.

I could not tell her how worried I was about my mother; I could not tell her that peace and harmony were two strangers on a distant shore never destined to enter my mother's life.

I could not tell her such simple sad truths.

That night I could not sleep. I lay awake thinking. My mind gave me no peace. I could see home; I could feel home; I missed home. My emotions were so intense that my body ached. I had been away from home before, but I had never been away for Christmas. The season served to intensify the pain.

I forced myself to direct my thoughts back to the present and to the family who had been so generous and so thoughtful. I thought of Christmas dinner; everything was so different from our home traditions —the food was different, the customs were different, the weather especially was different. Yet, with all these differences I was able to enjoy Christmas. Everything that could have been done had been done, and I was deeply appreciative.

While I was deeply appreciative, I was nonetheless miserable.

I was missing home and the million and one little things my family did on Christmas Day—traditions that I didn't even know were traditions until I left home: traditions I more fully appreciated having been removed from them for a season. Ma and the girls would prepare a large feast at lunch time on Christmas Day; that was the most notable tradition. No one dared miss that event—or even to be late. Ma did not make many demands on her family; nor did she make observing this tradition a demand; somehow we just understood without words that we were *expected* to be home by lunch time. We could have been visiting with royalty; nothing mattered; we were expected to be home and we made it home. This one expectation of Ma's was easy to accommodate, for Ma and my sisters never failed to create a spread of dishes that would charm even the most challenged of taste buds. Following lunch, I was free to visit or have friends visit me. I truly missed visiting friends. I was so forlorn lying in bed.

Thus perfectly depressed and miserable I lay on my bed wondering if other students felt such deep rooted sadness. They must. I made a vow to myself that next Christmas I would find a way to be home.

And, just before sleep claimed me, I remember thinking how privileged I was to have been a part of this amazing family at Christmas. Despite my homesickness, this Christmas would go down in my memory as a near-perfect *Whyte* Christmas.

11
A Blissful Catastrophe

The New Year came and the demands of university life were upon me once again. In Mr. F's class, marked assignments were regularly returned; never again was I called to his office for a 'meeting'. That fact alone led me to believe that I was not doing badly. My marks were improving gradually and I was still working part-time at the cafeteria. Everything seemed to be in order so I began to relax and enjoy the lovely predictability of my life.

My instinct to relax, however, was premature.

One day, shortly after I returned home from university, Mrs. Cloutier shocked me with this announcement, "Frank, I have something very important to tell you. Starting next month, you won't be able to live here anymore. You and the other Frank will have to find another home."

Her announcement caught me totally by surprise. I had to sit down to absorb the shock. My mind immediately imagined the worst scenario. I wondered what had I done. *Had I offended her? Had I inadvertently offended one of the children?*

After catching my breath, I finally asked, "Mrs. Cloutier, have I done something wrong? Tell me, please. If I…"

"No, no, it is not like that. You boys did nothing wrong. We were glad to have you. But we want to have our home to ourselves. You can understand that."

"But, I was so comfortable here; and you and Mr. Cloutier are so good to me. You have done so much to make me feel at home."

"Oh, Frank, you will do just fine in another home. I have contacted some friends—the Horns—and they are willing to have you. Here is their number. If you like, you can arrange to meet them and see their place. They live right here in Current River—just a few streets over. There is a bus stop very close to their house. Frank, you'll be fine. There's nothing to be worried about, really."

I listened to Mrs. Cloutier in shocked silence. Having to move, having to find another home, *was* a big deal. I don't think that she understood just *how* big a deal it was to me. I had become so accustomed to their life and so attached to the family; I couldn't imagine my life in Canada without them. They were a family around whom I could afford to relax. They were the perfect buffer between my world in Trinidad and this new Canadian world. The children, while full of playful energy, reminded me so much of the children back home. Mrs. Cloutier had complete control; her word was law. Each day after classes finished at the university and I was heading back to the Cloutiers', I felt that I was heading back *home*. That was a feeling that I did not take lightly. Now all that was to be no more and I did not know what was going to happen; I feared for the worst; this was nothing if not a catastrophe.

****

When I phoned the Horns they invited me to come over. I discovered that not only was their house close to the bus line, but it was also less than a block from the church I attended and within walking distance to a supermarket. While that discovery made me very happy, there was still the small matter of the Horns. *Would I like them? Would they like me?*

All fear evaporated the moment we met; I liked them both immediately. Mr. Horn, with his English accent was most engaging. Mrs. Horn won me over with her down-to-earth manner and her hearty, raspy tone. Mrs. Horn had a million questions for me but that just served to make her all the more endearing.

They explained that their home was a three bedroom bungalow. They offered to show me around; we started with their bedroom which was at the very front of the house. Mr. Horn saw me staring approvingly at the very appealing room and wasted no time crediting Mrs. Horn for her "unique touches." Then they led me to a bedroom located at the very back of the main floor. This room was a most attractive bedroom indeed. It had a double bed and a desk. A night stand and a lamp stood to the side of the bed. *Yes*, I thought to myself, *I love this room. I am going to be okay. Life is good*. I had little time to indulge my imagination for at that very moment Mr. Horn casually said, "I suppose you are anxious to see your room. Come. It is in the basement."

Oh, no, not the basement, I silently protested. *I want this room. I don't want to go to the basement.* They motioned for me to follow. I did so, reluctantly; I did not want to leave *my bedroom*.

The basement was dark; I did not like it at all. They showed me to a small bedroom that contained a bed and a closet. While the closet contained ample space, I was not drawn to this room in any way. *Why was I feeling so negatively about this room? Was it simply because I had never lived in a basement before? Was I feeling claustrophobic and shut off from everything?* I was not quite certain. Then the Horns drew my attention to the three piece bathroom and the modest kitchen. These two amenities were to be shared with their two other male tenants.

This information gave me some cause for concern. It was not as private as I would have liked and yet, it was almost too removed from the rest of the house. My feelings were quite mixed; I didn't truly know what I was thinking. As we came upstairs to the living room, Mrs. Horn asked, "Well, Frank, what do you think? Do you like the room? We would love you to stay with us."

I did not answer immediately; I had to consider the situation carefully. I *wanted* the upstairs bedroom. I really didn't know if I could survive living in a room in the basement. It was private, but not the kind of privacy I relished. That privacy invited sheer loneliness.

"Mr. and Mrs. Horn," I began, "I love your home, and the neighbourhood is great. It is just that…and I hope you understand…"

"What is it Frank? You can tell us," interrupted Mr. Horn.

Mrs. Horn added, "Frank, you don't have to hold back. We have three boys of our own. They don't live with us right now; they are away but we do have two other boys renting downstairs, so you might as well tell us…"

"Alright. I don't know if I could get used to being in a room in a basement and having to stay there all the time. I would prefer the upstairs bedroom. I am not used to…"

"Frank, is that what's bothering you?" asked a concerned Mr. Horn. "If you like, you come up stairs any time you want and visit us; we don't mind. The bedrooms upstairs are for our boys and their families when they come to visit. You are most welcome upstairs. Let's put it this way. You can sleep downstairs and live upstairs. What do you say?

That gesture spoke directly to me.

"And Frank," Mrs. Horn cautioned, "just one more thing; we really don't cook like Mrs. Cloutier. She is a very adventurous cook; our household is very conservative when it comes to cooking but you are most welcome to join us for meals. You may have to look after yourself sometimes but you certainly can join us whenever it works out. "

I could barely contain my appreciation, "Thank you, thank you both; it is more than I could ask."

We agreed on a price that was most reasonable for the accommodations. It seemed that Mrs. Cloutier *had* found me the perfect home after all.

Later, when I told Mrs. Cloutier how I felt about the Horns and how we had worked out a mutually agreeable arrangement, she, too, was happy for me. Furthermore, she offered me these words of encouragement, "Frank, you are a friend, so don't be a stranger. We do expect you to visit us from time to time."

The month ended and I packed up my things for my move to the Horns. My companions—my two suitcases and my faithful briefcase—were sufficient; everything I owned fit inside. Then it was time to say goodbye.

"Mr. and Mrs. Cloutier," I began, "I cannot thank you enough for all that you have done. I'll never forget your gourmet meals. And, Mr. Cloutier, I must say that I really enjoyed your many stories about life in Quebec."

"Goodbye, *mon ami*."

At the Cloutiers I had more than just a room; I had a home—my first home in Canada.

12

A New Home

Mr. and Mrs. Horn made me feel welcomed as soon as I entered their home. We required no adjustment time; we seemed to understand one another right from the beginning. The boys renting the downstairs however, were a different matter altogether; while they were friendly enough, they seemed to want to keep to themselves; they preferred their privacy and did not seek to establish a too familiar relationship with the Horns. That was never my goal; I soon became an extension of Mr. and Mrs. Horn; they included me in so much of their daily lives that I felt quite at home. When they had to be away for Mr. Horn's job, (he was a travelling salesman) they invited me to sleep upstairs in the guest bedroom. Whenever they were away, I had the complete run of the house. I particularly enjoyed their stereo system; it was most impressive indeed. The Horns' three sons had purchased it for their parents. The enormous wooden cabinet housed the stereo and a massive collection of LP records; giant speakers were attached to either side. Previously, the Horns had introduced me to both the system and the records, and had encouraged me to use the system whenever I wanted.

Whenever the Horns were away, I explored their vast collection of music. I felt as if I had struck pure gold when I unearthed the riches of their music. That was not all that was precious however; the Horns accommodated me richly in yet another manner.

On Sundays, they had a delightful tradition: the Sunday drive. Before we left for the drive, Mrs. Horn would prepare our supper and put it in the oven to bake while we were away. On Sundays, Mrs. Horn always provided a choice of lamb, fish, shrimp, or chicken. While Mrs. Horn always insisted that she was not a great cook, with the simple addition of Worcestershire and Tabasco sauce, our dinners were always delicious.

Sometimes we drove through the countryside, sometimes to a small town nearby. Always Mr. Horn plugged his eight-track into the car stereo system and we were entertained by Johnny Cash and Anne Murray and a delightful assortment of other country artists. Most of the time, they both added their voices to the ones radiating from the stereo. We were a very happy trio stopping for coffee along the way.

Upon returning from our Sunday drives, supper was always ready. Sunday drives were invariably followed by another Sunday tradition: dinner in the living room on T.V. trays in front of the television set. Every Sunday we watched Hymn Sing on CBC television followed by dessert and the Tommy Hunter show! These desserts were always rich, always tempting, and always completely devoured by Mr. Horn and me; soon my pants no longer fit; but then, back then, who cared? Such was my ease and joy living with the Horns.

Mrs. Horn must have felt extremely comfortable around me too, for one Sunday during supper she said, "Frank, you are going to like my boys. They are down to earth; and you are going to especially like the son who is Chicago. He looks very Italian. Why, in the summertime, he is *black* just like you."

I froze. *Black*, I was called *black*! I did not *know* I was black.

My face must have registered confusion for Mrs. Horn teased, "What's the matter Frank? You look like you've seen a ghost. You look white."

And then she started laughing; in her heart she was just having fun with me. She had only been joking but I wasn't accustomed to jokes like that. Mr. Horn, perhaps sensing some sensitivity in me regarding this area, attempted to redirect the conversation, "Frank, what is it like in Trinidad? I mean, there are so many people in Trinidad and they probably are descended from so many different backgrounds. In England, people come from all over the world; they represent all races, all the colours of the globe. What was it like for you in Trinidad?"

I knew what Mr. Horn meant to do. He was attempting to make up for Mrs. Horn's innocent comment that I was black. I took no offence at the comment, for she meant no offence. I had been momentarily startled by the comment for I had never thought of myself as black. By Trinidadian standards I was considered "fair of complexion". I was cognizant of the fact that my reaction had created a bit of an awkward moment. I considered Mr. Horn's question carefully and responded, "Mr. Horn, in Trinidad I was neither white nor black. It was that simple."

"How so, Frank?" asked Mr. Horn. "As far as I understand, the thinking is if you're not white, then you are black."

"I don't think it is quite like that for Frank," offered Mrs. Horn. "Frank, you explain it as you see it."

"Well, I grew up all my life knowing I was not white. That was very obvious. But I never knew I was black until I came to Canada."

I looked at both of them; their faces registered confusion. I continued, "In Trinidad, our Negro counterparts are considered black. We who are descended from India are regarded as neither white nor black; we are the brown people. To be sure some of our brown people are very dark and could be considered black, but, because they are Indian, they are regarded as brown. I hope this makes some sense."

"But Frank, how did you feel as a brown person—being neither white nor black?" Mr. Horn asked sensitively.

"For me brown and being brown were normal. Come to think of it while I never had the obvious advantage of the white people in Trinidad, neither did I suffer some of the negative consequences of my black counterparts. I was simply a person without colour; I was me."

"And how has your stay here in Canada been so far? How have you been treated?" Mrs. Horn asked candidly.

"Wonderful. I have had the most wonderful experiences here in Canada. Everyone has been just great. I wanted to come to Canada, and I chose Lakehead University. I am very lucky."

"Well, Frank, it is not only luck, my friend. But there is another matter I wanted to ask you about. I suppose you enjoy spicy dishes seeing you come from Trinidad," inquired Mr. Horn.

"Yes."

"I suppose you are used to curry cuisine."

"Absolutely."

"Well, it is just that it has been a long time since I have had a real curry dish. I mean an authentic curry dish. I was wondering…"

Then Mrs. Horn interrupted and finished his thought for him with this confession, "Frank, I can't make that dish. I am a simple cook. I don't venture out of my comfort zone if you know what I mean. But mind you, I don't mind if you boys want to experiment."

"Well, Mrs. Horn, I would be happy to oblige. It is not a problem."

There was however, one *slight* consideration. While I had been *present* when many a curry dish had been prepared, never did I *actually* make one.

In fact, never had I actually *cooked*.

13

My Hot Experiment

It was a delightful spring Saturday afternoon and everything that I needed to make the curry chicken was at hand in Mrs. Horn's cozy little kitchen. Mr. Horn was excited and expectant and mentioned repeatedly that he could hardly wait. The chicken had been cut up and dutifully seasoned by a variety of spices bearing unfamiliar sounding names. When it appeared that I was about to launch the whole cooking process, Mrs. Horn withdrew to the bedroom. Mr. Horn waited expectantly at my side ready to assume the duties of a *sous chef*. I had to get him out of the kitchen. I could not have him witness my ineptitude at the stove. I was nervous enough already just thinking about what I had to do; I could not have anyone witness my incompetence. I suggested to Mr. Horn that he might want to withdraw to the living room to enjoy a glass of wine. He seemed somewhat hesitant to follow my suggestion until I quickly explained that such a glass of wine would heighten his appetite and improve the general taste of the food. After that he gladly consented. The first major obstacle had been cleared and I was indeed alone in the kitchen. Now all I had to figure out was: *what do I do next?*

I had to dig deep into my memory bank for my first clue. I had to put myself back into Ma's rough hewn kitchen and remember all the sights and sounds that accompanied her cooking. *What did Ma do first?* Easy, she poured oil into a pot. A pot. I needed a pot. I looked in the cupboards and found several large shiny good-looking pots. I chose the largest and the shiniest and the best looking. I poured a generous amount of oil into the pot and turned the element on high. While waiting for the oil to heat, I peeled several cloves of garlic. I looked around for something to pound the garlic to release its pungent aroma. Nothing in my immediate eyesight seemed suitable to the task. I began opening drawers. Aha! A rolling pin.

That'll do the trick. I pulled it out and immediately pounced on the garlic. Mrs. Horn, hearing the pounding noises coming from the kitchen, left her bedroom to pay a brief visit. Satisfied that nothing was amiss, she then returned to her bedroom. Meanwhile Mr. Horn put a record on the stereo and a series of country and western hits followed. When he brought in a glass of wine for me and said, "For the master chef," I became empowered. I was in the zone; nothing could stop me now. The oil was sizzling on the stove; I added the crushed garlic confidently. Yes! The raw garlic reacted quickly with the burning oil. I was impressed. Cooking was much easier than I had thought. *Why hadn't I done this before?* My enthusiasm was short lived for soon a blanket of grey smoke enveloped the entire kitchen. It spread quickly to the living room and filtered under the door to Mrs. Horn's bedroom.

Mrs. Horn ran from her bedroom very concerned, "Frank is everything all right? Are you okay? You're covered in smoke."

I wasn't the only thing covered in smoke. By now the smoke had filtered through every part of the house. But what was worse than the smoke was the thin layer of oily garlic adding a shiny veneer to everything in the immediate vicinity of the stove. It was quite a mess.

Then the coughing began. Mr. and Mrs. Horn tried to muffle their coughs at first but soon the coughing escalated to the point where their bodies were unable to respond to their efforts to maintain calm. Mrs. Horn had to race to the back door to get some fresh air to allow herself to breathe. This action was quickly followed by the opening up of all the windows. Mr. Horn quickly came to her assistance. I stood helplessly by in the kitchen with a wooden spoon in my hand. Had I been exposed? Was my secret out? Would I be allowed to continue? I turned the heat down on the stove and awaited the verdict. While I waited I examined my actions. I had done exactly what my mother had done—well, almost. *Perhaps the heat had been a little too intense; I could keep it lower.* I wondered why we had never experienced the quantity of smoke in Trinidad the way we were here; then it began to make sense. The windows were always open when Ma was cooking. A fresh breeze always carried away the smoke. *Poor Mrs. Horn. What had I done to her kitchen? What must she think of me now? Would she let me continue exploring my culinary delight?*

I waited. The smoke cleared. Mr. and Mrs. Horn were talking quietly. No one came to me. Perhaps Mr. Horn had persuaded her that there would be no more surprises. I resumed my task. The oil and garlic now received a generous helping of chopped onion; the new mix of ingredients sizzled in perfect harmony. *What came next?* Again I searched my memory; the next step was the addition of curry. I put in a generous cup of curry powder; a familiar aroma immediately filled the kitchen. Once again Mrs. Horn visited the kitchen. Seeing that everything was relatively calm she merely casually remarked, "That's a strong spice."

Mr. Horn happily sauntered into the kitchen and confessed excitedly while clapping his hands, "Yes, Frankie, I do remember that aroma. I just love that aroma. Anytime soon, I hope?"

To which I responded, "In good time."

He smiled and withdrew to the living room.

I turned the heat up a little to ensure that all the spices in the heated oil were comfortable with each other; the garlic and onion did not mind the bold entrance of the curry powder. It was now time to see if the seasoned meat would be as well received. As I rested each piece of chicken in the pot, I sensed no protest, no hint of rebellion. I felt that I had found the right mix of ingredients.

I was proud of my creation. It looked just right; moreover, it smelled just right. Then my eyes caught sight of a stack of spices on the wall just above the stove. I checked through the collection and only one container claimed further attention. It was a deep red powder that bore a strong resemblance to a powder that my mother used to use in her stews. I looked at the powder again and decided to add it to my creation. If nothing else, it would add a bit of colour to the meat. I was right. Immediately it enhanced the colouring of my dish. I added more hoping for an even darker hue. It looked just about perfect and I had only used half of the bottle. It would be my secret ingredient. The presentation would be perfect. I turned the stove down to simmer and joined Mr. Horn in the living room. He wondered whether I had had a taste. He seemed disappointed when I said I did not; clearly he wanted a taste. I made him wait until everything was ready and on the table. I wanted to surprise him.

Soon dinner was ready; Mrs. Horn had added her touches to the table: oven baked vegetables, rice, potatoes, and a serving of fish. She had already informed me that she would probably not be eating any of the curry; it was all just for Mr. Horn and me. Mr. Horn came to the table. His eyes said it all as he surveyed the offerings on the table. "Frankie, I cannot wait another moment; bring on the creation!"

I hurried to the kitchen, transferred the curry onto a platter, and brought it to the table. It looked wonderful. Meanwhile Mrs. Horn excused herself as she said that she just had one more thing to add to the table. She came back with two huge candles and a can of scented spray. She shook the can and sprayed everywhere; then she lit the candles and brought them to the table.

"Thank you my dear; the candles are a lovely touch," beamed Mr. Horn.

I wondered if he knew that the candles were brought not merely for their ambiance, but also to absorb the strong curry aroma. Then Mrs. Horn announced, "Shall we?"

Those were the two words Mr. Horn had been waiting most patiently to hear. He reached out and helped himself to a generous serving of my curry. I did likewise. No sooner was the food on his plate then it was in his mouth. I was about two seconds behind him. Before I knew what was happening inside my mouth, Mr. Horn began to cough. I don't think that he had had his first swallow. He reached out for his glass of water; after nearly draining the glass, he took another bite. Once more he began to cough. By now I had had my first taste; my lord, my mouth was on fire. My entire mouth was consumed with a burning sensation. I couldn't understand it. *Why was this dish so hot? I had added only a small shot of hot pepper to the curry; that should never have made this dish that hot. Something else was responsible for this extreme hotness.* I looked at Mr. Horn who tried to speak reassuringly to me through brief gasps, "Lovely, Frank—quite spicy—yet lovely, thank you."

Another fit of coughing overwhelmed him. Again he reached for his water; this time the contents were emptied. Next, he retrieved his handkerchief from his pocket and dabbed beads of perspiration from his forehead. Because his hairline was somewhat retreated, he was left with what could be described as an extended forehead. This extension was gradually turning a distinct shade of red. Clearly, Mr. Horn was on fire. Yet he was not dissuaded from doing battle with the curry. He stood his ground and continued to push forward still praising my culinary talent. I was not nearly so convincing. I had already abandoned any further pretext of actually eating. All I could do now was pretend that I too had enjoyed the dish.

Then Mr. Horn asked, "Frank, the curry is tasty—delicious—yet a bit spicy. What ingredient did you use to make it so spicy?"

"Well, I added a bit of hot pepper sauce to spice it up. But that was not enough to make it this hot. I am at a loss; I don't know what to think."

Then Mrs. Horn walked in carrying a bottle. "Here is the culprit, Frank. You used this, and you used quite a bit. Do you know what this is?"

"Mrs. Horn that is a spice that's used to add colour and flavour; it's a kind of paprika; that spice is not hot."

"Frank, this is a bottle of Cayenne pepper. A heavy dose can kill you. I have had it for years—never touched it. I wouldn't. The boys might..."

"Oh, my! I used more than half a bottle! I had no idea... Mr. Horn, are you okay? I am so sorry."

"Frank, when I saw you enjoying your meal, I did not have the heart to tell you it was so hot. I thought that I had to keep up with you or something like that."

"Mr. Horn, that is exactly how I felt. It thought that if you could handle it then so should I. You were much better at staying the course; I did not want to abandon you. I was trying to be polite."

Mrs. Horn then announced, "I think that this would be a good time for dessert."

To this I can attest: nothing puts out a fire like a generous serving of apple pie and ice cream.

14
Finding that Elusive Job

The year was 1968 and it was spring. Spring meant more to me than just the promise of warm weather and green grass. Spring offered also the promise of work: legitimate work. Exams were over and finally I was free: free of the pressure of school; and now, finally free to pursue a job!

I could hardly wait to begin my search; I started immediately. I began with the construction companies: no luck. Next, I tried the department stores: still no luck. Finally I turned to the local fast food outlets: same result. Feeling somewhat discouraged, I talked with a friend who suggested that a job might be easier to land in Winnipeg. Since I already had a contact in Winnipeg, I decided that that could be a viable option.

Winnipeg was about 500 miles away; never having travelled that much by car or bus I rather relished the idea of the adventure. When I mentioned my plans to the Horns, Mrs. Horn suggested I take the route that went through the United States. She had a particular bias regarding this route because that route passed right through a border town called Rainy River; and Rainy River was the town in which she grew up. Mr. Horn expressed his concerns regarding that particular route, "I am not sure Frank should go that way. He would have to pass through Fort Frances, and if it is a warm day and the wind is just right, Frank is sure to be made most uncomfortable to say the least."

"Oh, don't be like that. Frank will survive. Besides, Fort Frances is a lovely town. Who knows, Frank may even love that place. Mark my words—you never know."

Later I would recall Mrs. Horn's words and marvel at her prophecy.

I decided to take Mrs. Horn's advice and travel through the States. I got a map and checked out all the stops along the way. Atikokan was to be our first stop. Strange name for a city I thought; I wondered how it derived its name. I was most curious to see this city and was looking forward to the stop. About three hours into the trip, we finally pulled off the main highway and travelled five or six miles north. The bus came to a stop in front of a small building on what appeared to be the main street. I was in shock—Atikokan was not the sprawling metropolis I had envisaged. Yet, in retrospect, Atikokan was small, yes, yet it was charming in its own way. I quickly adjusted my expectations. After about a twenty minute break we resumed our journey.

Mile after lonely mile unfolded before us. There was very little traffic along the two lane road stretching endlessly between Atikokan and Fort Frances. Trees, trees and more trees greeted the bus at every turn. Occasionally we'd catch a glimpse of a lake but there was not much else to break up the monotony of the trees; even the moose and deer kept their distance. Occasionally I would see an expanse of open land and would marvel that there could be so much unoccupied land anywhere in the world. It was such a foreign concept: space. But it was nearly impossible to fully appreciate the true magnitude of those open spaces from the confines of the seat on the bus.

Just before we reached Fort Frances we crossed a bridge spanning several small islands. The view of the lake was breathtaking; it was a thing of sheer beauty and I envied the people that had it all to themselves. Once past the bridge we came upon a beautifully manicured golf course. At the edge of the golf course was a Dairy Queen store. It was a surprise to find it there on the edge of the city. The bus stopped at the Dairy Queen and everyone piled out to grab a quick ice cream. I couldn't resist. Once back aboard the bus, we headed into Fort Frances. I waited to see what the town had to say for itself.

We turned right onto Second Street. The many trees bordering both sides of the street made it truly a beautiful street. There seemed to be just the right mix of sun and shade to make being outside a comfortable experience. The varied houses along this residential street added to the laid back charm of the avenue. I remember thinking that Fort Frances was lovely and I was impressed. As we entered into the heart of the town I became aware of a most unpleasant odour. It seemed to emanate from the front of the bus. The odour was so overwhelming that I thought that someone had accidentally released a *bomb* inside the bus. In all my life I had never encountered such a potently unpleasant smell. Someone explained that that smell came from the mill. I wondered how people could live surrounded by such a disagreeable odour.

It was a warm day and the potency seemed to be magnified. I remembered thinking that I could never live in such a town. Soon we were far away from Fort Frances and its most unwelcome odour.

We passed several smaller towns on our way to Rainy River, Mrs. Horn's home town. I couldn't get a very good look at it as the road did not lead into the town but rather around it. We crossed the bridge over the border to Baudette—the town on the U.S. side. Five hours later the bus pulled in to the Winnipeg depot. I felt it at once; Winnipeg was a city—a rather large city by Canadian standards. I was excited and felt very comfortable. My friends in Winnipeg welcomed me with open arms and I stayed with them for two weeks. For two weeks I explored every avenue in the hopes of finding employment. Nothing materialized however, and I returned to the Lakehead saddened and disappointed.

On the return trip, the bus took an alternate route. We did not pass through Fort Frances but through the towns of Kenora and Dryden. It was the all Canadian route. At Dryden, the driver informed us that we would be stopping for an extended period of time. I welcomed this break as the endless hours spent on the bus were taking a toll on my body. I needed to stretch. I did not follow the other passengers into the restaurant.

I began to walk; just window shopping and generally checking out the town. I came upon a large warehouse that bore a sign above the door: *Twin City Gas Company.*

With nothing to lose, I found myself walking through the door. A gentleman in a suit was standing in the outer office. When he saw me he looked up and asked, "How can I help you?"

"Find me a job."

"Well, you certainly wasted no time in stating your business. What can you do?"

"What do you need?"

"Can you use a shovel like your life depended on it?"

"Mister, I was born with a shovel in my hand."

"Really?"

"Yes."

"Where are you from?"

"The Lakehead."

"You don't look like you can use a shovel. You're all dressed up."

"I can."

"Where were you born?"

"Trinidad."

"I suppose you worked hard there. Can you do manual labour?"

"Yes"

"Really?" He sounded doubtful. "You can dig a ditch?"

"Mister I come from a family whose last name might very well be 'work'."

He looked at me for a while and said nothing. He was pensive; he seemed to be debating the pros and cons in his mind. With decisiveness, he approached and looked me squarely in the eye, "We will see just how good a worker you are. Come to the office in Inter-City."

Then he handed me a card with the address of the company on it.

"Let's say about 8:00 am. Tomorrow."

"Thank you, I'll be there. My name is Frank."

"Pleased to meet you, Frank. I am Bill Richards."

I hurried back to the bus depot; I didn't want to miss my bus. After all, I now had a job.

15

First Days at Twin City

When I arrived at the office the next morning, Bill Richards, the manager, was on hand to greet me. He rested down his cup of coffee as I entered and, after careful examination, declared, "I see you are dressed appropriately. When I first met you, I was not sure that you owned any working clothes."

Right at that moment, a young man of about thirty walked in. The first thing that I noticed about him was his mass of disheveled blond hair. His five feet five inch muscular frame seemed diminutive in comparison.

"Good morning, Boss," he uttered cheerfully as he rubbed his hands together.

"Good morning, Yogi," replied Richards.

Then Yogi inquired, "Hope you got me a good man."

"Yes I did; here, take a look. Yogi, this is Frank Maraj—the new guy—the last piece to the puzzle."

I was struck by Richards' choice of words, *the last piece to the puzzle* and I wondered just what it meant.

After hearing those words, Yogi examined me critically. I felt as if I were a piece of property being sold at auction. His dismissing grunts made me feel uncomfortable. I could already sense his disapproval. His words merely confirmed it, "This is what you give me, Boss? Does he look like the guy we need? Come on, Boss, he is soft. We have no time to waste. Send him home. I have another guy that..."

"No!" I yelled. "I am not going home. I am your man. I came here to work. Now take me to the job."

I wasn't the only one shocked by my reaction. Both Yogi and Richards were silenced. I wanted to scream, *Give me a chance please! Just don't send me away!*

I waited for someone to respond. Yogi was the first to speak, "Okay, Boss, you must see something that I don't."

Then, without even looking at me, Yogi barked his order, "Come with me."

I was relieved; at least I was being given a chance; that was all that I had wanted: a fair chance to prove myself.

I followed Yogi to the warehouse where several other workers were assembled. Two half ton trucks stood in wait, ready to receive their cargo. The men quickly piled into the trucks once they saw Yogi approach. Yogi directed me to the open flatbed section as the cab was already full. All ten of us headed for the same worksite in Fort William. As the trucks came to a stop I saw that a five foot wide trench had been dug and it continued on for about two city blocks. I noted that various pieces of equipment, a backhoe, a tractor, and a heavy roller were all parked awaiting drivers. Each worker hastened to a pre-assigned piece of equipment. I wondered how I fit in. *What is my job? I don't have a licence. I can't drive any of the equipment. What am I to do?*

Yogi handed me my answer—*a shovel.*

He growled his orders at me, "Frank, take a look at the bottom of the trench. See all the sand and pieces of dirt that fell in there overnight? Your job: clean it up. Then we can install the gas lines. Start at this end; we needed it done like, *yesterday.*"

"Like yesterday," I repeated the words to myself, what does that mean? I guessed that it meant get to work now. I looked around to see who else had been assigned clean up detail. There was no one else. I was alone.

I filled my first shovelful of dirt. I flung it hard hoping that the dirt would land well beyond the top of the bank. It didn't. This happened with each load. My efforts were proving fruitless. In fact they were considerably less than fruitless if one takes into consideration that not only did most of the dirt on my shovel fall back into the ditch, but also the dirt that made it to the top of the ditch dislodged the surface area of the bank causing even more dirt to fall into the trench. I now had even more debris to clear.

Added to the awkward mechanics of the job there was yet one more complication—my physical condition or more appropriately stated—my *lack* of physical conditioning. While it was true that I had done a great deal of manual labour in the past, that is exactly where it stopped, in the past. For the last several years, only my intellectual, emotional, spiritual, and social labours had been tested. Physically, I was out of shape. I was not the *master shovel specialist* that this job required. Having thus recognized my limitations, I was frustrated. But, being frustrated did not mean giving up; I just had to think of another way to accomplish this task. And I did exactly that.

I began by shoveling lose clumps of dirt into a pile starting from one direction. When I had gone as far as I could go in that direction, I started shoveling from the opposite direction until the two mounds met forming one grand mass. I jumped out of the trench and began to scale back the top of the bank. In this way I hoped that I could lower the top of the bank so that I would be able to successfully throw out the dirt from the trench.

Dave, another university hire, happened to be passing by my area with his grader. He looked, and understood immediately what I was trying to do; without so much as a word, he used his grader to level that part of the bank for me. Reenergized I set to work extracting the remaining debris from the trench. I had never worked that hard in years. I was near exhaustion when Yogi came by to inspect. He snorted something inaudible and then yelled, "Lunch time."

He had not said, "You're fired!" That was enough for me. Happily I joined the others sitting beneath a tree on a nearby lawn. I sat next to Dave. He moved a little to accommodate me and said, "I'm Dave."

I simply responded, "I'm Frank."

I looked at the crew chattering with one another and chomping away at their lunches; for the moment I felt a guarded peace.

For the next two days my life as the *master shoveler* continued without incident. Then, on the third day I was working on a trench that was not perfectly straight. This section had a curve to it and I was unable to see what was going on around the bend. Pipe lines had been laid on most of the trench and the process of welding had begun beyond the curved area. I continued my clean-up detail and, because of the curved nature of the trench, I was unaware that any welding was in progress.

I noticed that a section of the pipeline was resting on clumps of earth making it level with the rest of the line. I was not aware that a level line was crucial to a successful weld and that great pains had been expended to secure and level this section. I knew nothing about welding. I must have accidentally stepped on the pipeline thus interfering with its level. Suddenly from out of nowhere came a man, wrench in hand, red and angry of face. Expecting the worst, I braced myself for the inevitable reprimand. It never came. After looking me over for a moment he spoke. Although his words were curt, his tone was civil.

"Come with me!"

I did.

He took me to the area where he was welding; it was just beyond the curve, not far from where I had been working.

He pointed to the pipe he was welding and stated, "Look, it's ruined. I have to start over; when I am welding, stay clear."

Still confused about what had just transpired, I returned to my area. Luckily, Dave had overheard the conversation and explained, "Frank, don't take it personally. Jimmy gets irritable when someone is careless. He simply wants everyone to stay clear of the pipe."

"But Dave, what do I do in the trench when he is welding?"

"Find some other work; look busy. And stay clear of Jimmy. Don't worry. Everyone understands. It's the nature of the job."

After Dave left I understood that once again I had to manufacture a scheme to appear to be working. I would do anything to hold on to that job, the job that paid $1.50 an hour when the average wage was around $1.00 an hour only.

When the day ended, Jimmy came by and asked, "Hey, can you hold on a moment? I'll give you a ride."

"Sure. I would like that."

Then I spotted his rig—a truck fully equipped with propane tanks and welding equipment. This was most definitely the truck of a working man.

I knew that Jimmy lived in Fort William. I lived in Current River; to take me home, he would have to drive completely out of his way. When I explained to him where I lived, I expected that he would drive me to the nearest bus stop. Jimmy simply said, "I am taking you home."

As we drove, Jimmy asked, "Frank, you understand the situation when I am welding?"

"Yes, I do. Sorry, I was careless."

"Not your fault. It is Yogi. He should tell you about the job."

Jimmy was not one for long explanations, or for long sentences. He listened more than he talked. Yet I was able to learn that Jimmy was married and had children. I sensed above all, that he was a family man. Before he dropped me off, he asked, "Frank, you're okay?"

I nodded, he smiled and was off. I liked Jimmy Wilson right away. As the days progressed, Jimmy always found a moment here and there to communicate with me—*Jimmy style*. Once we spent an entire lunchtime sitting together and saying almost nothing. Every now and again Jimmy would say a few words, point something out, and smile. Everything that needed to be said was said in that smile, for in that smile was acceptance.

When the week ended, I was still part of the work force.

Monday arrived. Yogi approached me and growled, "Frank, do you have your licence?"

Without waiting for an answer, he left; I was confused.

At lunchtime I sat with Jimmy and told him what Yogi had said. Jimmy turned to me and stated, "Frank, get your licence. You need to have it. Do it soon, or else..."

Jimmy's tone sounded ominous...

16

The Much Needed Driver's Licence

The very next day over the lunch hour, Jimmy drove me to the Licensing Office located at the Inter-City Mall on Memorial Avenue near Simpson Sears. I took the written part of the test right then and there and passed. Many of the rules and laws were similar to those in Trinidad; this allowed me to pass the test with ease. Excited at having passed this first test so easily, I made an appointment to take the driving part of the test in two days' time. I did not give much thought to what was actually involved in taking a driver's test in Canada… I should have.

The two days passed quickly. I needed a vehicle in which to take the test. Again, my friend Jimmy came to my rescue. He drove me to the mall and handed me the keys to his truck; his precious welding truck containing all of his valuable equipment. I made my presence known at the office and waited. Soon, the officer came out; before getting into the cab, he carefully examined the unit both inside and out. Once satisfied he declared, "Proceed!"

I was curious about the comment: *proceed*. Nonetheless, I waited for him to tell me where to drive. After some moments, he finally ordered, "Proceed to Simpson Street."

Simpson Street was straight ahead. It was rather busy, and consisted of four lanes. I began my approach onto Simpson Street. The truck, heavy with equipment, chugged along; its gears ground loudly as I approached the entrance to Simpson Street. The inspector did not indicate which direction I was to take and when I asked, he dismissed my inquiry saying, "I shall tell you, thank you." *Had he just put me in my place?* Then, my reluctant officer commanded, "Negotiate a right turn."

His order was confusing. Why did he say, *negotiate a right turn*? Was that a Canadian thing: *negotiate*? In Trinidad one simply says, *turn right*. I guessed that he means turn right, and I completed a right turn. I was now on the inside lane and expected to continue in that lane for a while, when the officer once again ordered, "Negotiate a right turn at the next intersection."

There he goes again with that *negotiate* business. I thought that I had better get off the inside lane and occupy the outside lane to *negotiate* the right turn. I was a little uneasy for I found this instructor a little difficult to understand. I turned on my signals to indicate my intention, and when it was safe, I edged into the right lane. I was pleased that I had once again successfully *negotiated* a right turn. I smiled and began to relax.

Suddenly, ahead of me and heading straight for me, was a huge Pepsi truck; he was in my lane. *What a stupid madman!* I thought. I turned my head slightly to look at the officer seated to my right. His hands were on the dashboard in a brace position; his face was white. *Well, he's not going to be any help.*

"Idiot!" I yelled to the driver. "Get out of the way!"

He did not move. *Well*, I reasoned, *if he's not moving, then I will*.

To avoid what would surely be a head on collision, I moved to the other lane. The other driver did the very same thing. Again we were headed for a collision.

I must keep my cool; that driver is crazy.

I veered to the shoulder and stopped; he returned to his other side. As he passed by, he honked and delivered the famous finger to me. I couldn't understand why he would gesture so rudely especially since I had made such a valiant effort to avert an accident. *How utterly ungrateful!*

At last I had a moment to catch my breath. I looked at the officer; he was holding his chest and gasping for air. I then looked at the flow of the traffic. Everyone seemed to be going the wrong way. Then it dawned on me. I had been going the wrong way. When I *negotiated* that last right turn, I stayed on the *left* lane. For a moment, I was in Trinidad driving on the *left hand* side which is the correct lane in Trinidad, but was the *wrong* side in Canada. Inadvertently, I had put the driver of the Pepsi truck at risk. I was in the wrong lane. Horrified at my error, I turned my attention to the inspector. He was still in a state of shock. *I guess it is all over for me. How could such a dangerous mistake be overlooked?*

Hesitantly, I asked, "Guess you want to drive now? I am so sorry."

I half expected him to kick me out of the vehicle. Considering what had almost happened, it seemed only reasonable. At the very least I expected that he would take over the driving; all things considered, that action seemed almost mandated.

His response to my question shocked me, "No! You continue; you drive."

Had he just said, *You drive*? He must be crazier than I am.

Then I thought that maybe he was giving me a second chance. There was still room for hope. *Man*, I thought, *this Canadian officer is great*.

I started the rig and cautiously drove back to the office. The inspector never uttered a single word. *Yes, this kind officer is giving me a chance to make amends. Yes, I love Canada*. I parked the vehicle outside the office building and the inspector asked me to come in to the office. *Man, I love Canadians*.

Safely inside the office, the inspector asked me to have a seat.

Once I was seated, he continued, "Mr. Maraj, there is no question about your ability to drive. You know how to drive."

I was so relieved. *I'm going to get my licence. Jimmy will be so pleased*.

"But," then he paused to stress what came next, "*I want to save your life. More importantly, I want to save the lives of the people you are about to kill*."

"But, what do you mean?"

I was taken aback. What a reversal of expectation. He had more to say, "Tell me, on what side of the road do you drive in your country?"

"The left-hand side."

"I see. Do you have any experience driving on the right-hand side of the road, the right side of the road, the *correct* side of the road in Canada? Got it? Now, go practise driving on the right hand side; but, not by yourself. Have someone with you always. Remember when you are driving that you are now in Canada. I want you to stay alive. "

It goes without saying: I was denied a licence. It made sense. But, uppermost in my mind was this reality—no licence equaled no job.

Jimmy was waiting for me. He asked, "What happened, Frank?"

"The officer said I could drive, but never gave me my licence. I made one bad turn and drove on left side of the road. I almost had a bad accident."

Jimmy simply said, "I see. Sorry."

He was quiet as he reflected on the matter. Then he advised, "Frank, don't tell Yogi you failed the test. Tell him you need some practice. I will help you. Early next week we will be in Kenora. Take your test there. Okay? Don't tell anyone you failed.

I heeded Jimmy's advice and at the end of that day Yogi came to me a bit disgruntled.

"Frank, no licence?"

"Not yet."

"What do you mean, 'not yet'?"

Here I had to most careful and diplomatic. Yogi now had reason to get me fired since I did not have my licence. It was important that I do nothing to displease him. I remembered Jim's caution, *Don't tell Yogi you failed*.

Mustering up all my calm reserves I tried to be nonchalant as I replied matter of factly, "Yogi, the instructor told me that I was a good driver. He advised that I practise a little more. I need practice. Will you help me?"

"How so?"

"Well, you could supervise some practices. Do you think you could help?"

"I am a busy man these days. I will talk to Jimmy."

"I understand from Jimmy that we are going to Kenora next Monday? Is that right?"

"Yes. So?"

"Well, I will make an appointment to have the driver's test there during the lunch hour. Will you suggest the day?"

"Why?"

"Well, once I make the appointment, I will have to keep it and it would be helpful if Jimmy and I were both free to keep the appointment as I would need to use his vehicle for the test."

Yogi looked at me. I am not sure what he thought of me. What I could appreciate however, was the fact that he did not fire me; nor did he *threaten* to fire me. In truth I knew that the threat hovered over me like a dark cloud.

"Frank, make sure you get your licence. We are depending on you."

"Yes, Yogi."

17
At Last...

As we travelled from the Lakehead to Kenora I was struck by the beautiful although somewhat desolate landscape; to me it seemed awfully lonesome. Towns were so very few and so very far between. On my little island of Trinidad, I was always surrounded by people and towns and traffic. It was hard to find quiet. Here, it would appear that one could be smothered in solitude. One could travel miles without encountering a town or another vehicle. I quickly came to realize that to the residents of this part of Canada, this land and the people who chose it as home, was their personal pride; they prized it and their way of life above all else; while I, still a stranger, had yet to appreciate the full scope of its vast riches.

We began our trip early on a Saturday morning. A small convoy headed for the remote town of Kenora some two hundred miles away. (I still could not believe that we could travel so many miles and see so few signs of life.) When we arrived, Dave and I secured accommodation at a modest motel; the others were able to find more comfortable accommodations (albeit at a less comfortable price). I discovered that Dave and I shared many of the same values and life styles. He too was attending university and had to carefully monitor his finances. He too was not in the habit of drinking or smoking. He too was careful about his language; it was easy to get along with Dave.

The first thing that I did during our lunch break on Monday was schedule an appointment for my driver's exam. I was able to take the exam the very next day at lunch time. When I told Jimmy he was pleased; Yogi nodded his consent when he too was informed. Tuesday morning we started back to work bright and early; my task was to dig a trench by hand across private property in order to connect the gas line from the street to the house. It was an older home and the lawn was in meticulous condition. It was supposed to be an easy task for me to dig that trench.

And it was; well, it was for the first two hours and Yogi seemed pleased with the progress that I was making.

Then I encountered *the rock*; no matter how hard I tried I was not able to make any headway; that piece of granite seemed immovable. I was at a loss about how to proceed. The crew had dug the necessary hole to connect the gas line from the street; their task was done; but, there was no completed trench in which to lay the pipeline. By now it was almost time for lunch and my appointment was just minutes away. We were at a standstill; everyone assumed that we would break for lunch and then resume our task with a fresh vision. When Yogi came by I made the mistake of reminding him that I was on my way to the licensing office to take my driver's test.

Yogi's mouth exploded, "Frank Maraj, you lazy, son of a b****! What the hell are you thinking? You've been taking it easy for the past hour! I've got a good mind to fire your sorry a**! You want to have a lunch break. Get your f***ing shovel and finish the f***ing job.

I felt the pain of one humiliated. His explosive expletives were hard to digest.

My shovel was still in my hand and the temptation to strike back was strong; I don't think that I would ever have actually hit Yogi; nor would I have cursed him in the same manner that he did me; but I did want to tell him off.

That I had been sworn at, hurt; that I had been sworn at in front of my co-workers, hurt even more; that I had been sworn at by a *Canadian*, hurt the most.

Canadians in Trinidad enjoyed an elevated status; never had I encountered an ill-mannered Canadian. Yogi educated me that day and erased some of my naïveté. He helped me to understand that people are just people; no one nationality can lay claim to absolute *goodness or badness*. Yogi was but one Canadian; his behaviour was the behaviour of but one individual. Surely I could swallow my pride… *for now*. To do anything else would be foolish. I would most certainly lose my job and then where would I be? Penniless *and* jobless. Thus I chose to endure Yogi's insulting outburst; *"Another day, another time,"* I whispered.

Yet I needed to do something to assuage the raging emotion deep within; I threw my shovel and slammed it into the ground. In doing so it struck the rock with such force that people couldn't help but notice that the rock posed a huge obstacle. Jimmy jumped into the trench and began to dig. He soon recognized that the rock was virtually immoveable by one man and one shovel. Without saying a word, he gave the shovel to Yogi. He motioned for Yogi to start digging and see for himself. Yogi waved both him and the shovel away, while muttering something to Jimmy.

Jimmy came to me with a smile and said, "Frankie, let's go do your test."

****

On our way to the licensing office, Jimmy grabbed a marker from the glove box and gave the following instruction:

"Take it, and mark the letter R on two of your finger tips on each hand."

What a strange instruction; I did not understand; *how was this going to help me?*

Again Jimmy urged, "Go on, write the letter R."

Then it dawned on me: R meant right. Jimmy was offering me a clever way of reminding myself to drive on the right hand side of the road.

I received my licence thanks in large part to my good friend, Jimmy Wilson.

****

It was Sunday morning in Kenora and I was thrilled to have the day off. I planned to explore the town. At about 9:00 a.m. Dave invited me to attend church with him. I was not surprised that Dave was religiously inclined for this seemed to fit in with everything else that I was getting to know about him. While he was part of the crew, he stood apart from them in both speech and manner. He tended to spend time by himself when the others went out for the evening. That he asked me to join him at church came as a bit of a surprise, but I consented happily. An hour later, or so, we headed for church together.

His church was a new experience for me. Up until that day I had been familiar with only the Catholic Church in Trinidad, and the United Church in Current River. This church was a Mormon church. It was filled with families. The key element stressed in the service was *The Love of and for Family, and Neighbour*. As the service concluded, Dave was swallowed up by a small group of people. He motioned for me to come and join them. Two families had gathered around him; Dave introduced himself and me to both families; we chatted freely for some minutes when one family invited Dave to their home for lunch; the other family invited me to theirs. We both accepted our separate invitations and were immediately swept away.

It was the Campbell family that invited me to their home. The family consisted of the parents and four children: three girls and a boy. Almost immediately, Mrs. Campbell began with her apologies, "Frank, we are so happy that you accepted to come to our home. I hope you don't mind. We are in a state of repairs. There's insulation exposed everywhere and..."

I hastened to quickly assure her, "Mrs. Campbell, please do not worry. I will be comfortable. I am just happy to be with all of you, thank you."

When we arrived at their home, Mr. Campbell offered to give me a tour. The house was indeed in a state of repair and renovation. And, just as Mrs. Campbell had indicated, there was insulation everywhere. The walls were not yet covered and the floors were bare. But, the house was spacious. When we returned to the kitchen, we all sat around a table with a most unusual shape neither round nor rectangular; Mr. Campbell had designed it himself. I understood that this was the heart of the home and instantly that huge house was no longer just a house. Everything felt so right. Gone was the awkwardness of strangers. There was an inexplicable bond being rooted on that very first meeting.

Little did I realise then that *this* family would become my sanctuary: my shield from the raging tempest that was soon to come.

18

The Ear Falls Experience

On Monday morning our crew packed up and headed for Ear Falls, Ontario. Never having been there, I was most curious to see it. The crew expressed mixed feelings about this place for, while they were glad to have the opportunity to continue working, they grumbled about being sent to "the middle of nowhere."

Kenora came with its share of challenges; its hilly and often rugged terrain was not amenable to construction vehicles. The frequently encountered rocks and slopes were huge obstacles to overcome and demanded the utmost in patience and expertise from the whole crew. Yet, for all its faults, Kenora had enough in the way of *social amenities* to claim the attention of the crew and calm their frustrations at the end of the day. Because of that the crew was able to manage quite well when they were away from home.

By the way everyone was talking, I did not get the feeling that this could be replicated in Ear Falls. Ear Falls was being described as a wasteland and a barren outpost. There was a great deal of groaning and complaining. As the miles passed, I sensed a growing irritation among the crew. Yogi especially became visibly agitated and prone to volatility; he took to yelling and cursing at the crew. Accustomed to his outbursts, the crew returned fire in an equally colourful and vocal manner. It appeared that I was the lone exception and I did not go unnoticed. Apparently my silence further provoked Yogi.

There was no mistaking the sarcasm in his voice when he said, "So Frank, you don't drink, you don't cuss you don't go to the bars. What the f*** do you do?"

An awkward silenced ensued but he was not finished. "Frank, look at us . We are f***ing normal people. We do all the f***ing normal things.

You're like a f***ing stick in the mud. So I'm sure you're going to f***ing love Ear f***ing Falls. It's a son of a f***ing waste just like you."

Yogi's daggers pierced my heart; it oozed the blood born of isolation. *Should I have said something in my defence?* There was a certain risk in my avowed silence for it provided Yogi with an open invitation to pick on me at every turn. I was aware of his disturbing tendency to do just that. Yet, I swallowed his poison hoping that that my soul possessed enough of an antidote to prevent its certain death.

Then my mind drifted to the Campbell family and a sadness welled within me. *Why did thinking of them make me sad? There was something very special about that family; they made me feel special when I was with them.* That Sunday, when I told them that we were leaving Kenora and heading out for Ear Falls, Mrs. Campbell made me promise to contact them on my return. Already I was missing them and could not wait to rejoin the family. For now I had to find a way to survive the indignities hurled my way by Yogi.

That evening we secured lodging at the local motel in Ear Falls. Again Dave and I shared accommodations while the rest of the crew chose their own individual quarters.

The following morning we rose early, had breakfast, and then drove to the work site which was located in a new development. The Twin City Gas Company had been awarded the contract for installing gas lines in this new neighbourhood. The street was not yet paved and a strange mixture of mud and gravel covered the road. The members of the crew wasted no time in setting up their equipment and soon each piece of equipment was buzzing with activity.

I, on the other hand, was a little disquieted for I was not certain about my specific job duties. My work instinct kicked in however, and I grabbed a shovel and headed towards the nearest tractor; my intention was to assist with the digging of the trench. Yogi had other plans for me.

Before I could make it to the tractor, Yogi intercepted me and ordered me to get into his truck. He drove me to another work site at another recently developed area. The road leading to this development was not yet paved and the recent rains had made it a muddy mess of ruts. The main gas line had already been laid but there were some houses that were not yet connected to it. While a deep trench had already been dug, it was not yet ready to receive the pipe line. Huge clumps of earth and mud had fallen back into the trench and had to be removed. Thus Frank Maraj, the *shovel-engineer,* had been engaged; and Yogi delighted in reminding me once again as to why I was hired, "Frank, grab your f***ing shovel. Take a close look at the f***ing ditch. You have to clear the f***ing trench. We have to connect the bleeding f***ing gas today-after lunch; that f***ing rain over the weekend made a f***ing mess. You are the f***ing expert at shovelling. Now start f***ing shovelling.

He then turned around and walked back to his truck. In seconds he was zigzagging his way over the mud-packed road. Yogi's innate predisposition towards impatience overshadowed any basic common sense that he may have possessed.

Even though he was my boss, I found it extremely challenging to listen to Yogi. He seemed incapable of uttering a sentence without swearing. I climbed down into the ditch and tried to clear my mind of his profanities. Completely immersing myself in work proved to be a successful antidote. My resolve hardened as I applied my shovel to the bottom of the trench. The task was not an easy one for the muddy clusters proved to be nearly unmovable as they stood in steadfast rebellion against my shovel. They remained anchored firmly into the earth beneath, obstinate in their refusal to be disengaged. These mud packed pieces of earth openly resisted even my strongest efforts. It had been years since I had worked this hard; I was struggling.

When Yogi made an appearance some two hours later, he was far from pleased with my *progress*. The more he looked, the angrier he became. Again he hurled a volley of insults my way and I had to absorb them. I had nothing to say in my defence; I was the one who had claimed that I knew how to work hard; I was the one who had been selected for the job; I was the one whose performance was suspect. I was *the shovel engineer*. Yogi wasted no time delivering his ultimatum.

"Frank Maraj, I don't care who the f*** you are or what f***ing mother you came from. You are not holding up your f***ing end of the bargain. You're f***ing falling behind. If you cannot deliver then I cannot f***ing use you. Do you understand? I will fire your sorry f***ing a**. That is one f***ing promise. You can f***ing bank on it!"

Again and again I bore these insults resisting the temptation to use the shovel as an instrument to curb his profanities. I resisted the temptation to shove it down his throat, not in retaliation but rather as a means of silencing him. Yet, I recognized that Yogi did have a legitimate complaint; I had not made much progress and was not keeping up with my share of the work. If I had any hopes of keeping this job, I needed to prove myself. Thus I resolved to finish clearing the trench; to that singular task I plied myself tirelessly. Muscles ached with every stroke; exhaustion threatened but I was determined. Again and again I channelled my anger and my energies through the shovel into the ground below.

I recalled a time in my early life when I worked on that cane field; it took me nearly two full days to cut that cane. I had battled the elements—the rain and the heat—but I did it. I was focused and I had a purpose; I had to make money to pay my high school fees. I survived even though I was robbed of my wages by the very man who hired me. I reasoned that if I was able to survive that then surely I could survive Yogi. I developed a fresh resolve.

I needed the job in order to pay for another year of university. Once that reality became etched in my brain, I became an insane machine—body and mind were united in one singular focus: dig, dig; throw, throw. I was a one man chain gang.

Sweat poured off my body; every muscle ached in rebellion wanting to be rid of the task. The trench soon yielded to my will. With an uplifted spirit I leaned back against a tree to review my accomplishment. My shirt, saturated with perspiration, begged to be removed.

No sooner had I dispensed with my shirt than a young child, no more than six years old, happened by. When she saw me her eyes grew large and round and her mouth dropped open. I wasn't quite sure how to gauge her reaction: horror or surprise. When she abruptly left, I thought the former; but when she reappeared moments later dragging her mother along behind her I opted for the latter reaction—surprise.

Upon seeing me, the mother pulled back somewhat. This did not dissuade the child for she boldly walked up to me, extended her hand and began to rub the skin on my hand with the innocence of her six years.

And, with the innocent candour of a child she spoke, "See mommy? *The black won't rub off his skin.* Why won't the black rub off?"

I believe that the young mother was in a state of shock at her daughter's extreme openness. After somewhat regaining her composure the mother, too, approached me and offered an apology, "Oh, I am so sorry, so very sorry, Sir." She then turned to reprimand her child, "Catherine, you come here right now and say 'sorry' to this gentleman. You said something very bad...."

Upon hearing the work 'bad', young Catherine began to sob uncontrollably. I felt that the onus was on me to rescue her.

"Ma'am, no. She did not say anything bad. She is but a child; she was being a child."

When I asked the mother to bring little Catherine closer I explained, "Catherine, come and rub my hand." The reprimand seemed to have robbed her of her boldness and she approached most hesitantly. "Catherine, you are right: the colour won't come off."

"Why won't it rub off?"

"My colour is a gift, and I get to keep it forever."

"Who gave you that gift?"

"I'll let your mommy explain it to you. Okay?"

"Okay. Thank you."

With those few words I had managed to contain what could have been a very embarrassing scene. In those muddy surroundings I beheld the innocence of childhood. I felt uplifted; removed from the obscenities that had been launched earlier in the day.

Moments later, the little girl returned with a cool glass of lemonade for me.

Later, Yogi stopped by. Miracle of miracles, he did not start in with the cussing. Quite the contrary; he *seemed* pleased. He did not *say* he was pleased, nor did he smile. He simply did not cuss. He muttered something and took off. I did not hear what he said and it did not bother me in the least. I was at peace sitting under the shade of the tree smiling at the heavens sipping the best lemonade ever.

Nowhere could one find a happier *shovel engineer*.

****

On Friday evening, after having put in a seemingly endless work week in Ear Falls, the crew was ready to celebrate. They gathered in the lobby of the motel and decided to travel to Red Lake, a slightly larger town about sixty miles away.

Much to my surprise, the crew invited me to join them. Happy to be included, I accepted. And so it was that two trucks left Ear Falls for a night out on the town in Red Lake. When we arrived, most of the men headed for the bar. I went to the restaurant and ordered supper. Jimmy soon joined me. After supper, we joined the crew in the lounge. Music was blasting and neither Jimmy nor I was inclined to stay. When Jimmy announced that he was going to head back to Ear Falls, I opted to accompany him. We found Yogi and informed him of our plans.

Yogi's strong reaction caught me by surprise, "Where the f*** are you going? You have to f***ing stay. Jim, you go without Frank."

Jimmy looked at me. I could tell he really wanted to go. "Okay, boss." Then Jimmy left: by himself.

Feeling somewhat abandoned I rejoined the men in the lounge. As the band grew louder, so too, the crew. Everyone but me seemed jubilant. Yogi was especially happy, "Frank, are you having a good time? You must not have too much of a good time. You have to stay sober. You have to drive us back to the hotel. Got it? Now have some fun. Loosen up. Enjoy yourself, but stay sober!"

Yogi would never know how relieved I was to not be required to drink. He provided me with a legitimate reason to decline any drinks. When the waitress approached and asked for my drink order, I was able to look her in the eye and say with an air of manufactured disappointment that I could not indulge as I was the designated driver. She must have truly believed that I was disappointed at not being able to have a drink, for moments later she returned with a soft drink.

"This is for you; we can't have you be left out entirely now, can we?"

I appreciated the beverage. Soon the dense smoke, the loud crowd and the even louder band got the better of me; a massive headache seized me and I was forced to retreat to the restaurant which was now empty. I found a quiet corner and put my head down on the table. I remained undisturbed for quite some time until Yogi found me out.

"Frank, we've decided to spend the night here. We booked some rooms. So come on in and join the party. Have a drink. It's on me. Okay?"

While impressed by this new side of Yogi—the side that did not yell or curse—nevertheless, I did not wish to spend the night. I needed to be away from the smoke and the noise.

"Yogi, I'm not feeling well. I will be too much of a bother to you if I stay. I should go back to Ear Falls. Then you won't have to worry about me. Is that okay with you?"

"But we have no way of getting back if you take a vehicle to Ear Falls by yourself. We need you here, buddy."

"Oh, no problem. Jimmy and I will come back for you tomorrow, just phone. We would be happy to come back."

Yogi took a moment to reflect on what I had just said. Then he took another moment to empty his bottle. In a most agreeable manner he said, "Okay, Frank, my buddy, you go! I'll call tomorrow." He paused as he left the restaurant. Then he turned and offered once more, "Sure you won't have just a little? It might fix that headache of yours."

I shook my head to decline his offer and was left to wonder what was going on with Yogi. He was behaving like a normal human being; he called me 'buddy' and spoke with such understanding. Once again he never cursed or yelled. This establishment sure had an agreeable effect on Yogi. This was the very first time since I met Yogi that he was actually civil. He was more than just civil. He was downright affable.

I did not waste any more time thinking about it; I jumped behind the wheel of the truck and headed back to Ear Falls before the spell broke and he changed his mind.

It was a lonely stretch of highway: all sixty miles of it. I couldn't have gone more than twenty miles when I began to feel drowsy; I was straining to stay awake. There were no other vehicles on the highway; I was completely alone. I hadn't seen another vehicle for the past ten miles. There was nothing coming or going. I felt like I owned the road. Not a good thing for a recently reformed driver to feel. It could lull one into a state of dreamy complacency. It could make one feel that one was back in one's old country where the rules of the road were different. One's natural reflexes could revert to the old ways very easily. No one should be surprised about what happened next. Somehow I drifted over to the left lane. It felt so normal. I was completely unaware that I had switched lanes. Imagine my surprise to be suddenly faced with a set of headlights directed straight at me.

I do remember yelling, "Move over you crazy fool!"

The vehicle let out two huge blasts of its horn. In an instant I came to my senses and realized that the fault was within me. I was on the wrong side of the road. How long had I been in the left lane, I'll never know. Quickly I swerved to the right lane and avoided a collision. The hairs stood up on my neck and my whole body began to shake as I realized just how close I had come to totaling the vehicle. The other driver was in very little real danger for he was driving a massive transport; I, on the other hand, would have been most certainly on my way to my next life—whatever and wherever it might be.

What had I just done? I wanted to *walk* back to Ear Falls; I pulled over to the side of the road and remained in that truck for the longest while before attempting to continue. Once more I had been spared; once more I had been given a second chance.

19
Yogi Bear

Summer was well on its way and once again our crew had a contract for more work in the beautiful town of Kenora. To this very day, if someone were to mention the name, Kenora, I immediately think of the Campbells. To me, they are one and the same. The two were so intertwined in my mind that they became synonymous—thinking of one naturally led to thinking of the other. Thus it was only natural that I would try to contact the Campbells immediately upon our arrival in Kenora.

They wasted no time getting to the hotel to pick me up and take me to their home.

Once safely home, Mrs. Campbell became very serious as she asked, "Frank, we have a huge favour to ask you. We wonder how you would feel if we…"

Mr. Campbell interrupted and continued, "Well, Frank, it is like this. Margaret and Dorothy are having some difficulties at some classes at their high school. They could sure use some help. We wondered if…"

"I would be happy to help out. I would absolutely do it."

Then Mrs. Campbell interjected, "Frank, we were hoping by way of payment that you would stay with us. We hope that the two things would balance each other out. You'd be helping us, and hopefully, we'd be helping you. Would you mind such an arrangement? I know our home isn't finished, but do you think you would mind staying here…?"

"But, that is not fair."

"What do you mean, Frank?" asked a puzzled Mr. Campbell.

"You are not being fair to yourselves. You have to charge me…"

"No," protested Mrs. Campbell, "we do not have to charge you anything. We will have you to ourselves. You will be with us. That is all we need. That is payment enough."

Everyone was smiling. It was infectious.

"You need say no more. I accept. It's a deal. Although I think I am getting the better end of it. Are you sure you want to do this?"

Then Mrs. Campbell said, "We all want you to stay with us."

I felt most fortunate. I did not have to stay in a motel; I would now have a family that I could turn to for support. I needed their understanding for Yogi continued to take out his frustrations on me.

I sensed some resentment toward me from the crew when they discovered that I would not be living with them at the motel but with the Campbells in their home. They also took exception to the fact that I did not join them in their frequent get-togethers. It was never my intention to avoid my fellow workers, but I quickly realized that I could not live like they did—eating out every day and going out every night—and still expect to save money for next year's university courses.

I needed to avoid spending; it was that simple—I had to save every penny that I could. Again, my determination in that regard set me apart from the rest of the crew.

I don't know how many of them understood that the money I earned in the summer had to see me through for the following year. The only person I could have confided in was Jimmy but I don't know that I ever did. He seemed to understand me the best and he was the one who stood by me when it seemed that the world was against me. Jimmy's actions showed his understanding. He would quietly seek me out and just sit and have lunch with me. At other times, when his family came up to visit on week-ends, he would introduce them to me and occasionally I would be invited to go blueberry picking with them or some similar activity. Being with them always brought brightness into my world.

It seemed that Yogi took pleasure in yelling at me. It also seemed that he couldn't get enough. I often wondered why. *What was it about me that particularly incensed him? Was I doing something to cause him anger? Was he feeling offended that I chose to stay with the Campbell family? Did that action cause further resentment in him? Did I bear some responsibility for how he treated me?* At times when his words were especially cruel and personal I felt like a whipped and wounded animal. These were the moments when I wanted to walk off the job: quit—leave—walk away—make a statement, but I couldn't. Such an action would have cost me more than I could afford to lose; I simply *had* to work.

I hated myself for not standing up to Yogi; I hated myself for allowing him to insult me in that manner. One evening while walking back to the Campbell's, my heart seemed extra burdened and the walk extra tiresome; I was consumed with disgust and self-loathing; I don't know who I hated more: Yogi for what he had said, or me for allowing him to say it. Eventually I made it home. The walk had improved neither my mood nor my disposition. I did not know how much my condition had affected the family until I opened up my lunch box the next day and read this note from Mrs. Campbell: *Frank, you are not alone in this world. We know you are hurting. Hope you enjoy the cookies.*

While Yogi's words of derision shattered the soul, Mrs. Campbell's note flew to the spirit. Her note infused me with new strength, new hope and indeed a new spirit. She gave me hope to carry on for another day. That simple note, those few words of encouragement, powered up my spirit to endure another day in Yogi's trenches.

At this same time I had again been experiencing periods of homesickness. Trinidad seemed so far away, so remote. I longed to hear the familiar voices of Trinidad. I pined for *my* hometown. I had been melancholy for several days and I laboured hard to conceal that reality. But each night the caring faces of the Campbell family offered me a reprieve from the prison of melancholy that threatened to enslave me when my thoughts turned inward. Last night, however, I felt no reprieve. Mrs. Campbell must have sensed my extreme sadness and wrote the note. As I reflected on the note I could feel the acid of hate leaching out of me; it was overpowering, yet, at the same time, blissful. At that moment, nothing could touch me or hurt me. Basking in the warmth of her words of care and love I enjoyed my lunch quietly, under the shade of a tree.

Later that same afternoon when we broke for coffee, I found a seat under that same tree where I had had my lunch a few hours earlier. I was within earshot of the rest of the crew, but was not paying attention to what was being said. The crew loved to banter playfully all the time but especially during breaks. I was in a world of my own. When Yogi came by and asked me something I did not know that he was talking to me so I did not respond. When he increased his volume, I took notice.

"Frank, what do you want—a coffee?"

Yogi usually took orders for refreshments and would go to the nearest cafe and bring the drinks to the crew. When I realized that was what he was doing, I simply said, "Not today. I am fine, thank you."

"But we are all having a drink—coffee or juice. You already paid for it you dumb stupid f***. You paid for the f***ing drinks, now what the f*** will it be!

"Nothing, thank you, Yogi."

Nothing, are you stupid or something? You f***ing dumb? They don't sell anything called nothing you f***!"

I had returned to my own world. His swears ricocheted off some invisible shield and I was unmoved. Nothing was going to pull me back into his world.

Then Yogi moved in closer to me and yelled, "Frank, you deaf or something. Are your f***ing parents f***ing deaf too?"

Something in me snapped when I heard him denigrate my parents. To insult me is one thing; that I must endure. To deprecate my parents on the other hand, was something that I could not brook. I felt compelled to defend them. Some force pulled me to my feet and I declared, "Yogi, did I just hear you insult my parents?"

I was hoping that Yogi would offer an apology and the matter would end. Instead Yogi chose to be provocative. With a smile drenched in contempt he sneered, "And, what if I f***ing did?" Then he offered this challenge, "You going to do something about it?"

I took a step towards him; I seemed to tower over his small frame. In a measured tone I countered, "Yogi, it is obvious that you lack understanding. I do not know the language you understand best. Obviously it is not English; had you understood English you would have known that I did not want any kind of a drink."

Yogi said nothing; he just stared at me: confused.

I became bolder.

"And Yogi, don't think that you can get me to curse at you by swearing at me. It appears that you cannot speak English without cussing. It is obvious to me that the only school you have ever attended is the *School of Obscenities* and there you must have majored in *Cussing*. I did not attend that school and I do not like its graduate. Tell me what language I should use to communicate with you— one that *you* will understand—one without all that cussing. I would be willing to learn it if it meant that I would not have to endure your exceedingly limited and repetitive vernacular."

Yogi was still without speech.

"Go ahead, Yogi. Tell me the language!"

By now my voice had increased in volume, but I was not yelling even though I was incensed by Yogi's insults about my parents. The cauldron of depravity had been simmering within me for quite some time; it was now ready to be served. I took another step closer. I did not care about the consequences; all fear had vacated my anguished soul.

"Yogi, go ahead! Tell me! Look at you... so short in stature and understanding. Is that why you find it necessary to bully others? Do you think for one minute that your cussing and your bullying will make you a *big* man? Never! If anything, it makes you a pathetic bully."

There was complete silence; no one said anything. Even the crew was stupefied. It was never my intention to embarrass him in front of the crew. I had a sudden flashback to a time when I heard the crew call him a dumb Polack. I never understood the term but I sensed Yogi's discomfort and pain when he was put down in that way. Very often Yogi was the one to start the abusive remarks by calling one or more of the men dumb or stupid. They would counter by calling him a dumb Polack. Their retorts left him speechless. *Did Yogi just think that I had called him a dumb Polack?* I awaited Yogi's response. For a moment more he was silent, bereft of the mighty bravado that accompanied his fiery spirit. I appeared to be triumphant. *Had I not just silenced the volcano? Why was I not rejoicing? Why was I filled with guilt as though I was the one who had committed some heinous crime? Why had I called Yogi a pathetic bully? Had I not been raised to be better than that? Was I without civility?* A feeling of unease settled over me, indeed over the whole crew. Finally, Yogi found his voice.

"Hey everybody, Frank can actually speak up! I am not sure I understand what the hell he was saying, but this Trinidadian stood up. Well, well, I don't believe it!"

The whole atmosphere changed. Jimmy stood up and started clapping. Others followed suit. Hands were raised: some pounded the air as fists, others were raised in salute. There was no mistaking it; they were all rooting for me and for what I had done for myself. It was simply unbelievable. I struggled to contain my emotions.

That event happened on a Friday. The following evening I visited the crew at their motel; they had all gathered in Jimmy's room and were playing cards. When I knocked and entered the room, everyone seemed surprised to see me. I was carrying a bag in my hand. Before anyone could ask what was in it, I pulled out my gift and said, "Hey guys, I would like you to have one on me... just because."

I placed a bottle of scotch on the coffee table close to Yogi and left.

Jimmy came out and yelled after me, "Frankie, wait up!"

"Jimmy, all is well. Enjoy my friend. All is well."

I noticed that Yogi had followed Jimmy out of the room. He remained near the door and said nothing? *Why?* I wondered.

From that day forward, the crew seemed more attentive, more inclusive. Everyone reached out a little to me, each in his own way. What a difference. I was part of the crew, and I was pleased. I was accorded a certain respect, for there was a new found liking for me. Even Yogi exhibited a small change. Yogi continued to cuss, but it never seemed as frequent as before.

I am left to wonder if he had really changed or if it was merely that my perception of him had changed. Whichever it was, I was grateful.

20

Final Days of Summer

Summer was nearing an end. My time at the Campbells' home was also coming to an end. From the first moment we met I had felt an instant connection; this feeling of connectedness grew deeper with each passing day. They were so good for me; so good for my soul.

I was sad that the time to leave was close at hand. One evening during those last days, I was sitting in the living room looking out the window. Mrs. Campbell came in. She had made two cups of her special tea and as she sat opposite me, she offered me one. I had grown to love the tea and happily accepted the offer. For a few moments we sat in silence; I was staring wistfully out the window and she looking contemplatively at the back wall. Her whisper barely broke the silence.

"I am going to remember you whenever I see that wall, Frank."

"Really, Mrs. Campbell?"

"Yes, I will. I will miss you. We all will miss you. Don't you know why, Frank?

I had no words.

She continued, "Frank, it is the way you were with my husband, Andy. You were such a good companion for him. When you first came to us that wall was bare—unfinished. Andy never seemed to have the necessary energy after a long day at work to tackle the finishing alone. You expressed a willingness to help. Andy could not do it by himself. You were so willing to help with the sheets of drywall. He was so happy to have you help him. And, as tired as you were after your long day at work, you never showed it. You never complained and you stayed with him working side by side both inside outside the house. Frank, you are such a dear."

"Mrs. Campbell, are you trying to make feel good? All I did was help hold the gyproc; Mr. Campbell did all the work."

"Yes, I am. We all are going to miss you."

"Mrs. Campbell, it is I who will miss all of you. What will I do without you? Have you any idea what you did for me? Do you know that without you…"

She wouldn't let me finish my thought. "Never mind that, I have a favour to ask you. Do you mind, Frank?"

"No, of course not. Please, tell me how I can help?"

"Well, it's about your boss, Yogi. Do you mind if I asked a very special favour?"

What favour could she possibly want regarding Yogi? I had no idea. I asked her to continue.

"Frank, Andy and I know about Yogi. We know all about his insults. We also know that you never retaliated. Can you in your heart forgive him? I am aware that I am asking a great deal of you. Of course you could tell me it is none…"

"Mrs. Campbell, I value your opinion. I don't know at this moment that I can *forgive*. I can start by not *hating* Yogi. That much I *can* do. Because *you* ask I will try to not hate Yogi."

"Oh, Frank, you are a dear soul."

Before I could respond, the door opened the two youngest children walked in. Mrs. Campbell withdrew to attend to their needs. I regretted that our meeting had to end so abruptly but I understood. I had so much more to tell her.

I never did tell Grace Campbell what was on my mind.

****

This was our last weekend in Kenora. Many members of the crew were packing up to leave Friday after work. I planned to travel back to the Lakehead with Jimmy. I was excited for at long last I had a few extra pennies in my pocket and I was planning to offer to pay for our supper on the road. I anticipated my friend's objections and my counter; it was a great feeling to be able to offer to repay Jimmy's many kindnesses to me. Jimmy knew of my financial struggles and I knew he would never willingly accept money from me, but that wasn't going to stop me from trying. Jimmy was packed up and ready to leave the motel. I too was all packed and I had said my goodbyes to the Campbells. Mr, Campbell had brought me to Jimmy's room and helped me carry my bags in.

When Andy entered the room he immediately struck up a conversation with Jimmy. It appeared that they knew one another. I found it strange that

Jimmy had never mentioned it to me. *Well*, I thought, *I have the journey back to the Lakehead to unravel that mystery.*

Then Yogi showed up at the door and stunned us all with this announcement, "Jim, I'll bring back Frank tomorrow. Leave his things in your room. He'll be spending another night. I already paid for the room."

Before anyone could voice any objection, Yogi was gone.

Jimmy looked at me, shook his head in bewilderment and said, "Give me a call when you get in. See you." Then he too left. I was left alone to ponder unhappily this latest move by Yogi. I was not looking forward to the trip. *Was this how my summer was to conclude, punctuated at either end by the ill-temper of an even more ill-mannered Yogi?*

Alone in my room that night I had time to ponder this latest development in my life. *Why did Yogi have me stay back?* I could not understand his thinking. *If anything I should be last person he should choose to stay back with him.* Then, I began wondering, *Why did Grace Campbell ask me to forgive Yogi?* I remember wondering, *Are these two situations in any way connected? Was the hand of some unknown force at work here?*

Well, force or no force it would be most difficult to forgive Yogi. And, just before I fell asleep I thought,
It truly would be an act of
GRACE
If I were able to forgive.

Saturday morning Yogi picked me up and we headed out. Yogi had the radio on the whole way back and we had very little occasion to speak. I was grateful for I was spared the torture of listening to his expletives. The silence made the trip feel longer than it actually was. Yogi did however offer me some treats along the way. I accepted gratefully. Yogi dropped me off right outside the Horns' and by way of a final farewell he said,

"Hey, Frank, guess what?"

"What?" I asked.

"Today is Saturday. Had you worked today you would have received time and a half."

"I know, Yogi. It's okay. Thanks so much for the ride. And thanks for the treats along the way."

"Frank, you're not half bad. Good luck in your studies. I wish, I wish... Never mind! See you."

"Yogi, I want to thank you for something you did. You made a real effort to make me comfortable on the trip. I know it. I thank you for that."

(I was of course referring to the fact that for the duration of the trip Yogi never swore once.)

I reached to him with outstretched hands. He removed his driving glove and grabbed my hand and shook it strongly. His eyes betrayed a sense of unease and there was suggestion of sadness or regret in his demeanour as he drove off.

I no longer felt any animosity towards Yogi. I cannot explain why, but I began to feel sorry for him. Watching him drive away I felt a little bit guilty that I called him, a pathetic bully. Why I was filled with such remorse I cannot explain. I sensed that in some way I had misjudged him; perhaps it was I who bore the greater blame for I knew that I had been raised to act more charitably towards others. I could not help think that perhaps this man was really no bully after all. It would seem that he had buried himself in his own grave. It seemed clear to me now, that he too had a story—perhaps his was a story of hurt and affliction so cleverly entombed that no one was able to discern his troubled soul. With that revelation, any residual resentment evaporated; peace filled the void and calmed this once bruised soul.

I never saw Yogi again.

A few days later my paycheque arrived. Yogi had authorized payment for the Saturday that we had travelled back together—a full day's wages at time and a half. Indeed this rough Yogi Bear had become a Teddy Bear!

******

Looking back, I survived my very first summer; in fact I survived my entire year in Canada. I passed all my first year's courses—even the ill-fated English. My summer earnings might just be enough to see me through the upcoming academic year. There was a quiet promise of optimism as I prepared to embark on the next year.

PART II

Making Connections

21

Professor Cornell D'Echert: A New Experience

The registration process for my second year at Lakehead University proved to be much less of a trial than my first year. Summer earnings coupled with frugal money management ensured payment of my tuition and my university fees for the year. While I still had to be thrifty, I had room to breathe. A sense of optimism filled my world in spite of the promise of another dreadful cold winter. I was both relieved and ecstatic that I had succeeded in my very first year at university.

I looked forward with anticipation to all the new experiences that awaited me.

Then I met Professor Cornell D'Echert. Both within and without the classroom walls he was a truly gracious and distinguished individual. While his ability to walk was impaired by a noticeable limp, his ability to inspire and impart knowledge was superlative. He was particularly gracious to me to be sure.

I was enrolled in one of his French courses. Since it was described as a French grammar course, I anticipated that the actual speaking of the language could be avoided or would be minimal. I was mistaken. In his class, both the spoken and the written aspects were equally important. For the first few days, he allowed me to acclimatize myself. Once he determined my level of comfort (or discomfort) he called on me for an answer to some question he had posed in French. I responded in English. He asked that I answer in French. I froze. A horrible experience in Trinidad had scarred me and had permanently dissuaded me from ever attempting the language again. It is no exaggeration to state that I was terrified. Thus, I remained silent.

Professor Cornell came close and stood beside me. Years of suffering in the school system in Trinidad taught me to fear both his close proximity and his certain rebuke. For a moment he was pensive. My fears were unfounded. He spoke gently to me in English.

"Monsieur Maraj, your answer is correct. Thank you."

Then he whispered, "Perhaps another time, *en francais*, whenever you are ready."

The great consideration that he afforded me on that day established my deep respect for him. From that moment I knew that indeed this man was not just a professor; he was a *teacher*. He did not function merely to spout information; he encouraged with delicacy those who were timid or shy and celebrated with enthusiasm the achievement of each new milestone.

The passing of each day served only to confirm my initial assessment.

One day Professor Cornell asked me if I would stay back a little after class; he wanted to talk to me. Part of me fretted a little over this request for the last time a teacher wanted to talk to me I had been summarily rebuked for my many deficiencies. The rest of me was quietly assured that that was not the intent of this particular request. This quiet conviction proved to be correct. Not only was I not reprimanded, I was invited to the professor's home for supper—although he may have referred to it as *dinner*.

Professor and Madame lived in a large split level home on a hill just beyond County Fair Plaza in the northern part of the city. They picked me up at my home in Current River and took me to their residence. At the time, they were the proud owners of a grey Rambler. I was impressed with their car. In Trinidad, only the elite could afford such a prestigious vehicle. I recalled visiting car lots in the various towns in which I worked last summer and could not understand why there were so many Ramblers on the lots. In Trinidad these cars were in high demand and often were sold before arriving on the island. The story of the Rambler figures prominently later on in life but does not bear telling at this time. For now, I'll let the Rambler be!

Because of his injury and his great length of body, Professor never actually drove a vehicle. That job was aptly accomplished by his ever attentive wife. She was a diminutive five feet three inches but was every bit a match to the professor's energy and intellect. Her strong but quiet demeanour was the perfect complement to his outgoing personality. Their congenial interaction evidenced their total respect and support for one another. While Professor's massive height commanded any room, it was evident that he did not misuse this advantage in any manner. Frequently, he deferred to Madame's judgment and always actively supported her decisions. It was obvious that they had worked out many of the kinks of marriage and were very comfortable with who they were as a couple.

As we entered the house we were met with the unmistakable aroma of roasted lamb. As Madame entered the kitchen to put the finishing touches on the meal, Professor put on some classical music and invited me to sit. In order to accommodate Professor's great height, most of the furniture in the room had extremely high backs. Madame soon joined us and Professor poured each of us an aperitif. We sipped the liqueur in silence allowing the music to complete the mood. Soon Professor closed his eyes and rested his head back on the top of the chair. I followed his example. And so we three sat allowing the music to fill our spirits until it was time to dine.

Over dinner Madame gently broached the delicate subject of food and my *decision* to eat neither beef nor pork.

"Frank, I understand that you do not eat beef or pork. May I ask why? I don't mean to be rude. Is it okay to talk about it? I really want to understand."

Madame was neither American, like the professor, nor Canadian. She was French; her accent was so engaging. One could not take offence at anything that she said for she spoke so delightfully and with complete candour. Now to the question, why did I not eat beef or pork? I took a moment to reflect before answering.

"The members of my family are Hindu. As Hindus we do not eat pork or beef. I grew up that way."

Then Professor asked, "You mean you have never eaten pork or beef, Frank?"

"As far as I know I have never eaten them."

"Not even a small amount, Frank, even by accident?" asked Madame.

"If I have eaten it, I do not know it. What I know is I would not *knowingly* eat beef or pork."

"We have heard some explanation as to why Hindus do not eat these meats. Perhaps you might tell us your reasons," suggested the professor.

"Pierre, let Frank eat. He has hardly touched a bite."

Professor poured us some wine and we continued on with our meal. Baby potatoes and asparagus accompanied the roast lamb. The table was simply but elegantly set. In truth, I was terribly conscious about my surroundings and my two gracious hosts. I feared embarrassing myself even though neither one of them showed the slightest hint of criticism. They did their best to put me at ease. I observed closely how they attended to their meal and patterned my actions after theirs. I was conscious enough to pull out Madame's chair for her when she came to sit. For that small gesture, I was rewarded with a generous, *Merci*. I cannot tell you how charmed I was that she referred to me as a *gentleman*. When Madame picked up a portion of the ribs and ate with her fingers, I did likewise. Up until that moment I had been too shy to use my hands. Once I saw her take the lead, I happily followed—and with great relief. The lamb was quickly devoured. The question remains: *did Madame use her fingers to make me feel comfortable or was it genuinely in her manner to do so?* Perhaps I shall never know. What I do know is that she was most accommodating and I was most appreciative for I enjoyed my meal so very much.

After tea and some lighter conversation, Professor and Madame drove me home. Before I left, Madame asked,

"Frank, shall we do it again? Pierre and I loved your company. Would you come again? Say yes? And perhaps you would tell us about why you do not eat beef or pork. Yes?"

Of course I wanted to return. Who would not? As this charming couple drove away I reflected on our evening together. I felt that I had just dined with royalty. Their manners were impeccable and their attitude so accommodating; I knew that they were special friends; already they had impressed me with their genuine care for and interest in me.

That evening as I lay in bed I pondered Madame's innocent question, *why do I not eat beef or pork?* From as far back as I could remember our family had not eaten beef or pork. As a child I never questioned this fact; I simply accepted this practice and grew up that way. Now, Professor and Madame were asking. *Do I really know why I do not eat pork or beef?* My mind drifted back to the time of my childhood searching for an answer.

22
Poowa's World

We called my father's sister Poowa. She had a profound impact on our family. She ate no meat whatsoever. As a young child growing up I accepted her as she was. I did not question her reasons for not eating meat. I just accepted that it was her choice. That was who Poowa was.

Poowa's *choice* however, affected everyone with whom she kept close contact. She could not countenance anyone having any form of flesh in the home when she visited. My mother took extra measures to ensure that her wishes were honoured whenever she came to our home. Because we had no telephone, we rarely knew when she was about to pay us a visit. Thus, whenever she would take a notion to pay us a visit, she came unannounced. The fact that she would arrive without prior notice, did not alter her expectations upon her arrival. She expected that there would be no meat of any kind in our home; there was no thought of negotiation; her expectation was absolute.

My mother was vigilant in ensuring that Poowa would not be inconvenienced in the least whenever she visited. I still marvel at how this task was accomplished for each and every visit.

There is, however, some explanation for this phenomenon. The fact that Poowa lived in the southern part of the island and had to use public transportation to travel to us in the northern part of the island worked to our advantage. This lengthy journey required several stops along the way. One of the major stops was at Curepe Junction—only a couple miles away from our home. A stop there virtually ensured that she would be spotted by someone who would instinctively know that she was headed for our home. Such a sighting was immediately reported from person to person until someone actually stopped by our house bearing tidings that Poowa was close by.

If by some odd chance she was not spotted in Curepe, she would invariably be seen exiting a taxi at a nearby gas station right in Tunapuna. The workers at that station had an understanding with our family that any Poowa sighting had to be relayed to Ma forthwith. As I remember, there was never a failure in this regard as no one in that gas station dared face the displeasure of either my brother Clivey or my Pa.

Poowa expected that every trace of meat, fish or eggs would be removed before she stepped over the threshold. Oftentimes Ma had only minutes to perform this miracle. In spite of this fact, Ma never panicked. To be sure there was a sense of urgency and everyone at home was employed in this undertaking. All meat items were portioned off to various understanding neighbours for safekeeping and a thorough cleansing of the house was begun. There was to remain no hint of even the slightest scent of the *forbidden foods*—Poowa was most adept at discerning the slightest irregularity. Every task was executed without resentment. It was simply required of us and we all did our part to see that Poowa was made to feel welcome.

And were these items always returned to Ma...

When Poowa arrived at or close to a regular mealtime we were somewhat reluctant to surrender our food. But, we knew that it had to be done. Our neighbours gladly accommodated our need. Ma would then have to prepare a vegetarian meal. I never once heard her complain about the additional work that accompanied a visit from Poowa. We all accepted Poowa just as she was. Poowa herself made the task seem less onerous than it was; she specialized in the making of a special treat—*ladoo*—a kind of fudge. To make this fudge required a painstaking patience—a patience that Poowa possessed.

I can still see Poowa squatting on a small stool endlessly churning the hot milk, sugar, and butter. Only she knew when the mixture was just right for the next step. It would have to show signs of thickening slightly in the pot. Poowa would then remove this newly formed semi-hardness and create the small balls—ladoo—with her hands. It was the sweetest fudge ever and we were always anxious to taste a sample. But, with Poowa, there simply was no sampling. She would often service the neighbourhood with these prized treats before we got so much as a small taste. We protested to one another and together we children determined to mount a quiet form of desperate rebellion. Poowa generally placed these irresistible sweets on a tray and rested the tray on the floor beside the coal pot. Imagine a tray of sweets on the floor! It was almost sacrilegious. The floorboards in our home were not always secure; oftentimes there were sizeable crevices between them. It just so happened that there was a rather large gap between two of the floorboards located right beside the tray of sweets. The temptation for subterfuge proved too irresistible. We were of one accord—*those ladoos belonged to us too.* We had already given up meat without protest; we were not to be denied our fair share of the sweets.

Accordingly we devised a plan of sorts. One of us was elected to crawl under the floor until he reached the area that had the gaping hole. The rest of us then had the task of distracting Poowa while the tiny hand reached upward through the crack to seek its fair reward. Another one of us would sneak a substantial share of those ladoos into the outstretched hand. Once that act was accomplished, we all retreated below the house to do justice to Poowa's delightful creations. We got away with it every time so there was never any real resentment to Poowa's visits.

One day I was sitting beside Poowa on the floor as she was preparing to make a batch of her fudge. I was watching her every move very closely. Poowa then turned to me and asked, "Frankie, yo want to ask me something?"

"Yes, Poowa."

"What yo want to know?"

"Poowa, why yo don't eat meat."

"Because we is Hindu. Hindus don't eat meat."

"Ma and Pa eat meat. We all do. Are we Hindu?"

She paused and reflected, then answered, "Frankie, they can eat meat. Never pork or beef. *If you ever eat pork or beef, yo no Hindu.* So be a good boy. Be good and yo go to heaven, okay?"

"Yes, Poowa."

Thus the idea that I was never to eat pork or beef was firmly riveted into my psyche. I still did not understand *why* a Hindu did not eat pork or beef. I was given an understanding from a very early age that it would be an act of sacrilege if I were to consume such meats. None of that really mattered when I was with my Poowa. What really mattered was this: my Poowa handed me a ladoo, and I felt like a king. That was my little secret that I kept from everyone; Poowa gave me a whole ladoo—all of it just for me. I did not have to share. My beloved Poowa had shown me great favour.

23

The Sweet Pootigal Experience

On this subject of meat, there is yet another incident. It concerns the Pootigal experience. (I do not know the correct spelling for Pootigal except to say it was a small fruit much like a Chinese mandarin with one small exception—it is the sweetest of sweet.)

Directly across the street from where I lived, resided a widow affectionately called Miss Assina. It was generally believed that this elderly lady was blind. Soon we were to discover however, that this assessment was not completely accurate.

Our first clue should have been the fact that she was quite capable of doing her own laundry. We would often see her working on the task under the Pootigal tree in her yard.

As children we were taught to be respectful of our elders and to do their bidding whenever we were asked. Miss Assina was not shy about asking for assistance. Frequently she required me to run errands for her. My mother had amply prepared me to do such errands with a happy heart and without any expectation of reward. Ma repeatedly impressed upon our young hearts that our real reward was in heaven. "If the elder give no reward to yo, don' worry; yo reward go be in heaven."

Because of my mother's teaching, I would do errand after errand for Miss Assina; she always offered a polite "Thank you" or "God Bless"; never once did she offer a Pootigal from her overflowing tree. I often wondered why she would not share her fruits. I could see that many were on the ground and spoiling for want of attention. When I offered to gather them up for her, she dismissed me.

I so wanted a pootigal; one would be worth a hundred—no, a *thousand* of her verbal blessings. The reward that my mother had assured me awaited me in heaven seemed too distant and remote. I could not wait that long. I wanted a *real* reward *now*. Thus that shining orange fruit so abundant in

Miss Assina's yard constituted a constant temptation. Miss Assina seemed oblivious to my need and detached from my reality; I felt denied—perhaps even cheated.

Apparently I was not the only one frustrated in this manner. A small gathering of neighbourhood boys revealed a similar concern. One voice spoke for us all, "Miss Assina not fair. The pootigals fallin' and rottin' all 'round her. She don' care. She blind. Maybe she blind affec she mind. Wha we go do? How we go help her out?"

We looked longingly at the Pootigal tree and observed that Miss Assina was again doing her laundry under the tree. Right then and there we hatched a plan to rescue the rotting fruit. The four of us would form a squad. The lead person would engage Miss Assina in conversation while two of the others gathered up the oranges. They in turn would pass the oranges to the fourth member hiding in the ravine bordering Miss Assina's property. That fourth person would quickly deposit the fruit into a large bucket. There was just one problem. No one would volunteer to take the lead. Then, one of the boys asserted, "Frankie, you take the lead."

"No."

"Why?"

"Because... That's *your* role."

We continued to argue and debate the point. I absolutely refused. I did not want to be forever condemned to a life in hell.

Then one of the boys countered in a most disappointing tone, "Frankie, if you don' do it, we quash the plan. Yo the bes one fer it. Yo can talk to Miss Assina. She listen to you. Now, look at all those oranges just rottin on de groun. We *no steal*, we *rescue*."

There was a silence. All eyes were on me. I said nothing. Then one of the boys reached into his pocket and brought out a pootigal and placed it near my lips. It was irresistibly sweet.

"Frankie, yo no stealin. Come on man, help we out," he petitioned.

The sweetness of the fruit worked its magic and I weakened. I agreed to my role. In the back of my mind, however, I could hear my mother's voice warning, "If yo steal, yo go to hell."

And I offered a gentle explanation—a prayer for forgiveness, "God, I do not mean to do a wrong, forgive me."

My intention in my prayer was not to make a wrong seem right. It was my way as a child to help myself *feel* less guilty about what I was about to do.

We set out to execute the plan. The three boys made their approach via the ravine while I followed the regular path from the road to the pootigal tree. When I reached the tree, there was Miss Assina doing her laundry.

She appeared totally absorbed in her work. By now the three boys were stationed in the ravine ready to assume their *duties*. I looked at the many mandarins rotting on the ground. I looked at the fruit ripening on the branches knowing full-well that soon they too would be relegated to a place of dishonour on the ground.

It was not right; the fruit truly required rescuing. I think I heard the fruit calling out to me.

"Save us, please."

I had to act; the fruit deserved some measure of consideration.

I looked at Miss Assina and my heart started to beat quickly. I was not totally convinced of the *rightness* of our plan. A sense of discomfort started to spread; then guilt began to weave a web around my conscience.

I could tell that the boys were becoming impatient; from the ravine they motioned for me to get on with the plan.

I chose to ignore my conscience and approached Miss Assina. "Miss Assina, good morning. Ah notice your line for your clothes is falling down. I'll fix it."

I picked up a rather large rock and began banging on a nail in an effort to further secure the rope stretching about ten feet between the pootigal tree and a post. The noisy banging seemed to be the perfect ploy to create the necessary distraction. Miss Assina seemed to be directing her full attention toward me allowing the boys to pick a pail full of fruit completely undetected. Once the mission was accomplished, the boys signalled me to retreat. I could hear the scampering of feet and the breaking of twigs as the boys hastened away with the contraband.

I couldn't wait to make my escape. "Miss Assina, Ah fix the rope. It much better nh. Bye."

I could not have taken more than three steps when the commanding voice of Miss Assina pierced the air.

"Frankie, stop. Come back here now!"

I stopped dead in my tracks. When I turned around she brought her face right up close to mine and ordered, "Frankie, you tell your friends to bring back those pootigals. Now go on. I'm waiting and I don't have all day. Do you hear me, Frankie?"

"Yes, Miss Assina,"

I found the three boys waiting for me at the back of my house pail in hand. They were still admiring their 'catch'. Much to everyone's horror, I grabbed the pail and began to run back to Miss Assina's. Over their protests I offered the briefest of explanations, "She onto we."

I alone faced Miss Assina. "Miss Assina... here. Me bring back every one of dem. Every single one."

"*Every* one, Frankie?"

"Yes, Miss."

"Frankie, you've done a very bad thing. I can see the others try to steal my oranges. But you ... Miz B's son? How could you do that to me?"

My silence was an acknowledgement of my guilt. I could find no words to express how sorry I was for what I had done. I was so ashamed. I could only listen to her words of chastisement.

"Frankie, you used to be such a good son. What happened to you? A short while ago I asked you to do something for me. Do you remember? You never came back. I had to make another plan. How could you be so bad?"

I wondered how Miss Assina could be so smart and yet not know what she had asked of me. I wanted to tell her, *How you go ask me to do such an errand? Your errand is no ordinary errand. Did you forget? You asked me to go buy a piece of pig tail—pork meat! I cannot do that. I am Hindu. Poowa says a Hindu cannot and must not touch that meat.*

I honestly wished I could have done her bidding for it did seem simple enough. But, to comply would mean the surety of one kind of hell. To not comply resulted in another form of anguish. By not obeying my elder, it would appear that I chose one form of hell over another. I wish I could have communicated my dilemma to her in a way that she could have understood.

I started to form an apology, "I am so sorry Miss Assina. Please forgive me."

Before any more words were said, Miss Assina interrupted, "So, you are a true little Hindu. You will not bring me that piece of pork meat. When you did not come back, I talked to your Ma. She explained why you acted the way you did."

My relief was instant. I no longer felt that I was on any highway to hell. The roadblocks were all removed.

She continued, "You are not bad Frankie. You are a good boy still. Now I won't go against your father and mother. But, if you ever want a taste—just a teeny, weeny taste of pork—come to me. I'll fix it up good for you. You won't go to hell for eating pork. Some Hindus eat pork."

This was very strange. Was she tempting me? I did not know any Hindu in my world that ate pork or beef. No one on either my mother's or my father's side of the family ate beef or pork. My world was shielded from those types of meats. I grew up thinking that it was wrong for a Hindu to eat either of those meats. Furthermore, I grew up knowing that to violate that custom virtually assured a trip to hell. Miss Assina's offer left me in a state of confusion. Did she know something that I did not?

I thanked her and turned again to leave.

Once more her voice rang out, "Frankie?"

"Yes, Miss Assina."

"You forgot your pail of oranges."

I was stupefied.

Then Miss Assina herself picked up the pail and brought it to me.

"Here. Go ahead, take it. I know you will share it with your friends."

My 'thank you' was barely audible, but I am certain that she heard, for when I glanced up, a gentle smile played about her lips.

I hastened back to my friends. They were truly delighted with the return of the forbidden fruits. I marvelled at the quick change of events. In no time at all, that complete pail was emptied.

Later, I was able to reflect on these two neighbours whose beliefs were so dissimilar. First there was Poowa, my father's sister, who ate no meat. She believed that the eating of anything of the flesh was against God's decree. And then there was dear Miss Assina who not only ate all forms of meats, but also recommended that I try a taste of pork.

My ten year old mind could not reconcile these two ways of thinking. Each one was convinced in the rightness of her opinion. I wondered how God decided who was right and who was wrong. Life was most confusing back then.

Now, I was an adult attending university. *Was my mind any less confused? Did I have an answer for Madame and Professor Cornell regarding this subject?* My next visit to their home provided me with an opportunity for some explanation.

24

The Favour

It wasn't long before I was once again a happy dinner guest at the home of the Cornells. I really looked forward to my meetings with them. Their home, nestled in the woods and away from the noise of the highway, was a delight to visit. It was not too far outside the city limits and one could really appreciate the country feel that such a location afforded.

The greenery evident both on the ground and in the trees proclaimed that summer was not far away. Adjusting to the isolation and the coldness of winter had proven more difficult than I had anticipated and I was really looking forward to the promise of warmer weather.

Madame and Professor Cornell again proved to be both gracious and devoted hosts. After having visited there several times I was able to anticipate their routines and looked forward to them. Professor would put on the classical music, pour everyone a glass of wine and then we all would gently relax until it was time for dinner. Sometimes we chatted quietly, at other times, we allowed ourselves simply to be entranced with the music. Occasionally Professor would comment on the music or give a brief explanation of it. It was most evident that music was a very important element in his life bringing both physical comfort and intellectual stimulation.

When Madame announced that dinner was indeed ready, we hastened to the table. Over dinner, Madame picked up on the conversation concerning the eating or the avoidance of eating certain types of meat. She came directly to the point, "Frank, are you ready to tell us why you don't eat beef or pork? Pierre and I are so anxious. Yes?"

When I shared with them the stories about Poowa and Miss Assina and their comments regarding religion, they seemed to be both fascinated and intrigued. Professor expressed his concern for the agony of spirit that I went through as a very young boy. "How utterly dreadful for you, Frank.

To think that you believed that you could be doing something that wrong, that you were no longer a good Hindu... And furthermore, to think that your violation was so great in nature that its natural consequence was eternal damnation makes me shudder. What a terrible state for you to have had to endure."

Then Madame asked, "And Frank, what is your view now? Why do you not eat pork or beef? We want to understand and learn."

Sensing from her, the spirit of one who truly wanted to understand, I began to explain. "Professor and Madame, I intend to return to Trinidad, God willing, after I finish my studies here. I will be returning to the same community that I left. Since I was raised a Hindu and I did not eat those meats, I consider that it would be respectful if I honoured that tradition of the family. I know my ma would be most pleased."

Then Professor asked, "Frank, it is not the Hindu religion itself that is preventing you?"

"Professor, I am almost ashamed to say that I have no fully satisfactory answer for you. I too, have a great deal to learn. For the present, let us say that I am upholding a time honoured tradition. And there is much peace in this decision..."

Both Madame and Professor smiled graciously and I was relieved.

Apparently my explanation held some satisfaction for them. Stroking his beard, Professor changed the subject. "Frank, we have something to ask of you. Frank..."

Before he could complete his thought, Madame Cornell rose from her chair, came over to where I sat and, taking me by the hand, said, "Come, let us withdraw to the next room. We will be more comfortable there." Only after we all were seated and only after Professor had shared a little more of his wine, was the true reason for the visit unveiled. With his head held upright and an irrepressible smile playing about his lips, Professor continued, "Frank, Madame and I are totally of one mind. We want to ask you a favour. It would be a special favour. It would mean the world to us if you were able..."

"What favour, Professor? Just ask and I would be only too happy to oblige."

Of course I had no idea that the favour he was about to ask was one that I could never have anticipated.

"Frank, we have a very large house. It is spacious. We have an extra bedroom. We want you to come and live with us. We both have discussed this idea, and we are so very excited to have you live here with us. What do you think?"

Both of their faces were beaming with anticipation. I was in heavenly shock. *Imagine living with Madame and Professor. What a world that would be.* I was lost in thought and I could not respond immediately.

Then Madame excitedly interjected, "Frankie, my dear, you must be wondering about the pork and beef issue. It will not be a problem. Believe me when I say that we will prepare meals together. You will be satisfied with us."

Professor added, "Frank, do not worry about the rent. We have a plan. You help us; we help you."

"But, how…?"

"It is simple," continued Madame, "Professor and I can't get around anymore without much discomfort and pain. Perhaps you can drive us to the university and bring us back. Mind you, we would not want your schooling to suffer; it would be when it is convenient. You would be such a help."

"And Frank, my dear boy, you would, when you can, help us a little with the outside chores, perhaps clearing the driveway in winter. What a great help that would be."

Again Madame spoke, "Frank, you would be like a son, our son. We are so, so excited. You are just the person we need in our life. What say you, Frankie?"

Caught up in all the planning and excitement, Professor proclaimed, "And don't forget Frank, when we travel to our villa in France, and our home in America, you will be with us. Our son and his family would love to meet you. We would go sightseeing, we would attend concerts, and best of all you would not have to worry about money: my word what a scourge has money been to you; we will help you. Now, what say you?"

For a moment it felt like I had just won the biggest lotto of them all. From here on in it looked as if the Gods—who, up until the present, had been absorbed elsewhere—had at last appeared to champion my cause. The offer presented to me by my Professor and his beloved wife was cause for jubilation and celebration. I should have been ecstatic. Yet, I was not. In fact, I was almost at the other end of the spectrum. I was pensive. Deep inside, I knew that I could not accept their offer.

How was I to tell them? Where was I to find the right words to express to them my deepest gratitude for their extreme benevolence and goodwill? Immediately my stomach churned; I was in such turmoil. A wave of loving devastation just battered the shores of a grateful soul. I was searching for an answer when Madame asked, "Frank, you are not happy. Perhaps you do not, how shall I say, desire to live with us? No, Frank?"

Professor, sensing that I was not able to respond at that moment advised, "Perhaps, we need to let Frank think it over. He has much to consider. Frank, you would think on it some more? Do not worry so much my boy. It will be okay."

I was in such agony; my insides were being torn apart. I knew I had to give an answer now. I could not put it off. I prayed that I could find the right words.

"Professor and Madame, more than anything I want to live here with you. I want to be part of your life, your world. I desire it, yet..."

"What's wrong, Frankie?" intoned a saddened Madame. "What is the problem?"

"The problem is *me*; it is the way *I am*. I am not able to accept your offer—so generous as it is—I must try and do it my way. I don't know why, I just know that I must stand on my own two feet. At least I must continue to try. What you offer me is a gateway to heaven's joy. I am crushed that I at this moment am such a disappointment."

"Frank," a concerned Professor intervened, "you can never be a disappointment. Sad we are and will be. I wish I were more selfish then I would strenuously urge you to accept our offer."

"Professor and Madame, I am honoured by your affection. Your friendship I must preserve; that bond means something precious to me. Let me go, but let me be your friend."

Madame approached. Placing her hands on my face she consoled, "Of course Frankie, friends we are. But if ever you change your mind, if ever you just feel the need... just let us know..."

"I know that Madame. I know..."

Sadly overjoyed, I left Madame and Professor.

25
That Gift...

It was December, 1968 and Christmas was looming once again. A creeping melancholy invaded my soul. The inevitability of a second cold Canadian winter, coupled with an ever intensifying sense of homesickness heightened my melancholy. I wanted to be in Trinidad; I wanted to be surrounded by the familiarity of my home and the understanding of my family. My longings became so strong that I could no longer concentrate on my studies the way I should. My grades were beginning to suffer. Try as I could to concentrate, my thoughts constantly drifted back to the land of my birth; memories of family and friends were a constant plague. Trinidad beckoned. My mind knew that it was a financial impossibility to even consider going home; but, knowledge does not stop the desire of the heart. Perhaps more enticing than anything else was the fact that Trinidad, as always, was without snow; that year, snow was plentiful in the Lakehead.

Then, from out of nowhere, a letter arrived announcing that Ma was not well. The writer of the letter further suggested that: "Perhaps you should come home." While the letter suggested a certain urgency, I took it as a sign from heaven. I was *meant* to go home. The letter was merely my confirmation. I did not debate; I did not procrastinate. Finances did not even figure into the equation. I had enough money to get me home. I would worry about everything else upon my return. Up until receiving word regarding Ma's ill health, financial considerations reigned. The letter changed all of that. I had to go home.

When I informed my professors that I had to return to Trinidad and that I would be missing a few days at the beginning of the new year, two of them expressed concern. Both Dr. Doan, my professor of philosophy, and Professor Cornell d'Echert, shared their concerns.

Dr. Doan seemed to have taken an interest in me and in my welfare during my first year at Lakehead University. That was when I undertook a course that he taught: An Introduction to Philosophy. I truly enjoyed his class and found him most intriguing. The first year course was a rather large class and personal relationships were difficult, if not impossible to form. This second year with him had a much more personal tone about it. I felt that he knew us and we knew him. His manner, while mild and contemplative, in no way hindered the strength of delivery of his lecture series. He was a knowledgeable man and an impressive thinker. He captivated our minds. Students chatted often about the issues raised during the course of his lectures and, more specifically, about the manner of the man himself. His furrowed brow, his rounded shoulders and his predisposition to chain smoking made him somewhat of an enigma. His mind, always contemplative and engaged, made him even that much more of a puzzle. Even when he was all alone, one sensed that he was never truly alone for he was always thinking, forever contemplative.

I was being merely courteous as I explained to Dr. Doan that I was going to Trinidad for the holidays. We had spoken on a personal basis only a few times before. I don't recollect ever having mentioned anything regarding my personal financial state to him during the course of our discussions. Needless to say, it came as quite a shock when he mentioned, "Frank, what would a trip like that do to your finances? Would it not create financial difficulties for you?"

I was at once both amazed and embarrassed at his insight into my personal affairs. His question reflected a depth of understanding and compassion. I had no response to volunteer. I was not prepared to reveal the true state of my situation. I stood silently before him a thousand questions whirling in my brain. *How could he know? Why would he know? Why should he even care?*

Then he reached for his chequebook. He was about to write me a cheque when I gently but firmly stopped him. He protested, "Frank, I know you are thinking that I am trying to help you by issuing this cheque. That is true. But that is only one part of it. I would be helping myself too. You would be giving me a gift if you let me extend a hand to you. That means something to me. Can you allow me that small gift and accept this cheque?"

I was sad that I was unable to accept that gift from Dr. Doan.

I did not understand Dr. Doan's sentiment. I could not comprehend it at the time. I did not accept his cheque. I knew I was grateful to him for his offer. I sensed my action had saddened Dr. Doan. I was more humbled than ever before by his kindness.

Professor Cornell and Madame also reached out to me in a similar manner. They too wanted to help me. They too I denied. Professor and Madame, while understanding why I declined their offer to make my home with them, did however, question my wisdom when I turned down their offer to pay my air fare to Trinidad.

Professor and Madame, and Dr. Doan... I have no words to describe such kindness.

26

That Christmas in Trinidad

Piarco, Trinidad. Delirious with bliss, I was beyond happy as the plane was about to land. Throughout the entirety of my journey I blissfully anticipated the reunion with both family and friends. The whole island beckoned and I couldn't wait to drink it all in. The truth behind the phrase, "Once a Trini, always a Trini" resonated in my soul. Suddenly Trinidad and everything about her loomed large and all I wanted was to be consumed by her. I had missed everyone and everything so much. It was only now, moments before landing that I could allow myself to truly acknowledge the depth of my longing. Despite my good fortune at the Lakehead, I longed for Trinidad. The longing became a hurt, and the pain from that hurt was a pain like no other.

The wheels touched down on the tarmac.

The doors opened. A sudden blast of warm heat announced that I was truly home. To be anchored once again on Trinidadian soil felt good.

Before walking the short distance from the plane to the customs building, I took a few moments to stand alone on the tarmac and revel in the luxury of being home. Knowing that everyone was waiting inside to receive me invited a reverent euphoria. I was so excited, I wanted to explode. Moments after I cleared customs, Boysie grabbed my luggage. A crowd of family members had gathered. My eyes scanned the crowd for my mother. Finally they found her, standing at the back, all smiles. I'll never forget my delight at seeing her.

Then I saw Clive. He motioned for me to follow. I was a little nervous for I just never knew what Clive had in mind. As it turned out, my fear was unfounded for Clive merely wanted to take me to his home to "show me off." Clive proudly introduced me to those gathered at his home as his "younger brother who was studying in Canada." Even people attending a nearby function managed to find their way to the gallery to offer greetings and good wishes. That day I saw a side of Clive that I did not know existed. Happily I welcomed and embraced it. After a quick refreshment, we left for home. My visit was off to a good start.

Once home I noted how beautifully decorated it was for the Christmas season. Christmas was but two days away. The fridge too was filled to overflowing with special fare for the season. I peeked in at the freezer section—yes—the coconut ice cream was already in there.

Since it was supper time everyone gathered around the large table. It was the same table that I had helped make and it was still in relatively good health. An impressive feast awaited our appetites. Nothing compared to the feasts that Ma and the girls prepared. I was ecstatic and I did not, for one minute, try to hide my feelings or curb my appetite. That was a moment that I had long anticipated and I fully indulged my appetite. It was a moment filled with the spirit of laughter and gentle banter.

It wasn't long before Boysie began to receive visitors. He soon withdrew outside to entertain his friends. Once he was outside, the conversation inside the house took on a new complexion. The family started to voice their various opinions regarding Boysie and his governance. "He too stric," said one. "He way too rough. He have no patience or understanding."

A younger sister then boldly affirmed, "Frankie, when you coming back home for good? We need you. Boysie's too difficult."

Then Ma interjected, "Leave Frankie alone. You putting all kinds of ideas in his head. The boy just get home. You want chase him away already?"

There was a silence... for now, as everyone heeded Ma's words.

What was beginning to emerge was a picture of life at home. Ma certainly had her hands full. And over the course of the next days I learned more about Ma's situation. To Ma, the talk that was emerging from the mouths of her daughters seemed mutinous and she felt trapped in the middle: torn between a desire to honour a son who gave up so much to help out with the family and a need to protect the daughters who felt they were being mistreated. Emotionally this proved to be too much of a strain for Ma and at times she succumbed to the pressure coming at her from both sides and a type of depression would overtake her spirit.

Then did a loving neighbour take it upon herself to write to me and ask me to come home once again. That letter was just the prompt I needed to cause me to return home and now, in the midst of these quiet rumblings I felt assured of my decision to return; I felt needed. This revelation certainly now justified in my mind at least, that returning home was the correct decision despite the financial cost.

The next two days were filled with merriment. A spirit of happiness was infused in every meeting with family and friends. How heavenly was my visit.

It was Christmas Day. Ma and the girls were busy. Soon I was feasting over a breakfast of fried plantains, roti, stewed tomatoes and salt fish. Later that morning when I mentioned to Ma that I had to visit friends she cautioned, "Frankie, go. But remember, Son, to be home for lunch time. It is going to be good. Your favourites."

Her eyes twinkled; she was actually teasing. How happy was Ma; how content was I. More than ever I was assured of the rightness of my decision.

***

The family that I was about to visit had befriended me for some years now. While making my way to their home I recollected how welcoming they had always been to me. I reminisced about how much I had always enjoyed their company and their hospitality. I especially enjoyed where they lived for theirs was a home situated in very pleasant surroundings. There were several brothers and sisters that made up the family. In many respects it was not unlike my own family. I anticipated a casual and light-hearted visit.

I could not have been more wrong; it was anything but.

27
An Unexpected Offer

My friend Dev answered the door when I rang the bell. We both were excited with the reunion. He led me inside where the rest of the family had gathered for Christmas celebrations. I was ushered into the drawing room and was immediately offered a glass of wine. The mood was truly celebratory for even those family members who had been abroad had returned home for Christmas. I felt honoured to be among them and to be so well received. When Dev's mom announced that lunch was ready, I got up to take my leave. It was then that Dev's mother intoned, "Frankie, you can't leave. I've a special surprise for you. You are our guest. Come."

Dev's older brother pulled out a chair for me and motioned for me to sit. I did. Everyone was so happy; I was completely swept away by the emotion of the moment. The mood was so festive; the meal was so inviting. I knew I should not fully indulge my appetite for my mother was at home preparing a special Christmas dinner, but I had been away from this food for such a long time that I simply could not resist anything less than complete indulgence.

Everyone encouraged, "Frank, try this. Oh, you would like this. And you will die when you try this." What a prince I was made to feel. After the meal, Dev's mother brought out her special Christmas cake; it had been soaked in wine and rum for ages and was so moist and inviting. I wanted to resist; I should have resisted; but I could not resist. Christmas would not be Christmas without such an indulgence. Moreover, I did not want to risk offending my wonderful hosts.

The post dinner quiet was now settling in and I mentally prepared to take my leave for I knew Ma would be awaiting me for lunch. Everyone would be wondering where I was; I really *had* to get back home.

Suddenly Dev's mom stood and announced, "Frankie, we are happy to have you with us here. And we are proud of you. You are studying in Canada. Here is to Frank."

I was honoured yes, but I was beginning to feel slightly uncomfortable. Then an older brother, Harrilal, stood up and added, "Frankie, we like you like a member of our family…"

What is he saying? Please don't say what I think you are going to say, I silently prayed.

"Frankie, we know you like our sister, Meela. From our talks with her, she likes you too. So what do you say? Would you like to join our family? Do you accept?"

An awkward silence ensued. I was taken completely by surprise. Truly, Meela was a beautiful young woman, and the family was well established and very respected on the island. Under different circumstances it would have been an honour to accept such an offer. I met Meela as Dev's sister. As such, she became to me like my own sister. I could conceive of no other relationship. That is the standard that I expected in my family; I could expect nothing less of myself in these circumstances. In my mind, Meela and I were like brother and sister; such a relationship was so deeply rooted that there was no hope for a change.

Harrilal, was looking at me, awaiting my response—I sensed that he expected nothing short of acceptance of the offer.

Then I rose. I did not know what to say. I looked at Meela; she was sitting there quietly happy. Then I looked at everyone as I searched for a response. Then I began, "Harrilal, thank you and the family for such an honour. I have one small problem."

Everyone wanted to know the problem; each in his own way would make every effort to assist to solve the problem. Harrilal echoed the sentiment of all.

"Frankie, tell us, how can we help you?"

I was still silent. This was so hard. Then Dev's dad stood up and encouraged, "Frank, we know you have no father. You have a hard life. Well, we don't want you to worry about that. We are here to help you out…"

I had to interrupt at this point. I explained, "The problem I have is one that no one can help or solve. Not even me."

They were all quiet.

"I love Meela, but as a sister and that is the problem. From day one I did not dare have any other feelings for her. To do so would be to disrespect you. And I love her so much as a sister, as a beautiful sister. I am so terribly sorry. I have to go. I..."

Meela rose and whispered, "I will see Frank out." She then escorted me outside to the gate. I was silent; I did not know what to say to her. Somehow she knew, "Frank you don't have to say another word. I too accepted you as my brother's friend. Then I began seeing you differently—like more than a friend."

I looked at Meela; I was full of admiration for her, but I could not stay.

I hurried away.

******

It was now well past the lunch hour as I made my way home. Everyone was waiting for me and I could see by their faces that they were not happy with the delay. Ma's words as I entered the dining room indicated that once again she had assumed her role as conciliator, "See, Frankie did not forget about our lunch. He is here. Frankie, sit down. Everybody is hungry."

The clinking of glasses signaled the beginning of the meal. The disappointment felt about my being late seemed to have been forgotten. Genuine happiness and excitement once again filled the air.

Ma's eyes were on me and on my plate, happily anticipating my joy at all that she had prepared. I forced myself to eat. I mumbled rave revues about all that had been created. Only when my plate was completely empty was Ma satisfied. Apparently my ruse had succeeded. Then, from out of thin air, Ma produced another one of her specialty dishes—a huge serving of shrimps—a dish that I would normally die for.

"Frankie, Ah save this just for you. Nobody mind. You don't get this shrimp in Canada. It all for you. Enjoy."

Her smile went beyond a smile; she, in fact, became her smile. I could do nothing to destroy that. I looked at the shrimp. Then I looked at my mother. I thought I would explode, but respectfully, not at the table.

28
Old Year's Remembrances

I embraced new joy with the passage of each day. Christmas may have been over but preparations for the New Year's celebration were just beginning.

In Trinidad, New Year's Eve was always referred to as *Old Year's Night*. Previous *Old Year's Nights* held many fond remembrances. And now, once again, I was sitting on those familiar steps in front of my home. Sitting on the steps brought back one particular tale from those early days of childhood innocence: a time when the most innocent were frequently at the mercy of the more worldly among us.

Even as very young children we were allowed to stay up late on Old Year's Night. One such night a group of us gathered, excitedly awaiting the magic of the midnight hour. It was eleven o'clock, just one hour away from midnight. Old Boy Salim, one of our neighbours, saw us gathered outside and made his approach. After carefully surveying our faces he quickly discerned that we were but the babies on the block. Our older siblings had gathered with their friends. He then boldly declared, "Ah bet Ah can bring a block of ice right now and make it last all the way into the New Year."

Well, we all looked at him as if he were crazy. Salim was usually clever. Today he was talking nonsense and we wasted no time in telling him so. In almost one voice, we chanted, "No Way! Are you crazy?"

"Then I bet you one penny each. Put your money where your mouth is."

The moment took on a serious tone as every one of us frantically searched for a penny. Never before had a bet seemed easier to win. *A block of ice lasting a year?* Indeed, Salim had taken leave of his senses. There was some easy money to be made.

I was the last to find my penny. Suddenly it struck me as odd that Salim would be willing to lose so much money to us by betting on something so preposterous. It was like him to take advantage of situations and I wondered: *Why was he so interested in betting with us so all of a sudden?* Something told me be cautious in my dealings with him. I sensed that perhaps he was putting one over on us. I went over his claim once more. *What exactly had he said?* He said that he could make a block of ice last into the New Year. Suddenly it hit me—the New Year was actually Old Year's Night. And the New Year was but an hour away.

Of course he was correct; it was not obvious to us because of the way he said it. We all thought that he was talking about keeping the ice for almost a year. So, I challenged him, "Salim, I bet the ice would not last two days much less a whole year."

Salim's face fell as he realized that he had been found out. We had seen through his prank. He gave me a little tap on the head and murmured, "So you think you so smart?" Then he walked away.

To my friends, I was a hero. My status as hero lasted for the rest of the year.

All forty-five minutes of it.

29

Old Year's Night at Nani and Nana

No sooner did one nostalgic joy from my distant past surface, then another one vied to take its place. This time my memory took me back to my grandparents who lived on the mountains in the Northern Range. A married daughter and her husband lived on the edge of my grandparents' property. Without any neighbours nearby, they lived virtually alone. My grandparents' youngest child, my uncle, was just one year older than I was and I remember wondering, *How does uncle get along all by himself with no other children to play with?*

Travelling back in time in my mind was so easy now that I was home; my mind offered no resistance; if anything it summoned remembrances. One of my earliest recollections involves special preparations undertaken sometime during the Christmas holidays. My grandparents spent endless hours preparing and there was great expectation surrounding the event. When I asked what all the preparation was for no one would offer the slightest hint or explanation. My uncle knew but even he kept the secret from me. I had to content myself with keeping busy with other things. To distract myself I went to visit an aunt who lived at the edge of my grandparents' property. Not even my aunt would proffer one hint.

Mousie (auntie) and her husband, Mousa (uncle) lived in a small modest house about a hundred yards or so from my grandparents. When I first looked at it, the house looked so very strange; it had no roof! I wandered around it and inspected it from the outside. Mousa, witnessing my incredulous stare, asked, "Frankie, everything okay?"

I could not answer for I was too busy trying to figure out this house with no roof.

"Frankie, what you thinking?"

"Mousa, this house has no roof. How come?"

"Frankie, it hav a roof."

"But, I don't see a roof."

"But that is because you not lookin' in the right place. Look again. You see it?"

I looked and looked. All I saw was what looked like railroad tracks extending out from the house. Where the tracks ended, they were supported by thick beams that were buried deep within the earth. At the very end of the tracks was a roof. I was puzzled. I asked Mousa, "Why is the roof built out there? There is nothing below it. I don't understand."

"Frankie, follow me. I'll show you."

Mousa took me inside the house. There was a wooden stair leading upward. He mounted the stairs. I followed. At the top of the stairs was a flat wooden surface littered with cocoa beans. Then I became even more confused. *Why were these beans all over the floor?* It just didn't make any sense. No sooner had these thoughts come into my mind when I was immediately distracted by the sky overhead. Since there was no roof to block the view, I could clearly see the blueness of the sky and feel the warmth of the sun. For a moment I was captivated by the scene. Even at my tender age I was charmed by Nature. The trees stretched out endlessly before me in their various hues of green. I was so enthralled at the sight that I did not respond immediately when Mousa called my name.

He then gently reached over and shook me, "Do you see the roof?"

I smiled and pointed, "That roof way over there."

"Yes!"

Then we went back down the stairs and walked over to where the railroad track structure was located. We climbed up a make-shift ladder to where the roof was suspended. Mousa asked me to sit on a cross beam and hold on tight. I did. He then grabbed a beam that supported the roof and pushed on it. As he pushed, the roof began to move. Mousa had managed to construct a moveable roof using pulleys and wheels. The beams along the base of the roof were equipped with wheels which rolled along the tracks in much the same way that the engine on a train runs along the railway tracks. Soon the roof was resting securely on the house. It was magical.

Before I could fully form a question in my mind regarding the roof, Mousa was answering it.

"You want to know why we have a roof that moves. Simple. We used to store the beans in bags upstairs. Then we would haul the bags outside and spread them out to dry under the sun. Whenever it rained or threatened to rain we would have to put everything back in bags and lug them back up the stairs to store. We would have to repeat this process every day. Now, with this contraption, we simply move the roof."

"That's smart!" I yelled. I was most impressed by Mousa's inventiveness. The roof was truly fascinating.

Before I could ask any more questions, Mousie called from downstairs and signaled for both Mousa and me to come down for a snack. We sat outside the kitchen on a little bench. Mousie poured me a whole glass of sweet drink all for myself. Then she offered me a whole egg. That was unbelievable! Imagine, a whole egg and a whole glass of sweet drink. No other kid could have been as happy as I was at that moment. Just when I thought that things couldn't possibly get any better, Mousie teased me with the most tempting aroma of fresh sweet bread. She offered me a whole slice all to myself; I did not have to share with anyone. It was a moment stolen from heaven's gate. The world was a wonderful place with my Mousie and Mousa.

I tried to find out then what was the excitement—the special event for Old Year's Night. I was sure they would tell me. No such luck.

When nightfall descended, Mousie and Mousa came with me back to Nani and Nana's. We chatted, told stories, feasted and waited and waited. All that my grandfather would say was this, "Frankie, yo hav to wait till the stroke of midnight."

I knew enough not to argue with my grandfather. *What was going to happen? Why won't anyone tell me?* Uncle knew but would say nothing.

We were gathered in the living room, sprawled out in make-shift seats. It was close to midnight. I was becoming very tired and shamefully just about to fall asleep when I heard a voice singing—it was coming from outside. *How could that be? There was nothing there but deep darkness.*

As Nana approached the door the voice became a chorus of voices accompanied by the sound of a mandolin and guitar. Nana opened the door to greet and welcome in a group of neighbours from the nearby mountains.

In no time at all a special cherry brandy made an appearance. Sweet cakes and other treats were served round. A lantern burned brightly in the darkness and gentle voices broke the night silence with sweet melodies. I was entranced and mesmerized by the whole scene.

Then Nana went into the bedroom and returned with a gun. One of our visitors also retrieved a shotgun from his bag. What a sight! I had never seen a real gun before. I stared; I was so excited. *What were they going to do?*

Everyone burst out in song as we all marched outside into the black night. The strumming of guitars joined the voices and filled the fresh night air with sound. Then all sounds ceased. Utter silence prevailed. The two men with their guns stood side by side facing the mountains. They aimed their guns into the glorious darkness.

Bang! Bang! Bang!

A volley of fire blazed from their guns. The Old Night—the last night of the year—was shot, blown away to make room for the arrival of the new year. The dawning of the new year promised to envelop the land and render a blessing upon all who dwelled therein. From the perspective of my child mind nothing could have been more enchanting.

30

Boysie and Ma: A New Awareness

A melancholy stole over me as I realized that the holidays were quickly coming to an end. The magic and the excitement that had sustained me over the Christmas season gradually dissipated and I was left with the stone reality that in just a few days I would have to return to Canada.

My mind could not embrace my imminent return to Canada—to its harsh winter and to the solitary existence of a struggling student. At every turn I began to look for a reason—any reason to remain in Trinidad. I searched in vain for a reason that would make sense to my family. I could not understand myself. For most of my life I had made decisions that were readily accepted. *Why was I now trying to manufacture a reason to stay home? What was happening to me?* I began to brood.

One evening Boysie came home from work rather early. That he came home early meant that he had not had a full day's work. When he spotted me in the back yard he came over to me; his look was grave. We had not yet had a moment alone together to talk seriously—brother to brother. As he approached I could sense that this was our moment. I braced myself for *the chat*.

"Frank, tell me, how you're doing?"

"Boysie, I'm doing fine, and I am happy to be home. It is good to see you. How are you?"

"Well, Frankie tell me this. You are doing well at university? You studying hard? You passing all your courses?"

"Yes, Boysie. I have to work very hard, but I am passing."

"Then Frankie, it is worth it. I know you are worrying about me. You worry that you left me to take care of the family alone. I have it hard that is the truth."

That was it! That was my out. I could seize this glorious opportunity to explain why I would not return to Canada. Boysie needed me. I could not let him suffer alone. It was my *duty* to stay home and assume my fair share of the responsibilities. I had to seize the moment.

"I am so sorry you have to do it all alone, Boysie. It is not right that you have to take care of Ma and everyone else. It is too much for you. Boysie, I am prepared to do what is …"

Boysie would not let me finish, "To do what, Frank? Give up your studies? No! I will handle home; you handle your studies."

"But, Boysie…"

"No buts Frank. That's how it is written. Pa always wanted you to do something with your life. That's what you must do. I know that now."

With those words, I was silenced. Boysie withdrew into the house.

My plan had backfired; instead of me getting to offer my support to Boysie, he offered me his support. This was too much. Clearly Boysie was sacrificing his life for all of us. This was not right. I should be standing beside him—shoulder to shoulder. We should be taking care of our responsibilities together like brothers.

I was vulnerable and wavering; could I have been looking for an excuse to stay and abandon my studies?

Why hadn't Boysie complained about his hardships? Perhaps then he would have been amenable to my remaining in Trinidad and would have accepted my decision. Why did Boysie have to adopt such a supportive spirit and attitude?

The next morning I got up early. I decided that I needed to know more about this brother of mine. To this end, I determined that I had to go to work with him and experience some of the realities of his life. As Boysie was about to leave, I announced, "Boysie, I am going with you to work today. OK?"

Somewhat taken aback by my offer he countered, "No, Frank, you are not going to go with me. You crazy?"

"Boysie I would appreciate it if you…"

"No Frank, I'm not taking you. You make it hard for me and me workers. You get annoyed when we yell. And you go nuts when we cuss. You don't belong out there with me. My world is rough and…"

I was not going to be dissuaded, "Boysie, I am coming and I will not say anything. My mouth will be shut."

Boysie relented, "I don't know why you want to come, but okay. Remember any interference and…"

"Boysie, you can toss me off the truck and leave me to find my own way home. I won't interfere. I promise."

Still somewhat shocked by my assertions, Boysie stared at me. He said nothing as we boarded the truck.

As the day unfolded, I witnessed my brother at work. From the moment he arrived at the docks in Port of Spain, he was busy. First, he picked up his orders and then headed for the wharf. He had to load a shipment of rice and flour and potatoes and take them to the warehouse. Bags of rice, flour, potatoes were standing in wait on the docks. Watching him work, I gained an appreciation for not only his strength but also his rhythm and timing. The act of loading and unloading by hand demanded the cooperation of all who worked on the docks. I sensed their mutual respect and interdependence.

Their mouths were seldom still while their bodies toiled. The air was blue with the sound of cussing. It was as if the cussing was a necessary adjunct to the labour. I was tempted to open my mouth, but I forced myself to remain quiet. I had to be on my guard constantly and check my mouth; moreover, I was not to show one look of disapproval. That was exceedingly difficult; many times I was tempted to "chastise" Boysie, but I kept my promise and said nothing. Instead, I paid close attention to my brother. And what did I see? I saw a brother slaving to provide for the daily needs of his family. At that moment I had a new found affection for and appreciation of my hard-working brother.

Evening descended and Boyie was about to make his last delivery: a few cases of Solo (sweet drink) to a nearby restaurant. As Boysie and his worker delivered the last case, I headed back to the truck. Boysie called out, "Hey Frank, you want a cool Solo?"

I was honoured to be included. "Yes, please," I responded.

Boysie must have been happy with me to include me in that way. Then he produced a beer for his worker and one for himself. As he was opening the caps, Boysie turned to me and asked, "Frankie, you want a beer?"

Even though I really didn't want to have a beer, my answer to him was, "I sure do." Truth be told, I preferred the Solo pop. But, at this moment in time, the beer was more than just a beer. It was a symbol of Boysie's acceptance and approval. I had passed the test and I would have the prize that was offered.

By the time I had taken my second sip, Boysie's worker had downed his beer and prepared to leave. He was anxious to be on his way.

After the worker left, Boysie looked at me curiously. He ordered another beer for himself and regarded my bottle of unfinished beer. After finishing that one he then ordered another for himself all the while staring at my still unfinished bottle.

Just then, another dock worker, Butch, entered the restaurant and ordered a beer. His voice was harsh and demanding. When he spotted Boysie sitting in the corner he briskly approached our table and without an invitation, sat down opposite Boysie. No sooner had he sat when he began complaining to Boysie about some problem; his voice was loud and grating; his language was full of obscenities.

At first Boysie maintained an awkward silence in the face of this man's boldness. The angry visitor became even louder. After quickly downing one beer, he ordered another. It was apparent that he had put away quite a few before entering the premises. Soon his focus of concern shifted from his problem to Boysie's apparent lack of concern. He then began attacking Boysie.

"What the f***'s matter with you Boysie? You not paying any f***ing attention. You not even f***ing drinking with me. I thought you was my f***ing friend. Boysie man f*** you. And who is that f***ing person with you? F*** him too!"

Boysie's face turned red. I saw his jaw tighten and his muscles clench. Truly, he was disturbed by this man's words. When he stood up and looked squarely into the face of the man I became concerned. *Was Boysie going to blow up? Was he too going to start swearing? I had held my peace all afternoon. What would I do if Boysie too lost his cool?* Normally I would have prepared to walk away. Today I chose to stay.

I waited.

Boysie did not yell; neither did he cuss. He took in a deep breath and calmly introduced Butch to me. "Butch, I want yo to meet my brother Frank. He is my younger brother. He is studying in Canada. He is just here for the Christmas holiday. Frank is a teacher."

The unshaven and somewhat disheveled Butch stared at me, scratching his jaw. He took out a handkerchief and as he wiped the perspiration from his face he apologized, "Mr. Frank, I'm sorry man. I meant no disrespect to you. Ah so sorry. Excuse my language. I having a problem I can't solve. I was unloading me mind to Boysie. Could you excuse me, please?"

Moved by the simple earnestness of Butch, I stood and offered, "Butch may I buy you a beer? I would be happy to do so."

"No thanks, Frank. I can't let you do that. You a student. I want to buy a round."

Before I could protest, he ordered three beers. As soon as we were served, Butch raised his beer to me and professed, "Mr. Frank, I am happy to meet you. I congratulate you. You are going to be a teacher. You are going to be somebody most important. We are just ordinary workers. Boysie, you have quite a brother there. You must be so proud."

Before too long, both Butch and his beer were gone and Boysie was headed over to the bartender to order a snack. I was left alone with my thoughts. The experience was surreal. What an amazing turn of events. The situation that I had thought would escalate into an angry verbal exchange at the very least, had become a moment in which honour and respect were bestowed upon me by both Boysie and Butch. Butch's whole demeanor changed upon learning that I was studying abroad. He became apologetic and conciliatory. Boysie too, had shown remarkable restraint out of respect for me. By remaining calm in the presence of such disrespect, Boysie had honoured me.

I was moved.

Furthermore, Butch's assertion that he was *just a worker* both touched and saddened me. I realized that he was trying to honour me but I was saddened that he did not recognize the dignity inherent in his own work.

Soon Boysie returned to sit opposite me once again. He drew his chair in close and leaned into me. His face was intent as he spoke, "Frank, you never once meddled in my conversation today. You did not interfere and there was a lot of cussing. How come?"

"Let's say I grew up a little. Maybe Canada taught me a lesson or two."

"Really, Frank?" He sounded surprised but pleased.

My thoughts immediately transported me back to Canada to an incident that occurred while I was working with Twin City Gas in the small town of Atikokan, Ontario in the summer of 1968.

A disagreement or a misunderstanding erupted between two of the workers. Tempers flared and a heated argument ensued. The argument quickly escalated to the point of explosion. Their anger was palatable. Their rough and offensive language toward one another further fuelled their rage to the point where I truly believed that they might kill one another. Yet, only moments later, all seemed to have been forgiven; the two men emerged from the trench the best of friends once again.

Their world of work was a rough and challenging one; the intense language and intense emotion seemed to go hand in hand with the physical intensity of their jobs. Yet, their friendship was able to transcend the negatives and to somehow become strengthened.

From those two men I gained an insight into Boysie's world and through that, into my father's world. Through them I tasted the everyday frustration that challenged the life of the physical labourer; through them I gained some understanding of my brother. Boysie epitomized the consummate worker; he was immersed forever in the day to day struggle for existence; he was saturated in a life where there were few opportunities to indulge in philosophic contemplation and idealism. I, on the other hand, was the teacher, privileged to attend university, in large part due to the generosity of spirit of my selfless brother. Suddenly, I was overcome by a feeling of guilt; guilt borne on the wings of selfishness. It was selfish of me to have left Boysie all alone to care for the family. It was selfish of me to have dared to seek to pursue my dreams at his expense. I never should have left.

Boysie's words brought me out of my retrospective reverie. "Frankie, you okay? Yo looking worried. Frank, don't worry man…"

"Boysie, I can't help it. You have to work so hard to take care of the whole family. You are alone. You remind me of Pa."

"How so?"

"Pa had to work so hard. All his days he worked hard. And now you, Boysie, you are here doing what he would have done. I am so proud of you Boysie. But, maybe I should be here with you helping to take care of the family. Boysie, let me…"

"No, Frank. This is not your world. You belong at the university."

"Boysie, I cannot let you continue to do this all by yourself. I am serious…"

"Frank, you do what you started. I will do what I have to do."

"But it is too tough, too rough for you. Let me help!"

"No, Frank. I admit that life is hard. When you was here you handled the discipline. Everyone listened to you. That's because you had ambition and made something of yourself. Back then I took the easy way. Your mind went for education. I was not like you. I did not listen to Pa. I made my own bed… But Pa gave me a start. He passed on the truck business to me. And he gave me a roof over my head. I learn. Now I am responsible. So you must learn too. You *must* make something of yourself brother. Remember yo fader Frank. He wanted you to be a lawyer. But you is more the teacher type. Pa would be proud too! Clivey, your oldest brother and I talked. We agree. You better off in Canada. You got it? Now finish your drink."

The pep talk was over for the moment. Soon we arrived back at home where supper was ready and Ma was smiling. When Boysie saw her he teased, "Madame B, every time Frank here you happy. You young and energetic. Today you looking so good."

"Boysie, enough of that talk. Come, I want everyone around the table. I am happy; all my children are here, sitting together, around the table. Now Ah ready to make a toast. Fill your glasses."

When each of us had a refreshment in our hands Ma continued, "To all my children, sitting right here with me, I lost your father…" For a moment, she choked up but soon she resumed her toast, "I have all of you. I drink to your happiness. Try, all of you, to be one…"

We raised our glasses and toasted to her request. And I know that to this very day Ma's prayer still sits etched in the souls of all her children. Over the years, even though I was not always conscious of it, her simple petition has served as my guide; her simple request that we stay one reverberates for all eternity.

That evening as I prepared for bed Ma came into my room. I was not surprised for I knew she was waiting to speak privately to me. Time was running out and the moment was at hand. Gently she rested on the edge of the bed just looking at me for a few minutes. When she was ready to speak, she whispered, "Frankie I was thinking about you."

"No, Ma, you were **worrying** about me, right?"

"Yes, I can't help it. Here at home we have each other. Who you have in Canada? No one! You have to face everything in Canada by yourself. No one to help you. Frank, boy, I can't even see you—help you."

Ma broke down and started to sob. It was obvious that she had been carrying this burden for a long time. I sensed the pain that had long engulfed her soul. For so long she had been consumed with such concern for me that she could no longer keep it bottled up. She cried in a vain attempt to release the pain; I too felt her pain. I reached out to her—to my mother, to the woman who sought endlessly for ways to make life better for her children; to the mother who forever lived in order to give to every one of her children. As I held her in my arms, I felt helpless; I wanted to take away the hurt. More than ever the desire to remain at home and be a help to the family burned in my soul. In that very moment I realized that my place was not in Canada; it was here at this home in Trinidad. While I knew that Boysie would have objections I also knew that in time I would be able to prevail on him. Ma needed me; I reached out and held her. She needed me at home. I knew it. Her body trembled with the knowledge that

I would be leaving once again. I had to tell her that she was mistaken. I would never leave her again as long as I was needed. Her grip tightened and once again I was reminded that her frail body was very vulnerable—but forever she would be *Ma*.

Then she broke the silence, "Frankie, I know what you thinking. You want to stay home. You want to help your brother, Boysie. Right?"

"Yes, Ma."

"No, Son. You place is not here. Not now."

"But, Ma."

"No 'but Ma'. If I could go through life without you—as hard as it is—you must go through life and you must finish what you went to Canada to do."

"Ma, Boysie have it too hard."

"Yes, Boysie have it hard, but it would be harder for Boysie if yo did not finish your studies. You don't know how proud your brother Boysie is of you. Frankie most important yo must finish your studies for yourself."

"Ma?"

"Boysie tell all his friends that his smaller brother is in Canada. He tell them that you is going to be somebody. Frankie, Boysie is proud of you. You have to let Boysie have that pride. You understand?"

"Yes, Ma."

Her case was irrefutable.

After she left the room a thousand and one thoughts swirled in my mind. Unable to sleep I sat up in my bed and looked around at my surroundings. In the corner standing tall was the closet that I had built years before. The headboard of my bed and its hidden compartments gleamed with fresh polish. Boysie had made sure that everything was buffed, polished and freshly painted for my stay. A simple night stand, which I had built also, caressed the side of the bed; on it still rested the modest gramophone player on which I had always played my favourite single 45 record. As I reached into the compartments of the bed head, my fingers trembled. I was searching for that one special record; it wasn't there; my disappointment was immediate. That small record had been life-giving for me. For so many days and nights it had sustained me. I continued to search for it. Then I saw it… on the shelf of my night stand… one of my favourite pieces of music. I placed the treasure in the gramophone and adjusted the volume. Ever so gently Acker Bilk's "Stranger on the Shore" pierced the silence of my room. I had played that record a thousand times before, and each time was like the first time.

Frank Maraj

Each time elicited in me the same feeling of melancholy. Each time I was reminded of how much I had felt like a stranger on the shores of my own life. This time however, it was different; today, for once, *I was no stranger on the shores of my family.*

31

Back to the Lakehead

All too soon my holiday was at an end and once again my entire family gathered at the airport. I tried hard to hide my melancholy at leaving. As we exchanged goodbyes I looked for the face of my mother. As usual Ma hung back having retired to a spot near the rear of the group; her hand was raised in silent farewell. Just before I entered the terminal to begin my walk to the plane, I turned for a final look back at all that I was leaving. Ma had made her way to the front of the line. I gave her one last look; I sensed the toll my leaving had placed on her spirit. She released me with a slight smile; I tucked it in my heart along with her prayers for me. They would have to sustain me until I was home once more. Soon I was on board an Air Canada flight bound for Toronto.

During my journey I took time to reexamine my situation. *What events conspired together to cause me to return to the Lakehead? Had the care and concern showered on me by those two great ambassadors of good will, Dr. Doan and Professor Cornell, coupled with the strong affection and insistence of my family, acted in concert to negate my personal inclination to remain in Trinidad?* The totality of all their efforts seemed to pre-destine my inevitable return to Canada and the resumption of my studies. Thus I surrendered to the dictates of the Great Beyond. I determined that I would do whatever it would take to see me through this next portion of my life.

Within moments of making peace with my circumstance, we landed at the Lakehead. I steeled myself for the weather. Between the time the plane landed and the time it took to retrieve my luggage and head outside to secure a taxi, the weather had dramatically changed. A blizzard of white had woven its icy fingers around the city. The taxi provided little relief from the freezing temperatures. My body quickly lost any residual Trinidadian heat.

Earlier in the fall, I had left the Horns' and had found a small room at the Levesques' to rent. It was close to the downtown area.

As I vacated the taxi in front of the Levesque home, the full force of the hostile wind forced me into a struggle to remain vertical. Light summer footwear caused me to redouble my efforts with each step. In the short distance between the street and the back entrance to the house I lost all sensation in my feet and I wondered if indeed I still possessed any toes.

The house was empty. No one was on hand to greet me; no one to say *"welcome back, it's good to see you."* My empty bed and small dresser were small comfort for all that I had left behind. A sudden melancholy stole over me as my mind straddled two hemispheres. *How could life have changed so much in so little time?* Short hours ago I was surrounded by the boisterousness of an affectionate family. *And now?* Now I am alone; alone with my thought and my melancholy. I was feeling sorry for myself and allowed myself a moment's indulgence. That is when I recalled the voice of Ma, just hours ago, urging me, "Frankie, most important, you must finish your studies for you, yourself." That was when I realized that I had to dispel these visitations of sadness, loneliness, and uncertainty. There was something about Ma's loving insistence that I return to Canada and complete my studies. *Did she know me better than I knew myself? Did this angel of a mother recognize that she needed to protect me from myself?* On the anvil of time my mother's words hammered an unspoken truth that sparked a new resolve.

32
My Bond

The next morning I awoke to a new universe. For a moment I had forgotten that I was no longer in Trinidad. The cold realization that I was once again alone and in Canada settled reluctantly in my soul. Slowly I went through the motions of preparing myself to face this next new day. My first order of business was to visit the Royal Bank of Canada. My unexpected trip to Trinidad had drained me of my summer earnings.

Immediately upon entering the Royal Bank of Canada on Cumberland Street, I sought out the reception desk. A cool but nonetheless polite business voice greeted me, "Sir, may I help you?"

"Yes, I truly hope so."

"And how may I be of help?" the voice queried.

The receptionist gave me a good look over. I could not tell what she made of me. Did I measure up? Was I worth her extra effort? Her manner appeared somewhat distant and withdrawn and it was difficult to ascertain what her perception of me was. Her tone, while officious revealed a certain cautiousness which suggested that I had to follow proper protocol just like everyone else that walked through that door. She certainly had the right to such an opinion.

I must have passed visual inspection for with her next breath came the pointed question, "And your name?"

"Frank Maraj."

Without so much as a second look back, she proceeded to go directly to the manager's office. Like an obedient puppy, I remained seated awaiting her return. I became a bit anxious as people continued to flow in and out of the bank and the receptionist had still failed to return with the verdict.

Finally, an answer. But I could not read it on her countenance. I would have to await the words. "Mr. Maraj, Mr. Kennedy will see you in an hour.

And he indicated that the meeting was to be very brief. He is completely booked up and…"

"Miss, I am thankful to you for your assistance. I realize that I don't have an appointment. You are most kind."

"One hour from now, Mr. Maraj, at four o'clock."

She turned and resumed her duties at her desk.

Four o'clock came… and went.

At four thirty the same officious voice beckoned, "Mr. Maraj, Mr. Kennedy will see you now. Follow me."

I smiled for I really did not mind waiting; I was so grateful just to be granted an interview with the manager. Just before opening the door to Mr. Kennedy's office, the receptionist whispered, "Mr. Maraj, I wish you luck. I hope everything works out for you."

I had barely an instant to process the remark. I was struck for it seemed so out of character from my initial impression of her. I managed a simple, "Thank you, ever so much."

As I entered the office, immediately Mr. Kennedy rose from his seat, extended his hand and greeted, "Mr. Maraj, I am Mr. Kennedy. I am so sorry I kept you waiting. Won't you have a seat?"

His professional courtesy was most inviting. It gave me a good feeling and immediately I was put at ease.

"Mr. Maraj, how may I help you?"

"Mr. Kennedy, thank you, Sir, for seeing me on such short notice. I promised that I would be brief so I will come directly to the point. Sir, I would like a loan of $250.00. Can you help me?"

A heavy silence followed my request. Mr. Kennedy seemed caught off guard. Had I been too abrupt?

Mr. Kennedy quickly regained his composure and his next question revealed that he was back in charge. "What kind of collateral do you have? We…"

"None, Mr. Kennedy."

"Then, Mr. Maraj, how do you hope to have us lend you that kind of money without some form of collateral? At the very least, you need to have someone co-sign on the loan. Perhaps, then I might be able to help. Without either of those things I don't see how I can be of any assistance. I am sorry, Mr. Maraj."

"Mr. Kennedy, if you, the bank manager, cannot help me, then no one can help me. Besides, I do not know anyone from whom I could ask such a favor. Thank you for your time Mr. Kennedy."

I stood and began to take my leave. Mr. Kennedy reached out, "Mr. Maraj, if only you had someone, anyone to offer some type of collateral…"

"But I do, Mr. Kennedy?"

"And who might that be?"

"Me. You have the word of Frank Maraj."

"Mr. Maraj, business is not usually conducted on the basis of someone's word alone."

"Mr. Kennedy, my word is my bond. It is all I have to offer."

I reached into my briefcase and produced a folded sheet of paper. I handed it to him. On the paper was listed my address in Trinidad and my various business transactions conducted with the Royal Bank of Canada in Trinidad. Attached to this was my current address and phone number.

Without another word, I left the bank.

One, maybe two weeks passed and I had no word from the bank. Then one day upon returning home from school, my landlady simply said, "Frank, someone phoned and asked for you. I could not quite understand. But here is the number."

I returned the call and the voice on the other end belonged to Mr. Kennedy himself. He indicated that I should come to see him at the end of the next business day.

When I arrived at the bank the next day, I found myself occupying the same chair that I had on my former visit. I was greeted by the same receptionist but her greeting was very different from our first meeting. In fact, it was several degrees warmer. "Mr. Maraj, good to see you. Mr. Kennedy is expecting you. Come with me. How are you, Mr. Maraj?"

She escorted me to the office; Mr. Kennedy was at the door to receive me.

"Mr. Maraj, come in."

Mr. Kennedy came straight to the point, "Mr. Maraj, I am in a position to grant you a loan of $250.00. Simply sign the document. It is a promise to pay said amount completely in one year."

"Thank you, Mr. Kennedy, I will not disappoint you."

"I know that."

I looked at him; he was smiling. "I know a good deal about you, but I know something much more."

"And what is that Mr. Kennedy?"

"You and your word, Mr. Maraj. I believe you would rather die than not honour your word."

I could say nothing. I was overwhelmed with emotion at my good fortune. I quietly smiled as I left the office.

Someone was looking out for me.

I sensed a thaw in the weather.

33

A Job... Well, almost

Standing outside the construction site building somewhere near Memorial Avenue and Simpson Street at eight o'clock on a chilly Saturday morning, I still marveled at the fact that even though the sun was gloriously blazing, the temperature remained icy.

A truck broke the early morning silence as it pulled into the reserved parking spot at the side of the building. Its solitary occupant stepped out into the brisk morning air acknowledging me with only a cursory glance and a simple hello. Clearly absorbed in thought, he quickly brushed past me.

"Who was he?" I wondered to myself. His attire suggested that he might have been one of the crew members. His six foot frame looked a bit intimidating in those rugged jeans and jean jacket. *Looks can be deceiving* I reminded myself thinking back to my last summer and my encounters with Yogi.

Moments later this same person returned and asked, "Who are you? Why are you here?"

"The advertisement in the paper indicated that there was a job. It said to be here at 9:00 a.m."

"And you came this early?"

"Yes."

Julian invited me to come inside into his office. He began asking me about Trinidad. It was his expressed view that I was brave to leave Trinidad and come here to what he called "a frozen wasteland." I began to smile. He was very curious. I explained that I was actually settling in quite nicely in "this frozen wasteland." But, I had to confess that my feet frequently rebelled at the cold. His response surprised me, "In that case, let's get those feet working."

"Do you mean I got … "

"Yes, you are hired, Frank. You start tomorrow morning at 9:00."

"Great, and thank you ever so much. Is there anything I can do for you? Like… maybe you might want me to start *today* if it works out?"

He paused for a moment, then added, "The work here is dusty and dirty. You will be covered in cement dust all over. You will need…"

"Work clothes!" I said, finishing his sentence as I pulled out some work clothes from my briefcase.

I believe I impressed him with my initiative and preparedness for he gave me a smile and led me back to the floor of the warehouse and explained to me the nature of my job.

His explanation was straight forward. As trucks loaded with bricks came into the warehouse, they had to be unloaded. Front loaders were able to remove most of the bricks but individual bricks and broken pieces always had to be removed manually. Similarly, when bricks were being loaded onto trucks for shipment from the warehouse, again manual labourers worked alongside the machines by picking out individual bricks to complete the load count. Julian then confided that he was a bit of a "neat freak" and really liked to have a clean and organized warehouse. He readily admitted that given warehouse conditions that facet of the job would be hard to achieve. He hastened to add, however, that he would be very appreciative of any effort made to accomplish that end.

By now, it was nearly 9:00 a.m. and I had changed into my work clothes, ready to start the day. I noted that the truck on the far end of the warehouse was beginning to be loaded. The driver was counting out bricks from an open stack and carrying them by hand and depositing them on the floor just outside the truck. I joined him in his endeavors until everything but the individual bricks were loaded. The driver then jumped up onto the back of the truck and I passed him the bricks resting at the side. He smiled a thank you when the truck was fully loaded and then drove off.

The truck departed, leaving cement fragments littering the floor. Julian must have noticed me looking around and directed me to the area where the wheelbarrow, the brooms and other cleaning materials were stored. Soon that section of the warehouse was nearly spotless.

That pretty much describes how I spent the majority of my first day. Wherever a hand was needed my hand was there. No one had to tell me what to do. My eyes were open and my hands were busy.

Over the course of the next week, Julian hired three more students. It seemed that they needed direction at every turn. This need reduced the productivity of the more seasoned workers and I sensed a small hint of frustration in Julian. These three were made all the more conspicuous by their obvious lack of initiative. As for me, time passed quickly and I was happy. Even though the work was exceedingly hard and physically taxing, I was grateful to have a job. I was especially grateful to have a job with no supervisor constantly in my face. That, in and of itself, was pure joy. I was allowed to use my own discretion and trust my own initiative whenever there was work to be done. I kept my own counsel and was quietly content to be counted among Julian's workers.

When Monday arrived, Julian assembled all the workers together. Mr. Garbini, the manager and owner of the construction company announced, "The contract we had, or thought we had, has been cancelled. Sorry. Some of you will be let go. It's not your fault. Sorry."

After Mr. Garbini left, Julian called one of the new workers aside to speak with him in private. As Julian spoke, the worker hung his head, turned to gather his things, and then left. Over the next two days the other new hires were released. Work slowed down to a mere crawl. Many just stood around waiting for *the talk*. I grabbed a broom and swept the floor from end to end. I picked up every speck of scrap from the floor. Then I began organizing the warehouse. By Thursday there really was nothing left to do; I began sweeping the dregs from one end of the warehouse to the other end and then back again. Later that day Julian paid me a visit.

"Frank, I can't tell you how sorry I am to have to do this. Sorry, man. You did your best to keep yourself occupied. That is why you are the last to go. And your paycheck is for the full week. I am so sorry, I couldn't do more, Frank."

"Julian, I appreciate your support. I am so sorry that I have to go. I really liked working here."

"We liked having you… Frank, if things improve I will be sure to call you. I just wish…"

"I know, Julian, and I understand. Don't worry, something will come up. I thank you for your kindness."

There are many people out there who say, *I will call you* when they know very well that they have no intention of calling. Then there are those few who say it and mean it. I believe that Julian was bred from the latter stock. There is great honour in giving one's word and keeping it.

Conversely, when one fails to keep a promise, one brings dishonor to one's self and further erodes the very root of personal integrity.

I truly believe that had there been work, Julian would have called. Yet, I felt also that it would be unwise of me to wait. I needed another job… and quickly.

34

The Nor-Shor Experience

I walked along Memorial Avenue staring at the many businesses that lined the street. It wasn't long before I stopped squarely in front of the Nor-Shor Motel. There was something about this place that spoke to me, that drew me to cross the street and enter its doors. Perhaps it was the allure of its reputation for a great dining experience.

I had never been there before but as I walked through the door, I could just picture myself sitting quietly in the coffee shop sipping a cup of coffee. The urge was strong and the coffee beckoned. I even spotted the perfect table where I imagined myself sitting enjoying that cup. A waitress smiled as if to welcome me in. Everything was falling into place perfectly conspiring to make the drinking of that cup of coffee almost inevitable. Alas, I had to content myself with merely imagining having that cup of coffee for my resources were limited; more than the coffee, I needed a job. Sadly, I turned away from the coffee shop and retreated to the cashier's station. I must have looked lost or out of place for another employee noticed me and asked if she could be of any assistance.

"I'm looking for the manager," I explained.

She pointed to the pool area. I followed her directions and quickly located the pool; I saw no manager there. I returned to the cashier's station and advised the woman that the manager was not there.

"But I saw him there a moment ago. You must be mistaken; Mr. Zale has to be there."

"Thank you, I'll look again."

I went back to the pool and again I saw no manager—no Mr. Zale.

Yet, there was however, someone standing inside the pool mixing together what looked like some kind of chemical compounds and conducting some type of test. He had noticed me each time I came into the area but had said no word of greeting.

I decided to approach him and inquired, "Sir, excuse me. I am looking for Mr. Zale. Do you know where he might be?"

"Yes!"

Then this curious man dove underwater. When he resurfaced, I again asked, "Mister can you tell me where Mr. Zale is?"

"Yes, what do you want?"

"To see Mr. Zale."

"Yes, what do you want? I am rather busy."

"Oh, you are Mr. Zale? You?"

I realized immediately that my response would appear rather inappropriate and it left me feeling somewhat awkward. It implied a certain judgment and betrayed my Trinidadian mindset. I certainly had not expected to find a manager performing menial duties.

In Trinidad, the word "manager" conjured up images of a well-dressed man usually in a suit. A gold chain pocket watch dangling from the vest would complete the visual. Further, a manager would not deign to be discovered doing the work of a "common" labourer. He rarely left his air-conditioned office that boasted all manner of impressive and sometimes ostentatious, human comforts.

These "managerial" expectations would hold true especially at a fine establishment such as the Nor-Shor. As such, I was caught off guard completely upon finding the manager not only working in the pool, but working half-naked in the pool. Canada was quickly shattering many of my preconceived perceptions.

Perhaps made somewhat impatient by my bumbling initial remarks, Mr. Zale hurriedly asked, "What do you want?"

"A job."

"What can you do?"

"I can do many things. I can help clean your pool."

"Can you swim?"

Then he dove to the bottom of the pool once more as I reflected on his question, *Can you swim?* As he surfaced, I received his full attention when I announced quite confidently, "Like a fish, that's what I did in Trinidad all the time, go swimming."

"So you are from Trinidad?"

He seemed interested. My hopes were raised.

"Yes, my name is Frank Maraj."

"Well, Mr. Frank Maraj, I don't have any openings right now. Sorry, I wish I did."

"Thanks anyway, Mr. Zale," I intoned, my hope vanishing.

I guessed this man to be around fifty years old. His strong frame was fit and added an element of youth to his appearance. A massive blanket of thick hair crowned his head. But, that was not what commanded my attention. The fact that his piercing gaze seemed to be able to assess and define someone with the merest of glances, intrigued me. I started to leave. An indefinable urge turned me around. An uncharacteristic boldness seized my speech and I found myself asking, "Mr. Zale, how do you take your coffee?"

"Black, but..."

"Would you join me in the coffee shop? I would love to treat you to a cup of coffee."

"Thank you, but..."

"I know you are busy. I bet you don't know anything about Trinidad? Just a few minutes?"

"Sure!"

"Then, I'll meet you in the coffee shop."

I found a quiet spot in the back of the coffee shop near a window. A waitress came and took my order—two coffees—but poured just one cup for now. I then settled down to enjoy my coffee, but not before adding three sugars and two creams to it. The window opened up my mind to the world, and, while awaiting Mr. Zale, I allowed myself the luxury of another childhood reverie—my first swimming experience.

This memory was triggered by Mr. Zale's question, *Can you swim.*

I was but a child when I approached my brother Clive and asked, "Clive, teach me to swim. I want to learn. Please, Clivey."

"Not yet", he responded, "someday."

"But, I'm ready Clivey."

"No, you not."

For so long it seemed, my heart had been filled with sadness and longing as I watched my older brother, Clive teach all the neighbourhood boys how to swim. Later on, he would invite his special little entourage of swimmers to go swimming with him at Vanlow. (Vanlow was the nickname that had been given to that popular area of the river. Boys who just wanted to "hang out" and have fun frequented that popular spot.)

Unbeknownst to Clive, I would often follow him and watch him from a distance. I was always so in awe of my big brother; I couldn't get enough of him. He was a magnate—always surrounded by friends.

There was one thing that I did not understand however. I never understood why, whenever Clive and his entourage made an appearance at the river, everyone else who was there before them, left and moved to a new location. I never knew what hidden power the group possessed that allowed them singular access to this prized piece of real estate. (Why Clive in particular seemed to be granted such entitlement remains a mystery.)

The Vanlow area itself was a section of the river that was blocked off by the authorities in order to secure ample water for the irrigation of the surrounding sugar cane fields. This particular section of the river was on higher ground. Towards the middle of the river, a dam was constructed with steel gates to contain the water until such a time as it was needed. When the dam was opened, the collected water would stream downward onto a concrete floor that had a steep slope. The resulting cascade of water fell about ten feet, creating a magnificent waterfall. This provided the perfect location for adventure- seeking young boys. It was a rare occasion indeed that would render this location quiet. This spot could be counted on for inducing a reckless return to our primal roots. Yelling and excitement prevailed as the dominant mood as each boy took his turn at diving from the concrete ledge far above the swirling waters below.

My brother had taught many boys to swim; he employed a simple (and some might now argue, crude) method. Because inflated rubber tubes were always easily available, Clive employed them in his regimen. First, Clive lined up the several young enthusiasts; each was given an inflated tube. As each one in turn came to the edge of the bank, Clive first threw the tube into the water ensuring that it would land near the waterfall. Then he picked up the would-be-swimmer and tossed him into the water. Invariably, the boy would land a short distance from the tube; this required him to move his arms and legs in order to reclaim the tube. In actual fact, the boys were learning to swim and they were not even aware of it. Each one willingly "swam" to the other side of the pool where the water was shallow then breathlessly climbed out of the water and back up to the ledge, most eager to resume the "game".

Clive had taught Boysie how to swim. Why could he not now teach me? (I have to now wonder, was this jealously or just good old fashioned sibling rivalry at play here?) Nevertheless, I persisted far past the point of annoyance until Clivey finally agreed.

"So you want to swim, do you, Frankie?"

"Yes, I do."

"Then come here."

"But, I don't have a tube."

"You don't need one."

Suddenly his large hands grabbed me by my tiny waist. He swung my body back and forth making me exceedingly dizzy. Then he launched me like a missile head first into the waters below. I sank very close to the bottom of the pool near the waterfall. After what seemed like an eternity, I surfaced and immediately began looking for the customary tube. I don't know how I remained afloat; I felt desperate. I looked back up at Clivey and implored him with my eyes.

"Frankie, swim!"

That's all I heard before once again I was submerged by the waters. Upon surfacing, I panicked and began thrashing frantically about with my hands and legs. Before I knew it, I had reached the other side of the pool—safe.

I glanced up to the bank where Clive stood, smiling.

"Please, Clive… again."

Again and again he accommodated me, and I loved every minute of it for I was swimming.

What a thrill!

Then Mr. Zale's voice brought a halt to my musings.

"Sorry Frank, I was delayed."

After he sat, I motioned to the waitress to bring us coffee. Mr. Zale added neither sugar nor cream but stirred his coffee all the same. We exchanged notes about our backgrounds; I spoke about Trinidad glowingly and he spoke of Italy with melancholy. I was left with the distinct impression that he had wished to return to Italy permanently, but could no longer do so. Thus, when he asked me about my future plans, I assured him that I was here to further my education and that I had every intention of returning to Trinidad to live. Mr. Zale seemed so pleased by my assurances. He made me feel proud of my decision.

Our conversation came to a delightful conclusion and Mr. Zale motioned to the waitress to bring the bill. She simply stated, "It is already paid." He looked at me curiously and placed a tip on the table. Again the waitress advised, "That too is taken care of."

He looked sideways at me and left the tip anyway. As he left, he thanked me, "Frank, thank you for the coffee. So sorry I could not help you." In his words I detected a note of concern. I truly believed that he wanted to help me.

The entire bill (including the tip) was about $1.00. This was the equivalent of four bus rides. While I did not regret my action; I did wish that I had a job.

I soon finished my coffee and was about to leave the restaurant when the now familiar voice belonging to Mr. Zale hailed me, "Wait up, Frank."

I turned back; Mr. Zale hastened to meet me.

"Frank, this weekend we have an entertainer, Tommy Commons, visiting our bar. I expect we will have a crowd. Can you be an usher or something like that? I could use you to seat people."

"Absolutely."

"You might need to dress up a little… a jacket might do and dark pants."

"No problem."

"Then let me show you around."

As he led me from one area to the next, he introduced me to the rest of the staff. His introductions made me feel welcome.

My job as usher at the Nor-Shor was expected to last two days: Friday and Saturday. My one dollar investment proved to pay a rich dividend.

****

Antics at the Bar…

Now that I was living in downtown Port Arthur, I could have walked the few miles from there to the Nor-Shor; and, I might have had it not been for the simple fact that this was my first day on the job and I wanted to not only look refreshed but actually be refreshed to begin this new venture. I chose to take the bus.

Just before six I entered the bar. Mr. Zale was right there to greet me. He seemed pleased with my choice of attire: black dress pants, black shirt, and green jacket. I had passed my first test.

Inside the bar preparations were still being made for the evening show. Since there was as yet no indication that people were to *wait* to be seated, a few patrons had already taken up residence inside the bar. One single gentleman occupied a table for four; while another couple had seated themselves at a table designed for six. While placing a "Please wait to be seated" sign up, the bartender motioned for me to take my place at the entrance. A flood of people all seemed to arrive at once. While excited to be there to see the show, the customers were patiently gracious in awaiting their turn to be seated. It soon became evident that I could not merely seat people in the order in which they came if I were to fulfill management's expectations that every available seat be filled. People did not come in neat groups of four, six or eight. They came singly and as couples and in groups of three. Sometimes two single men arrived together and occasionally two single women arrived together. Successfully blending the demands of management with the expectations of the patrons demanded more than the simple escorting of people to awaiting seats as they walked in the door; it demanded some skillful maneuvering around that age-old adage of first come, first served.

Not wishing to offend anyone who may have been first in line by not seating them first, I adopted the policy of announcing that a table for four or a table for six was available for the next seating. This allowed the patrons themselves to form their own groups of four or six; this made my job considerably easier.

The night was filled with activity and I did my best to accommodate as many as possible. My efforts did not go unappreciated or unrewarded. Not only was I handsomely tipped by the patrons who were happy to be accommodated, but I was similarly compensated by the waiters who appreciated my efforts at taking drink orders and cleaning off tables. At no time did I ever handle the money; that end of the transaction was the exclusive domain of the waiters. *I* gladly served; *they* dutifully collected. Thus passed my first Friday night at the Nor-Shor; with his music blasting in the background, a beloved Canadian icon thrilled his increasingly appreciative audience.

Saturday night might have been a carbon copy of Friday night except for two things: first, Saturday night was a slightly busier night; and second, the curious incident which occurred around eleven o'clock that made the night stand out.

The incident involved a very disgruntled and somewhat inebriated customer. The man had just returned to the Nor-Shor and was complaining boisterously, accusing one of the waiters of having stolen his wallet. When he had left the establishment previously, he had not noticed that his wallet was missing. He didn't discover this until he was attempting to pay the taxi driver. Following this discovery, he ordered the taxi's immediate return to the Nor-Shor. Once there, he undertook to yell at everyone creating quite a scene. His voice was so intrusive and his tone so abusive that the band could no longer play. Wisely they opted to take a short break while Mr. Zale tried to resolve the matter.

Mr. Zale called the police; the taxi driver clamoured for his fare; the general anxiety grew. A sense of unease threatened to claim what was left of the night.

As we awaited the arrival of the police I took a good look at the complainant. I remembered him and I remembered where he sat. He was the man who sat alone at a table for two. He was the man who resisted having another person be seated at his table. His objections were large and discourteous revealing that he had absolutely no regard for the other patrons in the bar. Even then it was becoming apparent that he had had too much to drink.

I made my way over to the table where he had sat. I checked out the floor: nothing. A table for four was just behind his table. Thankfully, everyone was still enjoying the night out and was oblivious to the present circumstance.

Someone from that table, mistaking me for a waiter asked, "Waiter, can you get us a round, please?" And handing me a twenty dollar bill, continued, "There, that should take care of it."

In an effort to have him not pay me, but rather his own waiter, the $20.00 bill somehow fell to the floor. As I bent down to pick it up I noticed a dark shadow the size of a wallet under their table. While retrieving the twenty dollar bill, I was able to verify that it was indeed a wallet and then discreetly recover it.

Immediately I sought out the somewhat flustered Mr. Zale who was trying his best to appease the disgruntled customer and explain the situation to the police. As I handed him the wallet and a brief explanation of where I found it, Mr. Zale became noticeably relieved. He regained his composure almost immediately and graciously attempted to accommodate the distressed patron by offering to pay for his taxi fare.

The police were satisfied with this successful resolution and assisted the man to his taxi. Tommy Common and the band came back from their break and everything returned to normal.

The evening ended on a happy note. The event was a huge success.

When the crowd dispersed at the end of the night our final cleanup began. I was busy wiping down tables when Mr. Zale approached, "Frank, thanks." Then he handed me an envelope.

"Say, how you getting home?"

"The late bus, I hope."

"Just a minute…"

He left to talk to one of the waiters. When he returned he advised, "Frank, you have a ride."

"Thank you, Mr. Zale."

"You're welcome."

"Can you come see me on Monday, about five o'clock?"

"Yes, of course, Mr. Zale."

"Take care."

Soon I was in a car, envelope in hand, headed home. Alone in my room, I opened the envelope. It contained enough money to pay for a month's rent and then some... all in one weekend... only in Canada.

35

The Sunday Family

Monday's meeting proved somewhat fruitful. Mr. Zale, while he could not offer me full-time employment, tried to help me by offering me occasional shifts in the dining room. Janet, the dining room supervisor, made it possible for me to work on Sundays when they offered their special lunch buffet where I was able to witness first-hand the extravagant and always sumptuous offerings. The buffet seemed to be a family favourite. (My personal favourite at these Sunday buffets was the shrimp in garlic tomato sauce.)

The preparation of the cocktail drinks that accompanied the buffet fell in my domain. Once I came to understand how things worked I developed a way to generate a little camaraderie and good will among the staff. Knowing how many of the servers liked to taste a little of the special cocktail drinks, and they knowing how much I appreciated a little access to a prawn or two, we developed a mutually beneficial system: a symbiotic relationship of sorts. I made it a point of mixing the drinks in such a way that a little would always be left over in the tumblers. Whenever it was convenient to do so, one of the servers would enter the bar area, bend down as if to be piling up dirty dishes, and then help herself to the little taste remaining in the tumbler. The one precaution I took was to ensure that no one server partook too frequently on any given day. In return the servers would "misplace" a large prawn or two somewhere in my vicinity. We took pains to be reasonable in these dealings with one another and no one suffered. Our customers were equally well cared for and received our utmost generous and affable attention. Everyone was happy—including Mr. Zale.

Then one Sunday an older man came to the entrance of the restaurant and just stood there—alone and uncertain. He seemed to be about fifty; his suit had seen better days, and his thick glasses covered the greater part of his face. There was something about his shy and somewhat reluctant demeanor that struck a chord in me. Approaching him I asked, "How may I help?"

"Could I see the menu?" he asked hesitantly.

"Of course you may," I returned, handing him a menu.

As he perused the menu he started to speak, "It's my wife's birthday today. We don't usually go out but today is very special. I'm not sure that this is the place for us. We have five children…maybe we should…"

I hastened to put him at ease, "No. You stay. Bring your family. I will find a table for seven; everything will be just fine. You'll see."

After hearing my words he was still unsure. He turned around as if to leave. I quickly scanned the tables to see if the huge round table at the side of the restaurant was vacant. It was. It would be perfect for his family. I managed to have him follow me into the restaurant to check out the table for himself. He agreed; it was perfect and somewhat private. Just what a large family needed.

When he left and returned with his family, I was most impressed. His wife's shyness rivaled that of his own. The children, while not shy, were perfectly mannered. The older of the two boys pulled the chair out for his mother whilst the younger brother assisted the three girls. When I noticed that the youngest girl could barely see over the top of the table, I offered her a booster seat. Following that, I brought menus to the parents and explained the prices of the buffet. Allowing a few minutes for deliberation, I went to the back to get a pitcher of water for the table.

Then Janet approached, "Nicely done Frank; they seem relieved. You are doing well."

"Thanks, Janet."

When I returned to the family a couple of minutes later, they had not quite decided.

One of the children had become particularly enamored with what appeared to be a child's cocktail. These drinks were more than twice the price of a regular pop and I could sense that the father, who really wanted his children to have a wonderful dining experience, had to forego that particular indulgence for the sake of his pocketbook. I understood his dilemma immediately and knew instinctively how I could help. I suggested to the father, "Order two adult buffets, and three children's. Then simply order five pop. It will all work out."

"But we have five children."

"Yes, but the two youngest would hardly eat anything. I will bring you seven plates. Please allow me to help you."

"Okay, and thank you."

As they approached the buffet table, their eyes grew wide in amazement at not only the amount of food available but also the great variety. The dessert table proved to command the greatest interest with its assortment of cakes, puddings, cookies and the promise of ice cream with sprinkles. It would tease even the most hesitant palate.

When they returned to the table to enjoy their meals, I was standing nearby ready to deliver five very special glasses of pop: each one decorated with a tiny umbrella at the top and a little red cherry which settled to the bottom of the glass. Their eyes sparkled and popped with delight.

I took a step back to watch this family enjoying one another's company; the parents were attentive, affectionate and firm. The five children were amazingly well behaved and if anyone needed correction, no one heard for they required only the softest of voices in order to turn a questionable practice around. They claimed my respect.

When they finished with their final desserts, the gentleman asked for the bill; I presented it to him and his face took on a quizzical expression, "Excuse me, Sir," he asked. "Are you sure about the amount?"

"Did I make a mistake? Is it too much?"

"No! Quite the contrary. It is so…"

"Reasonable?"

"More than reasonable!"

"Then we are happy."

He paid the bill and offered me a handsome tip. I looked at the tip; then I looked at the family.

"Thank you for the tip. It is most generous and I appreciate it so very much. Would you mind if I asked you to keep this and buy some treats for the children at another time? It is indeed a rare occasion when such a beautiful family steps out together such as you have done today. Please, I would like you to take this money and use it for the children…"

The mother then intervened, "Young man, you deserve this gratuity. And today we would be happy if you keep it." With that she reached out and shook my hand. Then each child in turn shook my hand.

Quietly I retreated to the bar area. For a moment I was transfixed; feelings stirred within me that I could not understand. Then the fog of the present gave way to the clarity of the past. Watching the family sitting around that table returned me to a time long past where another family sat around another table.

The first table that I remember us having in Trinidad was small but initially it accommodated all our needs. But, however, as time passed and our family increased in number, we had increasing difficulty sitting down together as a family. For my mother, being together around the table was very important for as far back as I can remember.

Since I seemed to be the one around the house who was interested in building and fixing things, the task fell to me to somehow fashion a larger table. I had but a single hammer and saw. I never even heard of a square or a level. I just purchased planks of wood from a nearby sawmill and set about the task. The finished picnic-like table measured about six feet by three feet. Following that construction, I managed to build a bench for the table.

The finished product, far from professional, was extremely functional and made mealtimes more comfortable. Ma found a piece of plastic tablecloth large enough to cover the rough wood and put a vase of flowers at the centre completely transforming its awkward angles.

That table became a focal point in our home. Our lives were re-engaged at that table and the sight of Ma and all her children sitting around the table is forever imprinted in my mind. (In later years in my own home with my own family and friends, I too grew to love the idea of having all the family comfortably housed around a central table sharing stories and ideas. This was one of Ma's many unconscious legacies to her children.)

I even remember my father sitting at that table too! How happy he was sitting around that table with all his girls. Having six girl children meant that at times there would be even more than six girls in the house sitting around that table. Pa was especially happy visiting with his daughters and their girlfriends. He always found a way to entertain them. (This scenario never seemed to hold true for Boysie or for me.) But of those girls…Pa, was most protective.

I remember one particular occasion when a girlfriend of one of my sisters visited. The girls were sitting around the table talking and doing girl stuff. As I came near to the table, the friend said something. I did not know that she was speaking to me for I was headed out to the back yard to sit under the banana tree and read a book. Before I had become barely settled under that tree, Pa suddenly appeared. He was most upset.

"So, Frankie, you mannish (rude). You have no manners."

"Pa?"

"You make Indra cry. She say she said hello and you ignore her."
"Pa?"
"And you always insult her. She try to say hello and you act stuck up."

Pa was standing very near to a plum tree. From any branch on that tree, Pa could fashion a good sized whip. He did just that and before I could protest, he landed me a blow to my shoulder. Pa was strong and the whip was sturdy.

"Now, Frankie, you apologize to Indra. You say you sorry."
"But, Pa, I did not mean…"

Another volley of blows followed .

Reeling backwards from the force of the blows, I fell. Pa and the whip followed me to where I lay on the ground. As he raised the whip and prepared to strike me again, I yelled, "Stop!"

I guess my loud outburst caught Pa off guard for he did indeed stop and I was able to continue my thought. "Give me a minute; I will be right back."

I went inside and asked Indra to come with me to the back. As she followed me she noticed that my shoulders were beginning to swell and that I seemed to be in some discomfort.

"Frankie, stop. What happened? Why your pa beat you so? Because of me? Because of what I told him?"

"Pa says I insult you, and I am rude. He says I have to apologize. Indra, I don't know what I did. Tell me what I did wrong."

"Frankie, you didn't do anything wrong. I was trying to get your attention. I never thought your pa would beat you like that. I thought he would talk to you, that's all. I so sorry, Frankie." Her voice was so sincere and then she started to cry.

"You want me to get another beating?" I asked her.
"No!"
"Then you have to stop crying. *If Pa sees one teardrop, I am a dead man*."

When she stopped crying I noticed her curly hair and said, "Indra, your hair is nice."

"Really, Frank?" she smiled and then ran outside ahead of me, yelling excitedly, "Frankie likes my hair. I so happy."

Then she was gone. Pa, meanwhile, was still standing there holding the whip in his hand. I went up to him and reached out for the whip and said, "You don't need this anymore, Pa. Indra and I are better now."

Pa allowed the whip to be removed from his hand. Once out of his sight, I quickly discarded it.

Alone, I had time to reflect on Indra's words. She had said, *I was trying to get your attention.* While that phrase puzzled me, it stayed locked in my memory. It was only years later that I understood what it really meant. But, at the time, I wondered why she wanted my attention.

Her words, along with the words of another neighbour had my mind in a bit of a whirl. I had expressed some disgust to my neighbour upon seeing the cover of a romance comic. The front cover showed a picture of a young couple kissing. I remember asserting that I would never do anything like that. My neighbour, upon hearing my comment, smiled and calmly whispered, "Frankie I will live to see you take back those words. I will. And that day is not too far off."

Both Indra and my neighbour referenced a world that I could not even imagine at the time.

I would remember both these incidents in another time in my life when the first stirring of another type of consciousness was born. For now I was simply content.

36

The Couple

They walked into the restaurant and stood at the entrance—waiting. They were a rather attractive couple: he in his conventional suit and tie, and she in a modest dress. Although I was going to be occupied with other concerns for a few minutes, I hastened to advise them, "I'll just be a few moments, so sorry."

His terse comment, "Well, hurry up, buddy!" was not consistent with his attire. Both his tone and demeanor belied his conservative appearance. This impression received further reinforcement when next he spoke. As I returned to attend to their needs, he spouted, "Hey, buddy, get us a table; we don't have all day."

I spun around on my heels, primed with a retort, and then I remembered where I was and who I was. I was at the Nor-Shor and I was the server. "Right away, Sir," I responded with all the civility and politeness that I could muster under the circumstances.

As I showed them to their table I pulled out the chair to allow the young lady to sit. This courtesy used to be a simple matter of course, naturally extended at fine dining establishments. The young man's next comments revealed how little he understood. "Buddy, does she look like she's helpless? Save that for your mother. Now where is your menu?" Apparently, chivalry was a foreign concept.

Thus far the young lady had not uttered a single word. The thought flashed across my mind that perhaps she was not *allowed* to say anything. I had to watch myself. I had to take particular care not to appear to be challenging or offensive.

I brought the menus and handed one to each of them. I waited while he perused the wine menu. Soon, again he spoke, "Hey, buddy, are you familiar with this wine list?" Without waiting for a response from me, he answered his own question, "I suppose not," and added, "Well, let's see this wine. Bring it, then we will order."

The young lady looked up at me and uttered a simple, "Thank you so much."

The young man seemed to have a problem with extending even that little courtesy for he wasted no time in telling her, *"You don't have to thank him. He's only a waiter."*

I almost felt sorry for this young man. It was so obvious that he possessed not one modicum of the social graces that the wearing of a suit implied. How little he thought of those who served; how highly he thought of himself. He was the epitome of self-aggrandizement. *Careful, Frank*, I urged. *You need this job.*

I returned with the requested bottle of wine. I assumed the posture of a *maître d* as I poured a little of the selected wine into his glass for him to approve before I offered any to the young lady. I awaited his signal. His response was both surprising and telling.

"Hey, buddy," he complained, "what country do you come from? Don't you know that in Canada we always serve the lady first? Got it? You really should not be working at this job."

Since it was not my place to argue with the customer, (nor was it my inclination to educate him) I simply responded, "So sorry, Sir."

"You got that right."

I filled her glass with wine. Her eyes seemed to be pleading with me then her napkin *fell* to the floor. As I picked it up to return to her I noticed the word "sorry" written in lipstick on the napkin. Her gesture quelled some of the dissatisfaction and resentment brewing inside of me and I smiled. Glad was I that I had not returned his lack of civility measure for measure with a provocative remark of my own. I did however manage one act of quiet rebellion by filling his wine glass to the very top. He did not even notice; he was so intent on asking me questions perhaps hoping to catch me in "error". His tone was both haughty and condescending as he asked, "And what do you recommend for lunch? Are you at all familiar with the dishes?"

I decided that I did not want to be responsible for choosing his meal; it would make me far too vulnerable to further attacks. Sensing an ally in her, I looked to his companion for assistance, "Perhaps *you* might care to choose?"

"What do you recommend?"

"The buffet, Miss. It is enjoyable."

"Then we shall have the buffet."

The buffet was the perfect choice for it left me a little bit at liberty. I thought that it would relieve me of the exceedingly onerous task of attending to his every whim. To be sure, I dutifully attended to his requests for more water, more napkins and fresh silverware. You can be assured that there was no shortage of demands. He really seemed to be trying to make a point. Finally the meal was finished and the last thing he requested was the bill. After perusing it for a moment, he reached into his billfold. Then he fished around in his pocket for some loose change… just enough to pay the bill: not one penny more. He handed me both the bill and the money and proceeded to address me, *"Waiter, I will not complain about your lack of skills. Consider that I have just done you a favour and be thankful. And buddy you better learn to be a proper waiter before I come back here again."*

He then looked at his companion and ordered, "Let's go."

"I'll be just a moment," and she motioned toward the restroom.

As he headed to the door, I rushed ahead to hold it open for him. He thought that I was doing him a service. I knew that my action was self-serving; now I had him alone—all to myself.

"Well young man, you at least did something right. You know that you have a lot to learn. In this country there are certain things you should know…"

I could not let him finish; I could not stomach any more of his pompous drivel. "I beg your pardon, Sir; I believe that *you* are in error. What pains you take to dress your body with the clothes of civility. It is time you took the same care with your mind. I am sorry that you found me disappointing as a waiter; but, I am even more deeply saddened by your total lack of courtesy."

I felt no joy, no relief, in this exchange. I took no pleasure in those words. But, I felt compelled to address the situation. I could not live with the knowledge that I had allowed someone to devalue me in public and not do anything in my own defence.

As I returned to my station, the young lady passed by. She handed me a folded sheet of paper and then she quickly disappeared.

I opened the paper and read:

Mr. Waiter, Sir,

I apologize.

I am so embarrassed.

You were more than gracious.

Thank you for being the gentleman in all of this.

I am truly sorry.

Inside the fold of the paper was a sum of money that far exceeded my hourly wage.

I was stunned. Moments ago I was seeking redress for the injury that I had suffered; now I was humbled.

I will remember today, for today I met a young couple.

He lacked the spark of civility; she was its brightest gem.

37

A Good Intention

The prospect of obtaining fulltime employment at the Nor Shor did not look promising. If anything, it was likely that my hours would be significantly reduced since business tended to be slower in the summer.

A former neighbour from the Current River area told me about a possible opening for a well-paying job at the mill where he worked. After church one Sunday he met with me and we chatted about my situation. He told me that I might have a good chance at getting the job as he would be sure to put in a good word for me. As he phrased it, "My boss will consider my opinion." With much gratitude, I agreed to let him set up an appointment for two o'clock on Friday with the manager, Mr. Mc Clary.

So eager was I to have this opportunity, I arrived a half hour early for the appointment. I checked in with the receptionist but she had no record of any appointment for me. Before I could get too worried, she quickly explained that it was entirely in keeping with Mr. Mc Clary's character to forget to jot down the appointment in her book. She further explained that Mr. Mc Clary would be free from his meeting in about a half an hour. I felt optimistic.

An hour elapsed and during that time Judy and I became polite friends. She even thought to offer me a cup of coffee while I continued my vigil outside the office. By the time her day ended at four o'clock, she felt comfortable allowing me to stay and wait for Mr. Mc Clary. She reasoned that since I was expected, it would be alright. As she left she said, "It's been a pleasure to meet you. I am sure we will see more of you. Perhaps we'll meet again on Monday. Good luck."

Within ten minutes of her departure, Mr. Mc Clary appeared. He seemed startled by my presence. His words confirmed my impression. "Who are you? What are you doing here? Who let you in?"

I answered all his questions but his attitude still remained hostile verging on the belligerent. "Are you drunk? Out! Out with the likes of you!"

These final words caught me totally off guard. I was unaccustomed to hearing a Canadian, especially a Canadian in a position of authority, using such a tone. His words wounded me deeply. The words *drunk* and *likes of you* revealed a heart filled with utter disdain. His remarks were not merely sarcastic, they were meant to be hurtful. *Why? Why would he want to hurt me? He didn't even know me.* I headed toward the door intending to make a quick exit but stopped midway. I returned to his desk my heart pounding in my chest.

"Mr. Mc Clary, have you ever met a baboon or gorilla?"

He stared at me blankly.

I continued, "Neither have I... until now. Your plaid shirt makes you look *almost* human. Good day."

My legs were like rubber but I made it to the door and once outside I steadied myself against the wall. *What have I done?*

The only good that came from this incident was to point me firmly in the direction of New York.

38

Pigeon River Border Crossing

It was a lazy day in late June that I boarded the bus to begin my trek to New York. I carried but one modest suitcase. The bus was on time and soon the city was only a tiny spec on the horizon. The bus grunted in seeming protest as it made its way through the winding country road. Within an hour we arrived at the Pigeon River border crossing. The bus was ushered to an area to await inspection by an American officer. Similarly, an American bus carrying passengers destined for Canada was waiting for clearance by Canadian customs and immigration on the American side. Once both buses and their passengers pass inspection, the passengers continuing on to the U.S. would then board the U.S. bus while those on the American bus headed for Canada would move onto the Canadian bus. No one was authorized to move until clearance was achieved.

The U.S. inspector on my bus quickly moved through the passengers. He hesitated slightly after examining my passport; leaving me, he completed his check on the rest of the passengers. They posed no problem. He returned to me and briefly ordered, "Follow me, please."

Before exiting the bus he whispered something to the bus driver. I was unable to hear what was said. The officer then led me to a small windowless office where two other officers began to throw questions at me.

"Mr. Maraj, where are you headed?"
"To New York."
"Where in New York?"
"Brooklyn."
The officers looked at each other.
"Why?"
"To see my family."
"Who is your family?"
"My sister and brother-in-law."

Even though I was confused by the intensity of their manner, I answered every one of their questions with politeness and courtesy.

Finally one of the officers announced, "Mr. Maraj, you are attempting to enter the United States illegally."

I was astounded by the assertion. "What!"

"You do not have a visa."

"A visa? I need a visa? But I have a passport."

"Furthermore, you can be charged for trying to enter the U.S. illegally."

It was not only the words of the officers but also their intensely serious tone that suggested that I was in deep trouble. But, for the life of me, I had no idea why. I had not knowingly done anything of a wrong or illegal nature. I decided that I needed to do some kind of self-advocacy so I spoke. "Officers, I am sorry for this mix-up. I didn't know that I was doing anything wrong. When I went to buy my ticket from the travel agent he asked only if I possessed a valid passport, which of course I do. I do not understand why I was not advised that I would also need a visa to enter the U.S. I'm sure that the agent would not knowingly mislead me, would he?"

They conferred briefly then one officer left. Within minutes he returned with another, more senior officer. One officer began questioning me about my family in New York and about each of their occupations. His questions were pointed and direct. For some of his questions I had no actual answers. I did not know the exact nature of their jobs but I did have the names of each family member, all the addresses, and every telephone number; these I surrendered voluntarily.

Still not satisfied with my responses, all three began firing questions at me. I felt as if I was under siege; in some weak attempt at self-preservation I blurted out, "Please stop. Tell me what wrong I have committed. I am feeling as though I am some kind of criminal, and I don't know why."

My outburst seemed to give them a moment's pause. One of the younger officers pointed out, "At this point it would appear you did not mean to enter the U.S. illegally. Since you do not possess a visa, you will have to return to Canada. So follow me."

He then led me to the exit where I noticed that both buses were still waiting. That was strange; I thought that they had long since left.

The more senior officer came quickly to my aid and asked me to return with him to his office. He explained that he was trying to secure me clearance by phoning the authorities in Winnipeg and getting "confirmation." When this proved unsuccessful he seemed genuinely disappointed. I no longer felt as if I were under attack.

"Sorry Frank, I tried. I am afraid…"

Before he could finish his statement, the younger officer interrupted with yet another idea. "Listen, then maybe we could do something else." He scurried off to another office returning moments later with two thick immigration manuals. Each officer grabbed a manual and flipped quickly through the pages rapidly exchanging ideas. I could barely keep up with their dialogue. They were quoting numbers and subsections back and forth. Then as if by divine intervention one of them excitedly announced, "Yes, this will do. I am sure of it. Here, enter this code. This should do it." The code was dutifully entered into my Trinidadian passport. In essence this code gave my passport the legitimacy of a visa and I was rightfully accorded entry into the United States in June, 1969.

A strange destiny delivered me into the hands of these two accommodating American officers. Anyone else might have simply turned me back. I would not soon forget their efforts on my behalf. Nor could I forget my reception as I boarded the U.S. bus. But for me, everyone would have been long on their journey. Both buses had been detained for the outcome of my dilemma had remained uncertain for a good hour. I felt bad for keeping everyone back.

I entered the bus sheepishly, fully prepared to be greeted by angry stares and irritable voices. To my astonishment, everyone began clapping; the passengers were as happy as I was that I was allowed to continue with the journey. That recollection of those U.S. customs officers advocating for me on that hot day in June still stands out in my memory.

39

The Two Faces of Gratitude

When the clapping subsided, I took my seat on the bus. Immediately the differences between the American and the Canadian buses became apparent; the American version was much more comfortable. The seats were softer and somewhat roomier.

Relieved at having survived the ordeal at the border, I should have been free to enjoy that small victory. The turmoil in my mind was replaced with one of a more physical variety—the turmoil of the stomach. I believed that I was going through motion sickness. I became violently ill repeatedly. Fortunately for me, the restroom was located not too far from where I sat. After making three or more trips to the bathroom, some of the passengers at the rear of the bus offered up their seats to me so that I might lie down. That location also proved to allow for a more convenient access to the restroom. Other passengers were also sympathetic to my plight and offered me aspirins. I was too sick to show the true measure of my appreciation. I became worse, not better and desperately wanted off the bus; at that moment, I believe that I would have been happy just to lie somewhere on the shoulder of the highway.

Midway to Minneapolis the bus stopped so that the passengers could get off and stretch and enjoy a brief coffee break. When I got off the bus I dragged myself to the coffee shop and immediately became sick once again. I was so embarrassed. That time I never quite made it into the bathroom.

I began to wonder if something more than mere travel sickness was affecting me. Even the bus driver became concerned. He told me that once we reached Minneapolis there was a YMCA right on the route. He assured me that the cost was most reasonable and that I could stay if I needed to rest up a bit before continuing on my journey. Furthermore, if I needed medical attention, I could get it there. What he said made perfect sense and so I consented. Thus at Minneapolis the bus and I parted ways. In spite of all the goodwill that was afforded me on the trip, I am sure that everyone was relieved by my departure. At the YMCA I was able to purchase accommodations for ten dollars.

While it lacked the comfort and privacy of a bedroom, it did have an assortment of beds. I chose the one nearest the bathroom. The extreme violence which characterized my earlier outbursts seemed to have subsided somewhat and I attempted to claim some much needed rest. Sleep was completely out of the question and even the simple concept of rest proved elusive. I had to contend with not only the ruminations in my stomach but also with the cacophony of sounds emanating from the nasal choir occupying the beds next to me.

The next day I awoke—*unrested* and unwell. My insides bore a hollow ache, the reward of a long day devoted to vomiting. Afraid to have breakfast, yet needing to eat, I decided to go for a short walk. The briskness of the crisp morning air had a positive effect on my circumstances. Particularly refreshing was the sight of the few tall buildings that dotted the horizon. The streets were filled with people walking to or from work. Across the way, anchored by the bold letters announcing breakfast, was a nondescript café. The most notable thing about the café was the variety of clientele that patronized it. The café was filled with people from all walks of life and from all different races. The place was busy but I saw exactly where I wanted to sit. It was a spot just now vacated by a young couple. Even though the table had yet to be cleared, I headed straight for it as it claimed the perfect view of life in the city. And, I sorely missed the hustle of the city.

When the waitress came to clear the table, I ordered coffee and toast. Toast was all that I felt that I could comfortably handle. Returning with my coffee, she asked, "Where you from, man?"

"Trinidad."

"I am from Jamaica. Now let me give you some advice. You see this special – coffee, toast and scrambled eggs—same price as your toast and coffee. So you want the special?"

"Thank you."

Fearing that my coffee might initiate a revolt in my stomach, I merely sipped on it. Several minutes passed before I felt assured that the coffee would not make an unexpected reappearance. While awaiting the rest of my breakfast I entertained myself by looking out at the city. The city was vast and beautiful. I felt so at home just sitting there. True, the majority of the people was white, but, scattered amidst the whiteness was a hint of brown, and of black, and all the colours in between; I was looking at a tiny slice of Trinidad. Seeing this hint of colour everywhere in Minneapolis, made me realize how terribly and overwhelmingly white the Lakehead truly was; fewer than a dozen people like me made their home there.

My Jamaican waitress returned and set before me a platter of scrambled eggs, toast, and potatoes. Topping up my coffee she asked, "So where you coming from?"

"The Lakehead."

"Never heard of it."

"You heard of Duluth?"

"Oh, yes."

"It's about a four hour drive north of Duluth."

"Man you must live in the boonies."

We laughed. Then she asked, "Where you headed?"

"Brooklyn, New York."

"Brooklyn? All my family there. Man, take me with you."

"I wish I could. I don't know how I'm getting there."

"What you mean?"

"Well, I was on my way there by bus but when I became very ill I stopped off here to stay a night at the YMCA. How do I get to New York?"

"Don't take the bus. That's too long. Take a plane."

"But that must be so expensive."

"Not really. Not if you fly standby. And you in the right city for standby flights to New York."

She had to leave to attend to other customers.

I stared at the enormous platter of food and knew I would not be able to finish. It would be such a waste and an incredible shame to have such perfectly good food end up in the garbage. My Trinidadian roots protested against such an outcome; how many times had I heard the old adage, *waste not want not*. How many times had I recited those very words to my students! And here I was about to be tested on my own principles. Again the waitress came by.

"So, how you doing?"

"Very well. Great breakfast. Perfect Service. Any chance I could have the remainder of the platter to go?"

"Why, not a problem."

She took the platter. When she returned, she handed me a bag. "It was nice meeting you. And I sure wish I was going with you to Brooklyn. I have so much family there."

Then, with tears of nostalgia in her eyes, she added, "And if you see any of my family say hello. I miss them so much…"

She was so sad. And I felt her sadness. Had I been back in the Lakehead listening to her, I too might have been sad. But such was not the case. I was on my way to New York City, and a strong feeling of nostalgic longing, coupled with a strange excitement, stole over me. Now more than ever, I longed to be in New York with my family.

I picked up the bill. Across the front of the bill the waitress had written, "No charge. It's on me."

I wrote back, "Thank you. Here's a little something for a rainy day. P.S. I will be looking for your family. I will say hello."

What is it about traveling that engages me so? Every turn in the road is like turning a page in the novel of life. At each junction we can reflect on what we have thus far learned. Today, I was a passive observer and a receiver; my young waitress an active participant and a giver.

Life would soon afford me an opportunity to switch roles.

******

With my bagged breakfast in hand, I began walking the streets of Minneapolis. Impressed by the cleanliness of the city and the beauty of the scenery I walked on and on. Minneapolis truly was a beautiful American city. I loved it. Soon I noticed a change in the shops. They were smaller and more modest. It was there that I encountered a man who appeared as if by magic. He himself was far from magical. His clothes were worn and unkempt and his hair dull and lifeless.

"Spare a quarter. I have not eaten."

"Really?"

"Yes, I am hungry."

I offered him the bag.

I had no way of knowing the truth of his situation. Was he really hungry or was he merely trying to scam a quarter? Since I really didn't have any extra money to spare, I handed him the bag containing the rest of my breakfast. If he really was hungry, he would appreciate it. If he wanted money for something other than food, he would scorn it.

Without a word, I handed him the bag and walked away.

Curious, he opened the bag and examined the contents.

His next spoken words caused me to turn back and look.

"Sir, thank you! Thank you! This is some breakfast!" His waving arms, outstretched in praise and gratitude, touched a chord deep within.

In my pocket I had a quarter. I walked back to him, hand in pocket. As I put the quarter into his hand, I read the questioning look in his face. He did not need to say anything. I understood the look of gratitude.

40

Some Enchanted Evening?

I resumed my explorations and soon found myself in an area full of motels. The very first one stunned me with its ad announcing the price of a room. It advertised rooms were available for the low price of ten dollars. *That was exactly what I had paid at the Y.M.C.A!*

I had to check it out. I asked about the ten dollar room. I was surprised that it was still available. I took it: Room 10 upstairs. *I wondered why the room was so reasonable.*

I had no idea what awaited me.

****

My ten dollar room was quite the bargain; it came fully equipped with a full-size bed and colour television. I wondered briefly, *What was the catch?* The bed, however, beckoned and soon I was enveloped in its luxurious charm. The newness and largeness of the television set further enhanced the mood and I could not resist losing myself in its temptations. Soon I was settled in bed and willingly abandoned myself to the world of dreams. Just as I was about to drift into this other realm, the affectionate silence of my room was broken by a harsh banging and quickly I was summoned back to reality. Then the sound of voices joined the banging and the very floor of my room quivered in protest. *Where was that noise coming from?* I wondered. The banging pulsed throughout my room; the voices, while somewhat muted by the carpeted floor, could not conceal the extreme agony of the sound. I had to find the source; it seemed to be coming from the area directly below my room.

I dressed and started downstairs. I was barely halfway down the winding staircase when the puzzle was solved. The noise was coming from a band playing in the bar; my room was located directly above the stage. Then came the realization why my room was a mere ten dollars:

no one could get any sleep until the band stopped playing. I continued on down the steps and sat at the bar. The bartender asked, "What's your pleasure?"

My mind could not entertain his question. It craved sleep. I asked, "What time does the band stop playing?"

Sensing that I was not ready to order anything just yet, he attended to another customer and threw back the response, "Around two a.m."

Two! It was barely eleven! How was I to survive another three hours of such intense enthusiasm? I was in musical trouble. The night was just getting started. I sat there considering my options when an attractive young lady sat on the bar stool right next to me. She smiled and said hello as she sat down. I noticed immediately how gorgeous she was, and how stunningly she was dressed. It was with some reluctance that I rose to leave when she said, "Leaving?"

"Yes, I was about to."

"Won't you stay just a bit longer?" she prevailed upon me.

I have to admit that her voice was intoxicating and I was flattered by her attention.

"I see that you have not yet had a drink. May I join you for one? I would be ever so grateful."

Surprised by her forwardness and confused by her intent, nonetheless, I knew that I wanted to oblige her.

"Of course, I would love to buy you a drink."

The bartender was not oblivious to her presence and came immediately when she motioned to him. (Really, who could fail to notice her stunning beauty?) She stood up when he came by and I thought that I heard her whisper, "The usual."

Initially, this struck me as an odd thing to say, but when she again turned her attention toward me, the thought simply evaporated. "Where are you from?" she asked.

"The Lakehead."

"Where's that?"

"Port Arthur, Ontario."

"So you're from Canada. Are you just passing through?"

"Yes, I'm on my way to New York."

She repeated the words, *New York,* with such whimsy and delight that I immediately assumed that she had been there. Her next statement proved me correct. "I've been there on business trips; I love that city. But, now, tell me about yourself, Honey."

I was flattered that she would call me *honey* and sought to answer her question quickly, "I am a student and I'm traveling to New York to find a job. And you?"

"I am what you might call a *business* girl travelling from city to city."

"That seems very glamorous."

The bartender was taking an exceptionally long time to serve us. *What was he up to?* Having worked in a bar myself, I knew that it should not take so long to produce two simple drinks. When next I looked up, I was surprised to see him fashioning an attractive red cloth napkin around the neck of a champagne bottle. He then placed the bottle in a large container of ice. I looked around the room to see if I could discern who the celebratory company was who ordered such an expensive bottle. Having worked at the Nor Shor, I knew that such occasions were very rare and special ones indeed. No face however, seemed expectant; no one group stood out. Everything seemed extraordinarily ordinary.

That all changed the moment the bartender deposited the container in front of *me*. When he added two champagne glasses to the mix and announced, "That'll be twenty-five dollars, Sir," I was completely dumbfounded.

I looked up at him in disbelief. *Surely he was not speaking to me.* Clearly I had not ordered such extravagance. I had rented a ten dollar room; why would he think that I would order a twenty-five dollar bottle of champagne. Surely he was in error. I looked around behind me; there was no one there to lay claim to the bottle. Reluctantly I met his gaze. His eyes were stone. They pierced through me leaving me looking awkward and feeling intimidated. I appealed to the vision of radiance sitting beside me.

She seemed singularly unperturbed.

"Buddy, as I said, twenty-five dollars, and I don't have all day."

Never before had I faced a situation quite like this. Truly, I had no idea what to do or what to expect. My mind drifted immediately to a movie scenario. I had visions of men with specialized skills being summoned to grab me and search me, helping themselves to whatever cash or valuables on my person and then tossing me out into the street. Then they would follow me out into the street to kick and pummel my fragile remains and finally leave my lifeless body alone in the street. I wondered what I had done to initiate such a chain of events. I could not afford such an extravagance.

I turned back to the bartender. The reality of his six foot six, two hundred and fifty pound presence was ominous, to say the least. What easy prey my one hundred and forty pound body presented! Resistance would be futile if not suicidal. Such was my dilemma. I decided to use the only weapons I had: my calmest voice and a reasoned appeal to logic.

"Sir, excuse me. There must be a mistake; I did not order that bottle and the young lady did not order that bottle... Did you?" I asked pointedly as I turned to her. She merely stared blankly back at me.

"Surely this is just a simple misunderstanding." Again I asked, "Miss, did you order the bottle of champagne?"

Still no answer.

But, some of her radiance began to fade.

"Miss," I continued, "I honestly meant for us to have a drink together. I do not understand why the bartender saw fit to act in this manner and bring a bottle of champagne."

She looked at me earnestly, then asked, "Honey, do you not know what's happening? Do you not understand?"

"Understand? What is there to understand? I offered to buy you a simple drink. How could it turn into... *this*?"

When I stopped talking there was nothing but silence. A gradual dawning of awareness crept over me. It saddened me to acknowledge the reason for its existence.

"Miss, are you...?" The question remained unasked.

"Yes, I am; you did not know?"

"No."

"You did not even suspect?"

"No."

"My god, are you for real?"

Then, turning to the bartender, she signalled for him to remove the container.

He stared at me as he removed the bottle and grimaced, "You're some kind of lucky."

Her radiance, having been somewhat restored, I asked, "Would you have a drink? I would be so pleased."

"Honey, if only I had the time."

She started to leave then turned back, "You mean that you would actually have a drink with me knowing what you now know..."

"Miss, I know not your whole story. What I know is that I would love it if we could have a drink together—no more, no less. That would be my pleasure."

She came closer and gently whispered, "I don't know your name, and I don't I want to. What I want to remember is this. I have met someone who actually desired to have a drink with me... simply a drink. No strings."

"Yes."

"I wish my life were otherwise."

As she eased closer, she gently kissed me on the cheek and whispered, "Please, don't change."

Her words rooted me to my chair. Even after she left I found that I could not move... did not want to move. Even I did not understand my sentiments. Why was there such confusion in my spirit? I felt vulnerable yet oddly confident. For a moment I was allowed to feel somewhat appealing to a beautiful young woman. Yet, even after that illusion was shattered, and it was indeed shattered, some residual confidence remained.

I ordered a modest drink to avoid the awkwardness of my continued presence at the bar. As I sipped the drink I felt it soothe my wounded spirit. I had enjoyed her attention it was true, but to find out that everything was contrived was a bit of a shock. It left me feeling vulnerable and alone. Her final words however, seemed to return to me a measure of my dignity. Indeed, life was an unusual experiment, albeit full of confusion and contradiction.

41

Manhattan Memories

My bid to fly standby from Minneapolis to Kennedy Airport was surprisingly successful and inexpensive. Later that evening, I met with both Bob and Kay at the apartment in Brooklyn. The strong scent of stewed shrimp and curried lamb greeted my senses before I crossed the threshold. Once again my every culinary whim was gratified and I was so very happy.

We talked on into the night. I never wanted the evening to end. Kay put on some Trinidadian music while Bob poured the wine. Life was perfect. For a moment, that modest apartment became our castle. Then we had to settle down to reality. Bob took it upon himself to help secure a job for me. Kay handed me some pocket change with explicit orders to go to Manhattan and take in the sights. I was ordered to explore and enjoy New York City. I began my explorations the very next morning

I took the subway into Manhattan. My mind could barely process the sheer number of people that passed by me as I stood on one street corner. It was incomprehensible. I grew dizzy looking up at the tall buildings rivalling one another for a piece of the sun. The street vendors, pedalling their goods on small tables, claimed my attention and my admiration. It was unbelievable just how many products could be contained in one small space. Perhaps more than anything else, it was the prices that drew me to linger. Everything appeared so affordable: books, fruit, clothes, coffee, all these and more, begged me to part with my pocket change. The temptation to buy *something*, to buy *anything*, erupted at every corner. I walked on and on absorbing all the sights and smells. New York was just too huge to comprehend. I remember thinking that New York City was so big that it could easily accommodate several islands the size of Trinidad. My mind was simply amazed. The last place I visited before lunch was the Empire State Building. I had heard so much about it but I was not prepared to find it sandwiched between other buildings on the street. Its height is what made it stand out. At that time it was the tallest building in the city since the Twin Towers were still in their formative stages. I tried to look up at the very top of the building but somehow failed in my attempt. Looking up at its dizzying height made me somewhat disoriented.

I turned down a side street and was struck by an unusual sight. People were not bustling about. While there were still hundreds of people in the area, no one was moving. Curious to discern the cause, I slowly approached one of the storefronts. It was an electronics store and in the window was a huge television screen. The picture on the screen seemed to captivate every passer-by. Because that day was the anniversary of the death of Bobby Kennedy, the television stations were honouring his memory with a memorial documentary. The picture on the screen highlighted his casket; everything seemed to have been shot in slow motion, frame by frame. The people of New York were stilled by the haunting images from a year ago. Slowly and silently I continued to move along the street not wanting to disturb the reverence of the moment. This scene played itself out almost identically at every other electronics store for blocks around. I felt as though I were an intruder; I did not understand the full significance of the history between the American people and the Kennedy family. At one point, the television station replayed a portion of President John F. Kennedy's assassination. This, coupled with the footage from Bobby's assassination caused an audible gasp from the gathering community of onlookers. One woman's cries were heard above all others', "Bobbie, Bobbie, how do we go on; we've lost our Martin and John, and Bobby... how can we get to the mountain?"

The full significance of that lady's cry was lost to me. I did get the sense of some monumental grief and wished I had had a more complete understanding of her words, *"How can we now get to the mountain?"* A feeling that I can only describe as empathy seized my spirit; heaviness fell upon my soul.

Seeking a reprieve, I entered a nearby cafe and ordered a coffee. Sitting at a booth with a window to the street, I could still see the story unfold. Still moved by their collective grief I began to feel an odd sense of connection. I did not understand this connection; it really made no sense to me at all for I knew so little about the Kennedys or Martin Luther King. Back in my home in Trinidad, such news events had not claimed our attention the way it had in America. The main explanation for this was that our family did not have a TV at that time. Our radio picked up one station only, and, as I remember, it concentrated mostly on the local news. While we may have known of the deaths of these three important political figures, the fullness of the impact of their deaths on the spirit of the American people remained a mystery in my mind, a mystery that I never fully probed, until later years.

As I sat there drinking my coffee, my mind recalled the words a librarian had spoken to me when I was in the senior elementary class, "Frankie, you have been asking for special books, books that would interest you. Well I have found one."

She beamed as she handed me the book detailing the life of Abraham Lincoln. The front cover revealed a bearded man seated on an arm chair that seemed far too small to accommodate his lengthy frame.

"Miss, would I like this?"

"Frankie Boodram, you are going to love this book. I know it."

She smiled and I took the book. I read that book faithfully over the next several days; it told the story of the life and assassination of President Abraham Lincoln. Even after reading the book, I did not fully understand why he was assassinated. I reread the book, yet I still could not grasp the reasons why this saintly man was murdered. My lack of understanding made me sad. I did not know why I did not understand. Was it because I was somewhat intellectually challenged and was unable to grasp the deeper implications of the book, or was it because I was not sufficiently politically aware? What I do know was that I was enthralled with the particular circumstances surrounding Abraham Lincoln's life.

As a boy of thirteen I recalled being impressed with Lincoln's early years. He grew up in a rural area, in a rudimentary cabin without hydro or indoor plumbing. His mother taught him to read and write using a simple slate board. Having read this I could hardly believe that such a man could later became the president of the United States. But also, having read this, I began to see that we could dream and aspire to the greatest of heights. I realized that we are limited by our imagination, not our particular circumstance. I too, was educated in my very earliest years with the same type of slate board. A chill ran down my spine as I wondered about him as a young lad; *how faithfully had he held the determination to become educated? Did he ever rebel? Did he ever feel beaten down by his poverty?* Eventually he became an esteemed lawyer and then President of the United States. I remember pondering, *How could such a person, born into such poverty, lay claim to the highest title in the United States?*

When I first read that this unassuming president had been assassinated, I became sad. I could not comprehend why such an honourable soul, bent on doing right, could be so vengefully killed. The story of Lincoln, sealed itself in my subconscious, perhaps an unwitting instrument helping to form my own set of ideals.

Then another name, Mahatma Gandhi resurfaced in my consciousness. I was but a child of seven when he was assassinated in India. The event stands out in my memory because of how it affected the lives of my father and his friends. Sadness and anger joined forces with grief and misery to become twin towers of emotion consuming the people of Back Street, indeed consuming so much of the Trinidadian adult world. While I did not share in the grief for I was just a child, I sensed that something awful had occurred for Trinidad. It was as if the very light of life had been snuffed out and the world was left in complete darkness.

The librarian in Trinidad would never know how great an impact reading that biography of Abraham Lincoln had on me; it ignited a spark in my lost soul. That librarian offered me the key to the door of knowledge; gladly did I let myself in. Such is the intense recollection that seized me.

Here in this quiet cafe in Manhattan, the reality of the interconnectedness of Mahatma Gandhi, Abraham Lincoln, John F. Kennedy, Martin Luther King, and Bobby Kennedy struck my soul like a bolt of lightning. Each of those noble souls had been sent on to the afterlife through the instrument of an assassin! I began to comprehend a little of that which I had but little knowledge of at that time. Then I too understood the emotion of the New Yorkers for the loss of their beloved Kennedys and shared their pain. A deep sense of despair enveloped me as I understood that the cause of civility and humanity is under constant threat.

I resumed my walk.

42
WHERE'S THE CLASS IN THAT?

I walked and walked, taking in all the sights of New York. Walking soon rendered me famished and I began searching for a restaurant. This task was not particularly difficult as Manhattan was well known for its many restaurants. The restaurant which captivated me from the outset boasted a highly polished terrazzo walkway which could rival any piece of contemporary art; it invited me to follow its intricate design up three steps where it opened up to a curtained vestibule in which rich red curtains draped the far end. Two huge marble planters anchored the curtains at either side. I was only too willing to indulge in the pure luxury of the moment. It was with a sense of nervous excitement that I found myself entering this high end establishment.

I was quite surprised to find that this huge restaurant was filled nearly to capacity. I noted that the clients were well-dressed. Most of the men were wearing three-piece suits. I was wearing dress pants, a long-sleeved shirt and comfortable walking shoes. While not sporting the garb of the typical tourist i.e. shorts, runners and a camera, nonetheless I felt slightly intimidated by the presence of all those business suits. I began to second guess myself and wondered if I were dressed appropriately. That feeling of insecurity was reinforced further by the critical glare of the young server who greeted me. His unending stare rendered me most uncomfortable but I remained resolute in my intention to stay. Finally, he motioned to me and announced, "You...follow me!"

While several tables near the front of the restaurant had recently opened up, he led me to a table located near the bathrooms. It did not look like all the other tables. Whereas they were covered with a tablecloth, matching napkins, a flower arrangement and matching silverware, this table was almost Spartan in appearance. It did not match the austerity which characterized the rest of the tables and seemed somewhat out of place. Sitting there, I too felt somewhat out of place.

When my server brought me the menu he instructed, "You... order quick; we very very busy. I come back soon."

He was gone in a flash. Trying not to feel offended by his abruptness, I decided that he had gone unasked to retrieve for me the customary glass of water that graced every other table but mine. While awaiting his return, I tried to relax but was unable. I felt so removed from everyone else; I felt tossed aside as somehow lacking some singular ingredient that would make my presence acceptable. When I opened the menu I discovered that it was not written in English but rather in Chinese characters. There were no English translations and as a result I could not make my choice. When the young man returned he asked in a brusque and curt manner, "Which number you choose?"

"I have not chosen as yet. Can you help me please?"

"You waste my time. Now you choose; we don't have your kind of menu."

"What dish is plain chicken?"

"Number 5, you order number 5."

I ordered number 5.

He took the order and left. Sensing that I was not welcome, I too, wanted to get up and leave. Mentally, I toyed with the idea of leaving but before taking any action, I needed to locate the washroom. I was directed downstairs to an area far beneath the restaurant. Immediately as I opened the door, I was shocked by the condition of the washrooms. The lighting was totally inadequate, dim at best, and for good reason; it appeared that management thought that the dim lighting would hide the shortcomings of this inferior bathroom. Everything about it screamed sub-standard and second rate. It stood in stark contrast to the superlative design of the restaurant proper. It was a total disappointment. I hurried back upstairs where my server was depositing my dinner onto my table. "Here... you eat... quickly."

Again he was gone.

I could not begin to eat. In his haste to be rid of me, he had forgotten to provide me with a knife and fork. I waited for him to return but he was nowhere to be seen. I grew weary of waiting and took matters into my own hands and reached over to an empty table and grabbed a cloth napkin containing the necessary utensils. I began to eat. While tasty, my dinner was extremely spicy and still I had not been served anything to drink; not even a simple glass of water. Again my eyes searched out my attending friend. My mouth was burning and I sought to attract the attention of another young man clearing off an adjacent table. I asked him for a glass of water. He did not understand English. I grabbed an empty water glass from his table and pointed to my table shaking my head to indicate that I did not have one. He understood and moments later he brought me a glass of water; he even came back to refill it later. Because of him, I was able to enjoy my lunch—a little.

When my server eventually returned it was with my bill. He directed, "You pay cash, just cash!"

While his manner was less than civil, I was however, pleasantly surprised by the reasonableness of the bill; it was less than three dollars. I pulled out a ten dollar bill in a manner that suggested I owned a world of ten dollar bills and placed it on the table beside the check. My server reached out and grabbed both the money and the check and left. When he returned with the change he handed it to me expectantly. He could barely contain the smile on his face.

I pocketed the loose change while keeping the five dollar bill in full view.

I inched the five dollar bill toward him never letting it leave my control. His eyes grew large and shone with excitement.

I smiled at him as I lifted the bill.

He barely drooled in anticipation. His next action was best described as servile and ingratiating. All hint of his previous displeasure at my presence dissipated. His words, drenched in self-serving condescension failed to exonerate his previous bad behaviour, "Thank you, thank you so much, you good customer."

As he reached forward to take the money from my hand, I pulled the five dollar bill back a little and dangled it in front of his bewildered face.

"You like money? Yes? This could have been yours. Let this be a lesson to you. Treat *all* people with dignity and respect... "

I tucked the five dollar bill into my shirt pocket and left. As I strode down the aisle I noticed the server who had come to my aid previously. Remembering his attentiveness, I slipped a dollar into his hands and thanked him. By now, my server had regained his senses and rushed after me, instructing me in the protocol surrounding "tipping."

"Sir," he blustered, "you must tip. You forgot... everyone tips."

"You are so right. I did tip. Thank you."

He quickly returned to my table in search of the tip. His search however, yielded no reward.

Feeling vindicated, I walked out of that restaurant, head held high.

43
Hired ...?

Two weeks had already elapsed and the New York job market seemed impenetrable. It would appear that I had waited too long to come to the city and had missed my window of opportunity for work. While my first week in the city with Kay and Bob was amazing, my inability to find work and contribute to my own welfare, weighed heavily on my mind. Not once did Bob or Kay register the slightest resentment regarding my unemployed status. In spite of their best efforts, my morale began to ebb with the passage of each day, and I began to brood.

By the beginning of the third week, my spirits were lifted by the offer of a job. The job site was in the basement of a huge warehouse located right in Brooklyn; to say that I was ecstatic would be an understatement. The offer of this job meant the world to me. It marked the moment when I could begin to reclaim my worth as a person. No matter how menial the labour, my mind was prepared to accept it. The job proved to be very physical; I welcomed the opportunity to rebuild my muscle after months spent in a sedentary position studying.

On the main floor of the warehouse, one set of heavy machinery cut sections of steel beams; these, in turn, were transported to another section of the warehouse by yet another set of heavy equipment. So powerful were these machines that the vibrations could be felt blocks away. The job that I was hired for however, required no mechanical skill whatsoever. My job was in the basement of the warehouse where no heavy equipment could be accommodated. The sorting and ordering of the various lengths of discarded steel had to be done manually. That became my sole responsibility. I had a whole area to myself and I was happy in my solitude; I made my own rules and organized the steel beams according to my own judgment. Alone, I managed quite well.

Then along came Stoneface Mike. He also had been working alone in another section of the basement. When he approached me and directed that I accompany him to his area I happily obliged; he needed assistance in moving some larger lengths of steel that he could not manage on his own in spite of his massive size. Carefully I assessed the differences in our size and strength. Mike was pushing six and a half feet while I was a mere five foot ten. Even my thighs were smaller than his biceps. If I were to be of any use at all, it would require some careful management for we two, while not polar opposites, were significantly mismatched, not only in strength, but also in disposition. Mike was impulsive and impatient; I, calculating and prudent.

Mike expected that I would be equally suited to the task and that together we could bring order to the section containing the longer lengths of steel. Seemingly without effort, he hoisted up his end of the beam expecting me to do likewise. I was less adept at managing my end and he expressed his impatience by suddenly dropping his end of the steel beam. The full weight of the steel then rested in my hands; I was totally unprepared for his dangerous reaction. The sheer weight of the load knocked me off balance and some portion of the steel struck my leg. I yelled out in pain, grabbing the affected area. Stoneface then swore at me and told me that I was f***ing lazy. His reaction left me in a state of shock; *I* was the injured party; *I* should be the one who felt offended.

Within moments, we resumed our task. When it became obvious to him that I was no match for his strength, he became crazy with rage. Seizing a six foot length of steel, he headed straight for me. When I saw him coming, I quickly retreated to safer ground. Taking aim, he dispatched that missile straight at my head. Had I been less agile, I honestly think that I would have been struck dead.

Next thing I knew, Mike had gone to fetch the supervisor. The two of them approached; Mike, still seething, repeatedly launched insults against my person. Each crude invective sought to injure my character. The supervisor quickly waved Mike away for he wanted a moment alone with me. Once Mike complied, the supervisor asked, "Frank, you're not able to keep up, right?"

I was silent, for it was true. I hung my head, totally embarrassed.

He continued, "There is no shame if you are not able to do the work. But, I now have to make a decision. Do I fire you, or do you resign?"

I got the message, loud and clear.

I walked away. He called me back, but I kept on walking. I had nothing to say; I just wanted to be alone. He caught up with me, and explained that I had some wages to collect.

"Thanks, but no thanks."

Again I turned and walked away. Once more he caught up with me. Putting his hand on my arm, he forced me to stop walking and look at him. He looked at me as if I were from another universe. *Who turns down an offer of money* was the question that hung unasked between us.

Once more I began to walk away. He placed a hand on my shoulder, this time in a more fatherly fashion, as though he wanted to comfort me. Then he reached into his wallet and pulled out a bill and placed it in my hand. I would not let my fingers grasp it and it fell to the ground. He picked it up, and this time tucked the bill securely in my shirt pocket.

I had no words for him. I simply stared at him and walked away once more. I did not look back.

Hobbled by failure, my soul floundered.

I began making plans to leave New York. Back at the apartment later that night, Kay, sensing that something was amiss, cornered me and asked, "Frank, why are you really going back to Canada?"

I made some flimsy excuse. She did not accept it for a single moment and said, "Frankie, I know you, brother. You cannot fool Kay. Something happened. Yes?"

How could I tell her the truth about the job? *Hired and fired on the same day!* It was the lowest of lows.

Kay and Bob had been supremely generous toward me and had I had a job, I could have continued to accept their hospitality. Without a job, I no longer had joy.

Despite the protests of my family, I left New York and headed for Toronto, to my friend Roderick. Perhaps there…

44

Toronto Employment Centre

I knocked on the door.

A decisive voice returned, "Yes, come on in."

I entered.

"Can I help you?"

"I think not," was my weary response, "but I'm here."

The young man, barely into his twenties, hastily put down the magazine that had previously claimed his attention. My unconventional response took him by surprise. Quickly he removed his feet from their comfortable home atop the desk but not before I noticed that he was not wearing the traditional Oxfords. He was wearing runners, and, if I am not mistaken, his socks did not quite match.

I am sure that I must have appeared to him as a bit of an intruder who was not just an inconvenience but worse, a rude inconvenience.

Quickly gathering himself, he sat upright, and countered my rough assertion with an authoritative tone of his own.

"So, you don't think I can help you?"

"Frankly, no."

"Well, well, well. Do you know that I could interpret your comment as sarcastic – even rude?"

I softened my tone, "I would not blame you."

I could tell that he was not too impressed with my manner thus far but I felt beyond desperate and had nearly lost all hope. He may have had reason to dismiss me right then and there as someone who really didn't deserve help. He didn't. Instead he stood beside his desk and asked,

"What is it that you want?"

"I want a job that pays over four dollars an hour."

My outlandish assertion almost caused him to lose his balance. He grabbed onto his chair and sat down—temporarily dumbfounded. When he recovered from shock he unloaded on me,

"You have some nerve walking into this office and almost demanding a job that pays over four dollars an hour. Are you for real or just plain nuts? Who do you think you are?"

"Please, no insults."

"Look, man. I don't know what makes you think you're so special. Everyone who walks in here looking for a job is grateful if they get one that pays $1.50 an hour. And if they're lucky enough to land one that pays $2.00 an hour they're ecstatic. And you… you're asking for over $4.00 an hour. Tell me what makes you so special. You some kind of prince or something?"

"Please, no sarcasm. No insults. I am sorry you could not help. Thank you."

I headed toward the door.

"Wait up, come back. I didn't mean to sound insulting. Please…"

He motioned for me to sit down. After I calmed down he asked me to fill out a standard job application form. He explained that I had nothing to lose by filling it out and it would provide a written record of my visit. After I filled out the form, he scanned it carefully to ensure that all areas were correctly answered. The tension between us eased.

"Frank," he began and all sense of presumption evaporated. "You do have my attention. It would be helpful if you tell me why you stipulated $4.00 an hour. You do realize that you are asking a great deal. Why? By the way, my name is Allan."

He rose from his seat and came around the desk to shake my hand. Then he sat down beside me and waited.

Then something happened. The wall around my spirit crumbled. The anger and pent up frustration found a place to vent. Everything poured out, "Allan, I have perhaps enough money to get back to the Lakehead on a standby flight. My university fees will cost close to $600.00. As of yet I do not have one cent to dedicate to that cause. Futhermore, I have not yet secured a place to live when I do return to the Lakehead. I have the promise of a possible lead, but I have no money to advance to that cause either. I don't have one single penny to my name. If I sounded sarcastic or rude when I first came in, it was unintentional. Truth be told, that tone masked my growing desperation. Sorry, we got off on a wrong foot."

"Man, you sure have a lot on your plate, Frank. Do you have anyone – any family in the Lakehead?"

"No."

"Am I to understand that you are absolutely alone and quite literally penniless?"

"Yes."

"I get all kinds of people in this office and from all parts of the world, seeking jobs. I hear their stories. Man, you are in a boat by yourself."

"And my boat is sinking... fast."

"Frank. I do understand. Let me tell you plainly. The job you want—and brother you need it—is nearly impossible to find. I will be on the alert. What you need is a miracle."

"That I am here today—thus far in my life—has to be a miracle in itself, my friend."

"Tell me, Frank. What happens if you do not find a job?"

"Oh, I would prefer not to think on that right now."

"Sure, I understand. Look, hold on to this card. It is my personal number. I will be thinking about you."

Then he came close to me and shared, "I was wrong about you—dead wrong..."

"Allan, thanks."

I spent the rest of the day scouting Toronto for a job. No luck. Late in the evening I returned home to the place where my friend Rod rented a room. Rod was a long-time friend from Trinidad now living in Toronto and going to school. He rented a room in a house owned by another Trinidadian woman whom we affectionately called Auntie. Rod had made special arrangements for me to stay with him.

For three long days I awaited word from Allan regarding a job. For three long nights I suffered the agony and embarrassment of not having a job. Throughout this time, neither Rod nor his landlady made me feel anything but comfortable. They were encouraging and supportive. Auntie was especially assuring sharing whatever food she had with me. By whatever means she could she sought constantly to bolster my fading spirit.

By the time Friday came around I had made up my mind. This was to be my last day in Toronto. I could no longer impose on my friend's hospitality. I awoke early. I was packed up and ready to go before Rod left for work. Rod tried to change my mind but I would not be dissuaded. After he left for work I headed downstairs suitcase in hand to offer my thanks and to say farewell to Rod's landlady. When she saw me, she offered to make me breakfast. I declined. I needed to be on my way.

"Tell you what, Frank. Let's just sit here and have one final cup of coffee together. I have lots of carnation milk—the type you like so much."

"Thanks, Auntie, but I really must leave. Sorry."

As usual, she overrode any and all protestations with affirmative action. "Here, Frank. I've already poured it for you. Sit and have this cup of coffee with me. I like your company."

I sat down; before long Auntie had added fresh homemade muffins to the mix. And, if that wasn't enough, she brought out the big guns—guava jelly! She was a master at her craft and the two of us relaxed into the morning. The ringing of the telephone interrupted our chatter.

Handing me the phone, she said, "Frank, it is for you."

It was Allan, the man from the employment centre. He seemed intense.

"How soon can you get here?"

"Twenty minutes."

"Great. See you in twenty."

Auntie and I exchanged curious looks and I immediately set off for the office uncertain of my expectations. Fifteen minutes later I was face to face with Allan just outside his office. In his hands he held a piece of paper. I did not know it then but that paper contained the key to my future.

"Frank—here is an address. Here is the name. This is the telephone number if you need it. Now I have a map of the transit route for you. It seems complicated; it is not. I have underlined the route and the bus and train exchanges. Do you still have my number?"

"Yes."

"Get going."

"Allan. Thanks."

The address on the paper was that of Ontario Hydro; it took me close to forty-five minutes to complete the trip as laid out by Allan. The paper instructed me to contact a Mr. Glen Martin from the Parts Department. Once I found him, I started to introduce myself,

"I am Frank Maraj…"

"Excuse me a moment, Frank," he interrupted, "I need to attend to these two workers."

Quickly and efficiently he found the needed parts and dispatched the two workers; he then turned his attention to me, "Frank, thanks for coming right away. We are really in a bind. The guy who does this job just suffered a broken leg and won't be back for a good six to eight weeks. Let me tell you about the job. Basically, you're doing a lot of paperwork; you fill orders. When a part is needed on the jobsite, the manager of each section signs the order. That step is critical. Then you locate the part and check it off. You keep the carbon copy and store it here in this drawer. Let me show you."

He reached out and grabbed the pile. "Next it is imperative that you inform me when you are running low on certain parts. So far so good?"

"Yes."

"Let me show you around. I'll… " Again he was interrupted.

It seemed that he would never get away; the interruptions kept coming. Finally there was a lull in the demand and he showed me around the department. I was overwhelmed by the sheer number of different parts from the tiniest washer to the largest replacement pipe—each with its own special place on the six foot high shelving units and each with its own unique unit ordering number.

"Well, Frank, what do you think? I know it looks complicated at first. It does get better, I assure you. Are you ready to give it a try?"

"Yes. Thank you. I am."

"Oh, Frank, by the way, the job pays $4.25 per hour. Sometimes there is overtime. Good, eh?"

I nearly fell over.

"Can you start Monday?"

"Yes. Do you mind if I spend the rest of the day just observing? It would help me get to understand what is expected next week. Oh, and don't worry. There would be no expectation of pay."

"Sounds just great, Frank. Great spirit. I like that."

"Thanks."

I spent the rest of the day familiarizing myself with the job's requirements. By day's end I felt somewhat less intimidated by the challenge that awaited me on Monday. I couldn't wait to get home to Rod and Auntie and tell them about this dramatic change of fortune. Had Auntie not detained me, none of this would have happened. I would have been on my way back to the Lakehead to… I don't know what. Was Destiny intervening once again?

45
Caught... Big time

Now that I had a job—and a well paying job at that—I could allow myself to participate in a few social indulgences. Rod was part of a group that loved to socialize and occasionally I was invited to join them. Their main form of socialization consisted of making their way to the heart of Toronto where they would take in the all the lovely sights—especially the girls. Occasionally they were brave enough to approach the girls and begin an innocent conversation; behind this action was always the feint hope that it might lead to something more.

On one such night the boys focused their attention directly on me. Rod's friends were unanimous in their finding that I lacked the necessary social bravado that defined a man. They found me to be socially withdrawn. They sought to be the instrument of my makeover. To achieve this end they began to cajole Rod into pressuring me to take my turn at approaching the young women of Toronto.

In an attempt to put me at ease, Rod advised, "Frank, it is like what we used to do in Trinidad. It's just liming, man. Go for it."

"But, Rod... in Trinidad when we went liming, we didn't have to make a move. We..."

"Frank, this is just a small step. Do it, and you get the boys off your back. Okay?"

I knew that Rod was under pressure because of me and for that reason only I agreed to participate the next time we all went out to take in a late night movie in downtown Toronto.

I overheard one of the boys ask, "Rod, yo had a talk with Frank yet?"

"Yes."

"Well, what he say?"

"He going to make a move tonight."

"Hey guys, yo got to leave Frank alone. He will do it his own way."

"But he is a man, right?"

I was just a step or two behind the boys so I heard everything that was said. Rod was taking the heat on my account and still trying to defend my honour. I knew that I had to take the initiative or the comments would never end. I sped up my pace and soon passed both Rod and the others. Within moments I beheld the answer to my dilemma. Right in front of me was a group of five young ladies. They too appeared to be casually taking in all the sights that a Saturday night in downtown Toronto offered. I picked up my walking pace; when I felt that I was close enough to be heard, I boldly inquired, "Young ladies, can you help me please? I am with some friends and we are looking..."

The young lady to the extreme right of the group stopped dead in her tracks and spun around accusingly, "I know that voice!"

The other four girls followed suit and soon ten pairs of eyes were staring me down.

The first girl continued, "Is that you, Mr. Boodram?"

Mr. Boodram... It had been a good two years since I had heard myself referred to by that name. What were the chances that the first time I attempt to put myself out there to advance myself on the social scene that I would encounter one of my former students? And, to make matters worse, this was not just any former student; this was a former student who had also been the prefect in one of my grade eleven classes—a girl named Jocelyn.

The accusatory tone in her voice caused me to freeze on the spot. Memories of her flashed across my consciousness. She had graduated a few years ago from St. Charles Girls' High School and had left Trinidad to further her studies. I did not know that she too had come to Canada.

In her role as prefect she took charge of my class whenever I had to be out of the room. Jocelyn was one of the best prefects ever. What sad irony brought our paths together at this most inauspicious moment. Humiliation and guilt rendered me speechless.

"Mr. Boodram, I am so shocked," she continued.

My insides began to crumble and my legs felt like rubber. Whatever bravado I possessed earlier exited to another universe.

"I simply cannot believe my ears or my eyes. Is it really you, Mr. Boodram, my beloved teacher?"

Knowing that she knew that my motives for stopping them on the street and trying to strike up a conversation were not completely innocent struck a cruel blow to my psyche. I was wounded badly; I needed a way out. The respect that I had worked so hard for as a young male teacher at an all girls' school was about to be destroyed by this one compromising act; this knowledge weighed heavily on me. I prayed for a way out. Then Jocelyn said, "Girls, I want you to meet Mr. Boodram—my beloved teacher."

She introduced me to each of her friends and then, with a twinkle in her eyes, she gently teased, "And what kind of help did you need, Mr. Boodram?"

I could feel the blood rushing to my face but I hoped my casual response was enough to mask my embarrassment, "Oh, my friends and I were going to have a meal before we go to the movies. I was going to ask about a restaurant that you might recommend."

When she challenged, "Really, Mr. Boodram?" I knew that she was on to me. But, much to her credit she allowed me my dignity. The girls discussed my request and recommended a nearby Chinese restaurant. Then when Jocelyn found out that I was just in Toronto for a short while, she offered her telephone number. Soon the other girls wrote their numbers down also. We agreed to try to meet again. Then they were on their way.

Roderick and others had witnessed the scene from a little distance away. They were not privy to the words that were actually spoken. In their eyes I had passed the test. The little piece of pink paper with five telephone numbers on it was proof enough. As to what had actually transpired... well, I left that to their very active imaginations. I headed for the restaurant.

46

Last Days Toronto

"Glen, any chance I can speak to you today? You are so busy I hardly see you."

"Sure, Frank. Later in the afternoon—coffee break is the only time. You okay with that?"

"Sure. Thanks, Glen."

I hated to bother him; he was always so busy. He seemed to be the main go to guy at the plant. My feelings of guilt ran particularly deep because he was the first one I went to for help doing my job.

"Frank, what's up?"

"I need a favour. I hesitate to ask."

"Well, ask away, man. Out with it."

"Glen, I realize that my job finishes next week, the end of August as we agreed. Yet, I would like to stay on for another couple of weeks. Is there any possible way that you can help me?

"Now, let me see if I can help you. We may have one problem though."

"What problem is that, Len?"

"The Union. The Union and their dues."

I didn't understand.

"Frank. You didn't have to pay any union dues when you started working because of the time frame. If you work beyond this next Friday, you will have to join the union. The fees are high—so high that it would not be worth it for you just to work two weeks. Man, I'm sorry."

"Thanks anyway."

Disappointed, I went back to my duties.

Two days later Glen approached and asked, "Frank, you still want to work another two weeks?"

"Yes, absolutely."

"Well, here's the deal. Mind you it is not official. But you will be allowed to work on a day to day basis beyond Friday. I am, however, going to ask you to keep a low profile. It would be best for you not to have lunch in the cafeteria from here on in."

I looked at him quizzically.

"Yes, I know you are wondering why. I don't want anyone to start asking questions. If you keep a low profile you won't be exposed to any uncomfortable questioning! Got it, Frank?"

"Yes."

"Frank it'll be good to have you around a little longer. You need a little extra cash for fringe benefits? Some beer perhaps?"

I merely smiled at his presumptions and we both headed back to our posts.

Glen had no idea what that two extra weeks would mean to me.

Thus I worked on a day-to-day basis at the plant for the next two weeks. He even managed to secure me some overtime hours. I was most happy to oblige. At time and a half, my paycheque was considerable.

****

The work came to an end and it was time to bid farewell to Toronto and to my friend Rod. I did not know how to thank him for all that he had done for me. We were having a final meal dining out at a fine restaurant when I broached the subject with my friend. Rod wasted no time in assuring me that I owed him nothing extra. "Actually, you owe me nothing, Frank. You have helped out with the bills—more than what I expected. And just to be clear, this meal is on me, Frank."

"Rod, this is a fancy restaurant; it's costly... "

"Never mind that; it's my treat.

Early the next day, I was off to the airport hoping to catch a standby flight to the Lakehead. Eventually I was successful. Once on board, I remembered that Auntie had given me an envelope just before I left, with instructions not to open it until I was on the plane. As I opened the envelope there was a note.

Frank I know you insisted on paying for your meals and accommodations.

Now I insist you accept this small gift.

Auntie had included some money along with her note. I welcomed her generosity.

Now, settling in my seat, I began to reflect on my good fortune and wondered, "What new adventures await me at the Lakehead."

How little did I know…

PART III

Life Change

47

Is My Room Ready?

"*L*en, is my room ready?"

Most anxious to know about the room, I hastily blurted out my question. I had arrived at the Chaykowski home on a Saturday evening in late September, 1969. Len met me at the door.

My bluntness lacked any hint of social propriety and Len was caught off guard. His surprise was only momentary. Quickly recovering, he apologized, "Sorry, Frank, we have already rented it out to someone else. Someone who worked at the bank with my sister, Linda."

"You rented it out? But I thought that the room was promised to me."

"I know, Frank, and I am sorry. We waited to hear from you ever since you left in the summer. When we never got any word, we didn't know what to think. Linda knew of this girl at the bank who was planning on going back to school in the fall. She thought that my mom might need another girl in the house so when we didn't hear from you, we agreed to rent it to **Diana**. Actually, she's here right now, helping out with the shower. Sorry to disappoint you, Frank. But, Dad does have some other ideas to accommodate you in the house..."

"We'll talk later," I interrupted. "You seem to be busy with company right now. What's going on?"

"I started to tell you about the shower. We are having a shower for..."

My mind wandered, *A shower? What's a shower? It cannot be that all these people are getting into a common shower, can it? What an unusual custom...* and I failed to hear Len's full explanation.

Then Len suggested, "Come on in and join the guys downstairs. All the family is here. The girls and Diana are upstairs. You should come in and meet Diana. I don't think you all have met. Have you?"

"No, we have not."

I did not particularly want to meet this individual who had staked her claim on my room and usurped my place in this home. But, I was a tiny bit curious and wondered about this Diana.

Deep down I knew that Len and his family had every right to give "my" room to someone else. Before leaving the Lakehead to seek work in the U.S. (and ultimately, Toronto) I had secured a tentative promise of a room from the two Chaykowski brothers, Len and David. They also attended Lakehead University and we had developed an enduring friendship. Their sister, Linda, was getting married over the summer and they told me that her room would be available for renting in the fall. I was excited to move back to the Current River area and to finally share accommodations with other young university students like myself.

I certainly did not contact them, yet I did not mean to take them for granted. I realized that it was my fault. Sad were the circumstances of these last weeks that I was so preoccupied with work and did not contact either Len or David. I guess I had to accept the consequences.

Accepting consequences however, in no way diminished the disappointment that I felt. I was so looking forward to living with the Chaykowskis. Now I had blown away my own luck. I had never even considered that "my" room could be occupied by another. I guess that I had taken our friendship too much for granted. It was a friendship not just with the two boys, but with the entire family.

Our first chance meeting occurred one morning in downtown Port Arthur when the two boys dropped their father off to work. Mr. Chaykowski was a barber and owned a modest shop in the downtown area. I lived a short distance from the barber shop at the time, and the two boys offered me a ride to the university when they saw me hitchhiking. Over the course of time, a real friendship developed and, eventually, I came to meet the entire family – Mr. And Mrs. Chaykowski and their daughter Linda, who still lived at home. An older sister, Alice, was already married. It wasn't long before Mr. and Mrs. Chaykowski began referring to me as one of *their* boys.

Mrs. Chaykowski loved to cook. She especially loved baking bread and frying doughnuts. Cinnamon buns and honey dipped doughnuts ranked high on my list of favourites. Fortunate I was too, to be invited for Sunday dinner. The family showed genuine interest in hearing all about Trinidad. David had such an adventurous spirit that he encouraged me to plan how he, Len and I could find a way to travel to Trinidad by car. Excitedly we planned our dream trip. The boys decided that they would retrofit the engine of their father's Dodge before using it to take us from Thunder Bay through the United States and Mexico. From there we planned to continue on through Latin America, ultimately ending up in Venezuela. From Venezuela we determined that we could catch a ferry across to Trinidad. What a dream plan. I loved it. I really wanted it to materialize.

This Diana person however, seemed to be putting all that in jeopardy. I was not inclined to be favourably disposed to her.

Len then brought me into the kitchen and announced, "Everybody, look, Frank's here."

Mr. and Mrs. Chaykowski came quickly; they seemed genuinely happy and excited to see me. "Frank you dressed up – nice clothes," noted Mrs. Chaykowski.

I must admit that I did look different from how they last saw me. I attempted to spice up my wardrobe by replacing the traditional shirt and tie look with a more casual western scarf style tie. To complement my new look I also adopted a new way of talking. I put on a Torontonian air and declared in a very *unFranklike* manner, "Yes, just came from To-ron-to. Great city. Just loved it!"

The Chaykowskis laughed at my new persona. They knew my true character and saw this as me just having a bit of fun. I carried the new character one step further and boldly reached out to everyone in the room. Then I saw *her*. She appeared as if from nowhere. When Alice moved forward to receive me, ***she*** was revealed. I liked her immediately; my heart skipped a beat and a new sensation came over me. What was this new feeling? Really, I did not know the words for this feeling; but I knew this much… **I was smitten.**

She, however, seemed unmoved by my presence. She appeared to pay me no heed until Mrs. Chaykowski encouraged, "Diana, come. You have to meet one of our boys – Frank. He is like family."

Obediently, but somewhat reluctantly, she stepped forward. I believe that she managed a polite *'hello'* before going back to whatever task had occupied her when I entered the kitchen. I was left with the distinct impression that she did not care for me. I wondered what I had done.

Then David asked, "Frank you want to come with us? The boys are leaving to take in a show. The girls are having a shower."

There was that unusual shower talk again. *A shower? Why would the girls be having a shower? Was this some strange Canadian practice?*

David stood there urging, "Frank you coming to the show with the guys? It'll be fun…"

"No, thanks, David, you go ahead. I have some things to do."

At the top of my list was finding a new place to live.

As the boys left the house I quietly stole away and headed back to Port Arthur on foot. I knew that the guys would have readily offered me a ride to downtown but I needed to walk; I could not get that girl out of my mind. Hopefully the walk would free me from her clutches. *Did she have any idea what she had done to me?*

48

Planning for the big day

October 4, 1969 promised to be a day of extravagance at Lakehead University. It was an event called Cote-ci, Cote-la. Because I was a member of the West Indian Club, I became involved in some of the planning. Each different ethnic group was going to be represented in some manner at the event. The president of our club, Angela, sought input as to how we should be represented. After some informal discussion, I suggested, "Angela, what about a steel band?"

"A steel band? Great, but impossible. Who? Where? How much? We could not possibly afford…"

"Angela, maybe you should approach the executive council – see if they might help."

Everyone was in agreement. Then Angela declared, "Frank, it's your idea! You're coming to the executive meeting! You have no choice. Everyone in agreement?"

There was a unanimous cheer. So much for speaking out!

A few days later, I went to the executive meeting with Angela. There was a definite positive buzz around the table the moment the idea of securing a steel band for the event was mentioned. Angela introduced me as the man behind the dream. While there was great enthusiasm, there was also great scepticism and many questions regarding the logistics of pulling off such an event.

"Frank, bringing a steel band here is so awesome. Is it really possible?"

"Yes!"

"But, how can we afford it? It must cost a great deal! Where'll we raise that kind of money, and do we have the time?"

"Well, I have already made inquiries. I have contacted that leader of the band in Toronto who is willing to wave all fees. If we can be responsible for transportation and accommodation, the members of the band will be willing to perform for free at the event."

This bit of news created quite a stir. Then I added, "And, Ladies and Gentlemen, I phoned the Prince Arthur Hotel and the manager there is presently considering offering a substantial discount to house the performers. Air Canada has also consented to a discount fare to fly them in."

Then an amazing spirit of sheer energy pervaded the assembly as every affiliate pledged its support. Then the president declared, "We are going to make this happen. I will approach the University; they will help; they have to. Look everyone else is. Frank, Angela, we need to talk further."

Later on, the three of us met over coffee to iron out the details. The president asked, "Shall I take the lead and follow through and contact the Prince Arthur Hotel and Air Canada?"

I was about to say, "Yes," when Angela suggested, "Let Frank do it. It is his baby. Something tells me we are in good hands. Besides your plate is already full!"

"Well, Frank, she's all yours. We'll talk later."

What just happened? I wondered briefly how I could deliver on all the promises. With no time to lose, I went to work right away. I convinced the management of both the Prince Arthur Hotel and Air Canada about the wisdom in heralding a *first* in the Lakehead – a Trinidadian steel band. After due and quick consideration, both corporations offered deep discounts. I was ecstatic. I shared my news with Angela; she was speechless.

At the next meeting, Angela declared, "Frank is amazing. He did the unbelievable. Frank you do the honours and take the floor. Share your findings."

When I revealed the amount of the discount that both Air Canada and the Prince Arthur Hotel were offering, a hush fell over the room. The silence was broken eventually by little pockets of whispering which soon exploded into a fervent outburst of accolades interlaced with expressions of incredulity.

"Frank, how did you do that?"

"Frank, you are the man!"

Then the president announced that the university board itself had offered a generous amount to defray costs. After each individual organization declared its offer, we discovered that the total amount pledged exceeded the anticipated expenses. When the President smiled and asked, "What shall we do with the extra funds?"

I volunteered, "Would it not be a nice gesture to offer the band members some pocket change since they are donating their services for free?"

There was a unanimous *yes* response to this suggestion; again I soon found myself in the centre of all the excitement with all eyes focused on me. Man, these accolades almost sent me into another orbit. Soon a new category was being created on the executive and I was being declared the *Honourary Public Relations Officer*."

More praises and accolades followed the announcement.

Now, truly, I was propelled into another universe.

As word spread regarding my new position, members from every group adopted me as their advisor. Suddenly I was *someone* and *everyone* was seeking me out. What a turn of events! *Should I not be ecstatic, revelling in the adoration of my supporters?* Yes, I should, but sadly that was not exactly the case, for my mind was still bearing the rejection of a certain young lady. I could not get her out of my mind. She had been most polite but not at all inviting. Feeling powerless, I brooded still. The man of the moment was momentarily feeling rejected.

How was I to repair this situation?

The answer came inadvertently from Angela, when, at our next meeting, she presented me with several complimentary tickets to the event.

"Frank, you are one lucky guy. Here are eight tickets. Man, you sure are getting the recognition. Enjoy. Any idea who you are going to invite?"

Yes, I said to myself, *I do have an idea.*

I began to hatch my plan.

****

Almost immediately, I contacted Len and urged, "Len, let's go out as a group to the Cote-ci event at the university. I have complimentary tickets; two for your mom and dad, two for David and Janice, two for you and Nancy and another one for Diana. Please include Diana. What do you think? Do you think she'll agree to come?"

The very next day I met with Len and asked about the progress regarding my plan. He responded, "Mom and Dad won't be coming. Sorry. But, David and Janice are definitely coming and Nancy and I can't wait."

"And Diana?"

"Frank, give her time. She'll come around. Right now, she is a little shy. But don't you worry."

Well, I did nothing but worry after that. I worried because I knew that I had handled the situation all wrong. *What had possessed me to go through someone else to ask for a date?* That was not my style. I guess I was so afraid of being rejected by her that I sought to soften the blow by going through a third party.

I had worried about asking her outright but doing it through Len I risked looking underhanded and sneaky. In my soul, I had this uneasy feeling that something was not right.

I was not wrong.

49
Cote-ci Cote La

Len called to let me know that Diana would be coming with us. Not content with knowing that she was coming, I pushed to find out more about her state of mind.

I should not have.

"Len, how is she? Is she happy to come?"

"Frank, she will be fine. Don't you worry. You have to give her time until she gets to know you. Everything will be fine."

Fine! Everything is not fine! Diana does not wish to come. And I am to be blamed. I did not ask her out properly. I felt compelled to correct the situation. Accordingly, I resolved to visit the Chaykowskis' and talk to Diana myself.

When I arrived at the Chaykowskis', Mrs. Chaykowski answered the door. Immediately she invited me in and offered me coffee and a doughnut. This gave me a temporary distraction while Mrs. Chaykowski went to inform Diana that I was waiting to see her. Minutes passed. Both the coffee and the doughnut had been consumed. Still no Diana.

My solitary presence in the kitchen became awkward and finally Mrs. Chaykowski offered, "That is strange, Frank. I go get her for you."

Just as she started up to go, Diana came downstairs. She appeared distant and cool. I smiled and offered a hello, automatically reaching out to shake her hand; she did not respond to my outstretched hand. She seemed unaware that I wanted to shake hands and politely turned away temporarily distracted. I could not figure this girl out at all. She did not seem rude. Was she just shy as Len had indicated? Or… was it just that this girl did not like me at all. I opted for the latter conclusion and made some hasty excuse to be on my way and departed.

My soul was in turmoil. Truly convinced that Diana had no interest in me whatsoever, all past insecurities were resurrected. I began to obsess that she found me unattractive… perhaps even *ugly*. I was rendered awkward and inept. Our "date" was tonight. Somehow I had to find a way to get through.

Later in the day, I received word from Len that his girlfriend, Nancy, had become ill and that neither of them would be coming with us tonight. Now there would only be four of us. Already I worried how I was going to get through the night with just David and Janice to save me from Diana's inevitable rejection.

Diana too, appeared somewhat apprehensive now that plans had changed and it was going to be just the four of us. I was *allowed* to open the car door for Diana and she seated herself in the back. When I went around the car to get in on the other side, I noticed that she was huddled up as close as she could be to the door. Staring blindly out the side window, she never once glanced in my direction. In the quiet discomfort of the back seat, I had ample time to reflect that another couple could easily be accommodated in the huge distance that separated us.

David and Janice were talking and at some point drew Diana into their conversation. Any opportunity that I may have had of initiating a personal one-to-one conversation with her was effectively erased.

I felt every fibre of her being silently cry: *you… keep away! Don't touch!*

After David parked the car, the gentleman in me took over. I jumped out and immediately rushed to Diana's side of the car to open the door for her. While opening the door with one hand, my other hand reached out instinctively to assist her in her departure from the vehicle.

Then I remembered who I was dealing with. *Foolish hand, withdraw,* I commanded.

Too late, for despite the obvious fact that my hand was extended only in an effort of assistance, Miss Diana recoiled slightly at my touch. I took that as further proof that she wanted nothing to do with me. Her action screamed, *Frank, keep your distance.*

I got the message. *Yes, Miss Diana, I will comply. Lord, help me make it through the night.*

No sooner had we entered the venue when I was bombarded by a multitude of requests from various quarters. The band wanted my final approval on the set up and various clubs were anxious for me to taste their food. I welcomed the thousand and one distractions that greeted me. Everyone made me feel so important and I was accorded such recognition. It seemed that I was the man of the hour– that is, to everyone except Miss

Diana. The distractions kept my emotions in check and lessened the dismal burden of failure.

Soon it was time for the dance to begin and everyone was anxious to hear and see the performance by the steel band.

As we sat down, the student president approached and asked me to introduce the band. I thanked him and advised that it would be a better idea for him to introduce the band since he was the president. I no longer wished any further recognition. Now that I was at the table with my friends and Miss Diana, I simply wanted the evening to end.

The band began playing. David and Jan got up to dance. Almost everyone else followed their lead. Everyone wore a smile and seemed to be having a great time. Diana consented to my offer to dance and soon we had joined the others on the floor. I cannot say for certain if we were truly dancing. I can only attest to the fact that we were *participating* in what could only loosely be called *dancing*. To be truly dancing with a partner implied some sort of physical proximity but Miss Diana ensured that some sort of invisible barrier remained between us and I could not get within ten feet of her without her moving off in another direction.

At one point in the evening the band began to play a classic island rhythm. Someone in the room came up to me and entreated, "Frank, we don't know how to dance this piece. What do we do? Show us."

A crowd gathered around. All eyes were on me. The onus was on me to do *something*... I reasoned that almost anything I did would be appreciably received by this predominantly Canadian audience. I had nothing to lose.

I moved out onto the dance floor and began to move; my hands went up, my head bopped from one side to the other in time with the music and my legs kicked out at various intervals. Someone grabbed on to my shoulders and mimicked my actions. Then others joined us and soon we were a veritable ocean of waves moving and swelling rhythmically to the music of the drums.

Everyone seemed to enjoy this type of line dance. It took the pressure off the one-to-one commitment of dancing with a single partner. All too soon it was over and a slow dance took its place.

I could not believe how beautifully this band was able to conduct itself through the various melodies. Normally I would have been just thrilled to be up dancing to this lovely ballad. I restrained myself and took deliberate pains to conceal my desire to dance. I did not even allow myself to tap my toes. Everyone from our table was up dancing—everyone save Miss Diana and me.

Then something happened and I honestly do not know who initiated the action but soon we too were up on the floor dancing. I am inclined to think that it was she who initiated the act because by that point in the evening I had pretty much given up all hope of capturing her genuine interest. And, never for one minute did I think that a slow dance with me would be the dance of choice for this young lady who was given to adopt a strictly *hands off* policy. Once on the dance floor, I was sure to keep my distance. Had my arms been longer I would have attempted to maintain the ten foot rule that she seemed to have implemented for the majority of the evening thus far. I did not want to appear presumptuous.

Something truly remarkable happened during the course of that number; I simply cannot account for it. By the end of that particular dance, were no longer ten feet apart; perhaps we were only five feet apart. And, truth be told, I was not the one who initiated this closeness. I was far too conscious about maintaining a most acceptable distance. By the time the last dance of the evening concluded we could have passed for a near-normal couple.

Then David informed us that we all were invited to a get together after the dance.

I hesitated to give consent. My brain cautioned, "No way!"

While my mind battled the alternatives, shy little Miss Diana looked up at me and asked, "Shall we, Frank?"

Shall we, Frank? Had I heard correctly? Was she seriously contemplating extending our evening?

In an attempt to conceal my utter shock at her unexpected response I replied most nonchalantly, "Yes, let's."

As we drove to the party Diana was no longer hugging the opposite side of the car as she had in the beginning. That, in and of itself, was progress. To say that she sat beside me would be a bit of an overstatement. She maintained a normal distance from me; however, she began *speaking to me*.

Shortly after arriving at the home of David's friends, Diana and I sat together on a couch facing David and Janice. Inexplicably our hands touched and before either one of us had time to think, they became enjoined. We were actually holding hands!

I don't remember anything that was said after that.

I do, however, remember wishing that the evening would never end.

50

My Landlady, a stranger or just strange ...

Since Diana was living in *my room* at the Chaykowskis' in Current River, I had to find other accommodation. Mr. Chaykowski had indicated that he had had another idea regarding my living arrangements. The Chaykowski home had what appeared to be two living rooms on the main floor. The second room was probably intended to be a dining room but since the family did all their entertaining in the large kitchen, Mr. Chaykowski was prepared to give serious consideration to turning the second room into a bedroom for me. I could not believe how much thought had gone into this accommodation. I was honoured that they still wanted me to live with them.

But to live with them, meant that I would also be living with Diana. Because of how I was raised in Trinidad, I would have had to regard her as a *sister*. I wanted none of that. I already had far too many *sisters* in Canada. The daughters of every family that I met in Canada were, by extension, *my* sisters because of the relationship I had with the parents. This is a direct result of the conditions I put upon my own male friends and my sisters. If my friends came to my house as my friend, their intentions toward my sisters had to be above reproach. They could not use our friendship to get close to my sisters. I carried this same expectation in my own person and it immigrated to Canada along with me. If I hoped to pursue a real relationship with Diana, I had to find other accommodations.

I managed to find a single room within walking distance of downtown Port Arthur. The room itself came with no cooking facilities but my new landlady offered, that on occasions, I could dine with her. She appeared respectful and friendly and at times, did provide a most delicious meal. Mealtimes however, proved to be extremely unpredictable, almost as unpredictable as my landlady's moods. One day she would greet me at the door upon my return from school and offer me lemon tea and dessert. Another day she would barely acknowledge my presence.

About two weeks after I took up residence in her home, she took me aside and explained that she no longer wanted me to flush the toilet after 11:00 at night. Truth be told, she did not merely *explain* it; she virtually *commanded* it. It would seem that the noise *disturbed* her and she did not like being disturbed. Attached to her command was an implied threat that I would be asked to leave if I did not comply.

I tried my best to honour her request but one night I needed to use the bathroom and indeed it was after the appointed hour of eleven. *What was I to do?* I could not ignore the dictates of my body and I did not want to break the house rules. Thus I dressed quickly and headed downtown to a corner coffee shop that was still open and used its facilities. I found that I had to stagger my visits between two different cafes in order to avoid being detected as one who was merely taking advantage of the store's conveniences. On occasion, I would even buy a coffee.

Then, one day I brought Diana home to meet my landlady. The landlady seemed pleased to meet her and offered us orange tea and cookies. The next day, however, her character was a complete contradiction of the previous day's presentation. When she saw me coming up the path to the home, it was obvious that she was displeased. She shut the door to the living room veritably shutting me off from all contact with her and the kitchen. She never spoke a word to me. I had no dinner that night. I do not understand what I could have done to displease her so suddenly and so completely. I assumed she wanted me out.

I determined that my days at this home were numbered and began scouting the Current River area for alternatives. It was at the Coopers that I found my next home.

I packed up my suitcase and informed my landlady that I was leaving. She looked slightly confused and affectionately inquired, "Frank, why are you leaving? Did I do something wrong?"

I merely smiled, leaving her to draw her own conclusions.

51

Thanksgiving at Diana's

All was going well in my relationship with Diana, perhaps a little too well. We saw one another every single day and, when we were not in class, spent every waking hour together. Now that I too was living in Current River, the anticipation of seeing one another on the bus first thing in the morning was a very real possibility. Although it had been a mere two weeks since we first met, I felt that we had known one another for an eternity. I was excited to the point of distraction; I was neglecting my studies. Truth be told, I was on wings, flying high. Canadian Thanksgiving was just around the corner and Diana had already invited me to go home with her to Rainy River to meet her parents. Far from being scared off by this development, I welcomed it. I was excited at the prospect of going to her home; needless to say, I was even more distracted from my studies. My studies suffered happily.

In the midst of joyfully anticipating meeting Diana's parents, a sobering reality dawned; I came from humble roots in Trinidad. Diana came from a Canadian home. Thus far in the infancy of our relationship, there was nothing about her to suggest that she would shun me or my roots, but I wondered if I would fit in with her family. *Did her parents live a life of privilege? Would I feel comfortable at her home? Did Diana live in a mansion?* Somehow Diana must have sensed that I was having some concerns regarding the impending visit. She started to tell me a little about her home and about her town. She explained that her town was small and that her home was quite modest. These assurances helped me to relax. En route to the bus depot, Diana decided to alert me to the water conditions in her small town. She joked that in the spring, if you wanted to take a bath, (they had no shower) there existed a very real possibility that one could emerge dirtier than one went in. The water was known to turn quite brown with the spring run-off and there was often a sandy residue left in the tub. When these conditions arose, she explained, they had to get their drinking water in jugs from a free-flowing spring.

"I hope you don't mind our water, Frank. Please, don't change your mind about coming," she entreated.

"Never!" I assured her as I hugged her. Secretly, these details made me happier than ever—if that were possible.

On the bus Diana told me a little about her dad. He owned his own insurance business, was a Notary Public, and was a Justice of the Peace. I was very curious about this man and I wondered if he was very strict.

Our seven hour journey was delightful—full of conversation and anticipation. As we neared Rainy River, however, Diana became less conversational. She seemed concerned but would not disclose what might be troubling her. She became quiet. I wondered why.

As the bus pulled in to the parking spot in front of the CN Hotel on the highway, we saw three people standing outside, waiting. One was her girlfriend, Penny; the other two were her parents. When the bus stopped, Diana burst from its doors, leaving me behind to exit alone. *A most curious move*, I thought. I dismissed it as mere excitement at once again being home. (Much later, she divulged the real reason for her anxiety.) As I exited the bus Diana had already gravitated to her girl friend's side and then, hastily, she introduced us, "Mom, Dad, Penny, this is Frank." (A shorter introduction, I had never witnessed.)

Diana and Penny immediately whisked off ahead of us, leaving me to face her parents alone.

The Hammonds came toward me and extended their hands in greeting. Neither of them seemed the slightest bit phased by their daughter's action. I decided to not worry about it either and together we retrieved the luggage and then proceeded to walk to their residence some three houses away down a back alley. We chatted delightfully as we walked and when we came to their home, Mr. Hammond said, "This is it, Frank… our castle."

Our approach was from the rear of the property. Indeed, this *castle* was no mansion; was I ever relieved. The first thing that I noticed and wondered about, was the wooden plank bridging the gap from the top of the back step to another deck. (Actually, that's not true. The first thing I noticed was the shiny green new model Cutlass Supreme parked in the driveway.) I later observed Mrs. Hammond, gingerly making her way across the plank to hang towels on the clothesline. I tried to wrap my head around the contradiction.

Once inside, I was even happier. The kitchen was homey and inviting. I could smell something cooking in the oven. The cupboards were few and the counters were full of dishes and gadgets. Each room was equally inviting and without pretention. After depositing my luggage in the bedroom, we settled down at the kitchen table for a cup of tea. Still no sign of Diana.

Some time later Miss Diana made her entrance. Penny left for home and Diana asked, "Frank, is everything okay?"

I was struck. What a strange question; why wouldn't things be okay? After assuring her that nothing was amiss, Diana, noticeably relieved, became her old self. Whatever had been bothering her, seemed to have been resolved, and soon Diana and her mom were serving up supper- turkey and all the trimmings. It was truly beautiful and I noted the wonderful array of dishes on the table; *Inviting,* I thought.

I waited for a signal to begin. Diana's dad uttered a brief grace after which he reached out for the salad dressing... my first introduction to French's Original Western Salad Dressing... sweet *and* addictive. Great with the baby shrimp and green onion toppings!

Then came the turkey event. Everyone was happy and took generous portions. They all seemed to be enjoying supper.

A bit too bland for me... I wonder what can be done?

I asked, "Mrs. Hammond, might you have any Tabasco sauce?"

"What's that, Frank?"

Then Mr. Hammond interjected, "Mother, just get out the bottle of Worcestershire sauce from the fridge. Let him try that."

Presenting me with the half-filled bottle, she asked, "Might this do, Frank?"

After a generous splash of the sauce, supper was no longer bland. Yes, we all feasted. After a pumpkin pie dessert, Mr. Hammond announced, "Let's all go for a drive. We'll give Frank the grand tour."

We all piled into the shiny green car and began our excursion. Mr. Hammond first drove down Main Street pointing out the highlights— a bank, café, a furniture store, a grocery store, the theatre, and the post office. Just as we passed the post office, Diana asked her dad to stop in front of his office. Curiously, I looked around. All I saw were empty spaces and then one tiny old building. That tiny old building was his office. Certainly it was not the office I had imagined. The tour continued.

Next, we were back out on the highway. Mr. Hammond explained that we were going to the Pines. *Great,* I thought, *that's where the real town must be.*

As we drove along, I noticed that we were going further and further away from any populated area. We seemed to be entering a wooded area, not a town. After turning a few corners and driving several miles over graveled roads, Mr. Hammond stopped the car and everyone got out.

Although the location was extremely scenic, I was puzzled. This was no town. These were trees—pine trees. *Where was the town?* Then it dawned on me. *We had already seen the town; those few streets that we drove down before getting back onto the highway **was** the town.* Now I finally understood. When Diana explained to me earlier that she lived in a very small town, she really meant it. It wasn't just a figure of speech. From then on, the concept of small town had a new meaning. It had to; I came from a tiny island with over a million people. The whole of the island could probably nicely fit in the area between Fort Frances and Rainy River. Now I understood what in meant to come from small town Canada. I took everything in stride, just learning and appreciating. And to be honest, as my mind adjusted, I found the Pines exhilarating and refreshing.

Next day Diana's dad took me out for coffee at the local café. His friends were there and I was introduced. I noticed that when the waitress was occupied Mr. Hammond got the coffee and served us all. Then when we were about to leave they simply left their quarters on the table with a little extra for the waitress. I was charmed, how delightful was this home-style café!

Later that afternoon, Diana and I headed down to the park which overlooked the Rainy River itself. How beautiful and peaceful was the view. The river itself was pure poetry reflecting the beauty of the landscape back to us. As we stepped out onto the dock, Diana pointed out toward the water to indicate the area where a young man from Trinidad had drowned. One of her sister's friends had been a lifeguard there at the time and tried to save him. The boy was the son of a family I knew well back in Trinidad. I was still living in Trinidad when news of the drowning was received and well remembered the shock and pain that accompanied the revelation. How strange indeed, that I would come all the way from Trinidad and discover in a remote small town in Canada, the very site of this tragedy. In silence we moved on.

As we walked the streets near the park, Diana noticed a dime at the edge of a sidewalk. She was about to pick it up when I put my hand on hers to stop her. She looked up at me quizzically, and I said, "Diana, leave the dime there. Please."

She gave in to my request without understanding why. I continued, "Diana, let's leave that dime for a child to discover. Just think of the happiness it would bring to a child who might come across it in the spring after the snow melts. It would be a real treasure."

She smiled and gave my hand an extra squeeze. Instinctively I knew that we belonged.

The next day, I went for a walk by myself. I wanted to experience this town on my own. I met so many friendly people working in their gardens. I just had to stop and chat. I was well rewarded for my efforts and when I returned home to the Hammonds', my arms were full of fresh vegetables. Everyone was struck. Diana asked, "Frank where did you get all those vegetables?"

"Oh, the neighbours offered it to me. I met so many friendly people – and so generous."

Diana quipped, "Frank, you have probably come to speak with and know more people here in one visit than I have throughout my entire life."

We laughed… because it was so true.

All too soon our visit came to an end. Diana had been so excited to come; now she was sad to leave. She did not have to say a word; I understood her sadness. As the bus pulled away she snuggled closely. The Hammonds accepted that Diana had to leave. I sensed they were accepting of the fact that Diana had to go and make her own way. But I knew something else; I recognized that Diana was a daughter connected to her parents strongly. And I was not going to attempt to sever that bond. I felt at peace for her and loved her even more, if that were possible.

After boarding the bus, we rode in silence for a while, each one absorbed in our own reveries.

Somewhere between Fort Frances and Atikokan, Diana asked, "Frank, are you hungry?"

"Starved!" was my immediate response.

Then out popped two sandwiches from Diana's carry on. She handed me one. Hardly waiting a minute to check it out, I bit into the sandwich. It was like no other sandwich I had ever tasted. It was tasty, but, different. Before devouring the second half, I took a moment to examine the creation. It was about two inches thick. Sandwiched between the two layers of white bread, was a layer of cranberry sauce, followed by layers of stuffing, turkey, and stuffing again. Everything had been amply soaked with Worcestershire sauce. Unbelievably good. I must have been ravenous, for my sandwich disappeared before Diana had managed to take a couple bites from her first half; I had to restrain myself from offering to help her with her second half… which I know she would have gladly surrendered. How delightful was this Thanksgiving with Diana.

After leaving Atikokan we snuggled down in our seats in silent reflection. There was something about the weekend that I never shared with Diana until years later. From the first moment that I met her father, I was struck by how much he resembled the physical essence of my own father. And my thoughts drifted to my father who had passed on so suddenly. How did I wish that he were alive today… he was not. Mr. Hammond was here…

Not knowing why, I kept these musings to myself.

52

Hospitality... Trinidad-Style

Life proved to be very good at the Coopers. They allowed me the use of the upstairs bedroom and complete access to the kitchen whenever I needed to make myself a meal. The Coopers would share the occasional meal with me and as time went on, Mrs. Cooper took it upon herself occasionally to do my laundry. These things were not part of the original agreement between us, but Mrs. Cooper, not one to make a production out of anything, would just quietly perform these tasks on my behalf. I was grateful. An added bonus in living at the Coopers, was that they lived only a few blocks from the Chaykowskis—the place where Diana lived.

My history with the Coopers dated back to the time when I first moved to Current River. Not only did they live right next door to the Horns, but Mrs. Cooper also attended the same church as the Jensens and the Vesters whom I had met when I first arrived in the Lakehead.

The Coopers were church friends with the Mackenzies who also lived in Current River. One day Mrs. Cooper invited me to go to church with her so that I might meet Aili and Rod Mackenzie. She told me that the Mackenzies, along with their friends the Monroes, were planning a trip to Trinidad. Upon discovering that I was from Trinidad, they had expressed an interest in meeting me and in seeing if there was anything they could do for me while they were in Trinidad. They said that they would be more than happy to deliver a message to my family or to do anything else for me if they could.

I believe that they were going to leave on their vacation within the week, so I had to think quickly. As we visited over coffee, I felt the genuineness of this family and told them that I would very much appreciate it if they could call on my family and say hello from me. I took a moment to write a brief note for them to deliver to my brother, Boysie. I handed the letter to Rod ensuring that they had all the names and addresses correct. I was able to explain to them where we lived in relation to where they were going. They seemed happy to have met me.

Some weeks elapsed.

Then one day I received a telephone call from the Mackenzies.

After confirming that of course I remembered them, I asked them how their trip to Trinidad had gone.

"Excellent!" replied Aili. "That's why we are calling. We want to talk to you about it. The Munroes are coming over for supper this Sunday. Can you join us?"

"I would absolutely love to; just let me check my book for a moment."

(I had special notebook where I jotted down all my upcoming commitments i.e. invitations to dinner. I lived by the motto: *Never say no; find a way to make it work.*)

After checking my appointment book, I realized that I had already committed that Sunday to another engagement. Saturday, however, was free. And so, I responded candidly, "I have an engagement for Sunday evening. Do you suppose that it could work for any time on Saturday? I am so looking forward to seeing your family and meeting the Munroes."

"We want to see you too, Frank. I'll call you back in a few minutes. We'll do our best to make it work." It wasn't long before Aili called again; this time to confirm that Saturday would work out just fine.

I was thrilled at the prospect of meeting everyone. Yet, a part of me was anxious.

In my letter to Boysie, I had indicated that I had met these Canadians. I took care not to say that we were friends, but I did hint that they were most friendly and agreeable and had shown a friendship toward me. I was not sure what my letter would mean to my family, for no one had ever sent "white friends" to our home before. I trusted that my family would be most hospitable to anyone at anytime. But, I did harbour some slight reservation because our home had never really received white visitors. I wondered briefly if I might have created an awkward situation by suggesting that these "friends" visit my family.

When I arrived at the Mackenzies', the Munroes were already there. The children were busily playing in one of the bedrooms, leaving the grownups free to enjoy the living room without interruption. The four adults were enjoying a Trinidadian Rum and Coke. Assuming that a Trinidadian Rum would be my drink of choice since I came from Trinidad, they offered me one. To honour the occasion, I accepted their kind offer. I was most eager to hear details about their trip.

In response to my query Rod noted, "Frank, it was a good trip. We had fun... until the end of the trip."

My heart jumped. *Did something go wrong? Had they been accosted or robbed? Had my family been a disappointment?*

Seeing the look of alarm on my face and not wishing to extend my discomfort, Peggy exclaimed, "We had the best time of our trip when we met your family."

"Really?" Relief flooded my body. I was all smiles. I could finally relax after that ringing endorsement.

Aili could not contain herself, "We should have gone to your family at the beginning of the trip, not at the end. Frank, did we ever have a blast!"

"What happened?"

Then everyone began speaking all at once. Everyone had a favourite story to tell. They were quite animated recounting the events. Peggy even tried to adopt a little of the Trinidadian dialect into her story telling. For a brief moment I felt like I was back in Trinidad. Their stories made me so happy.

It was late in the afternoon on Sunday when they arrived at my home by taxi. It was the last week-end of their trip and they felt obligated to bring my letter to Boysie in person and let him know that I was doing okay.

Boysie read the letter immediately and declared to the whole family that these visitors were friends of Frankie. As soon as my family heard the words friends and Frankie in the same sentence I knew what their reaction would be. In no time Ma and the girls had prepared supper and a delightful evening ensued. Boysie ensured that everyone was comfortable sitting outside enjoying the cool shade of a mango tree. The girls even managed to make some home-made ice cream to top off the evening.

When it was time for the visitors to return to their quarters in Port-of-Spain, Boysie volunteered to take them to the city. He would not take no for an answer. En route to the hotel, Boysie discovered that they were not due to leave the country until Tuesday.

"What yo plans for Monday?"

"We have no plans. We're free."

"Yo not free any more. Yo comin here."

Knowing that the rest of the family would back up his decision, Boysie laid claim to the Canadian visitors for the whole day.

The fact that Monday was a working day for Boysie and some of the others was of little concern to him. Being hospitable to visitors took precedence over work most of the time, but being hospitable to Canadian visitors required no second thoughts whatsoever. Everyone was of the same mind. Monday was officially declared a "holiday" in honour of Frankie's friends from Canada.

Sylvan, Pinky, Kay and Boysie all took time off work. Ma and the girls immediately set about preparing a huge chicken stew and rice pilaf. Everything was transported via Boysie's truck and Sylvan's car to the famous Caura River. Everyone took refreshment first in the water and then on land over generous servings of both food and drink.

Thanks to their very vivid descriptions, I could easily picture Boysie serenading our visitors after a day spent indulging the appetites. They recounted the tale of him driving the truck back home while standing half in and half out of the cab. At every turn in the road, the horn on the truck would ring out loud to announce that someone was on the road. The Canadians were assembled loosely on the flat bed at the back of the truck cheerfully greeting all and any passers-by.

Upon returning to Back Street, everyone was exhausted. Peggy and Aili were shown to the room that had previously been mine and immediately fell sound asleep on *my* bed.

Reluctantly, my friends took their leave and headed back to Port of Spain.

From all accounts it was obvious that my family loved our visitors and the visitors adored my family.

It was obvious, too, that all four visitors were stricken with the bug – Trinidad's legendary *hospitality* bug, courtesy of Boysie and the family.

And now, I was proving to be the greatest beneficiary of all that good will, for I had just acquired four new friends.

53

My Rubbery Experience

The Munroes and MacKenzies were not shy in expressing their love of the new cuisine that they sampled while in Trinidad. They especially loved Ma's curried shrimp. Aili, a wonderful baker and cook in her own right, tried her hand at "Canadianizing" one of the island's trademark dishes—curried chicken.

I was invited to their home to partake in this modified but still exceedingly tasty dish. Canadians seemed to prefer using the oven for all their creations. Aili was no exception. She used a combination of stove top frying and oven baking to create her unique taste. We all loved it. But, everyone still remembered Ma's cooking, and longed to sample the authentic cuisine once again.

Aili represented the group when she commented, "I really liked the curried shrimp your mom made for us when we were in Trinidad. She didn't make it very spicy – just spicy enough. She gave us something – hot sauce to add – but we only had a very small amount. Not Rod. He took more than a sample and he paid for it. I really wish that I had picked up some of that pepper sauce when we were in Trinidad. It would really add to the flavour."

"I have some hot pepper sauce at home, Aili."

"Really, Frank?"

"You're welcome to use some of it if you want. Are you planning to make a curry dish?"

"Yes, and no."

"Aili, what does that mean – yes and no?"

"Yes, I am planning the meal, and no, I am not cooking it. We all were hoping that you – Frank – seeing how well your mom cooks ..."

"No problem, Aili. I'll do it."

She smiled.

After agreeing so readily, I started to have second thoughts. I remembered my last attempt at cooking for others. But, I had learned a grea deal from that experience and was determined not to repeat the same mistakes. Besides, it was shrimp, and I had been told that shrimp was really easy to cook. I admitted to myself that the only reason that I had never made shrimp before was because it was so expensive to buy. But the Munroes and the Mackenzies were taking care of that; all I had to do was cook. I relaxed. No problem.

At the appointed hour on Sunday the MacKenzies picked me up and together we travelled to Fort William – past the airport and into the outlying countryside. I always marvelled at seeing the outline of Mount Mc Kay as we approached Fort William. There was something almost comforting and protective about its looming presence. I could not help but think how fortunate these Canadians were in having such a varied natural experience of nature within minutes of the city. I felt fortunate to share in that experience.

The Munroes greeted us with smiles and bottles of wine. Everyone was most excited about capturing one of Trinidad's most exalted dishes— curried shrimp. When I had occasion to glance at the shrimp, I marvelled at their size. They were huge. I believe that the girls had purchased prawns, not shrimp. Shrimp or prawn they would taste the same. The prawns just had to be cooked longer because they were so much bigger. No problem.

Adopting the role of chef, I took the lead. I would do all the cooking, but the prep work was to be done by everyone else. Aili cut up the onions and crushed the garlic. Peggy peeled the potatoes and prepared the vegetable dishes. A simple lettuce salad was already melding its flavours in the fridge.

The two Rods ensured that our glasses were always full. A real celebratory spirit prevailed.

Soon it was time for the master chef to create his masterpiece. I needed to have my privacy so that all my creative juices could be free and uninhibited. Accordingly I ushered Aili and Peggy into the living room.

Thus I began the creation.

Having profited from my previous fiasco in the kitchen, I avoided the cayenne pepper. I also avoided putting the stove on too high a heat, opting for a medium temperature. No splattering grease and smoke were going to blemish Peggy's kitchen. I made sure of that. All was going well. The welcome sound of a gentle sizzle filled the room as the garlic and onion were caressed by the oil.

A mental image of my mother in her little kitchen entered my mind. I saw her putting in the curry allowing it to cover the onion and the garlic. Following her example, I poured just enough curry into the pot to cover the onion and garlic mix. What a wonderful aroma filled the air. Anyone entering the house would just know that an expert was at work in the kitchen. I added a little water to the mix to ensure that the curry powder did not burn. Another sizzling sound, more acute than the first, pierced the quiet of the kitchen. A familiar aroma filtered into the living room; curious appetites attempted to disturb the peace of my kitchen begging for a sample. Each was gently admonished and told that nothing was ready yet for I had not even added the main ingredient!

Next, I added the huge platter of giant prawns. They sizzled as their moist bodies encountered the hot curry. I turned up the heat and added a little more water. I determined that those giant prawns needed more heat and lots of boiling in order to be thoroughly cooked.

Then I noticed the potatoes. They too, needed to be added. No problem! They were already cut and peeled. I merely threw them in and let the contents receive heat. I put it on high to ensure that the potatoes got enough heat. Again the aroma enticed everyone to the source.

Peggy entreated, "Frank, I think that it's ready."

Rod added, "I'll try it now, exactly how it is…"

Once again I marched my reluctant friends back to their drinks in the living room assuring them that it wouldn't be too long now. We just had to wait for the potatoes to finish cooking. As the minutes passed I kept checking the potatoes; still they were not yet fully cooked. I added more water, ensured that the heat was on high, and covered the pot and just let it boil.

A good twenty minutes had elapsed. I joined everyone in the living room and assured them that all was well; everything was going to be just fine. After all, it was just a curry dish. Nothing could go wrong. Minutes later I returned to the kitchen and tested a piece of the potato—perfection! I poured the curry into the awaiting serving dish and brought it to the table. The curry was perfectly cooked and the prawns looked large and magnificent.

After raising a glass to the master chef, each one took a generous serving of the curry.

My bottle of pepper sauce was well displayed at the center of the table but all opted to defer adding anything to the dish until they had the opportunity of sampling the original creation. Soon everyone had been served. In unison we took our first taste. The flavour was perfect.

I was ready to receive my accolades.

Then we began to chew on the shrimp. We chewed and chewed and chewed.

One by one, my friends politely raised their serviettes to their lips and deposited the remnants of the *unchewable* shrimp. Disappointment marked each of their faces. The shrimp was no longer shrimp. Rod lightened the mood, when he congratulated, "Frank, I didn't know you knew how to make **rubber**!"

To this day, shrimp remains noticeably absent from my culinary repertoire.

54

Friendship Abounds

An enduring friendship with the Aldrich family in Fort William began with the family matriarch, Lyn Aldrich. While still a very active and involved mother of four teen-aged children, Lyn decided to return to university to pursue a degree. Her dedication to life-long learning made her an avid reader.

We shared a history class during my second year at university and came to know one another during our group study sessions. While we chatted a little about Trinidad, our most obvious bond was our abiding interest in history. I had no idea that she was considering inviting me to her home. Her invitation to Sunday dinner came as a most welcome opportunity to have another meal with yet another Canadian family.

I liked this Mrs. Aldrich and looked forward to meeting her family. A woman of strong principles herself, she raised her family to be independent thinkers and confident individuals. This was evident from my very first meeting with the family.

She had given me both her address and telephone number and noted that while dinner was at five I was most welcome to come earlier to visit.

My landlord began to explain to me how to travel from where we lived in Current River to the Aldrich home. The explanation proved slightly complicated so Mr. Horn decided to drive me there himself. I was grateful for the ride as it gave me time to walk around and get a feel for this new neighbourhood. The homes were large and stately. The grounds were impeccably maintained. One was left with the impression that those who lived in such a distinguished neighbourhood were among the socially elevated in Canadian society. It was with some degree of nervousness that I rang the doorbell. Mrs. Aldrich, herself, answered the door and welcomed me warmly. Her bright eyes sparkled as she introduced me to her husband, Jack.

"Frank, I am happy to finally meet you. Lyn has spoken of you a good deal."

I liked Jack Aldrich immediately. His grey tweed jacket suited his sturdy frame; his hair was still rich in both colour and texture. When he spoke, his voice was clear and expressive. Everything about him asserted his self-assurance. He was a man comfortable with his own identity both as a business man and a family man.

Mr. Aldrich then invited me into the living room and Mrs. Aldrich introduced me to their teenagers, Rob and Mike, and Sherry and Kim. We all sat and immediately everyone began asking me questions about my background. The energetic atmosphere induced by the teens' genuine curiosity made me feel right at home. I loved their forward banter both with me and with one another. Mr. Aldrich sought to protect me from their intense inquisition, but, truth be told, their interest made me feel relaxed and a little bit important.

Soon it was nearly time for supper and Mrs. Aldrich retreated to the kitchen. Michael received the okay from his dad to start the music for supper. Mr. Aldrich had installed a state of the art music system and was able to pipe selected music anywhere in the house. I was most impressed by it and Michael showed great pleasure in being the one to play this most treasured piece of equipment.

In due time all the dishes for supper were simply displayed on the table; the linen tablecloth and serviettes lent a feeling of elegance to the dining experience. Soon everyone was seated except for Mrs. Aldrich. In my home, someone would have immediately begun serving himself. Not so, in the Aldrich home. When Rob reached out to retrieve a bun from the basket, Mr. Aldrich cleared his throat and manufactured a slight cough. This was all it took to correct Rob who was about to commit a faux pas. Immediately Rob dropped the bun, expressed a hasty but sincere, "Sorry, Dad," and as his mom approached, Rob went around the table to pull out her chair for her. This polite act of chivalry was not lost on this Trinidadian. Without their knowing it, I learned a great deal from their everyday acts of simple consideration for one another, especially at the table.

Supper was magnificent and when it came time for dessert, again, the teacher became the student. Everyone received a share of the dessert. Not one of the children began to eat. I too waited. I did not know why, but I waited. Then Mrs. Aldrich picked up her fork and had the first taste. All others followed suit. I marvelled how the family had found and then reinforced in their children a multitude of little ways to honour the mother in the home. What a wonderful tradition to observe.

When it came time to clear the table and attend to the dishes, both Mr. Aldrich and I were excused. The children all pitched in and helped the mom. Mr. Aldrich and I relaxed and enjoyed some quiet conversation in the living room until Mrs. Aldrich was able to rejoin us. One by one the children came into the living room and politely excused themselves as they had to begin preparations for school the next day.

After the children went their various ways, Mr. Aldrich quietly prodded, "Frank, Lyn tells me you are studying to become a teacher."

"Yes, I am."

"Will you stay here in Canada when you graduate?"

"No, I plan to return to Trinidad and work there."

"It seems to me that Trinidad is a developing country."

"It is a poor island in some respects. But it is rich in a number of other ways. Trinidad has a rich supply of oil as a natural resource. The other natural resource in Trinidad is its people; they are most hospitable. Mr. and Mrs. Aldrich, you will have to visit Trinidad and experience the island's hospitality."

Mrs. Aldrich interjected, "We can't wait. We would love to visit Trinidad. Both of us love to travel."

"Someday, Lyn," echoed Jack in agreement.

After chatting on for a while about Trinidad and my ardent desire to return there to work, Mr. Aldrich quite nonchalantly advised, "Frank, if it does not work out, stay in Canada. We understand your wish to return to your own homeland. But, speaking as a Canadian, we would love to have you with us here in Canada."

It was refreshing to hear Mr. Aldrich speak to me so candidly; I appreciated his words and I was most honoured to have the approval of this man for whom I was feeling such respect. The pull, however, to return to my native land and work with and for my own people remained strong. Thus that evening, and many subsequent ones, ended on a high note for me.

I knew that I would always be welcome in this home in spite of the fact that I never managed to get the names of the girls straight. For whatever reason, I invariably called Sherry, *Kim* and Kim, *Sherry*. My average percentage was 100% wrong. The girls must have grown tired of witnessing my struggles to differentiate between them and came upon a way to solve my difficulty—they wore name tags.

While I may have forgotten names, I have never forgotten the girls, the family, or the friendship.

55

Christmas of '69

Both Diana and I were looking forward to our first Christmas together in Rainy River—the Christmas of 1969. After our exams were finished and our assignments were handed in, we made plans to take the bus to Fort Frances at which point Diana's mom and dad would pick us up. We did not go home directly as I recall. We made a brief detour to Diana's aunt's house where I first met her Auntie Doris (Diana's mother's sister). I'll never forget that first meeting, for Auntie Doris was most forthright in manner.

Immediately after I was introduced as Frank, Auntie Doris asked, *How old are you?* I guess that I did not travel well and was probable sporting a five o'clock shadow at the time. She seemed satisfied with my response for no mention was ever again made referencing my age. The fact that Diana had barely turned twenty and that I was twenty-nine, seemed inconsequential; we were both in our twenties and that seemed to be that. Nothing more was said. (I noted how different Auntie Doris was from Diana's sister, Arlene. When I first met Arlene, I was struck by her down to earth and agreeable manner. I liked her right away and looked forward to our future visits.) After a brief visit with the family, we headed out in the green two-door Cutlass Supreme. Diana's brother, David, and his girlfriend, Linda, were with us for the trip home. We had to make a brief detour north of Stratton to take Linda back to her parents' home. Again we visited briefly with Linda's family and it was nearing midnight when we finally got back on the road. The snow was falling quite heavily at this time and the roads were exceedingly icy.

We had not gone more than a few miles when we noted that a car had skidded off the road and was stuck in a ditch. We all went to help rescue this disabled vehicle. It was my first venture as a good Samaritan— Canadian style. With all our combined efforts, we managed to get that car back on the road within minutes. It felt good to be part of the rescue effort. It was there that I first learned of the unspoken ethic that exists among Northerners— never forsake a neighbour in need.

This ethic was further reinforced only minutes later when we encountered yet another car in distress. This car had gone off the road completely and no amount of manual labour was going to alter the situation. Diana's dad stopped at a nearby farmer's house and explained the situation. Soon both the farmer and his tractor were on their way to the rescue. To alleviate the blackness of the night, Diana's dad positioned his car in such a way so that his headlights acted as spotlights lighting the way in the darkness. When the light from the tractor was interwoven with the lights from the two vehicles, a unique brightness was created amidst a universe of darkness. The beauty of the falling snow was captured by this light and I marvelled at the sight. (That is the memory I try to keep with me when I am struggling to keep my driveway clear of snow in the slushy ugly month of March.) After determining that all was well with the other vehicle, we headed to the Hammonds' home in Rainy River.

At some point during the holiday, Diana's mom and dad were entertaining friends around their dining room table. There was much camaraderie and joke telling. For most of the time I was merely an interested observer rather than an active participant. At some point, Diana's dad decided to tell a joke. That fact was no surprise to me for I was beginning to be aware of his propensity for telling jokes. What was surprising and somewhat startling, was the fact that his joke was directed at me.

"Well, Frank," he commented, "I would not feel too badly if I were you."

I looked and was puzzled as I did not understand where this remark was headed. I was uncomfortable for earlier auntie Doris had made a comment that had startled me somewhat. What was he about to do, now?

"That is about your colour, I mean," he continued.

Everyone settled into a quieter mood wondering just where he was going with this line of thought. He then continued, "You see Frank, about your colour… God forgot, for a moment, to take you out of the oven; this explains your pigment."

Everyone laughed, albeit, quietly.

A rare inspiration overtook me and I responded quickly, "That explains it, Mr. Hammond!"

"Explains what?" he asked.

"Well, looking at you, I would have to say that God took you out of the oven a little too soon."

This quick comeback brought forth peals of laughter from all gathered around the table. I worried that Diana's dad might fall off his chair as he was laughing so hard. And that, I believe, was a decisive moment for me as well as for Mr. Hammond. At that moment, he recognized that I had a sense of humour and that I could take care of myself. Well, I always knew that I could take care of myself, but as for me having a sense of humour… to that I could not attest; which explains why *I* was the most shocked by my own retort.

56

The Quarter

The spring of 1970 came not a moment too soon. While the crushing reality of academic responsibilities may have been behind me, the worry regarding my level of achievement was a constant preoccupation. Sparse finances further complicated my life and became a constant plague. Every day I searched for work.

Diana was already working at a bank in the downtown area. We had arranged to meet one evening to go out for dinner and a movie—a rare treat. While Diana knew that I was struggling financially, I could not divulge the true extent of my desperation.

It was a special occasion for the two of us. I believe that it may have been an anniversary of sorts. We always did something special to highlight each month on the anniversary of our first meeting or the first date. Usually it was something simple, like the sharing of an orange Popsicle or a peppermint flavoured Aero bar.

I wanted today to be different; today was a special anniversary and I had been saving my pennies, nickels and quarters for the occasion. I kept the money in a jar under my bed at the Coopers'; it was my special piggy bank. Today I was going to break into it.

With great anticipation I mounted the stairs to my bedroom. My heart skipped a beat when I felt under the bed for the familiar jar and it was not there. Panic set in as I went to the opposite side of the bed and it was not there either. I could find it nowhere.

I went downstairs quite perplexed by this most recent misfortune. Mrs. Cooper commented on my gloomy disposition, "Frank, you look down. What's the matter?"

"Mrs. Cooper, I must be losing my marbles!"

"Why, what happened?"

"I had a piggy bank of loose change under my bed. I don't know what I did with it. I can't seem to find it."

"Oh, *that* piggy bank."

"You know about it?"

"I have it! I hope you don't mind. I was cleaning your room and I knocked it over. And I needed change for our Girl Guides club. So I exchanged all that loose change for this." She reached into a cupboard, took an envelope, and handed it to me.

I was so relieved; I have no idea what I said to her; I just remember grabbing the envelope from her hands and tearing out of the house. There was just enough money in it to take care of the evening's expenses. I had to be careful for I did not wish to appear to be cheap in Diana's eyes. I contented myself with the thought that someday I shall have enough pennies in my pocket; someday I shall spend liberally, someday, but not today!

I could barely contain my excitement. Tonight we were going out on a proper date and I was treating!

Diana looked so happy when I met her just across from the Golden Dragon restaurant. She was so beautiful and I couldn't help thinking how lucky I was to have someone like her in my life. We strolled happily down to the corner where we were met by a shabbily dressed and unshaven man who asked, "Mister, can you spare some change, please?"

I looked at him. I did not have any extra pennies to spare.

Then he continued, "I am trying to catch the bus home. I've fallen on some bad luck. A quarter, surely you could spare a quarter."

Diana looked at me. It was obvious what she wished I would do, or *should* do. I was out on a date, and I wanted Diana to be proud of me. I wanted to be proud of myself. I reached into my pocket for a quarter and, albeit with some reluctance, I parted with it.

The man bowed his head and thanked me and walked away.

As he turned the corner, Diana said, "That poor man, he must not have gotten all the money he needed to make his bus fare."

"Diana, what do you mean?"

"Frank, that poor beggar must have been out here begging all day."

"How so, Diana?"

"Because, when I was on my way to work this morning, he stopped me and asked for a quarter too. I gave him one and when I got to the bank I talked with others who had also given him money. He must not have made enough yet because he is still out there. That poor man. I'm so glad you helped him too. He really needs the help."

"Excuse me, Diana."

I walked away and followed the beggar around the corner. Diana was just a little bit behind me as I caught up with him. Trying hard to maintain my composure, I commanded, "Give me back my quarter."

"What?"

"You heard me. Give me back my quarter. Put it in my hand, right now!"

I could see that Diana was perplexed by my action.

The beggar was stunned.

"You crazy or something?"

I raised my voice decisively and clearly reiterated every word of the command, syllable by syllable: "Put my quarter in my hand, NOW!" There was no mistaking my demand.

After considerable hesitation, he reached down into his pocket and pulled out the quarter. It was with great reluctance that he finally placed the quarter into my outstretched hand. He mumbled something inaudible and turned to leave. Loath to let him pass unscathed, I sought to detain him further and boldly ordered, "Now, you give *me* a quarter from *your* money."

"What? Are you crazy? You want me to give *you* a quarter? Why?"

"Because, I believe that I need the quarter more than you. You have no idea what I was willing to sacrifice to give it to you. And now that I know exactly what kind of a person you are and what you were going to do with it… Now, give me the quarter."

His hand was in his pocket…

57

Looming Finals

It was the spring of 1970. Examinations for the B.A. degree in English and Philosophy were close at hand. *Was I adequately prepared?* I admit that when I first met Diana, I had been distracted, and at times, lacked concentration… at the beginning. Then Diana steadied me and helped me considerably.

One way she helped was by proof-reading and editing my papers; it continues still today. I discovered that according to her, I did not always say what I intended, nor did I often finish what I was trying to say. Of course I protested, for a while that is, until I had the good sense later to see that she was right! Indeed, Diana possessed a competency in language and a polish that was second to none. Thank goodness I had the sense to recognize this, for it certainly heightened our academic relationship.

Thus, as the semester grew, whilst we were absorbed with each other, we did manage to attend to our studies, almost always faithfully.

The time came to write my examinations. I dearly hoped to be successful. At this particular time, I almost despaired, as so much was at stake. And exactly what was at stake? After all, for others, it was bandied around – "It's just a B.A.", or "That's no big deal." In essence, this B.A. degree was supremely important as it marked a pivotal sign staked on a post on the highway of my life. Successfully obtaining this degree was not just vital to *me*, it was important to my mother and to other members of my family as well. Perhaps more than anyone, this degree was essential to my brother Boysie.

Did he not shoulder the responsibility for supporting the family without me to help? Did he not release me and free me to pursue my studies? My brother would be overjoyed at my success. In a sense his investment in my freedom would entitle him, and quite rightly so, to a sense of pride. He could stand tall in our neighbourhood and proclaim to all that I was doing well.

I could just imagine hearing him say to his friends when they asked how I was doing, *Frankie doing great; he has a Degree…* and I did not wish to disappoint him.

Nervously, I awaited the results of my examinations.

58

Freed at Last

Early in my high school career, a teacher had assaulted my spirit with multiple condemnations. His words loudly proclaimed my ignorance and his position of authority lent credibility to his assertions. These two things acting in tandem, confirmed in me a belief that I did indeed belong in the house of the stupid.

In spite of such denouncements, some spirit within me fought hard against the tide of derision. There were people along the way who championed my cause and believed in me even when I doubted myself. I succeeded in some small way and managed to graduate high school by passing the dreaded Cambridge exam, and eventually assumed a teaching position in my beloved community, Tunapuna, in Trinidad. And now, here in Canada, I was about to be awarded my Bachelor of Arts Degree with a double major in English and Philosophy. The secret dream that I nurtured from my earliest years was now becoming a reality. I was overcome. What a moment in my life! I could not help but recall how my spirit protested inwardly when the teacher called me *stupid*. I would tell myself, *Ah don't know that I am smart, but I know I ain't that stupid.*

That quiet protest became my mantra; it became etched into my psyche allowing me to battle those elements that would have me believe that I was descended from a long line of the inferior.

Now, graduation day was a day not just of celebration, but also a day of gratitude. Today I had official proof that I had finally been released from the mansion of the stupid; I was freed at long last. Inwardly my spirit soared, and yet in the very midst of such ecstacy, I recalled that today was also a day, when I must return once again to my roots—to Trinidad—to

Ma. This humble achievement must be shared with her; it was the right thing to do; it was what I *wanted* to do.

It was nearing Mother's Day and I made my plans.

Trinidad, here I come.

59

Surprise Visit

She was scrubbing a huge pot outside in the corrugated cement sink next to the drainage ditch and was completely absorbed in the task; she did not see me approach, suitcase in hand. One of my sisters was standing in the gallery and burst out, "Oh, my gosh, Ma, look! It is Frankie. He come home."

Ma turned her head slightly to peer over her left shoulder and then she saw me. She dropped the clothes and came to me, "Frankie, Frankie yo home. Look at my hands. They dirty."

Grabbing her hands, I whispered, "Ma, you could never have dirty hands."

It was early evening and everyone except Boysie was home. One by one they came out to see what all the commotion was about. In the midst of the greetings, Ma asked hopefully, "Frankie, yo home for...?"

Before she could finish her sentence, *home for good*, I whispered, "No Ma, I still have to finish my studies. I came home for a short time only. I have good news."

By then we had been joined by a few of our neighbours; their appearance heightened the celebratory atmosphere. Usually Ma was patient at awaiting her time to talk privately with me. Today, she broke tradition and snatched me away from everyone and escorted me to the front steps. Never before had we two, sat together on those steps. I waited for her to speak. "Frankie, what's the good news, Son? I'm so happy to see you... and you have good news? Tell me, Son..."

"Ma, I passed my first big exam. I now have a degree, a degree in English..."

"Yo passed yo exam. Yo is qualified."

"Yes, Ma – but I still have another year to go. This extra year will help me to become better qualified."

"So yo have to go back, Frankie… Well, Son, yo always know what is best. Ah so happy to see you. Ah so proud of you."

Tears began to well in her eyes; before they could overflow their banks I attempted this distraction, "Well, Mother dear, are you going to help me?"

"Help yo, Frank? What yo talking about?"

"Help me celebrate."

"Oh, yes, Frank. What yo have in mind?"

"Ma, what do you think I should do to celebrate my success at university?"

"Ah know what we *have* to do. We will have prayers, Frank. But," she cautioned, "to do it right, we must invite the beggars."

"Yes, Ma," I agreed, knowing how important it was to her that she observe the traditions of her religion as she understood them.

Her happiness became my happiness.

60

A Lesson Taught by Ma

My time in Trinidad was limited; to label my trip as a vacation would not be accurate. True, I always managed to have a good time when I went back home and always seemed to be reinvigorated and refocused but this time, I actually returned home more on a mission than a vacation.

No sooner had I agreed to the idea of a prayer then Ma began initiating preparations. I knew that Ma had always advocated for me and on my behalf every time she bowed her head in prayer. Her prayers had been answered and it was proper to offer the gift of gratitude to God to acknowledge his role in our lives. This was to take the form of a prayer. In Trinidad, in our religion, a prayer is not merely the bowing of one's head in silent thought and meditation. It was so much more; it was an *event*. To host such an event required the preparation of special foods, the invocation of special prayers from ordained pundits, and the participation of special guests—the beggars. The fact that I returned home to honour this tradition gave Ma a sense of pride. To see her so happy made the trip well worth the cost.

At some point during the preparations Ma specifically requested that I approach a certain Hindu priest to request that he conduct the prayers.

To this end, she urged, "Frankie, yo better go and ask Pundit Manu to do the prayer. He is a busy man. Yo better hurry."

I, however, was conflicted about the reputation of this supposed religious man and expressed my objection to my mother, "But Ma, I do not want that man in our home; I want another pundit."

"Frankie, why yo object to Pundit Manu? Yo have a good reason?"

"Ma, Pundit Manu is not a true pundit. He is a scoundrel. He is..."

"Frankie, why yo call this priest a scoundrel?"

"Ma, I don't want to say why... He has a bad reputation."

"And, *Mister* Frankie, just what is this reputation that Pundit Manu has? Tell me."

"Ma, I'm sorry to talk this plain to you. Pundit Manu has a wife and children. He has another..."

I hesitated. I had never spoken like this before – I now found myself speaking or shall I say "judging" another human being.

"Frankie, finish yo thought."

"Ma he flirts with other women; moreover, he has another woman outside his marriage... "

I was embarrassed to be this direct with my mother... and on such a delicate subject.

"Frankie, what yo say, do yo know if it is all true? Do yo know this for a fact?"

"No, Ma, I do not really know this for a fact. I am told so."

"So, Mr. Frankie, yo went away, Son, and yo got a higher education. And now yo are ready to judge and condemn another person. That is not yo job, Frankie. *Let God do His job.* Let me do what I know is right. It is right for me to have this pundit do our prayer. If pundit is not faithful, that is between he god and he. I must do what is right. The right thing is to ask him to make the prayer. Understand?"

"Yes, Ma."

And humbly I bowed to her wisdom!

61

Bureaucracy Redefined - The Beggars' Demands

Inviting beggars to a prayer was as important a part of the ritual as having a pundit preside over the event. Honouring the beggars by inviting them to the prayer and sharing one's bounty with them, honoured God. This reminded me in some small measure of Christ's teachings when he said, *Inasmuch as you have done it to one of the least of these my brethren, ye have done it unto me.* Beggars were omnipresent while I was growing up. They were the truly unfortunate and had to beg in order that they might live. In my Hindu upbringing, I was taught that caring for the beggar class was an expression of one's obedience and devotion to God. It was with this mindset that I now resolved to approach the beggars and extend an invitation to our prayer.

Things, however had changed during my absence. No longer were the beggars visiting individual homes begging for portions of food as they had in the past. Boysie explained that I would find the beggars if I visited a certain rum shop in Tunapuna. I followed his direction and made my way to the designated site and entered. Immediately upon seeing me, the bartender asked, "What will you have?"

"Nothing right now, thanks. But, I could use your assistance."

"What yo need?"

"I need some beggars at my home for prayers. I was directed to your shop. Can you help me find them?"

"Wait here. I will get the Head Beggar."

A Head Beggar? Things certainly had changed. More than I had thought. My musings were interrupted when the bartended returned advising, "Mr. Gentleman, this is Mr. Ramkisson. He is the Head Beggar; he's in charge. Talk to him."

Wow! Things really had changed. This man before me looked like no other beggar I had ever seen. His clothing, while not state of the art, was far from tattered and worn. His hair, while perhaps not shining, was nevertheless, combed and lay nicely in place. I certainly never would have taken him for a beggar.

And now, yet another new concept. Not only is there a head beggar, he is also "in charge". *In charge of what,* I wondered. *Am I to understand that there is now an Association of Beggars?*

Mr. Ramkisson wasted no time with idle chatter as he commanded, "Follow me to my office."

He led me to a small table at the far corner of the makeshift bar. After asking me to take a seat, he then summoned the bartender and directed, "The usual."

Soon the bartender returned with two bottles of Carib Beer. After placing the beer on the table he remained standing in front of us—waiting. Mr. Ramkisson looked first at me, and then at the bartender. At first, I did not understand. It was only after he pulled out a wad of single dollar bills and nodded his head in the direction of the bartender that I got the message... I paid the bill.

Shaking his head, Mr. Ramkisson declared in a rather disparaging tone, "Most people catch on fast. Yo slow. Way yo from?"

"Right here, in Tunapuna."

"No, no. Yo born here. I know. But yo from away. Where?"

"Canada."

He rubbed his face and said nothing as he downed a good gulp of his beer. From a box on the table he retrieved a calendar and a pencil and asked, "What yo name?"

"Frank Maraj."

"Maraj, yes, that's quite a name. So you are a Brahman. Right?"

For me, answering this question in the affirmative posed a bit of a dilemma. Some Brahmans consider they are God's *chosen* Hindus – a superior class; such Brahmans succeeded in kindling resentment in others. Wanting to avoid inciting such a reaction, yet needing to answer him truthfully, I explained, "It is true that I am born the son of a Brahman; I, however, do not deserve such recognition."

"Yo wise. Now to business. What date yo want to book us?"

I indicated a day and a time.

He checked his calendar.

Snapshots II

I was quite perplexed by this new development—having to pre-book. As a child, I remember encountering beggars roaming the streets begging for something—grateful for anything. Ma always shared what little she had whenever she could. I remember her saying, "Giving to a beggar is like giving to God."

That simple precept was locked in my consciousness. It is the reason I returned to Trinidad. I wanted to honour my recent success at university knowing that Ma would be most pleased by such an acknowledgement.

At the moment, however, the joy I initially experienced in wanting to honour Ma's beliefs, was fading. This most recent development with the beggars added a new and invasive bureaucratic layer to what should have been a simple process. My task was becoming increasingly onerous and I was close to cancelling the whole thing when Mr. Ramkissson grinned and said, "Brahman Maraj, yo in luck. All ten of us will be there."

"Thank you, Mr. Ramkisson. Good day."

I turned to take my leave when Mr. Ramkisson's voice called me back, "Mr. Maraj, we not finished. There is the question of transportation."

"Transportation?"

"Yes, yes."

"What do you mean, Mr. Ramkisson?"

"Well, we don't walk like in the ol' days."

"But, it is not far..."

"Yo want us. Yo provide transportation. It is policy."

I was shocked. This beggar was no beggar; he had all the earmarks of a hard-nosed bureaucrat. In spite of a strong inclination to do otherwise, I conceded.

"I will make arrangements to have you picked up."

"No need. I arrange transportation. We don't want anyone to pile us on some ol' truck. No. We have our own contact."

"I understand. When you come, I will pay the fee. Thank you."

Once more I turned to leave when he yelled, "That ain't all."

I stopped and turned around.

"Mr. Maraj, son of a Brahman, there is something else."

"Something else?"

"It is the question of payment."

"Payment?"

"Oh, yes. It is important. We do not accept gifts of flour, rice, cloth, that kind of thing anymore. That's the ol' way. No, my friend, we accept cash only."

"Cash only?"

"Yes. Yo see if yo wants us, yo has to pay. Cash… a Brahmin must pay up real good. No, yo don't look like a cheapskate as so many Brahmans. Yo not?"

He was grinning. This beggar was so street smart, so clever and learned in his own way. Perhaps he was a bit too clever, too self-assured. He demanded, "Now yo need to give me a good down payment. Yo give me some good cash and we – all of we – poor beggars that we are—will see you."

"Sorry, Mr. Ramkisson. I will *not* see you."

"But, but why? Yo need us."

"Yes, I do need you, but… I am too poor.

I cannot *afford* you."

62

Ron French

The Prayer was just a couple days away. Ma had asked me to travel to south Trinidad to invite some relatives to the event. I obliged willingly.

It was whilst I was visiting the family in south Trinidad that I remembered a friend from Canada, Ron French.

At some point during the spring of 1970 I met Ron French. He was as uniquely inspiring an individual as I have ever had the pleasure of meeting. He had a mission and a vision in life; both were intertwined. He had been a teacher in Thunder Bay and was about to embark on a quest to Trinidad. Knowing this, someone decided that it would be good if we were to meet. Ron was making it his mission to bring a technical school to the island where the students would not only attend school, but would actively participate in building their own school.

Ron French was endowed with the gift of charisma. This gift combined with his genuine passion to make a difference in the world, drew others to him and to share in his vision. Diana and I were privileged to be counted among his many admirers.

One evening, Diana and I were invited to his country home as dinner guests. His wife, Betty was very cordial and their children were delightful. At that time they had two children of their own and one adopted child. I was enthralled at the reality of how they were truly living their philosophy. Their hearts and their home were open to those who wished to be a part of it.

Later that evening when supper was concluded, Ron and Betty withdrew to the living room. Diana and I followed. The conversation that followed caused me to understand more clearly what Ron had been up to lately. He had been seconded by an organization whose primary objective was to aid in the cause of education in the developing world. As such Ron was commissioned to help establish a school specializing in technical studies in the south area of Trinidad. I was deeply curious; to think that Ron here in Canada was about to travel to Trinidad to help build a school. Ron must have caught the sheer excitement in my visage for he asked, "Frank, how would you like to join me in Trinidad? I could use your help."

I was flabbergasted.

"Me, Ron... with you... in Trinidad?"

"Why not, Frank? We would be a team and I would love to have a person from Trinidad with me. We would build the school. I have a parcel of land already purchased for the school. Well, Frank, what do you say?"

I don't know which emotion I felt stronger: flattered or shocked. My mind was a tornado of thought as I tried to comprehend just how I could fit in to this new world with Ron.

Ron continued, "You know, Frank, we are going to need someone to take over the school when I leave... someone who is qualified. You are about to graduate from university, are you not? You would be quite suitably qualified." And then he added, knowing just how serious Diana and I had become, "And, I am sure there would be an opportunity for Diana also. It would be perfect for both of you. Frank, you would be paid a professional wage."

Ron's logic was convincing and his passion was intoxicating. I had to stop myself before I was swept away by his dream for I knew another reality. "Ron, hold on for a moment, please!"

Ron had painted a magical picture. He placed me as he envisioned it, in a position of privilege. There was one problem however, and I did not know how to voice it delicately. I was not *white* and as such I did not possess the obvious passport of approval that a foreign white professional was accorded. A white person from abroad involved in any capacity at a school would not be questioned, even if such a person did not have a degree. The fact that he was white, trumped every other credential. A local Trinidadian occupying any job in a leadership capacity would have to possess not just a degree; such a person would have to have additional qualifications. Therefore as much as I was tempted, I sensed that I was not ready. Besides, Diana claimed a special consideration; I just could not walk away from her. She was not yet ready to graduate. Regretfully, it was clear to me what my response to him would have to be.

"Ron, my friend, I am so sorry. I am not yet ready. I need to complete my teacher's credentials before I could presume to entertain such a thought."

I did not want to burden him with the other realities. After expressing his regret, he said that he understood.

Later, I would wonder if I had made the right decision by shutting myself off from the window of opportunity that would surely have led me back to Trinidad. *Had I indeed slammed the door of destiny on myself?*

63

The Prayer Event

Pundit Manu's flashy new car delivered him to our home. When he first stepped foot outside the vehicle, it was immediately apparent that his attire was no less pretentious than his car. His sparkling gold jewelry and garish costume stood in glaring contrast to our modest home. Furthermore, it was a stark reminder as to why I had been reluctant to have one such as he conduct prayers on my behalf. I pushed all such thoughts away, however, and made a determined effort to carry through with the original plan.

Ma and Boysie had invited close friends and family for the prayer of thanks and all were gathered outside under the shelter of a small tent. The tent consisted of a roof made from galvanized tin and supported by several lengths of wooden stilts. Under this shelter, Pundit Manu offered up prayers of thanksgiving to Brahma, the creator. Because he conducted the prayers in Hindi, I understood very little. The ceremony contained all the familiar trappings: incense, chanting, bells, and song. While the pundit's voice was most melodious and tuneful, I sensed that there was something amiss. He conducted himself as one in haste. In the past, such prayers required a dedication of no less than two hours of time; this event lasted a mere half-hour. The pundit apologized for his hastiness but quickly sought to justify his behaviour by saying that he was needed elsewhere.

He did, however, take time to *wait* while Ma retrieved a special bag in which she had placed the customary and obligatory offering – a portion of rice, potatoes, fruit, and cash. Instead of acknowledging with gratitude her modest offering, he took his time to advise her, "Bea, today I am on the go. Sorry, it would be better to have just cash."

This request of *just cash* further delayed his departure as Ma went off in search of more money. Before she could complete her search, I reached into my wallet and pulled out a Canadian bill to supplement her offering.

Seeing the Canadian currency, the pundit's eyes beamed happily and he uttered a hasty, *Thank you, thank you,* as he left. The Canadian bill was worth five times the Trinidadian currency. No wonder he was ecstatic.

I, however, remained sad; I had wanted the priest to stay for I had many questions. There was much that I needed to understand.

I looked appreciatively at the gathering of family and friends knowing that they had come to celebrate with me and to honour my mother. They smiled at me and I smiled back at them. Each smiling face brought me further and further away from the image of the counterfeit pundit.

Then I looked at Ma; her face was aglow; her smile could not be contained. Her happiness was childlike and real. The veil of white that draped her head proclaimed her innocence. I could not help but think that surely this mother, this Ma of mine, was to be counted among *the pure of heart,* and I was moved.

In spite of everything, my prayer had been answered. Now, I must return to Canada.....

PART IV

Explorations & New Horizons

64

Mindless Danger

Upon returning to Canada I immediately began my search for a job. While I was anxious to find one, I was not desperate. Since receiving my Bachelor degree, my status in Canada had changed; I was now considered to have *Landed Immigrant* status. As a landed immigrant, I was no longer restricted to working during the summer months only. I was now permitted to work without restriction throughout the entire year.

While my trip to Trinidad had proven costly, I had no regrets about making it. When I made the decision to return home, I knew that I would be able to accept work—any work—at any time. This knowledge eased the emotional burden of the financial debt that I had recently incurred. This knowledge, in and of itself, proved exhilarating.

Within days of my return I had secured a well-paying job with Brayshaw Steel. The business was located between the two cities of Port Arthur and Fort William on Memorial Avenue. It appeared to be quite a huge company. The workers at the Memorial Street location prepared steel beams for sale. When the beams first came into the plant they were of one uniform length. In the building where I worked, these beams were cut to order according to the specific needs of the local customer. My job was simple. I was responsible for cleaning the edges of the freshly cut beams; I accomplished this with the aid of a special electric hand held grinder. The job itself required little skill; the execution was simple and quite routine. It was purely physical; there was no mental challenge to the task.

The work day began at eight-thirty and ended at five o'clock. The first few days went well, but soon the task of grinding became routine. I was the lone worker in my station; I could hear happy voices coming from other areas in the plant.

The clock on the wall directly in front of me soon became the enemy. The first few days of work were days of adjustment and passed fairly quickly. Rarely did I have occasion to look at the clock. Once I had my routine down pat, I found myself looking at the clock quite regularly. Time seemed to be standing still.

The routine quickly turned to drudgery; this, in turn, escalated to boredom. I was in trouble. I was not enjoying my job at all. In an attempt to alleviate the boredom, I invented "the mind" game. Each day as I began my work, I imagined myself in a variety of situations. On this particular day I began imagining that I had just come into a massive fortune. Rich beyond measure, I was planning what I would do with my fortune. Thus engaged, I did not see, nor feel the tug on the electric cord when another worker walked past me and accidentally walked into the cord. This action caused a slight jolt to my right hand, the hand that was holding the grinder. Before I knew it, the grinder had slipped off the beam and had struck my left wrist.

I remember the tug at my wrist.
I remember falling.
I remember blood oozing.
Then I remember no more.
Hours elapsed.

I awakened in the emergency room of the Port Arthur General Hospital. I was surprised to see both the manager and my supervisor from Brayshaw Steel present in the room. They seemed very concerned. My supervisor approached and set a box of chocolates on a side table. Then the manager spoke, "Frank, so good to see you awake. How are you feeling?"

"Fine, thank you. So good of you to bring a box of chocolates."

"You are welcome, Frank. I have a matter to talk over with you. Perhaps another time?"

"No, it's okay. We can talk now."

"Well, it concerns your job. I know you may not wish to work at the steel plant anymore. A bit dangerous, don't you think, Frank?"

"Sir, it was probably my own fault. I should have been more..."

"Nonsense, Frank. It was an accident."

"Thank you."

"And, Frank, I want to help you."

"Help me, Sir?"

"Yes. If you need a recommendation for another job, I would gladly provide one."

"Oh, thank you. That would be most helpful."

"Meanwhile, hold onto this." He handed me an envelope and said, "I hope this helps. See you around, Frank. Good luck on your new job."

After the men left, I opened the envelope and discovered a cheque for a week's worth of work. I was touched by the kindness of this gentleman. Not only had he gone out of his way to see me, he also had offered me an extra week's wages—wages that I had not yet earned. I was unaccustomed to such generosity in the work place. (Weeks later, and purely by chance, I happened to discover that I could have sued the company for my injury and my loss of ability in my left arm. Would I?)

After I was sufficiently recovered, I set about the business of finding another job.

If nothing else, the job at Brayshaw steel proved to me this one irrefutable fact: the most difficult job for me would be one that is boring. Accordingly, I set my sights on finding one that engaged both my mind and my body.

65

Roach's Taxi Experience

Prepping for the New Job

Roach's Taxi was located on Cumberland Street in downtown Port Arthur directly opposite the Prince Arthur Hotel. It was a warm spring day and two of the cab drivers had their vehicles on the lot facing Cumberland. The drivers were actively engaged in conversation with one another. Each driver looked very professional in a shirt and tie. What impressed me the most however, were the hats. Each driver wore one that proudly displayed his badge. There was something about that scene that proved to be irresistible to me; I wanted to be one of those drivers. Imagine those two drivers chatting away and getting paid. (Such was my naïve thought. Little did I realize that when one was not driving, one was not earning.) I wanted a job driving taxi.

The question remained, how does a Trinidadian who is a relative newcomer to the city and who does not know the city very well, become a taxi driver?

Just like everything else in my life, I knew that I needed to study. I needed to study, yes, but not in the ordinary sense. I needed to feel the city and read the city. I got a city map and studied the main arteries and located where all the main points of interest were in relation to the main roads. I committed these to memory. Next, I boarded a city bus and rode it from beginning to end, noting all the major intersections and major points of interest. I took my notes home and studied them and was able to address the more obvious sites such as the airport, hospitals, malls, clinics, hotels and bars. Not so obvious were individual street addresses. However, once I mastered the major arteries, with a little help, I knew that I could find almost any address once I could associate it with a particular area of the city.

I made up various tests for myself. I would take the names of specific addresses and try to visualise how I might get there. Having formed an answer, I then looked at the map to check my accuracy. I did quite well.

I decided that it was time to take the exam. To that end, I determined to make my way to Roach's Taxi the very next day.

******

The Interview

The dispatch centre and main office of Roach's Taxi was located in the basement of the building. A steep set of stairs led directly down to the basement offices. There was a bench situated along the wall and several chairs were scattered randomly about the room. I came to the office of the dispatcher first. The dispatcher saw me and asked, "Are you looking for a taxi?"

"No, I'm not looking for a taxi. I'm looking to drive one."

"Excuse me?"

"Sorry. I'd like to see the person in charge. I'm looking for a job."

"A job?"

"Yes."

"Then you must see Mr. Carl Roach," whereupon, she wheeled around in her office chair and called out into the next room, "Carl! Someone here for you." She then motioned to me to take a seat.

A moment later, Carl Roach came out of his office and pulling up a chair beside me, asked, "You wanted to see me?"

"Yes."

"What can I do for you?"

"Give me a job."

"Give you a job? You came here to ask me for a job—to drive taxi?"

"That is correct."

He appeared shocked. He was quiet for a moment as he considered my request. When he spoke, he chose his words very carefully, "I am sorry; I don't have any job to offer. But what kind of a job were you interested in?"

"I want to drive taxi."

"Drive taxi?"

"Yes, very much!"

"But you are not from here. Where are you from?"

"Trinidad."

"Trinidad, that is British, is it not?"

"Yes, it is."

"Don't you drive on the left side of the road?"

"Yes, we do."

"Well, I am mighty curious. What makes you think that you can drive taxi here at the Lakehead? It simply would not work; you need another type…"

"No, Mr. Roach, I want to drive taxi. Your taxi… Roach's Taxi."

He was pensive for a moment. Then he explained clearly, "Frank, it would be near impossible for you to drive taxi here. You are at a distinct disadvantage. You're a newcomer to the Lakehead, and you would not know the area. It takes…"

"Preparation!" I finished his sentence for him and then added, "Of course, what you say makes perfect sense. For the moment, please go along with me. Test me."

"Test you?"

"Yes. Assume I lived here; now select some places any taxi driver should know and ask me if I were a taxi driver, how I get there. But start at the obvious places."

Again he was thoughtful. So far I felt that I still had a chance with this man. I had a feeling that I would enjoy this type of work. It was a far cry from my previous job. I would not be required to handle heavy machines. I would be working and interacting with people all day long. I would not be bored. In that respect, cab driving was like teaching. I would be exposed to a wide variety of people and personalities.

I looked at this man called Carl Roach and knew instinctively that I wanted to work for him. He struck me as a very honourable and decent man. Mr. Roach now looked at me and stated, "Well, Frank, I will go along with you for a moment. Are you ready?"

"Absolutely."

He began to test me on the most obvious places, such as malls, hospitals and the airport. Gradually he redirected the focus of his questions to the major arteries and highways. All these I answered correctly. He smiled then added, "Frank, I am impressed. How do you know so much?"

"Mr. Roach, I bought a map and rode the buses learning the sites as I travelled."

"So you came prepared. You actually *studied* for this test I gave you."

"Yes, Mr. Roach."

"That's the easy part of the test. Here comes the hard part of your test. Are you ready?"

"Yes, Mr. Roach."

"I would like you to go to, let's say, Elm Street. What is the route?"

I got out the map and checked the index. I located the coordinates and applied it to the map. I found it and responded, "Go to High Street, cross Red River, and it is located close by."

He proceeded to challenge me with some more addresses, and I followed my procedure taking care to be quick in the execution.

Mr. Roach voiced his surprise in a compliment, "Well, well. I am impressed. I cannot believe that you, a student from Trinidad, actually bought a map, studied, learned, and prepared for this job. Frank, I feel that I must at least give you a chance."

"Oh, Mr. Roach, thank you. I am so happy."

"Now, Frank, I am Carl. No more Mr. Roach. Wait a moment while I give you a *referral* to get your badge – your taxi badge."

"My own taxi badge, Carl?"

I had difficulty calling my future boss by his first name, but I managed. Rules seemed so much more relaxed here in Canada. In Trinidad, most bosses wanted to be addressed as Mister. This was the preferred custom of the day. In my mind I practised saying the name *Carl* over and over. I liked both the man and the name and I wanted the word to flow respectfully from my mouth.

Carl smiled as he handed me the address and the referral note, "Here is the address, Frank, and a signed referral. You will be asked to take a test. When you have your badge, come see me."

"I will, Carl, I will."

"Now, don't get your hopes up, Frank. I don't have any openings at the present time."

"Carl, I have a good feeling about this."

"Frank. Good luck."

I just couldn't wait...

******

An Opportunity

Several days later, with beaming face and pounding heart, I returned to the office of Carl Roach. When he caught sight of me in the outer office, he approached. Proudly I displayed my Badge #101.

A broad smile came easily to his face and I felt his genuine happiness for me, "Congratulations, Frank. You are now officially a cab driver." Then he added more solemnly, "But, you are a cab driver without a cab..."

Not dissuaded in the least, I responded, "Not for long, Carl. I'm not going anywhere else for a job. I am staying with you. It will work out. I know it."

The dispatcher, Jerry, heard me and interjected, "My, Frank, you certainly are optimistic."

Carl returned to his office to resume his duties. I was happy that he had come out to acknowledge me. I was at peace and was content to just remain in the office soaking in the day's routines. I took advantage of the opportunity to just witness how the business was run. I watched Jerry as she conducted her dispatches over the phone. I marvelled at her ability to resolve a variety of situations with calm efficiency. Such competency was the daughter of experience and confidence. When a driver did not know how to get to a certain address, she did not panic or berate the operator; she actually assisted him by informing him as to the best route. She accomplished all this in a most professional manner. She was very good at her job and I reminded myself what a wonderful resource she could be if I were to run into difficulties. From that moment on, I regarded her and the job she did with utmost respect never doubting for a moment that we would become coworkers.

At various times, Carl would leave his office and come in to talk with Jerry. I noted how he did not just sit in his office and bark out commands. He treated his staff with respect and consideration. I paid attention to every word, every nuance. More than ever, I knew that I wanted to work for this man.

After some time had elapsed, I sensed that it was time for me to leave. Not wishing to disturb anyone, I rose quietly from the bench and was about to climb the stairs when one of the younger drivers hurriedly brushed past me, nearly knocking me over. He appeared emotionally distraught. I turned to follow him back into the office as the drama unfolded. I heard him say, "Carl, I cannot finish my shift. My girlfriend is in the hospital. She...."

Carl appeared quickly from his office, reached out with some reassuring words and directed, "Percy, calm down. Now explain to me what is happening."

Hurriedly but more calmly, Percy recounted his story to Carl. When he was finished, Carl released Percy from his duties so that he could attend his girlfriend. Seconds later, Percy was once again rushing past me. I doubt that he even noticed me; he truly was a man on a mission.

Looking up, Carl saw me in the doorway and declared, "Well, Frank, how would you like to finish Percy's shift?"

"I would love to. But… will Percy be okay?"

"Oh, yes. It's just a minor matter really. Percy just…Don't worry. He'll be okay. Now, let me tell you how the business part of cab driving works."

"I'm ready."

"Better yet, let me take you to Percy's car and explain things."

Outside, stood the cab—a burgundy and white Chevrolet Impala. The hood of the car and the writing on the doors were burgundy; everything else was white. It was beautiful. Even the seats were burgundy. Compared to the cars back home, this one was huge. I delighted in its spaciousness.

Carl then briefly explained how the radio system worked and I nodded my understanding. He further warned me that if I received any speeding tickets, I had to pay the bill myself—not the company, regardless of the circumstance. About that one point, he was most emphatic. Again I nodded my understanding.

Then came his final point.

"Frank, for every dollar charged to the customer, you receive forty percent; the company nets the remaining sixty percent. Do you understand?"

"Yes."

"Do you have any questions?"

"Just one."

"What is your question?"

"Carl, I was under the impression that your drivers were paid a salary or an hourly wage."

"Wherever did you come up with that idea, Frank? No, Frank. I am afraid that taxi driving is no piece of cake. To make money in this business, you have to hustle. Hustling is the name of the game. Now, are you ready?"

I nodded.

Carl left.

I marvelled at how quickly my illusions about cab driving were being shattered. But, it was just the illusions that were being shattered, not me. My world was not collapsing, just evolving. I had to adjust to my new reality. Although I was somewhat disappointed, I understood the economics from the owners' point of view. They could not pay their drivers if there was no money coming in.

Then I caught sight of the hat that Carl had left on the seat of the car for me. I attached the badge to the hat and put the hat on my head. I looked at myself in the mirror in the cab and thought, "Not bad, not bad at all… for a Trinidadian."

66

My Fare Lady

Within minutes I was dispatched to my first call—to the local Safeway store. And so I began. When I was negotiating my first right turn I had to quickly readjust my driving technique. Having been accustomed to only manual drive back in Trinidad, I was totally unprepared for the ease of movement of this automatic. As a result, I over did the turn and the car veered strongly to the right. I braked so quickly that my head nearly hit the dashboard. Once I realized that this vehicle had *power everything*, I adapted my style accordingly. I had only moments to adjust as Safeway—and my first passenger—was only a few blocks away.

My fare must have been watching for me, for no sooner had I pulled up to the store when I was being hailed to come into the store. The lady had a minimum of twenty bags of groceries in her cart. She explained that she had a bad hip and needed assistance getting everything into the cab. I gladly accommodated her and even made my heart be happy throughout the execution. *It was the right thing to do*, I told myself.

She lived a couple of blocks away only so I turned off the meter as we arrived at the house. I grabbed the first few bags and headed for the front door. She directed that I should bring the bags around to the back door because that was where the kitchen was. After letting herself in the front door, she walked back towards the back of the house to instruct me further. She was unable to come down the four steps from her kitchen to the back door landing. She thanked me ever so much for my assistance, but *there was no one else at home so could you please bring the rest of the groceries around?* Without a word of complaint, I grabbed the rest of her bags and placed them on the floor of the kitchen.

Then she asked me to carry three of the bags to the basement.

I opened the door to the basement. The steps were narrow and dangerously steep. I obliged this lady and her ailing hips.

When I finished this final task, she asked me what the fare was. I answered, "The meter reads eighty cents."

She reached for her change purse and carefully counted out two quarters, two dimes and two nickels—eighty cents exactly.

She did, however, say a very sincere *thank you*.

Climbing back into my cab, I could not help but wonder, "Am I back in Trinidad doing favours for the elderly? Am I wrong to hope for a tip?"

Oh, well, I sighed, *I really must look on the bright side of things. After all I did just earn thirty-two cents; a little more than enough to buy me a first cup of coffee.*

67

Her Highness Mrs. P

As the summer of nineteen seventy rolled on, at first, I was just getting an occasional shift here and there at Roach's Taxi. Gradually, they began to add in more shifts. When I first started working there, I noticed that the crew kept a respectful distance from me. Entry into their ranks was not freely offered. While I wore the outward trappings of a cab driver, I knew that I would have to earn my entrance into their exclusive "club" by proving myself. How I was actually supposed to do that remained a mystery. I kept alert for any opportunity. Meanwhile, I tried to give everyone time to adjust to my presence. Thus, I too, kept a respectful distance; endeavouring all the while to remain polite, friendly, and obliging.

From bits and pieces of "overheard" conversation, I quickly learned that previous "educated" drivers may have assumed an air of superiority among the less "formally" educated drivers. I took extra precautions to guard against giving out such an impression. Having worked at a variety of jobs both in Trinidad and Canada, one thing I knew for certain was that we could all learn from one another irrespective of our educational qualifications.

The fact that I was a university student often worked against me… in the beginning.

I'll never forget the day or the incident that precipitated a change in attitude from the drivers. It was Saturday and dispatch directed me to a pick up from a hairdresser's salon. I was given very specific instructions about how to conduct myself while picking up this fare. I was told that it was imperative that I not remain sitting in the cab when I reached the salon. I was to go inside and *accompany* Mrs. P to the vehicle. The dispatcher took special pains to stress the importance of that last step on my psyche. I assumed (wrongly) that Mrs. P had some sort of disability and required assistance and I was indeed happy to comply with the order.

The salon was just a short distance away; I made it there within minutes of being dispatched. Following orders, I parked the vehicle and proceeded inside to await my fare.

Within seconds, a voice proclaimed, "About time, Sonny."

The voice belonged to an elegantly clad lady. I could not help but reflect how ill-suited her voice was to her vestments. Her hair, however, was a complete match to the voice as it too was at once both offensive and conspicuous. Her hair was piled layer upon layer and extended well into the atmosphere. The sight reminded me a little of a movie clip I had once seen about a birdcage that had been securely positioned amongst a similar layering of hair. (For a moment I wondered how I might fit her and all her layers into my cab.)

With the echo of her words still reverberating in my brain, she commanded further, "Come here, Sonny. Lend a hand."

"Yes, Ma'am," I obliged as I quickly moved to her side.

She clasped hold of my arm and I escorted her outside to the awaiting taxi. Knowing that many Canadians preferred to sit up front in the cab and chat with the drivers, my hand almost reached out for the front door out of sheer habit. Something inside me screamed that this lady was no front seat fare.

There was something about her demeanour that transported me back through time to Trinidad where distinctions according to "class" were a daily reality. No sooner had I opened the back door then I was rewarded with, "Well, Sonny, good for you. You know where a lady sits."

Closing her door, I returned to the driver's side. Even before I could turn to ask for her address, she announced, "Now, Sonny, I do like your attire. Very professional—not like—well, that's a completely different matter." Then she instructed, "Take me to the Towers. I believe that you know where that is."

"Yes, Ma'am." Everyone knew the Towers. At the time it was the tallest building in the city… and among the most exclusive places to live.

As I started to move the car out of *park,* I turned on the meter. No sooner had I done so when she announced, "Sonny, no matter what route you take to the Towers, the fare will be ninety cents, and not one penny more."

"Yes, Ma'am."

Just before we got to the Towers, I hit a red light. During the time that elapsed waiting for the light to turn green, the meter reached the ninety cent mark. Not willing to risk facing her possible ire at a fare higher than that which she had previously stipulated, I turned off the meter. I drove right to the front of the apartment building and stopped the car. I went around to her side of the vehicle and, after opening her door, I extended my arm out to her to assist her from the cab. I escorted her into the building and marched her right up to the elevator located in the lobby. Still she made no move to pay. Wondering what else was required of me, I pushed the button to summon the elevator. Then she reached into her purse and pulled out a single dollar bill. Without saying a word, she handed me the dollar. I reached into my pocket, produced a dime, and placed it in her hand. Somewhat surprised, she looked first at the dime and then at me. "Now, Sonny, you were a very good boy. This tip is for you." And then she attempted to place the dime in my hand.

I reached out and folded the dime back into her hand, declaring, "Mrs. P, if you *expect* to be *treated* royally, then you must be prepared to *remunerate* in an equally royal measure. It appears that *you* need this dime even more than *I* do."

When I left, she was still standing in front of the elevator doors with her mouth open.

Once in the cab, I started to head to the office. Before I made it back to the stand, the solemn voice of Carl Roach himself came over the air waves, "Frank Maraj."

"Yes, Carl."

"Please come to the office, immediately."

"Yes, Sir."

The tone of his voice inspired me to call him *Sir* rather than the more conventional *Carl* that I had been using up until that point. Something was up. I wondered if it had anything to do with me. I didn't have long to wait for my answer.

Before I could reach his office, Carl came out to confront me, "Frank, what on earth did you say to Mrs. P?" Then, not waiting for a response, he continued, "Did you say something about tipping royally? And then, did you insult her by giving her back her dime and by telling her that she needed it more than you?" When I did not answer immediately, he pushed, "Well, Frank, did you?"

I had never seen Carl so animated, so emphatic. Words failed me; my face revealed all. Carl, however, wanted confirmation in words. "Frank, it is easy," he continued. "This is not a complicated question. Did you tell her those things?"

Looking Carl squarely in the face, I responded, "Yes, Carl, I said those things. I am sorry that my remarks were misunderstood."

"Misunderstood?"

"Yes, Sir."

"Frank, do you know who Mrs. P is?"

"No, Sir."

"I thought not. She is the mother of a very distinguished man here in the city. And you insulted her."

"I am so terribly sorry I have caused trouble. I did not mean to do so, Sir."

"Alright. I will phone her and apologize. Whatever made you say that to her, Frank?"

Jordy, the veteran driver, had been downstairs and had overheard everything. He had his hand over his mouth trying to contain his amusement. When Carl went back into his office to make the call, Jordy asked, "Frank, did you really tell *her majesty* to *tip royally*?"

"Jordy, I'm sorry; I did do that."

Then Jordy surprised me by saying, "Don't be sorry, Frank. You did all of us a favour. If you only knew how long we have all wanted to say something like that to her. Man, I gotta hand it to you Frank. You really delivered. You defended us; you are our hero."

Thereafter, I was welcomed into the drivers' inner sanctum.

68

A Taste of Winter… Driving

Summer had long since gone; fall weather descended on the Lakehead ever so quickly. Carl retained me on a part-time basis. Car number 7—that shiny Chevy Impala—was officially designated as "Frank's," whenever it was available. I loved that car. Whenever I could, I would take it for a wash; now and then I would take it in for a service check. Number 7 had to be impeccable.

But, one day, I very nearly destroyed Car 7.

Everyone familiar with Port Arthur and Fort William knows that Fort William is flat and Port Arthur is hilly. Along with the spectacular views that the hills provide, come some unique winter driving challenges. Up until then, all my driving had been done on summer roads only.

On this particular day, I was sent to an address that was located near the top of a hilly street. After picking up my three fares, two in back, one in front, it started to snow… heavily. In minutes the road was completely covered in white. As a pedestrian, I welcomed the snow and delighted in its beauty. As a new driver in Canada, I was as yet, uninitiated in recognizing its inherent dangers. As I made a turn from Red River Road and neared Port Arthur Collegiate High School, the road was steep and all downhill. At first, the road ahead of me appeared free of traffic but just as I was about to negotiate my turn, a bus appeared directly in front of me. We were on a collision course. I applied the brakes… forcefully. Car 7 did not stop. In fact, it appeared to pick up speed and then spun into a three hundred and sixty degree turn. Finally the car came to a stop in the middle of the street narrowly avoiding disaster. Pulling over to the right, I stopped the car and apologized, "Sorry about that. Everyone okay?"

I waited for the chastisement that I was certain was coming. To my great surprise, the passenger in the front remarked, "Man, that was some driving. Brilliant."

The other two nodded their agreement.

I alone appeared to be the dissenter.

I alone knew that brilliant driving technique had nothing whatsoever to do with what had just happened.

Pure and simple good luck had been with me on that day.

Would an equal measure of good fortune await me at university?

69

Ye Cannot Enter...

I am not likely ever to forget the Anglican Minister who taught a course in comparative religion at the university; his name was Dr. Morris. The class was relatively small and we often met in a seminar room around a long table. Because the class was small, we came to know our professor very well.

Although Dr. Morris was a minister with a Christian background, I sensed that he tried very hard to present the religious material of the course without bias. Not one of us would fault him if occasionally it appeared that his Christian views dominated. We all knew him to be a man of deep faith and conviction. While he never tried to impose in any overt manner, his Christian viewpoint on us, we understood that unconsciously he would lean toward the Christian perspective.

During one particular lecture, Dr. Morris was instructing us in a segment regarding the early phase of Christianity. Towards the end of the lecture, he offered up the following quote for our consideration:

Except ye be born of Christ, ye cannot enter the Kingdom of God.

Following the lecture, he asked, "Students, any questions?"

Not one person had a question; I had a million.

But, I was unable to give my question a voice for I did not know quite how to frame it.

Since there were no questions, Dr. Morris continued on with his plans and passed out a list of essay topics and announced that the essays were due at the end of the semester. The groans began immediately following the announcement. *"Not another essay, again!"*

I perused the list of topics carefully; not one of them struck a chord. Perhaps my mind was still distracted by the statement made earlier by Dr. Morris; nothing seemed to be able to shake it from my mind.

In a matter of minutes, everyone had left the room. Only Dr. Morris and I remained. Noting the troubled expression on my face, Dr. Morris inquired, "Something the matter, Frank?"

Even if I could have spoken, I am not sure that I would have been able to adequately articulate my concern regarding the words that Dr. Morris had quoted. Thus, I remained silent. Dr. Morris persisted, "Frank, you look so lost, so troubled. How may I help you?"

And then a thought came to me and I acted on it at once, "Dr. Morris, may I do my essay on a concept you raised in class, *Except ye be born of Christ, ye cannot enter the Kingdom of God*?"

"Frank, I don't know. Let me think."

As he thought, a flood of questions filled my mind regarding this essay. I even questioned myself regarding the wisdom of the request. *If he agrees, how would I begin to investigate? What am I getting myself into?*

Before giving me an answer, Dr. Morris had a question for me, "Frank, do you have any ideas about what you wish to do?"

In a flash an answer came to me, "Yes, Dr. Morris, I know what I would like to do."

"Good, good. Tell me."

"Dr. Morris, I would like to explore the main tenets of Christianity, Islam, and Hinduism. I would like to explore these in the hopes that I can explain the statement, *Except ye be born of Christ, ye cannot enter the Kingdom of Heaven*."

Satisfied, Dr. Morris consented, "Frank, I look forward to your essay."

I could hardly contain my excitement and I couldn't wait to delve in to the essay.

Thus, I began my research on the three religions. As I read I made an essential discovery regarding how we are to treat one another during our brief sojourn here on Earth. Each religion emphasized that we are to be of service to our fellow man; this was crucial in determining entry in God's kingdom. Now what remained was to address the singular Christian claim that Christ was the sole port of entry to Heaven; because this precept was so specific and restrictive, I was somewhat stymied as to my next move.

Some time later, I was studying the Gospel of Mark at the university library in one of the carrels. For a brief moment I was lost in reflection just staring out the window while holding the book loosely in my hands. Someone came by and accidentally bumped into the desk. This unexpected action caused the book to fall to the ground. As I knelt down to retrieve the book, I noticed that it had opened to a different page. The words underlined on that page caught my attention.

I know it is written an eye for an eye...but I say unto you. For him that striketh thee on one cheek, offer him the other.

I remember that in high school my teacher had explained that those lines meant that one should not retaliate. I understood what my teacher said, but in my heart I wanted to know more; I wanted to go deeper into the concept... beyond the idea of not retaliating.

I reflected on those lines for a while. Did Christ mean for us to offer up our faces so that someone might beat on us freely? I knew that that response was without merit. But, what exactly did he mean? What message were those words meant to convey? When the answer came to me it was like a revelation. Christ was ushering in a new order that transcended the old way of thinking about justice as an "eye for an eye". According to Jesus, it is not enough to just not retaliate; we must find a way to heal by not hating the person who has transgressed against us. Not only must we not hate the transgressor, we are to let go and forgive the transgressor. It is in this very act of forgiving that our soul becomes sanctified.

And what did Hinduism offer regarding this same subject? According to Hinduism, the ill act of your offender essentially must be blotted out of the soul in order that the soul can attain a closer union with the great Atma. A warring soul falls down and unwittingly descends yet closer into the dark pit of oblivion. Thus, at the heart of human conduct, both in Christianity and Hinduism, is the promise that Grace and Civility are the twin powers that enshrine all humanity. This same concept underscores the spirit of peaceful Islam.

Once I reasoned that Jesus did not mean literally speaking, that we were to offer our cheek to our enemy, it took that same train of thought to examine the edict, *except ye be born of Christ, ye cannot enter into the Kingdom of God.*

There is a sadness in me for the one who holds that concept like a loaded gun and aims it directly at our hearts. Proponents of this philosophy threaten us to accept the mere *literal* translation of these words—*accept it as is – here it is from the Christ himself –* or die. To refuse to accept these words as the *only* truth is akin to being shot down by a gun forged in ignorance and fired in arrogance. How must Jesus Christ weep to witness such conquest in His name!

I cannot reconcile that the utterance of St. Augustine then is proclaimed so boldly as an ultimate exactitude. Then how does one explain

St. Augustine's edict. In one sense, Augustine was right in that *except ye be born of Christ, ye cannot enter the Kingdom of God*.

It is my understanding, and I might be mistaken, that some three hundred years after the death of Christ, St. Augustine delivered this edict. He delivered it to a people who were not far removed from the stories and the time of Christ. The world that existed then bears no resemblance to the world of today. Augustine did not know that beyond his country existed the landmass of Asia, nor did he know that the continents of the Americas existed. When Augustine spoke of the world, he essentially was addressing a world – a familiar world of the Judeo-Christian domain. In such a context, the essential claim of his text is valid. He singled out a people from his own era who had gone astray and admonished them severely. His remarks were directed at those inhabiting his world; he told them that unless they abandoned their worldly and reckless ways and return to Christ, then they would not enter the Kingdom of God. It was my conviction then, and remains so still today, that we must not take the utterances of St. Augustine and use them as a badge to be flashed to a non-Christian as if to say, "If you don't have the badge of a Christian, why then, you are a sinner and hell awaits you." How must Christ weep at the misplaced understanding of his followers.

I believe that anyone, yes anyone, who is *Christ-like* can enter the Kingdom of God, for God created the world.

For whom did God build His world?

This question needed to be addressed. I did not wish to presume that I knew the mind of God, for indeed I did not. Did I have a faith in the Almighty? Yes! And it was that very faith that lead me to believe that God existed and that He created us *all*. He gave us the gift of free choice; all He asks of us is that we all make good choices whilst we are here on our earthly sojourn. His mansion has several rooms; there is room for us all: for the Christians, for the Hindus, for the Muslims, and for all who seek God. Indeed we are now in a mansion without walls. When we are in God's mansion, we are truly with God and are part of his *Godness*; hence we have become one with God.

The question remains, however, how do we discover this sense of God?

There is an acknowledged authority that argues the existence of God. For every such advocate that clearly argues the existence of God, there is another advocate from the other side who, with equal or superior competence, argues against the existence of God. The question of the existence of God must never be relegated to the domain of the academic. Therefore, the question of the existence of God becomes one of personal faith and conviction.

At high school in Trinidad, I pondered this issue. And, it was right there in the place of my birth, that I did behold the intimate glory of God. It was all around me; all I had to do was look; it was present in the rising and the setting of the sun; it was present in the mists on the top of mountains; it was present in the promise of the seed; it was present in the newly born and in those about to die; it was present in the little unremembered acts of kindness that are performed each day... whether or not the person who renders the act of kindness is "a believer" is immaterial... the act itself is evidence of a power beyond ourselves. Any selfless act of sacrifice, regardless of race, religion, or creed is Godly; the fact that someone who performs these acts may not profess a belief in God, in no way detracts from God's Godness, for God is God regardless of what we believe as individuals. These are my musings of the Creator of us all. It was on this note that I concluded my essay.

I awaited the judgement of Dr. Morris.

The day soon arrived. Dr. Morris returned all the essays—all, that is, save one—mine. Dr. Morris asked that I come to see him in his office after class. This was eerily reminiscent of my disastrous encounter with Mr. F. my first year English professor. It was thus with the utmost caution that I ventured to knock on the office door of the esteemed Dr. Morris. I was prepared for the worst.

Dr. Morris answered my knock and invited me to sit down. I did so with the utmost trepidation.

I steeled my body for the negative comments that were sure to follow. His first words proved the correctness of my assumptions. "Frank, your essay is not typed. It is a most difficult writing to read."

Heart sinking, I remained nervously silent. He continued, "Frank, I do not understand why your essay was not typed. Had you typed it, you would have made it easier to read. As it is, I had to labour through the content."

Just how bad was my essay, I wondered.

Once more, Dr. Morris looked up from my paper and this time he smiled. "You barely..."

And he hesitated. I was confused. Why was he smiling? Dr. Morris did not strike me as a sadistic man who delighted in tormenting students. I braced myself for... I knew not what.

"Frank Maraj, you just barely received an *A*!"

Not daring to trust my ears, I queried, "What was that you said Sir?"

Then he turned my paper to reveal the A written in red on the cover of the essay.

While I daren't trust my ears, I trusted my eyes. In seconds I jumped up from my seat and in joyful elation shouted, "An 'A'! Yes!"

Then, suddenly remembering that I was in the presence of a very serious-minded philosophy professor, apologized, "Sorry, Dr. Morris, please forgive my antics..."

"Think nothing of it, Frank. I understand your excitement. But, let's get back to your paper. What original thought. To be honest, I never, not even once, entertained your sincere notion and conviction about Augustine's claim. You have given me much to ponder."

"Sir, thank you. Thank you for giving me the chance to offer a response to St. Augustine."

"Frank, your answer is more than a response. It is as if you have opened a door of understanding. I, for one, am happy to enter such a door. What grabs my attention is your explanation of *Except ye be born of Christ* – you were able to see into that statement and equate Christ-like as Christ. Thus, in essence, your conviction – given that anyone who is Christ-like can enter the Kingdom of God. Yet it might have been to your advantage had you given a description of what it is to be Christ-like. Do you understand my point?"

"Absolutely, Dr. Morris. And, what it means to be Christ-like is simple to demonstrate; it is a much more difficult task to put into practice. Consider Jesus' teachings on the Sermon on the Mount, and his parables, especially here, the parable of the Good Samaritan. Anyone, regardless of creed, colour, religion, and background adopting the essence of this parable has to be a living testament of God's creation and as such, is a shining example of the best that is humanity. And thus, the Kingdom of God is open to anyone..."

"Frank, once again I applaud you. I am a Minister and have never even considered ever stepping out of my comfort zone. You are my student. At this moment, it is I who am learning a lesson in religion."

Then Dr. Morris did a curious thing. He reached up and retrieved his bible. The he thumbed through the Gospels until he came to the Sermon on the Mount and read it aloud, as though he was reading it for the first time. Then he paused and pondered. A moment later, he shared, "Frank, it is your conviction that Jesus gave the world a way to find the Kingdom of God – and you do not have to be a *Christian*..."

"Yes, Sir. Consider what Jesus has just advocated, *Blessed are they*, several times. He never meant *Blessed are you "Christians"*, because he was addressing a nation that was not yet Christian. Sir, this Sermon on the Mount is a blueprint for human conduct, and as such, there is no exclusion of any."

"Frank, I cannot say that you are right; neither can I say that you are wrong. What I can affirm is that you have a point of view that is difficult to dismiss. Having said that… I now have a favour to ask of you."

"Sir?"

"I am giving an address – on the subject of "God and Religion." I will be travelling to Southern Ontario to deliver my talk. May I borrow your essay and quote from your writings?"

"Of course, Dr. Morris. I am honoured. Sir, I do have a favour to ask you if I may."

"What is it, Frank?"

"Sir, use my essay, please. But I would ask that if anyone were to inquire as to whose work you were quoting, please leave out my name. I would prefer to keep it that way."

Having said my piece, I left.

As I walked away, I couldn't help but reflect how not so long ago, someone commanded me to *sit down and shut up*. That person had no idea what he had done to my psyche. He made me feel dead, less than human; he treated me as if I were nothing more than a corpse and he was about to bury me in the grave of stupidity. And now, just moments ago, Dr. Morris paid me such a high compliment that it placed my emotions at the other end of the spectrum. Truly, this man has played a pivotal role in my growing confidence at university.

Thank you, Dr. Morris.

You allowed me to think.

70
Deja vu

My first year in university in Canada had been rough. My first year enrolled in an English course with Mr. F as my professor had been even rougher. It was he who made it his duty to inform me that my standard of English was found to be lacking in both proficiency and skill. It was he who had suggested that university might not suit me. I heaved a great sigh of relief when I emerged from the class with a clear pass. I delighted in the knowledge that I would never again have to take another course from this man, and indeed, throughout the rest of my four years at Lakehead, I was able to do just that. I was relieved that I would not have to come under his intense scrutiny ever again.

My relief, however, was premature. Although I was never again a student in another one of his classes, he, nonetheless, came to pose a very real threat to my academic success.

In order to fulfill the requirements of an Honours Degree in English, I was required to complete a research essay of about fifty pages. That was a challenge that I accepted without protest. The head of the Department of English assigned an advisor to supervise the process, conduct the final interview, and then grade the final product. As Fate would have it, Mr. F was chosen to be my advisor; I had no say in the matter.

Not only had Mr. F loomed large in my past, he was now promising to loom even larger in my future. For the present, I had nightmares; nightmares in which Mr. F played a prominent role. The dreams were vivid and ongoing. Every night he would attend me in my sleep, dressed in dark flowing robes, and hold my university degree high into the air and chant, "Frank Maraj, you shall never ascend to the chamber of the enlightened... return... return..."

I awakened from my dream in a state of panic; trapped in my bed sheets and sweating profusely. Then came the day for my first scheduled meeting with Mr. F. I don't know how I made it through the day without incident. My heart was still anxious and my mind was racing. I tried as best I could to compose myself before the interview. *Was I ready to meet him?* Hardly. I would never be ready. Extreme anxiety over meeting this man prevented my mind from relaxing… I could barely think straight. *Was I sufficiently prepared for the interview?*

I entered his office.

He awaited me politely.

"Mr. Maraj?"

"Yes, Sir."

"So, you are completing your Honours English Programme?"

"Yes, Sir."

"Splendid."

"Now, Mr. Maraj, may I see your *proposal*?"

I handed him my proposal; he scanned the several pages carefully.

"It seems that you have a solid plan here. All is in order. The question remains however, will you be able to follow through with the necessary literary proficiency?"

He paused. I recalled that years ago he had assigned a failing grade to my essay because it lacked proper literary structure and style. *How much of our early transactions did he remember?* I wondered. *Was he sending a message?*

Assuming a near normal expression, I fought to control my nerves in his presence.

"Well, Mr. Maraj, time will tell," he continued. "I expect that we will see one other from time to time. Do you have any questions or comments for me?"

I had to know if he remembered me.

"Yes, Sir. Just one. Are you in any way pleased with the topic I have chosen?"

"Why, of course I am delighted you have chosen Shelley – the giant."

Satisfied that he was completely without guile or duplicity, I took my leave. "Thank you, Sir. Goodbye, for now."

In the Spring of nineteen seventy-one I wrapped up my final courses for my honour's degree. All that remained was for me to successfully complete this last task: this final essay and interview. Here, it is only fitting that I acknowledge Diana's assistance in my success up until now. Together we spent many hours going over our respective essays giving assistance to whichever one of us needed it at the time. Diana always knew what I was *trying* to say but never quite said. She would go over my writings with a critical eye pointing out the areas that lacked clarity. Often she would advise, "Frank, you are not saying what you want to say. It is in your head. You have to complete your thought on paper too, so that others will understand."

At first it was extremely difficult to accept her point of view. Eventually I came to recognize her area of expertise and accept her valid criticisms. Over time we came to understand one another's shortcomings and draw on one another's strengths. We did all of our essays together and together we were very successful. I believe that neither one of felt that we could earn an A simply by our own effort. Each of us soon had an opportunity to prove that we could do just that independent of the other. Diana's came the summer I was called to Trinidad and she remained in the Lakehead taking a Spring Intercessional English course. My trial came during the period when my final essay was due for Mr. F. While Diana had been instrumental in guiding the production of the initial essay, some twenty pages in length, this longer version fell to me and to me alone. Diana had returned to Rainy River during this critical period and I was left to complete the bulk of the work without her assistance. I tried my best to review my essay with Diana's critical eye. I hoped that I was expressing on paper what was in my mind. It was hard to be objective for I was far too engaged in the project. But, I persevered, and soon all fifty of those pages were completed. Finally, and with great trepidation, I submitted my paper for examination to my professor. My future rested in his hands.

Hours of uncertainty turned into days and still there was no word from Mr. F. After two weeks with no communication, I took it upon myself to call Mr. F to inquire about the status of my essay. Professor F indicated that he was about to leave the university campus to go home. He suggested that we meet later that afternoon at his home. As it turned out, I did not live very far from him and I decided to walk to his residence.

As I walked, I tried to work out my ambivalent feelings regarding this professor. I could not shake that meeting that we had had so early on in my academic career. In his presence I became disquieted. Thus, it can be readily understood then, why I was somewhat reluctant to meet with him. During the course of my writing, the two of us had met informally to discuss the progress of my paper. Because I did not submit a preliminary paper, this essay became, in essence, everything. The more I thought about that, the more nervous I became.

I was somewhat relieved to discover that his home looked rather normal and really quite average. There was nothing ostentatious... at least, not on the outside. I rang the doorbell. The door was opened, by none other than Mr. F. He was surrounded by his three very active but delightful children. As he invited me in, I recognized that there was nothing to fear inside his home either; inside, it was simple and inviting. All that remained was for me to find my own sense of simple calm.

He prepared tea; I did not wish tea. I wanted the result of the essay, then tea.

Then he served the tea... in his best china no less. Normally, I would have loved this notion of drinking tea from lovely china with my professor. But, today, was no normal day. My mind was consumed with questions. Questions to which only he had the answers.

I lamented the fact that we were not in his office where we could be private and speak plainly and come to the point quickly.

We were in the kitchen, and we were not alone. Mrs. F was busy preparing a special dessert for us. I did not want dessert; I wanted my essay.

The two of them were making pleasant small talk and asking me about Trinidad. I did not want to engage in small talk; I wanted my essay.

After what seemed like an eternity of waiting, Professor F suggested that we retire to his office.

My final judgement awaited!

He took his place behind his desk. He looked comfortable.

I took my place on a high-backed chair opposite him. I turned slightly sideways so that we would not appear to be in direct opposition to one another. I wanted to give myself the benefit of all things positive.

He picked up my paper from the top of his desk and started turning the pages slowly.

My mind went straight to the negative, "Oh no!" I thought. "Not again. Too many errors. I'm doomed!"

My heart sank.

Please, say something, I silently pleaded.

In utter silence, he continued to turn pages.

In utter silence, I continued to brood.

Then I read the look on his face—a look that I had become all too familiar with—a look that I will never forget; it was the look that suggested disappointment.

Before he had a chance to speak, I was already having a talk with myself, trying to prepare myself for that which was inevitable. *Mr. Maraj, you will have to do over the essay. As it currently stands, it is unsatisfactory.*

Mentally resigned to this fact, I merely awaited his verbal pronouncement.

I did not want to hear what he had to say. I forced myself to stay in the moment. Here it comes, "Mr. Maraj, I am afraid..."

Then he paused. My mind took off and finished his thought; *I failed. Go on, Mr. F, give me the bad news. Then let me be gone. I can't handle any more uncertainty.*

"I am afraid," he repeated, "that you have errors."

"What's new?" I quietly admitted.

"Mr. Maraj, you have some errors – mind you – they appear to be typing errors—on three different pages."

What? my mind screamed, *Three errors – three typing errors! The essay is acceptable?*

"Have those pages redone, and the essay, Mr. Maraj, is completed – successfully."

"Successfully, Sir?" I asked incredulously.

"Yes, Mr. Maraj. You seem surprised. You shouldn't be."

I had no verbal response; I was completely overwhelmed by this change of fortune.

"And Mr. Maraj, be assured you have submitted an "A" essay."

I could hardly contain my excitement. I could not wait to share the good news with Diana!

I hoped that I remembered to thank the professor for all his time before I left his home. I could hardly wait to announce my happiness to the world. Without regard to where I was, once outside, I yelled, "Yes,—An A! Yes! Yes!"

The Lakehead Psychiatric Hospital was not far away. I did not care. Anyone could call me mad, for yes, I was mad—mad crazy with happiness. I had just drunk a large portion from the cup of Redemption.

71

Fate Beckons: Culture Threatens

Once again, I graduated. This time it was with an Honours Degree in English. I was ecstatic. Everything was finally falling into place. I had my degree; I had the security of a job with Roach's Taxi, and Diana and I were still evolving in our relationship. Life couldn't get much sweeter.

Thus, I again began to assume full-time driving duties during the summer of nineteen seventy-one. Full-time, that is, until my presence was needed back home in Trinidad.

Once again, it seemed that Fate had stepped in and I had no choice but to comply.

The situation was this: my second youngest sister, Basdaye, and a young man from our neighbourhood named Prakash, were "courting" one another without official permission. This created strained relationships. The strain was resolved when all parties mutually agreed to a marriage. Since my time was limited, I suggested that the marriage take place soon.

The date was set: Sunday, July 18, 1971.

There was much to be done.

****

Because we had recently suffered a death in our family, it was not deemed appropriate to conduct a festival of celebration in our home as tradition dictated. It was decided to host the reception at the home of the groom so that one tradition could still be honoured.

Because the venue for the reception was not going to be held at our home, did not mean that we were absolved from responsibility for the event. Boysie ensured that we did all that was appropriate.

We needed bamboo to form the structure of the tent for Prakash's back yard. Boysie and I, along with several friends and neighbours, climbed aboard Boysie's flatbed truck and headed to Valencia to get the required bamboo.

Boysie was driving; two of his friends were sitting in the cab with him. As I sat in the back of the truck, I leaned my back against the cab. I felt comfortable and safe assuming this very familiar position. Sitting there brought back many memories of my youth. It also brought back a very recent memory of an incident that happened only days ago.

72

Revisiting Mr. B...

I decided to visit my former principal, Sister Dorothy. She was most excited to see me and learn about my recent successes in Canada. She told me about an important bazaar that was being held in Port-of-Spain that very weekend to raise funds for the school. When she extended an invitation for me to come, I was thrilled to accept. When the appointed day arrived, I eagerly set out for Port-of-Spain. No sooner had I arrived when I spotted Sister. Immediately she approached me with a request. After greeting me, she explained that we were not very far from the home of one of my former teachers, Mr. B. He was going to help out with the bazaar and was home waiting for her to pick him up. Because she was unable to get away from her responsibilities for the moment, she asked me to take her car and pick him up. She added, "Frankie, I am sure you must be excited to see your former teacher, Mr. B. Would you be so kind as to assist me with this matter?"

Sister had no idea what she was asking of me.

"Yes, Sister, I will do what you ask."

Sitting behind the wheel of her station wagon I began to tremble at the very thought of coming face to face with the man who had come to live in my nightmares. The shame I felt as a result of his many denunciations pulsed through my veins. The feeling of rejection was as strong as it had ever been. My vision was clouded with the scars of all past humiliations. The mere thought of seeing Mr. B paralyzed me.

I had to force myself to start the car. I had to steel my trembling hands on the wheel. My mind was distracted with so many negative thoughts of Mr. B that I could not focus on the road.

Eventually, I pulled off the road and stopped the vehicle.

How can I do this?

Why would I do this?

Why would I consent to throw myself into the lion's den once again?
I would not consent to being the fresh meat that was certain to be devoured by the famished lion.

I turned the car around and headed back to the bazaar.
Should I not be feeling better?
Why was I still uneasy.

I tried to reason with myself, *Frank, you are no longer sixteen years old. You are nearly thirty-one. You are a grown man, and you are successful at university. Then why are you so nervous? Go and see Mr. B. Perhaps he will be happy to see you…*

I listened to my own rationalizations and managed to safely drive to the residence of Mr. B. Garnering all the courage I could, I knocked on his front door.

A voice from within responded, "Yes, come in."

Ever so cautiously I opened the door and entered.

I tried to sound casual and matter of fact, "Good afternoon, Mr. B. Sister Dorothy asked me to come and escort you to the bazaar."

"Oh, yes, that is so good of you."

"It is my pleasure to escort you, Mr. B."

"That voice, that voice, I recognise it. Let's see… ah, yes… were you not my student once some time ago… You were, were you not?"

"You are correct, Sir."

"Your name… it will come to me… I do so remember you… you are… oh, I cannot remember your name. What is your name, young man?"

"Sir, it is Frankie Boodram…"

I was not quite finished speaking when Mr. B suddenly become animated, "Oh, yes, I remember… Boo-oo-dram. Yes, yes, Boo-oo-dram. Well, Boodram, what are you doing now? What are you up to in life? Tell me, tell me.

"At the moment, nothing, Sir…"

"Boodram, my boy, what did I tell you? Did I not tell you to go and work and make something of yourself? Nothing *begets* nothing. Look at you – no purpose. You need a job. Tsk, tsk…You are in quite a losing situation. Boodram, Boodram, why did you not listen? Why?"

All the while he was speaking to me, his finger pointed accusingly at me. This man had not changed one iota. He was as self-absorbed as ever. Once again I was a sixteen year old boy being lectured by his third year high school teacher. Shades of his previous diatribes flashed before me.

His voice seemed to be gaining in strength as his memory of me became clearer. He rose from his chair, took two steps toward me and cautioned, "If only you had listened, Frankie Boodram. You young people did not heed my advice..."

"Sir..." I began.

"Yes, Boodram. What is it?"

"I need your advice now. May I ask for your assistance?"

"Of course, Boodram. It would be my pleasure. What advice do you need?"

"Sir, for the past few years I have been in Canada, and I..."

"You, Boodram? Went to Canada? To Canada? You?"

"Yes, Sir, and I graduated with a degree in English..."

"You? You graduated in English? You... the stupid little Frankie Boodram? Forgive me. No, no, I don't mean stupid..."

"Well, Sir, actually I am now a graduate with an Honours Bachelor of Arts in English."

"An Honours Degree you said? An Honours Degree..."

Mr. B was gasping a little; he was out of breath, and, totally out of sorts.

"But, Sir, I do need to ask you..."

"To ask me? What do you wish to ask me, Frankie Boodram?"

"Sir, do you suppose that it is a good idea for me to return to Canada and complete a Master's Degree?

Mr. B then collapsed into the nearest chair repeating my last words over and over, "You, Boodram, a Master's Degree."

No longer coherent, his eyes glazed over.

"Sir, you seem indisposed. I shall ask Sister Dorothy to excuse your absence."

I left.

Once, a boy

I was drowning
In an ocean, dirty with rejection.

Now, a man
I rise
From the depth

Frank Maraj

*Of those murky waters
And claim my share
Of fresh air.*

****

A smile played about my lips as I recollected that moment. I was gently pulled out of my reverie by someone calling my name. I looked up. A young man was approaching from the back of the truck, "Hey Frankie," he repeated.

It was Malpit – yes, that same Malpit who gutted my insides with his homemade leather shoes. I spewed blood when he propelled my body against the rough wire fence all the while kicking me with his shoes.

"Hey, how you doing?" I asked.

"Frank, you remember that years ago we had a misunderstanding?"

I feigned innocence, "What you talking about, Malpit?"

"You know, when I was rough a little bit."

"Oh, that."

"Well," he continued, "I want yo to know ah sorry." Then he returned to his own space.

Left to my own musings I remembered how I had struggled with the idea of forgiveness. There was so much that I had to learn; it was so hard to do by myself. Malpit's acknowledgement of the hurt he had caused was a true gift to my soul; he gave me a chance to heal. My mind was free; my spirit liberated.

73

Diana and Trinidad

My mind reflected on Diana. Our relationship had developed to the point that we both knew that the arrow was pointed in the direction of marriage. Even if neither of us spoke directly on the subject, I felt we both knew where we were headed.

Diana and her family had had the opportunity to meet me. They were able to come to know me and accept me. How can I speak so confidently in saying that they accepted me? The answer is really quite simple. I saw a recipe that Mrs. Hammond had cut out of a newspaper and left for Diana on their dining room table—Diana's mother was saving *lamb* recipes for Diana. The Hammonds didn't eat lamb; I regarded that as an act of acceptance—unspoken, yet loudly proclaiming their expectation.

Diana had yet to meet my family in Trinidad. If we were to have a future together, it was important for me that she visit Trinidad so that she could see what life had in store for her. We both knew that it was always my intention to return to Trinidad eventually. Basdaye's wedding would provide the ideal opportunity for Diana to meet my family. Accordingly, we communicated, and she agreed to come.

******

There was much to do.

On the one hand, we were all consumed in making preparations for the wedding day which was only mere days away. Added to that was the anticipation surrounding Diana's arrival... now only *hours* away.

A small army of people ventured to the airport to see the girl who had captured my heart. The flight was on time, but there was no Diana in sight. Time passed and practically everyone had cleared customs. Everyone except Diana. There was a great deal of chatter and commotion as to why we were not seeing her. I ventured to the area where the passengers had arrived and thought that I caught a glimpse of her being taken to an interrogation room. What was going on? Why were they taking her away? Five minutes passed. No Diana. Ten minutes, and still no Diana. Fifteen minutes later she emerged carrying a piece of paper. It seemed that Trinidadian immigration personnel frowned on people travelling without a passport and without verification of updated vaccinations. The paper was an order for her to get a vaccination booster within the next few days.

As I saw Diana walking toward me, I was suddenly struck by just how white she was. When we were together in Canada, her colour was never an issue. Everyone looked like her. It was only now, here in Trinidad, when I was surrounded by all of my family that I began to consider that her colour might be a cause of some concern. I wondered what my family would think? I had some concerns with Ma and Boysie, but my greatest anxiety was reserved for Clivey. *What would Clivey say? He had a mouth and he would not hesitate to put me in my place..."*

I barely had time to be nervous for here she was already approaching… a vision of shy loveliness. Boysie and Clivey were exchanging words. I could not hear the nature of the conversation but their smiles put my concerns to rest immediately. I need not have worried about their behaviour. They were downright gracious. *Was all this real? Was Diana really here? Were my brothers really that agreeable?*

I don't remember much about the ride home; I was just so happy having her here beside me. She too, seemed happy. She did, however, express one note of disappointment. Since her flight arrived at eight o'clock in the evening, she had expected to be able to see Trinidad in the brightness of the evening. This was her first taste of education in equatorial reality. The sun rises at six in the morning and sets at six in the evening. It got very dark very fast. She missed the Northwestern Ontario evenings already. I am sure that there were other things that were strange and overwhelming for her on this first night in a new country but she smiled through it all.

We gathered around the table in the gallery. Clivey sat at the head and placed Diana at the side to his immediate right. Boysie sat directly opposite and I was relegated somewhere down the line. My two elder brothers took the lead in attending to her every need. For the most part, Diana just smiled her most accepting smile while everyone chatted. I'm not sure she understood everything that was being said, because our family tends to speak quickly and revert to colloquialisms when we are all together. Clive took extreme pains to be perfectly clear when he broached the subject of the upcoming marriage between Bas and Prakash. He looked directly at Diana and asked, "So, what do you think about making it a double wedding? Bas and Prakash and you and Frank?"

Without missing a beat, Diana smiled, looked at me, and then back at Clive, "I don't know… Frank hasn't asked me… yet." Diana delivered what amounted to be a bombshell!

All eyes turned to me. Then Clive spoke up, "Well, brother, when yo going to marry Diana? Make up your mind."

And Boysie added, "Frank, we could have a double wedding, Bas and yours. Just say the word."

I was in quiet shock. It seemed that the Forces had allied themselves for a common purpose – marriage. What had seemed a distant idea – somewhere in the future—was now at hand. And, it seemed that all the Forces that conspired to bring Diana to Trinidad would have their way. Indeed, sitting at the very helm of the "marriage boat" was none other than my mother. Later on in the evening we had a private talk in the bedroom. "Frankie," she began, "Diana is gentle. She likes you. I know that you like her. You want to marry her?"

"Ma, how can I think of marriage? We have not spoken of it in any permanent way. Diana knows that I have responsibilities at home, here, with you and the family. She understands that all my sisters have to be taken care of first before I can think of myself. She has accepted that."

"Yes, Frank, that is true - if you was here in Trinidad. You have a chance for happiness. Yo like Diana."

"Yes, Ma, but I can't marry yet. I have to finish university first. I have to have a job and…"

"And what, Frank? You go marry in Canada? What's important is that I see you married for myself. I want to do my part as yo mother. And ah is alive. Yo here, now. Diana's here, now. Yo go away and God knows what go happen. I could be dead, Son. Yo think it over…"

She left. I did not have to think it over. I knew what I had to do. That very night, when we had a moment of privacy, I proposed. Diana accepted.

The next day we went the Maracas Beach in the northern part of the island. We spent the day on the beach and in the water. I waited on the beach for Diana to emerge from the water. She emerged naturally and was beautiful. I proposed once more right then and there.

Under the warmth of the equatorial sun I found myself on my knees. I had no ring to offer—only my intent.

I do believe, in spite of everything, that I did manage to surprise her with this second proposal. Without a moment's hesitation, she consented a second time.

Now, we were able to discuss marriage openly. We discussed the idea of sharing the day with Bas and Prakash but we both determined that we did not want to infringe on their day. Also, we wanted a day to call our own. We decided on a date. It would be the Sunday following Bas and Prakash's wedding, July 25, 1971. Having addressed that very important detail, it was now time to take care of one equally important consideration—I had to ask permission to marry Diana; I had to contact the Hammonds who were still a world away in Rainy River.

******

The Telephone Call

Like many homes in Trinidad in nineteen seventy-one, we did not have a telephone. Hence, Diana and I travelled the eight or so miles to Port-of-Spain. There was a telephone company in the city from which people could go to make long distance telephone calls. We explained the nature of our business and we were granted access to two adjoining telephone lines. (Diana was anxious to listen in on the conversation to gauge her parents' response and she was on the extension phone in an adjacent room.) I made the call. The phone rang.

Diana's mother answered, "Hello?"

"Mrs. Hammond, this is Frank."

She responded with a guarded, "Yes, Frank."

"Mrs. Hammond, I am calling to ask your permission to marry Diana."

"Pardon me, Frank? You want my permission to what?"

"I am requesting your permission to marry Diana."

"I don't know, Frank. You had better ask her dad."

I could hear her say, "Jimmy, it's Frank," as she then passed the phone to Mr. Hammond. "Hello?"

"Hello, Mr. Hammond. I am asking for your permission to marry Diana."

Silence… then…"Well, you had better speak to her mother…"

"I just did and she said to ask you."

"Oh." Then he added, "This is rather sudden, Frank."

"I know that and I am sorry. We will have a ceremony here in our tradition and when we return to Canada we will get married again in your church. We will do that willingly."

"I suppose it's okay."

"Thank you, Mr. Hammond."

It was now official. We were going to get married. There was much to do. But first we had to see to Bas' wedding.

74

Our Trinidadian Wedding

Diana had arrived on Sunday, July 11th. Basdaye's wedding was one week away. During the week preceding her wedding, Bas and Diana became close because the two of them shared my room up until Bas' wedding day. Following Bas' wedding, my youngest sister, Kalie, assumed the role of Diana's room-mate. Because of this, Diana was able to form a close relationship with these two sisters. Boysie made it his business to bring fresh milk for Diana every morning and he always managed to bring her some sort of sweet treat in the evening. Because of these kind gestures, Boysie too, cemented a place of honour in Diana's heart. My young nephew, David, became highly protective of her and never failed to be alert to her slightest sign of anxiety. Everyone in my family extended themselves to Diana in an effort to make her time here in Trinidad a good one. In fact, the entire neighbourhood rallied favourably to her side; Diana was dubbed a princess. Such was the charming spirit that prevailed throughout the entirety of her visit.

In spite of all this good will, there was one sobering reality that had to be faced.

Again, it was money.

Money, as always, was the formidable dark cloud hanging over my head.

Once Diana had agreed to come to Trinidad, I immediately visited the Royal Bank in Port-of-Spain to secure a loan in order to purchase a ticket for her trip here.

While I personally did not bear any of the financial costs for Basdaye's wedding, (Boysie, Prakash and Prakash's family covered those expenses) there was now the additional expenses associated with our upcoming event. While Basdaye's wedding was not a large wedding, it was by no means, small. Being very conscious of Boysie's financial situation, in no way did

I wish to extend his burden even further with our wedding. I approached Boysie with my concerns.

Boysie's response was immediate annoyance... with me. "Frankie, what yo worried about? What yo mean yo don't want to have too many people. No, man, yo got to have people. And I will take care of everything. Yo don't worry."

"No, Boysie. You not inviting a big crowd. We can't afford it. It will be a very small wedding."

My protest was ignored. Boysie became infuriated and bellowed, infusing his language with some colourful epithets. "Yo come from Canada, and yo will tell me, the elder brother, what to do? No way. Yo are my brother – my *younger* brother. I want you to have a proper wedding."

"Boysie, be reasonable..."

"I am reasonable. Look over there, Frank. Look how worried Diana is. Yo making trouble. You worried about cost. Man, what is some extra food? Frank, ah proud of you, ah happy for you. Ah glad to do this. I am the big brother. Now go to Diana. Make her smile."

"Yes, Boysie."

Boysie won, but I was no loser. How could I lose? My brother's affection for Diana and me was overwhelming. I was humbled by the extent to which I knew that he was prepared to sacrifice to honour us with a *proper* wedding.

Feelings of goodwill extended from every quarter. Dolly took Diana to Port-of-Spain to secure her wedding dress. Diana had loved Basdaye's red wedding sari and decided to choose the white twin to Bas' red one. The cost was twenty-five Trinidadian dollars which, at that time, translated to about twelve and a half Canadian dollars. Dolly purchased a gift of silver sandals for Diana to wear with the white sari. Dolly's assistance was invaluable during the proceedings and her calm demeanour kept everything running smoothly. Dolly willingly stepped in as Diana's big sister and assumed a primary role in guiding Diana through the ceremony.

Earlier in the week, Diana and I had ventured once again to the city to look for our wedding bands. My only stipulation regarding the bands was that they had to be made of *white gold* and not the traditional yellow gold. Diana found the perfect bands at the very first jewellery store that we entered. I remember making her go to several other stores just to be sure. She was. She remained with her original selection. I believe that I managed to pay for the rings with the final settlement that I had been offered following my injury at Brayshaw steel. The settlement just happened to come in during the period of our visit to Trinidad. It was enough to cover the cost of the rings.

Meanwhile, at home, Ma was busy preparing for our wedding – a Hindu wedding which was to be performed in the proper Hindu tradition. She was ecstatic to do her part.

Now that I knew that Diana was properly outfitted for the wedding day I turned my attention to what I, as the bridegroom, was to wear. I knew that I dare not approach either Boysie or Clive for I knew that they would find a way to outfit me in brand new wedding clothes no matter the cost. They were already stretched to the limit and I could not, would not, knowingly add to their burden. I decided to approach my new brother-in-law, Prakash to see if he would loan me his wedding outfit for the day. He agreed, happily. I was a bit taller and slightly heavier than Prakash but managed to squeeze into his outfit (just barely). Things were looking up.

Another matter needed my attention. This matter involved my own neighbourhood friends, the boys with whom I grew up. It was important to me that I personally invite each one. As I went to each home to extend the invitation, I explained, "It matters to me that you come. You are my friends—my first friends. I want you with me on this very special occasion."

Since the bride and groom could not both come from the same residence, it was necessary for Diana to be away at another home, and on that account, Prakash's parents extended that invitation for her to spend the day of the wedding at their home. I believe that Kaylie spent the day with her helping her dress and get ready for the ceremony. Thus, I was not to see Diana until we both arrived at the *Mandir*, the Hindu temple, located in Saint James.

I took my place at the altar as Pundit Krishna, brother to Clive's wife, began the ceremony. Once we were seated, Pundit signalled for Diana to take her place beside me at the altar. I could not contain my pride as I watched this bride dressed in a white sari and veil and approaching. From beneath her veil I could see hints of her dark beautiful hair. From head to toe, she radiated, and I felt that I had the loveliest bride ever.

Pundit began the ceremony taking care to explain to Diana the meaning of his every move. I was grateful for I knew that Diana would appreciate the opportunity to understand some of the customs that governed the ceremony. In less than an hour the proceedings came to an end, and we were whisked away in the wedding car. Atop the car, were loud speakers announcing to the world that a wedding had just taken place through the playing of traditional Indian wedding music. We were driven back to my home at 26 Back Street where Ma welcomed us and gave us her traditional blessing.

All of the trappings that served to build the reception tent at Prakash's home last week, were magically transported to 26 Back Street to serve for our wedding. Because the bride, Diana, was from away, there was no other option but to have the reception at our home. So once again we broke tradition out of necessity and we were allowed to have a "celebration" in spite of the fact that a death had occurred quite recently within the family.

Following Hindu tradition, a vegetarian lunch was served on freshly washed leaves. Once again, following tradition, no knives or forks were offered for use during the meal… we all ate with our hands.

A surprise awaited us following the meal. My long-time friend, Dickie, microphone in hand, began to speak, "Ladies and Gentleman, let us congratulate Frank and his most lovely wife, Diana, on this, their wedding day."

Dickie clapped, and the audience joined him with hearty congratulations. Someone yelled out, "We clapping more for Diana," and everyone began clapping again.

Dickie continued, "I am so happy to see you all in a good mood. You know, Frank and Diana are students going to university…"

I wondered, *What is Dickie doing? Where is he going with this?* I think I knew what he was up to and I was becoming a bit uncomfortable. Just as Dickie was about to continue, another voice interrupted, yelling, "Ah, but Diana is the bright one… After all, she is beautiful."

The audience smiled and laughed heartily. I looked at Diana who was so shy, so embarrassed. I whispered, "Smile, Diana."

And she did.

Dickie continued his remarks, "As I was saying, Frank and Diana are going to university. I know you have already bought your gifts. But I am asking you to help out." He paused and looked out the congregation of friends… my poor friends. I froze. He was doing exactly what I feared. He was asking people to donate cash. Then, Dickie reached into his pocket and pulled out a bill and placed it in a basket. He then looked out at those gathered and encouraged, "Whatever little, whatever you can, I am asking you to give. I know that I am embarrassing Frank. He did not know that I was going to do this. How about it?"

Members from the community came forward and gave generously. My own neighbourhood friends came, every one of them, and contributed. They looked at me, smiled and veered off. I cannot describe the joy I felt. I looked at Diana beside me glowing: I watched my mother radiating happiness; I witnessed my brothers and sisters just basking in the moment. Right there and then I thought that Heaven had descended. That event came to an end, and our guests wandered freely in the yard and on the street. Music started. Diana was now the major center of attention. A friend approached and asked, "Frankie, we having a drink at the back of de yard. Come have one with the boys."

"I want to have this drink with you, my childhood friends. Let's go."

They were so happy. They poured me a glass of rum and coke, and I was about to raise it to my lips. Then, I remembered why I should not drink and explained, "Everyone, today I am married and today I took a sacred vow from Pundit Krishna. I must not eat meat, or have alcohol on this day. I am so sorry. If only you knew how much I wanted to have this time with you."

One of the boys exclaimed, "Frank, tomorrow we are going to be here. We will have that drink together. We are so happy *we* did not take that vow. Yo can go, it's okay. See you tomorrow."

The next day, we awoke to the sound of loud noises coming from the yard. As I went to investigate the source of the commotion I could see that the tent from yesterday's celebration had already been dismantled; many hands assisted in the removal of the borrowed benches and chairs and arrangements were being made to return them to their owners. I could not believe it. In a matter of minutes, the yard was almost back to normal; there was no evidence that a wedding had taken place the night before.

The promise of continued celebrations at Caura River had everyone motivated to complete the dismantling process as quickly as possible. It seemed that the whole of Back Street was engaged in the endeavour. Everyone who had a job, was taking the day off; it seemed that they had *unofficially* designated Monday as a holiday; once the work was completed, a parade of vehicles made its way to Caura River where the *real* celebrating could officially begin.

There was an abundant supply of food, drink, and sun. When we had had our fill of all three we refreshed ourselves in the waters of the river.

The gift that I received on that day was the gift of their unconditional acceptance of and affection for my new bride. It was real. Diana was real. Our marriage was real. My happiness was real.

We spent the entire day exhausting ourselves in the river and with our friends and family. When darkness descended, we headed home to a blissful night of sleep.

Just before falling asleep, a sobering reality struck me: *as of this moment, I am no longer Frank Maraj. I am Frank Maraj plus Diana Hammond. We are Frank and Diana Maraj. So be it. I'll just deal with the future as it comes. No longer am I alone; Diana is at my side....*"

75

Back in Canada... Preparations

When Diana and I returned to Rainy River, Diana started making preparations for our Canadian wedding: September 4th, 1971.

Diana and I were of one mind: a small, modest wedding.

I returned to Thunder Bay and immediately began working for Roach's Taxi. I worked as many shifts as I could to garner enough money to start our new life together. For the wedding essentials, we were almost totally dependent on Diana's parents. Diana's dad had always managed to provide for his family but never had a reserve of funds at his disposal. This wedding, coming as it did, seemingly from out of nowhere, caught him by surprise. He was not prepared for extra expenses, much less the expenses involved in a wedding. Both Diana and I were very aware of his concerns and therefore we were even more determined than ever to keep costs down... for everyone. Diana had advised her attendants not to worry about buying new matching dresses. I believe that she told them to "wear whatever dress they wore to their last wedding when they were a bridesmaid."

Betty Grynol, a long time friend of the Hammonds played a significant role in planning the wedding and in the wedding itself. She had agreed to be one of the bridesmaids. While she appreciated what Diana and I were attempting to do to keep the costs of the wedding down, she could not begin to fathom a wedding in which nothing matched. It was she who came to Diana and expressed her concerns in this respect. Betty, an accomplished seamstress, wanted to investigate making simple dresses to outfit the attendants. They were able to purchase simple cotton material at the Ben Franklin store in Baudette, Minnesota (just across the river from Rainy River) for fifty cents a yard. Each peasant dress required about one and a half yards of material. So, for about seventy-five cents a dress, they made the three bridesmaid dresses. Diana's white sari and silver sandals would make a reappearance at the Canadian wedding. The ladies in Trinidad who had helped Diana with her sari took great pains to teach her how to tie the sari for herself since there would be no one at the Canadian wedding who would know what to do. In fact, they even stitched the front folds on her dress so that she would not have that particular worry. The Chaykowski's daughter-in-law, Janice, offered Diana the use of her very beautiful wedding veil. This offer was gratefully accepted.

Since purchasing fresh flowers for the wedding was completely out of the question for financial reasons, once again, our ever economically astute friend, Betty Grynol, came to our rescue. Betty just happened to be perusing the various gardens in town when her eyes fell on the very beautiful gladiolas growing in the First Street garden of Bertha Murray. Thinking that they would be perfect for the wedding, she approached Mrs. Murray and received consent to cut them for the bridesmaids' bouquets. I believe that Betty herself accomplished this task on the day of the wedding and kept them fresh until the appointed hour—five p.m.

Diana carried a single velvet rose instead of a bouquet. The rose was donated by one of Diana's best friends, Penny Metza. In fact, through Penny, we broke with traditional wedding protocol. Traditionally the bride invites a close male family friend to make the toast to the bride. Unfortunately, the men who had come to know her best during her growing up years had either moved away or had passed away. There was little time to find an appropriate alternative when Penny offered to assume the role. Diana quickly agreed as she too thought that this was a brilliant idea and a great way to include Penny in the proceedings.

I chose to wear one of the two suits that I owned and thus incurred no new expense in that regard for this wedding. My long time university friend Paul Paularinne gladly agreed to be my best man. Betty's husband, Bob, and Diana's sister's husband, Jim, were groomsmen. My two friends, Len and David Chaykowski, consented to being ushers at the wedding. It seemed that everything was coming together.

Diana's mother, an active member in their church, arranged for the women of the church to cook a turkey dinner for the reception which was to be held in the basement of the church; again, another first tradition— holding the wedding reception in the church's basement.

Extensive and generous were the offers of assistance made by both Bob and Betty Grynol. To me, personally, they offered lodging in their home in the days immediately preceding the wedding. To my friends from out of town, they offered the use of their property for setting up camp. Bob even offered up his prized black Dodge for us to use on our "honeymoon." I was grateful for their help and their solid support.

While Diana was back home making wedding preparations, I returned to the Lakehead on a mission; I needed to secure an apartment for Diana and myself. Up until now, I had need of a simple room with kitchen privileges only. Upon our return as a married couple, that was about to change. I now had to find not just a room, but an apartment. Thus I began my quest.

Initially I undertook this journey on my own. I visited several apartments but quickly discovered that the cost of renting them was prohibitive. Thus far, I had been paying about forty dollars a month to rent a room. The apartments I had looked at started at one hundred and twenty dollars a month. I began to seek out cheaper apartments—some of these did not have even the simplest of kitchens. One apartment that I looked at had no easily accessible bathroom and no real kitchen facilities. The owner of that particular apartment wanted an outrageous one hundred and thirty dollars a month. I was getting desperate and just looked at the landlord in disbelief. He, in turn, looked at me and said very matter of fact, "You want it or you don't want it? Doesn't matter to me. Somebody will take it. What do you say?"

I could only shake my head and walk away.

Diana and I had the good fortune to live like members of the family in the rooms that we rented from families in Thunder Bay. I wanted nothing less for the two of us as we began our life together as a couple. I could not bear the thought of bringing Diana to live in any form of substandard accommodations such as the ones I had just witnessed.

Up until this time, Diana and I had been riding high on an emotional whirlwind of happiness. I had been able to escape the truth of my financial reality until I started looking for an apartment. The summer was gone. Not only had I not worked, I had also incurred more debt as a result of my trip to Trinidad and the subsequent request for Diana to join me there.

I resumed apartment hunting.

I saw an ad in the supermarket for an apartment in the Current River area. It was reasonably priced and I was excited as I made my way to the address. It was encouraging to think that we could find a place in the area that had become home to us both over the past few years. The neighbourhood itself was pleasant and the house was close to the bus line. Judging from outward appearances, the house looked decent. Earlier on in the day, I had phoned the home and made an appointment to view the apartment. When I knocked on the door, the landlord came out and after careful scrutiny, invited me inside to check out the apartment. From his demeanour, I assumed that he had not been expecting a person of my Caribbean ethnicity. He ushered me down some stairs to the basement apartment. The stairs were a harbinger of things to come. They were narrow and dirty and dangerously steep. At the bottom stretched an uneven floor of cold concrete. At the far end of the room, and I use the term loosely, hung a curtain, torn and dirty. This curtain served as privacy divider for the bedroom. There had been no effort to conceal the water and sewer pipes which ran along the walls loudly proclaiming the owner's lack of aesthetics. A second curtain to the far right was a poor attempt at screening the bathroom from immediate view. No curtain, no matter the thickness, could mask the most unpleasant odour emanating from the bathroom. The *kitchen* held a makeshift counter; atop it, a single hot plate served as a stove. Despair claimed me momentarily as I wondered, *Is this where I am to begin life with Diana?*

This is not what I had imagined. But, this is all that I could afford. I found myself reminiscing about our very modest home in Trinidad. It is true that it was modest, but we took pride in keeping it clean. Even amidst our deepest poverty, we were surrounded with cleanliness.

My finances seemed to be dictating our next circumstance. This apartment, I could afford. I seemed to be left with no other choice. Before officially sealing the deal, something within me advised, *Frank, go see Dot Jensen.*

I told the landlord that I would be back shortly. He shrugged his shoulders as I left. I was not far from Dot's house. I asked her if she would mind accompanying me to see the apartment. She did not hesitate for one single second. Dot simply beamed; she loved that I had asked her opinion. Together we returned.

Within minutes we were back at the apartment. Again I knocked and again landlord answered. He seemed surprised to see that I had brought someone with me. This time I took the lead going down the steep staircase. Dot, however, stood at the top of the stairs looking most displeased. I was afraid that she was going to refuse to come down.

She announced, "Frank Maraj, I don't wish to come down those stairs." Then, as she held on to the walls and started the downward descent, proclaimed, "I am not going to like this."

Once downstairs, her eyes became darts. Nothing escaped her critical examination. Her feet moved quickly through the *apartment*, but her tongue moved even faster. Within a matter of seconds she made her views known. Not one to couch the truth, Dot asserted, "This is sickening. Frank, you're not thinking of bringing Diana here to this dump, are you? This is Canada, Frank, and this is a dump. I have never seen anything like it."

The landlord, having overheard the word dump, became agitated. He got close to Dot and protested, "You, lady. You call my place a dump? You know what dump is? This is good place. It is no dump. You can't see well; your nose is too stuck up – You think you are better..."

Dot didn't let him finish; she exploded, "You call this an apartment? This is a pig sty and I am going to report you to the authorities. One Hundred Dollars! Frank is not staying here even if *you* pay *him* one hundred dollars! Frank, let's get out of here. This place is getting to me... it smells..."

Once outside, Dot became calmer but did not hesitate to chastise me, "Frank, I can't believe that you would consider bringing Diana to such a hellhole."

I was in a state of shock; Dot held nothing back.

Still agitated, still feisty, she continued, "Yes, Frank, don't be so naïve. That place is a hellhole. No way are you bringing Diana there. If you can't find a place, you bring Diana to our home. We will make do until you find something decent. You hear me, Frank Maraj?"

"Yes, Dot." (One did not argue with Dot.)

The search for an apartment resumed. But, it had one more stipulation; not only did it have to meet my financial restrictions, it now also had to pass *the Dot test*. The word was out now, and all of our friends were actively on the lookout for any leads. Soon, information reached me that there just might be an apartment available to the right tenants. I was told that the owner of the apartment had had some bad experiences with tenants in the past and was in no hurry to rent the space out again. Once I received the exact address, I ventured to the home. It, too, was in Current River.

Standing on the road outside the home, I was more than pleased. It was located in a quiet cul-de-sac and again it was very close to the bus line. From the outside, the house appeared very attractive. But, I had learned my lesson and did not allow myself to be too hopeful that what appeared on the outside was an indication of what was on the inside. I knocked on the door. There was no answer. I knocked again and waited. Then, this little sprite of a woman opened the door. Her hair was grey but her eyes had a youthful sparkle. My presence at the door must have taken her somewhat by surprise for she simply stared at me. I guess she was waiting for me to speak. It took me a moment to find the right words to say for I had not thought the situation through. *Do I start with small talk about the lovely weather or do I just come right to the point?* I guess my inner deliberations took too long for she asked, "What is it?"

Her voice betrayed a strong hint of an English accent, and immediately I relaxed. I decided to come straight to the point. My experiences in England helped me to understand that generally they preferred a direct approach. "My name is Frank Maraj. May I rent your apartment?"

I could see that she was quite surprised with my forthrightness. The fact that she did not close the door in my face was encouraging. I had not been in any way diplomatic in my manner. After recovering from her immediate surprise, she responded, "Well, we do have an apartment, but it's not really for rent. How did you know..."

"I found out completely by chance. And I understand that you may not be very anxious to rent it out. If it is not too bold to ask, may I enquire as to why that is?"

This lady was still standing in the doorway and I had not made a single step closer. I wanted to remain respectful even though I was dying to get a glimpse inside the house. Then, as if reading my mind, she invited, "Come on in – but just for a moment."

As I entered the home, I noticed that the steps leading to the basement were wholesome and appeared easy to navigate. Everything looked spotless. Then this lovely little lady led the way up the two steps to the kitchen. She moved easily and delicately up the steps. It was hard to place her age. Everything in the kitchen was neat and attractive and I thought, "I love this place!"

She invited me to sit at the kitchen table. When next she spoke, I commented on her accent and asked if she was from England.

She responded, "Yes, but a long time ago. I am Mrs. Hebden. This is my daughter's home. Muriel makes the decisions and I am afraid that she is not likely to want to rent..."

"Please, Mrs. Hebden, I don't wish to appear intrusive but may I ask the reason that she does not wish to rent?"

"We have had a most unpleasant experience with our last tenants. More trouble than we... We certainly do not depend on the income... Oh, I am getting carried away. Forgive me."

"Mrs. Hebden, may I put to you a proposal?"

"I suppose, I could at least listen."

"I am getting married on September fourth. I am very interested in your apartment. I absolutely love the neighbourhood and your home – what I have seen of it. I am asking that you give me a chance. Give us a chance. I am willing to offer a deposit and the first month's rent. If you do not approve of Diana and me – for whatever reason – ask us to leave. We will leave–without any kind of trouble. And you keep the deposit."

"My, my. Your proposal is very honourable. I believe you, Frank, but that decision is Muriel's. I suppose you would like to see the apartment."

I could have exploded; such was my curiosity, my anticipation. I answered in the affirmative. She led me down the steps to the basement. Just as expected, they were easy to navigate. The steps gave way to a wide corridor which in turn opened up to a tiny but well-appointed kitchen. A wholesome three piece bathroom adjoined the kitchen to the left. And, beside the bathroom was the door to the bedroom which again was spacious and most pleasing to be in. As we headed back to the kitchen, Mrs. Hebden showed me the coziest looking living room tucked away around the corner and off the kitchen. It was the perfect apartment. *I had to have it; Diana would love it. More importantly, Dot would love it. The problem remained, however, how do I go about getting it?*

When we returned upstairs to the landing, Mrs. Hebden invited, "Frank, would you like a cup of tea?"

Eagerly, I accepted.

Within minutes Mrs. Hebden had made the tea. She served it with English muffins and jam. Her hospitality confirmed in me even more strongly than ever the desire to live in this home. Before I left, Mrs. Hebden suggested that I phone later that day and advised, "Frank, I will talk to Muriel. I will do my best on your behalf. We'll just have to see what she says. I make no promises."

That is all I needed—a chance. Later that evening, when I knew that Muriel would be home from work, I made the call. Muriel invited me to come over the next day after supper. She wanted to meet me. She made no promises.

At the appointed hour, I knocked on their door. Muriel answered. Immediately she impressed me as a very pleasant and accommodating Canadian with only a slight hint of English reserve. As she led me into the living room she introduced herself and added, "Mom tells me that you are soon to be married. Congratulations. She also told me that you are looking for an apartment."

I liked Muriel right away. She was so down to earth, completely without airs. "Thank you, Muriel. I am not looking for just *any* apartment. I want *your* apartment. I love it. I love your home, and I adore your street."

"Well, Frank, we do have a bit of a problem."

"A problem? What problem would that be?"

"My father... He is elderly. He wanders all over the house. He is going through a difficult stage..."

What a relief. The problem was not with me. Muriel was not saying *no* to renting the apartment to me. She was explaining the difficult situation that would result if her dad wandered and disturbed her renters. I understood her predicament and volunteered, "Muriel, your dad is not a problem. It seems to me that you and your mom might be a little too protective. I might just be what your dad needs..."

When she broke out in laughter at my suggestion, I relaxed and allowed myself to be hopeful.

Please, Muriel, just say, 'Yes', I yearned.

"Well, Frank, we have not discussed the rent."

"Whatever you wish, Muriel. If I can, I will take it. And I am willing to help around the house with your dad, with the grass and the snow. Whatever you need... that is... if you wish my help."

"Well, Frank, since you are willing, we will give it a chance. The rent is normally one hundred dollars; I will reduce it to seventy-five dollars..."

This was more than I had dared dream of. "Thank you, Muriel...thank you. And Mrs. Hebden, I know you put in a good word for me. Thank you both."

I reached into my wallet to offer a payment when Mrs. Hebden intervened, "Frank, go get married. We will see you in September."

Quizzically, I looked at Muriel; she quickly assured, "Don't worry, the apartment will be here waiting for you newlyweds."

Of course, I had to bring Dot to see the place. When she saw it she beamed, "Yes, Frank. This is beautiful."

Her approval was the final blessing that I needed.

76

The Canadian Wedding

It was September the fourth, the day of our wedding. Early that morning, Bob and I were busily engaged outside washing his car, preparing it for the wedding. As we worked, Bob teased, "Don't worry, Frank, I made sure the car was gassed up... properly. You shouldn't encounter any problems with it tonight."

He was enjoying one final laugh on me.

Last evening, I had borrowed Bob's car to drive to the cabin that I had chosen to take Diana to for our "honeymoon". Since I had no idea where Budreau's camp was, I needed direction. Betty's younger sister, Peggy, volunteered to be my guide as she was familiar with the area. It was very late in the evening when Peggy and I set out on our mission. We had been driving for a short while when suddenly, the car stalled... in the middle of nowhere—at least that is what it felt like to me. In my haste to leave, I had completely forgotten to check the gas gauge. No one thought to check. We did not know that the needle was registering on empty. Stopped out there in the dark, I was completely out of my element. I had no idea what to do to solve the problem. Thank goodness Peggy was with me. She knew exactly what to do. She had a general idea of where we were, and knew the people in the area. She could not however resist the temptation to tease me. After assuring me that everything was going to be okay that all we had to do was walk a few miles to the nearest house, she couldn't resist adding, "All we have to do is stay clear of any scavenging bears."

Panic must have registered in my eyes and Peggy assured me that we were perfectly safe if we stuck to the road. Soon, we were rescued from our plight by one of Peggy's friends and a can of gasoline. Peggy never fails to tease me about that night whenever we happen to meet.

And Bob was quite happy that the car was shining. While it had been raining during the day, by the time five o'clock came, the sun broke through the clouds as if to bless our wedding.

I took my place at the front of the church awaiting my bride. The music began the familiar wedding refrain. As I turned around to catch my first glimpse of her, I thought quietly, "Diana, how beautiful you are."

Within minutes the service was over. Our vows had been exchanged and we were being introduced as Frank and Diana Maraj."

As we walked arm in arm down the aisle amid the applause, I was delighted to see so many familiar faces in attendance. The friends that I had made in both Thunder Bay and Kenora filled the pews; these wonderful friends lifted for a moment the sadness I may have felt not having any of my own family there in attendance. They made me feel as if I were among my very own. I treasure the memory of that moment still.

Dinner in the church basement immediately followed a picture taking session in the park. Everything went well except for one tiny detail. In my desire to keep the knowledge of the honeymoon cabin as a surprise for Diana, she had no idea how to plan. In the morning I asked her if she had brought any food for breakfast. I should have known that she could not prepare for an event about which she had no knowledge. Her answer was a disappointed, "No. You never told me where we were going."

The camp owners, the Budreaus, were very accommodating and offered us coffee and toast—our very first breakfast together. Nothing has ever tasted so sweet.

77

The Three Cases

The Case of the Missing Wallet

After returning to Thunder Bay, I headed directly to Roach's Taxi to see Carl Roach. I told him that I would be available on week-ends for part-time work. (Diana and I were both returning to university for one more year. Diana wanted to complete her B.A., and I, my B. Ed.)

Carl agreed.

Once more, I assumed the role of a taxi driver. An uncomfortable encounter awaited me.

There is no other profession quite like taxi driving. To be successful at it, one has to hustle, for the wage that one earns is directly proportional to the amount of money one takes in from the various fares.

The taxi driver encounters every personality type from the very shy and reticent to the overbearing and argumentative. A good driver must often leave his personal prejudices at the door of the cab. Inside the cab, the fares are to be treated with equal respect: the good, the bad, and the ugly. Frequently, I was lucky and met mainly the good. Occasionally the bad and the ugly combined forces; those occasions were hard to forget.

One weekend early that fall, I was dispatched to a local bar to pick up a passenger. When I arrived at the establishment, no one was waiting for a taxi. I parked the cab and went inside the bar to check. I soon found him... completely inebriated. I assisted him to the car, and eventually discovered where he wanted to go. When we arrived at his address, I checked the meter and announced, "And that would be one dollar and fifty cents, please."

His head was wobbly and his eyes kept on closing as if he was fighting to stay awake. I repeated my request ensuring that my tone showed no hint of disrespect. When it finally registered on him that I was waiting for him to pay the fare, he began searching his pockets for his wallet. He found none.

"Don't have no x%$@ money. Some son of a #*%(@ stole my wallet."

I suggested that it may have fallen out and offered to help him search the back seat.

I got out of the car, went around the back and helped him out. I, too, could find no wallet. The back seat, however, was wet and reeked with the strong scent of urine. He stumbled as he attempted to walk to his house. I assisted him to his door, then left… without having received payment.

Once back in the car, I radioed dispatch. Margaret was on duty. She asked, "And your fare, Number 7?" (I was driving car No. 7—my favourite.)

"A negative one dollar-fifty."

"Oh no, Frank. Not again. Oh, wait, Frank, Carl has a question for you. Hold on."

"No. 7?"

"Yes, Carl?"

"The police just called. That passenger you just picked up claimed you stole his wallet. Question… did you steal his wallet?"

I could hardly bring myself to answer. I had just tried to extend a helping hand to this stranger, drunk as he was. I managed, "No, Sir."

"Thanks, Frank. That would be all."

Is that it? 'That would be all?' What are Margaret and Carl thinking? I began to fret. I had a long night ahead of me and I needed to keep my composure.

Later that night when I eventually went home, I was unable to sleep. Memories of people drinking and falsely accusing—surfaced. I had witnessed such behaviour in Trinidad when I was growing up. I did not expect this conduct in a developed country like Canada. Again I was learning a lesson, that people are people wherever you go.

But, I also knew that I had a choice in how I would react to such accusations. I could choose to be angry, explosive and reactive… or not. I chose not.

The passenger had been drunk and accused me falsely just because I was the one who happened to be on the spot when he discovered his loss. I knew that I was innocent; some other Presence knew it too.

The next day, the police called Roach's Taxi once again. They left this message, "Wallet of said passenger was found. Identification and other cards intact. Wallet empty."

For now, I had to be satisfied with partial vindication. Such was the life of a taxi-driver.

The Case of the Despairing Damsel

The night was quiet as I returned late one night from dropping off a fare. A few blocks before reaching the dispatch centre, a young lady flagged me down. I stopped beside her and rolled down the window to speak with her. She looked at me for a moment before speaking.

"Are you free?" she asked.

"Yes."

She opened up the front door, climbed in, and instructed, "Please, driver, just drive."

"Your address, please," I enquired.

My question seemed to unnerve her. Her demeanour changed and she appeared anxious. Her voice heightened in intensity as she begged, "Please, I don't know what to do, where to go. I am new in the city. I don't know…"

Her voice was approaching the hysterical. I tried to calm her. "Miss, how can I help you?"

"I need a place to stay. Please, can you help me? I don't know what I am going to…"

I was quick to reassure her, "Miss, I can help you. I have a place. You can stay at my place."

My assurances seemed to calm her and everything about her changed in that moment. Quietly, she assured, "Thank you, thank you. Believe me you won't regret it. I promise I will…"

My thoughts had gone straight to Diana. I knew that she could help this unfortunate soul. I couldn't wait to tell her about Diana. "Miss, you are going to like my wife, Diana. She will understand if I bring…"

An inexplicable hysteria seized her once more and she exploded, "Stop the car! Stop the car, now!"

"But, Miss…"

"Stop the car right now!"

Although still somewhat perplexed, I stopped the car.

Immediately, she jumped out screaming some profanity. All I truly understood was the word, 'stupid' which I heard repeated over and over until she was out of view.

I could not shake the incident from my mind and I worried about the girl and her circumstances. After my shift, I went straight home and related the strange encounter to Diana. After hearing the few details, she cocked her head to one side, rolled her eyes slightly, and asked, "Frank, haven't you figured out by now what she was after?"

"Diana?"

She smiled, "Oh, Frank...you truly are—"

Enlightenment dawned, "Never mind, Diana."

The Case of the Coveted Coat

After picking up a sailor from a local bar, he directed me to the shipyard. While driving, he shared with me that his ship was due to leave shortly. He seemed to be quite an agreeable young man and I was happy to have him as a fare. The distance from the bar to the ship was quite lengthy and I anticipated that this sailor would do right by me. Traditionally, sailors had the reputation of tipping handsomely and I had no reason to think that this man was any exception.

When we pulled up to the dock area all was quiet. It was so quiet, in fact that I felt like a bit of an intruder. The sailor reached into his pocket for his wallet.

I smiled in happy anticipation.

He frowned as he opened his wallet. Then he started talking to himself. Then he cursed. Slowly, he closed his wallet and returned it to his pocket. Sheepishly, he looked up at me and muttered, "Well, driver, I am afraid I am flat broke. Did not know I spent it all. Maybe someone helped me spend it..."

My first thought was one of relief; relief that I was not accused of being responsible for the empty state of his wallet. Then he continued, "So, what's the deal now? What do we do?"

I explained the procedure, "Well, you have to leave something of value – something well worth the fare. You have ninety days to claim the item and pay the fare or you forfeit the collateral."

"So, what shall I leave you? I cannot leave you my wallet; I need my shoes. They are a must for work."

I looked at him. He was wearing an attractive camel coloured three-quarter length coat. It was a beautifully tailored coat and was perfectly fitted to his body type. I couldn't help but notice that we were close to the same height and body size. In my mind I wondered what he was thinking. I knew what I wanted him to offer as collateral—his coat. Immediately, I felt guilty. That coat was a prized possession. I knew of its value in a Canadian winter. *Was he going to ask me to wait while he boarded the ship to see if he could raise the money by borrowing from some of his shipmates? What was he thinking?* Then he said, "Tell you what. Here, hold this coat. I will be back for it. Is that okay?"

"I suppose. But don't you need that coat?"

"Not really. I've got another on the ship. Is that okay with you?"

"Yes, definitely."

He boarded the ship and I left.

When my shift ended for the night I took the coat to the office and reported the incident. Margaret explained that I had to pay the fare myself. Then, in ninety days, if that fare with some interest was not paid, the coat automatically became mine.

Another driver had been taking in our conversation and made me an offer on the coat. He proposed, "Frankie, you need the money. I'll pay his fare. You can have the cash. I'll even throw in a little extra for you. What do you say? Is it a deal?"

Obviously he loved the coat, too. He looked at me expectantly. True, I could use the extra cash; but, I coveted the coat more than I needed the cash.

"Thanks for trying to help me. I'll be okay."

As was the custom, I surrendered the coat to the office.

Nearing the ninetieth day, everybody agreed that it was time that I took the coat home. We had had no word from its owner.

I brought the coat home and hung it up. I did not dare try it on. I did not want to get too attached. With each succeeding day, I thought more and more of the coat. Still I refused to try it on. It was not mine. The ninety days were not up... yet.

Then, on the ninetieth day, I took down the coat. I tried it on. It fit perfectly. Diana loved it. I dared to hope that it could be mine. Just a few hours to go...

Then, within the hour, we were summoned from upstairs by our landlady. There was a call for Frank.

(Since we had no phone of our own, our landlady allowed us the occasional use of their phone.)

Mrs. Hebden urged, "Hurry, Frank. The man sounds impatient."

It was the sailor.

"Hello, Frank. I am the guy from the ship. You have my coat?"

"Yes, I do."

"Well, I would like to make arrangements to get it back. Where can we meet to make the transaction?"

"It would be best to do it at the office."

"Great, how soon can you get there? I will pay your taxi fare from your place to the office and return. I am also prepared to compensate you for your time."

"I can be there in forty-five minutes. Is that okay with you?"

"Great. I'll see you *and* my coat in forty-five."

I needed the forty-five minutes because I was not taking a taxi; I was taking the bus.

We met at the office and made the exchange. He seemed very happy to have this prize back in his possession.

The sailor, true to his word, compensated me handsomely for both my time and the fare to and from the office.

It was with quiet dejection that I took the bus back to the apartment. Diana knew just how I felt and gently embraced me whispering, "Frank, it was meant to be…"

Perhaps it was meant to be. But happening as it did in the last hour of the ninetieth day was hard to accept. Just when I had begun to allow myself to think that the coat could be mine, it was snatched from my grasp. For one blissful hour, I dared think of it as mine.

Indeed we mortals are "the sport of the gods".

78

Two Faces of Respect

As a child I had been taught to be most respectful of the elderly. Such respect was given both dutifully and freely. I carried those teaching with me into my new life in Canada, most of the time such teachings were a blessing; sometimes they put me at risk.

One snowy night I received a call directing me to pick up two elderly ladies at a bingo hall. When I arrived at the hall I noted that they needed some assistance to make their way to the car. That, I gave dutifully. Upon reaching their residence, I stopped. The distance up the walkway, and the suspicion of slippery conditions prompted me to advise them that I would escort each one of them individually to their front door. They seemed appreciative. The fare was close to three dollars. Each of them handed me a two dollar bill (back when two dollar bills still existed) and directed me to 'keep the change'. A dollar tip for a three dollar fare was quite a substantial tip and I thanked them for their kindness. I remembered wondering at the time whether those ladies could afford to be so generous.

Driving back to the taxi stand I was feeling very blessed indeed. Then the voice of Carl Roach himself came over the intercom and ordered, "Frank."

"Yes, Sir."

"Please come directly to the office. Make no stops," he directed.

"Yes, Sir."

I hurried down to the office wondering what the nature of the emergency was. Once inside, I noted the presence of two uniformed police officers.

"Frank, these are two police officers are here to ask you some questions," explained Carl.

Immediately I became uneasy. *What kind of questions? What do they think I have done?* I repeated, "Some questions, Carl?"

"Yes. You do not have to answer their questions if you don't wish to. I will let the officers explain."

Then, the more senior of the officers spoke. "Frank, a complaint was made by the two elderly ladies you just dropped off..."

I interrupted, "Complaint? What is it that they claim that I have done, officer? I have tried to be kind and respectful toward them."

"They claim that they gave you two twenty dollar bills by mistake. They say you took the money and drove off."

This accusation silenced me. It was so far removed from the truth that I had no response. Then, the younger officer spoke, "Frank, may we ask you to empty your pockets? And may we see your wallet? It would clear up matters."

I hesitated. I knew that the women had not given me two twenty dollar bills. That did not mean, however, that I had no twenty dollar bills in my possession. I wondered whether I would be incriminating myself if I agreed to the officer's request; my wallet might very well indicate guilt.

Then the younger officer added, "I know what we ask is difficult. We do it not because we think that..."

Before he could finish, I agreed, "Officer, I will."

I emptied both my pockets. In one pocket I had a collection of bills, but no twenty dollar bills. Then the officer opened my wallet. In the front compartment, I had a couple of singles. Behind that, I had three twenty dollar bills, and a ten dollar bill. The twenties were very crisp and new. Before the officers could wonder, I explained, "Officers, my rent is seventy-five dollars – it is due in just days. I am trying to save up to pay it. I just need five dollars more."

Then the senior officer spoke, "So sorry to put you through this. Of course, you are innocent. Those two old ladies have tried this before… with another taxi company. Sorry about what you must be going through."

After they left, the dispatcher was close to tears. She didn't know whether to cry or scream. She was so incensed by the behaviour of people whom we have been taught to respect that she opted for the latter reaction and yelled, condemning their action. "What tricksters those women are, Frank. I am so sorry you had to go through that. They probably thought that you were an easy mark. Frank, don't let that get you down. Don't let that change you. There are still good people out there."

Before I could respond, Carl commanded, "Frank, give me your wallet."

Surprised, I complied. He took a five dollar bill from his own pocket and placed it inside my wallet alongside the three twenties and the ten. "There, Frank. Now you have enough for your rent."

****

Earlier on in the summer I was sent to pick up a passenger from a local residence. When I reached the address, an elderly woman was already standing on the steps in front of her house just waiting for the taxi to arrive. No sooner had I pulled up when the woman descended the stairs. She had made it all the way to the curb before I had the back door opened. She motioned for me to open the front door.

I thought that that was a bit unusual. Most of my senior fares preferred to sit in the back. I guess I neglected to even say hello, so absorbed was I in my thoughts. I started up the car; still I had not spoken. Before I even pulled out, the woman asked, "Are you not going to ask me for my destination? And how come you have not turned on your meter?"

"Sorry, Ma'am. Where to, please?"

"Look, just drive along Oliver Road. Is that okay? And put your meter on, young man."

The most unusual thing about her was her directness and it was rather charming. She seemed to be looking out for me. I liked her right away.

"Young man, you are not from Canada. Where are you from?"

"Trinidad."

"Trinidad? A warm climate. Whatever are you doing here?"

"A long story, Ma'am."

"Well, we will have time for that story. Drive me to Kakabeka Falls."

This announcement almost caused me to swerve off the road. Kakabeka Falls was over thirty kilometres away; the cost of such a trip would be considerable. I was not sure that my passenger knew what she was asking. I thought it best to advise her.

"Ma'am I am doing as you asked, but you should know that that is a very expensive trip. You can still change your mind. Perhaps I could drive…"

"No, no. Kakabeka Falls. Now what happens if I choose to stay there and not book a return trip?"

"Then I radio it is as a one-way trip. Then on my return trip I can be booked for another call."

"I understand. Now, young man, explain why you have left your sunny climate to come to this frozen country."

We chatted amiably all the way to Kakabeka Falls. When we arrived at the falls, she instructed me leave the meter running while she strolled around taking in the beautiful scenery. Upon her return she suggested, "Now, if you don't mind, you may stop the meter." I saw her look at the meter and feared that she would protest the display. My fear was groundless. There was no protest. Then she advised, "Young man, you will take me back home. If you were to be called for another passenger, why, I will pay the return fare also. Now let's go!"

"Yes, Ma'am."

I did exactly as she directed. On the way, I spotted an ice cream shop. I asked if she would permit a quick stop at the parlour. She agreed. Then I asked, "What flavour ice cream you like?"

"Love Cherry."

"Cherry it is."

I bought two cones: a vanilla one for me and a cherry one for her. She giggled with the delight of a child as I presented her with the double-decker cherry cone.

No sooner did we arrive back at her residence when she opened her purse and gave me the exact amount that was recorded on the meter.

I turned and thanked her for the trip.

When I opened her door for her she alighted nimbly from the vehicle. I escorted her to her door and opened it for her. Then, I tipped my hat to her ever so slightly. She knew that she had made an impression on me and she smiled as she entered her home. Once across the threshold, she turned and asked, "Please let me see the palm of your hand."

Obediently, I opened my hand to show her the palm.

She pointed, "There is a line in your hand and it tells me something."

"What?"

"That you could most certainly use this."

Then she placed a twenty dollar bill in my palm and shut the door.

79

The Will of Mr. C

Such were some of my experiences as a taxi driver. Now I must return to life at the university. Mr. C taught Language Arts at the Faculty of Education. A seasoned professor, he was ultra conservative both in dress and in manner. In class, he never seemed to deviate from his prescribed way of doing things. There was a firm gentleness in his voice but all in all, he was a likeable instructor inciting neither great passion nor resentment.

Christmas Exams were just around the corner and some students were stressed out. I kept up a friendship with several of these students; often we discussed language arts issues during group sessions. The subject of teaching poetry seemed to pose particular difficulty. One student in particular complained, "It will be the death of us all, except you, Frank. You dig that stuff, right?"

I was able to calm the group enough to ask, "What has been the main idea that Professor has advocated in almost every session? Can you remember any story or poem in which he did not touch on that one particular theme?"

Suddenly, I had their complete attention; they were totally focussed and soon they identified the theme that our professor was sure to advance on the upcoming exam. The group was noticeably happier. One of them announced confidently, "So, no matter what the poem, stick to that idea—his idea—and make it fit. We can't go wrong, right, Frank?"

"It should work," I said. "Let's hope so. It's worth a try."

I knew that in this particular course, the teacher's predictable and pre-scribed approach was not amenable to the creative mind or insightful thought. It was best to stick to the basics; it was a case of survival.

Exam day arrived. The poetry section counted for fifty percent of the total exam. I read the poem carefully and discovered that the very theme that Professor had been advocating all year, while it was certainly present, it was not emphasized. I then turned my attention to the accompanying questions. First, we were asked for our interpretation of the poem. We were required to express this interpretation as the topic of the poem. Secondly, we were required to draft five questions with accompanying answers to reflect the stated theme of the poem.

I was thrilled that Professor asked us for *our* opinion. Thus, I offered my own interpretation of the poem and framed a series of questions that would lead to that particular interpretation. Each question was accompanied by appropriate responses indicating the level of inquiry I expected from a student. When I finished I was pleased, confident that I had answered the question fully; I left the exam feeling optimistic.

After Christmas break, the exams were marked and waiting to be returned. Each member of my study group received his paper; noticeable relief was present in their smiles as they regarded their marks. I had not yet received my paper. My friends were looking at me as Professor handed me my work. He leaned over me and whispered guardedly, "I'll see you briefly after class." Initially, I didn't know whether to be pleased or alarmed at the invitation. One look at my mark in the poetry section took away all uncertainty—zero out of fifty. Alarm was the proper response.

After class, I remained. Professor called me to his desk and pontificated, "Mr. Maraj, all semester I had been harping on a certain theme. You did not offer an answer resembling anything I taught. Were you not paying attention?"

I was confused, lost, and bewildered. I was wondering whether I was in a university setting where critical thinking was esteemed as one of the highest virtues to be sought, or was I in a cookie factory where molds stamped out pre-scribed thoughts and actions.

I asked, "Sir, did you not in the very question ask us for our opinions, for our interpretation. When you stated, *'What is your interpretation'* did you really want my opinion? I thought that that was what that question meant. Did you not ask *me* for what *I* was thinking?"

"Mr. Maraj, the answer that you submitted is not what I was looking for. It was not what I thought when I devised the exam. Sorry."

I was not to be dissuaded. I pressed my point. "Sir, let's assume that the topic I offered is *incorrect*. Could you not review the questions I devised and see whether they were legitimate in as much as they were framed to highlight my interpretation of the topic."

Professor clung tenaciously to his position. "Mr. Maraj, if the topic is wrong, then the subsequent questions are all incorrect."

"Professor, before you go, Sir, allow me to share this thought, please. I have been a teacher for seven years. This university has bestowed upon me two degrees—a B.A. in English and Philosophy and an Honours Degree in English. Everything in me tells me that there is an error here. If you ask a student, Sir, for his opinion, then you must consider the student's opinion. Sir, if you wished the student to give you your opinion, all you had to do was change that one word: exchange the word *your* opinion to *my* opinion. Sir, I mean no disrespect to you. I cannot believe that what has just happened has occurred in a classroom in Canada. I honestly believed that our university... your university... was an institution of enlightenment."

I did not tell my professor that it was thinking like his that forced students, our future teachers, to perpetuate what appeared to be the archaic ways of teaching. I did not tell him that without his knowing it he was a serious threat to forward, critical thinkers. I did not tell him that his lack of vision condemned students such as me to feel that we were not fit to live and walk among the *educated elite.*

I did not take the matter any further; I fought hard to let it go; I needed to go on.

80

My Idol

Mr. Femar taught Senior English in the Education Department at Lakehead University. I liked him from the moment of our very first meeting. In both appearance and attitude, he commanded the respect of all his students. His distinguished look, coupled with his intellectual competency, made him a most remarkable teacher. As the weeks progressed into months, my admiration for this very learned professor grew exponentially.

The end of the year was approaching and we had one final essay to prepare for our very learned professor. I chose my topic and began my research immediately. I was most determined to give this final essay my very best effort. I was determined not to disappoint the most distinguished Mr. Femar.

Mr. Femar had recommended a number of authors for our final project. I chose one of these authors and, in the interest of clarification, I need to paraphrase the author's viewpoint briefly. He pointed out as he saw it, the realities of the everyday world regarding human conduct. Then he postulated that there was an ideal world wherein human conduct was elevated to such an advanced degree that the attainment of a new reality was possible. In his estimation, such a reality was akin to a paradise, indeed a Utopia. As I read his work, I became more and more excited and absorbed in his views. He was advocating a transcendental view of life. I was intrigued with the possibility of attaining such a state and was eager to discern how we could aspire to those heights.

Then I began my critical reflection of the work. Not critical in the sense that I wanted to criticize, but critical in the sense of a full examination of the thesis. In my reflections, I noted what I considered to be a gap in the author's thinking. While he grasped with complete authority the *real* world and glowingly testified to the *ideal* world, nowhere in his dissertation did he advance a proposal that would provide a bridge between these two worlds. That omission troubled me a great deal. I went through his writings many times ever searching for the answer to this most basic question: *How does one get from the everyday world to the transcendental world?*

This question became the focus of my attention as I neared the end of my paper. It was with the utmost respect and thoughtful consideration that I voiced my concern. I stated that I had hoped that the writer would have provided us with a blueprint or a ladder by which any man with sufficient will and reflection may scale one rung at a time from the bottom most rung rooted in the everyday realities of this world, to the Utopian view of the world as proposed by the author.

I supported my view by referring to the works of the celebrated author and poet, Matthew Arnold. In his writing he provided the very concrete steps which one must take to achieve a better world. The reader was free to agree or disagree with his view but he provided a foundation upon which we could achieve a better world. Agree or disagree with Matthew Arnold as one chooses. One cannot, however, contest the fact that he provided his readers with the necessary foundation for achieving this better world.

I had spent a great deal of time and care fashioning my argument and I was pleased with the results. My essay expounded the thoughts of the author as I understood them, but it also went further with its critical analysis of the basic thesis. I was most anxious to have Mr. Femar read my essay. I looked forward to his feedback with eager anticipation. The two week wait seemed endless.

Then the greatly anticipated day arrived. Mr. Femar marched into the classroom with a bundle of marked essays. I waited for a smile; nay, for even a hint of a smile. I waited for any little indication of acknowledgement that my submission had pleased him. I waited in vain. He gave nothing away.

My paper was returned to me face down just like everyone else's. At long last, the wait was ended. I turned my paper over.

There must be some mistake. The grade circled on the front of the paper mirrored neither my effort nor my expectation. While I did not fail, the mark was most disappointing.

The comments that accompanied the mark served only to further increase the pain of my disappointment.

Mr. Femar charged that my expectations of the writer were not only unfounded, but also unfair. Moreover, he asserted that my inclusion of Matthew Arnold and his views was both unwarranted and extremely *'prudish.'* On that basis, he downgraded my paper. I died that very instant of utter humiliation.

I could not look at, much less approach, Mr. Femar. I accepted my mark and my fate; they were somehow inextricably intertwined with one another. So fragile was my confidence that this one mark sent my spirit crashing once more upon the shore of the unintelligent. *How dare I presume to think that I had or ever could escape?*

I tried to hasten from the classroom. Mr. Femar stopped me before I reached the door. I did not wish any conversation. Out of respect for his position as teacher, I stayed.

"Frank," he began, "I believe you wrote an excellent paper for most of your essay. Your ending was critically flawed. It appeared that you attacked – and without basis – the writer. Why would you deign to do that?"

I could hardly speak. I could muster only a, *Sorry, Sir*.

He continued, "Frank, why did you choose to end your essay with such negative remarks about this writer? What were you thinking?"

I did not wish to explain, or argue. I wanted to be alone. Mr. Femar would not let me leave. He insisted, "I know you, Frank. At heart, I thought I did. Tell me, why you ended your essay the way you did?"

"Sir, do you really want to know?"

"Yes!"

"*You* did, Sir. It was because of you that I ended it that way!"

"I made you end your essay like that? Please explain yourself further."

"Sir, let's leave it at that. You have made your determination, and I have accepted it."

"No, Frank, please explain."

"Sir, it seems that all my life I have had to regurgitate and memorize and give information back to my teachers. For so long my mind was in the locked position. In my brain somewhere was the key to thinking. I came into your class and you unlocked my brain."

"How did I do that?"

"Sir, your style of teaching was fresh, liberating, and demanding. You wanted your students – tomorrows' teachers of English – to *think*... to become *original*."

"I did?"

"Sir, that day you introduced Robert Frost's poem *Stopping By Woods on a Snowy Evening*... do you remember that poem, Sir?"

"Yes."

"I remember the lesson you taught that day. I remember how excited you were when you felt that our class had grasped the essence of the poem contained in the line, "I took the road less travelled." I remember so well your unfettered admiration and confirmation that any and every student must dare to make a choice and stand by that decision. I recall only too well your challenge that such a student must think through each decision and stand by that choice if even it is not the popular choice. You emphasized that the road less travelled can be indeed very solitary."

Mr. Femar remained quietly pensive.

"I applauded you then. Today you used the word *prudish* to describe part of my essay. The word cut me deeply. I would have thought that you, Sir – above anyone else – would have recognised that the ending of my essay reflected that I had taken the road less travelled. Sir, how could I have been so utterly mistaken, so totally wrong? Goodbye, Sir."

And I left.

Sadness and confusion prevailed in my spirit.

Much had been lost.

81

Denied, yet...

"Frank, most Fridays after class, some of the staff go for a cool one. Can you join us this Friday? We'd love to have you."

"Mr. K, I am sorry. I would love to join you all but I do have to hurry home. My wife, Diana, is due soon and I need to be with her…"

"Frank, it is understandable. Before you go, I wanted to tell you personally that there will be a vacancy opening up at our school for an English position. Be sure you apply. I am not the only teacher who wishes you to join our staff. I can make no promises. We all really enjoyed you. Let me congratulate you and your wife, Diana. What are you hoping for?"

"Why, a girl, of course."

"Good luck."

Mr. K. was the chairman of the English department in this local high school. I had the good fortune to find a student teacher placement in his school. He, along with the other teachers in the department, welcomed me to their midst and I was elated to be considered part of the fold. At the conclusion of my placement, Mr. K. issued a glowing report on my behalf. I was more than pleased. That, in and of itself, was sufficient recompense. That he would seek me out and encourage me to apply for a teaching position within this very school, was beyond my scope of comprehension.

As soon as the position was posted I submitted my application. Mr. K's words of encouragement gave me hope that I might be considered a worthy candidate. And so began my journey of hope. From the outset I had to acknowledge—albeit reluctantly—that there would be dozens of applications for this position. In those days in the early seventies, there were very few jobs coming available. And, for the jobs that were advertised, there were hundreds of graduates eager to apply. The competition would be formidable.

When my landlady learned that I had applied for a local position, she almost begged me to apply for my Canadian citizenship. She recognized that times were hard and that employers would be under pressure to hire a Canadian over a perceived outsider. At the time, I could not entertain her entreaty.

In due course I received news that my application had been placed among those whom the senior administration wished to interview for the position. Ten names had been selected for interviews. Following the preliminary interview, the list of ten was shortened to three. I was one of the three.

The university year had officially ended and I had returned to driving taxi for the time being. The very real prospect that I might have the opportunity of teaching English right here in the Lakehead had me excited and somewhat distracted.

Soon, Mr. K contacted me and announced that the list had been shortened from three to two. My name was one of the two. Final interviews were scheduled.

During the initial stages of the interview I was quite nervous. The principal soon put me at ease. The fact that Mr. K was part of the interview team further eased my anxiety. I gained in confidence as the interview progressed. By the time the interview was over, I dared to be quietly hopeful. As Mr. K ushered me from the room, he confided that I had interviewed very well.

Some time later that day, Mr. K contacted me to advise, "Frank, I'm so very sorry but you did not get the job."

Silence.

"Frank?"

"Yes."

"Could I see you for a few minutes? Can we meet after school today?"

"Yes, I will be there, Mr. K."

I was so very sad that I did not get the job. The knowledge that I had made it to the very short list gave me reason to celebrate that I had been recognized as someone worthy of hire. I told myself that not getting the job was not the same as failure. While I was sad, I was not crushed.

When it was time to meet with Mr. K, my mind was clear. He was quiet when I entered his classroom. His manner was serious and subdued when he spoke and I knew he was taking care to be sensitive to the conditions surrounding our meeting. "Frank, thank you for coming. How are you?"

I appreciated his thoughtful concern. "I am now composed. Earlier I was sad. I was beginning to allow myself to dare to dream that I could work here at this school."

"I know, Frank. We are sorry you were not selected. I wanted to share some information with you. First, how many applications do you think we received?"

"Dozens?"

"No! More than a hundred. Now think on that for a moment. And you made it to number two. What an accomplishment, Frank."

The reality of what he had just explained—more than a hundred applications and I made it to number two—sank in.

"Mr. K, I did do well then, didn't I?"

"Not so fast, Frank. You recall that I said that my recommendation was overruled. Well you were my number one choice! You still are!

"Now what are you going to do, Frank... any leads on any teaching positions? Please feel free to ask me for a reference."

"When the time comes, I will be sure to contact you. For now, I must be going. I have job applications to fill out. Meanwhile, I do have a job that I must get back to."

"A job? Doing...?"

"Driving taxi for Roach's of course."

"Frank, before you rush off, allow me one more moment of your time. You are going to be challenged in your search for a teaching job. There are not too many out there right now. Yet, you must not give up."

"I won't."

He then paid me a supreme compliment when he said, "Here you are being groomed to be a teacher. No, Frank, you already *are* a teacher, and a very fine one at that. I know. I have witnessed it."

Hearing those final words, I took my leave.

No. I did not get the job. That was not to be. Instead, I received a shot of inspiration.

Long embedded in that corner of my soul were strewn the tattered fragments of rejection and stupidity. Such a garment old and worn, held obstinately strong for so long, now stirred a little. Someday, the disintegration of that tattered garment that still threatens my spirit might be complete and my dream to be free, free to think, free to feel normal, shall be realized. Until then, I continue to forge my way forward.

82

Our Reluctant First-Born

It was Father's Day—June 18, 1972. Diana indicated that it was time to go to the hospital. I was almost certain that we were going to have a girl. Both Diana and I were looking forward to the birth of a girl. We had no boy name picked out yet, so far we could agree on a set of initials only, if the baby were to be a boy.

After the initial signing in, Diana was ushered into the labour room. I was excited to think that our first born was to make an appearance on Father's Day. I was one lucky man.

Eventually, I took up residency in the waiting room with the other expectant fathers. We all were pretty much in the same boat: waiting. One by one the hours passed and one by one all the other fathers were rewarded with their little bundles of happiness. All, that is, save for me. New dads replaced the old dads. The only common thread uniting us was the anxiety of waiting. Men who had come in hours after me were receiving news of their child's birth. I did not understand. What was taking so long?

There was now just one hour remaining before mid-night. There was still time for me to become a father on Father's Day. Now, only two of us were left in the waiting room.

The other expectant dad could not sit still. He paced back and forth incessantly. I appeared composed, just sitting, waiting.

At some point in his pacing, he stopped to ask, "Your first?"

"Yes."

"What you hoping for?"

"A daughter."

"Not me, man. I want a son. I already have three girls." He continued his pacing. Just before midnight a smiling nurse peaked into the room and announced to him, "You have your boy, a healthy bouncing boy. Congratulations."

He let out a yell and danced up and down. "Yes, yes." Before either of us knew what was going on, he grabbed me and lifted me off the ground. "Man, we finally did it. We have a boy—here, have a cigar, Buddy."

After handing me a cigar, he vanished. His excitement at having a son, lingered in my mind and I began a new scenario and I began to think, *Well, it wouldn't be so bad if we had a boy. Boy or girl is okay. I just hope everything goes smoothly and the baby is born healthy.*

By now I was all by myself in the waiting room and the clock on the wall indicated that it was well past midnight. I guess our baby, boy or girl, wants me to *earn* my father's day. He or she was ensuring that I don't get to claim title to the day for the next year. I released the thought.

I started to worry. This birth was taking a long time. No one had come to inform me about Diana. I ventured to the nurse's station. The nurse explained that all was well and that I should just relax. The baby would come when it was ready. I tried to relax.

It was now just after three in the morning and a nurse approached. I looked around. I was the only one left in the waiting area. She had to be coming to me.

"It's a boy."

"A boy. Just what I wanted."

I was ushered in to see them both. They were both well.

Diana looked up at me expectantly. Wondering how I was doing with the news that the baby was a boy. I told her that at just about three hours ago I had changed my mind. I wanted our first-born to be a boy. Diana chose the name Trevor.

Now our baby had a name of his own—Trevor-Jay... and a mind of his own for he took twenty-seven hours to make his way into our world.

Seven days later it was time for Diana and the baby to be released. A nurse announced to us that our taxi was waiting. This was not just any taxi; it was a Roach's Taxi. And, the driver was not just any driver, it was my associate and friend, Howie. Earlier on in the week, we had mutually agreed that he would be the one to bring us home from the hospital.

"Congratulations to both of you. The baby looks just fine. I thought I might come up and help out."

Howie grabbed the suitcase. I collected the many extra packages that came with having a baby and Diana carried the baby. Howie held the door open for us and for the first time our little family was all together in the back seat of a Roach's Taxi. Howie drove with extreme care. When we arrived at the apartment he helped us carry everything inside. I thanked him for all his assistance and I reached for my wallet. Howie extended his hand to stop me.

"No, Frank. No charge. This one is on me."

83

Destiny?

It was now nearing midnight. Both mother and child were asleep. For me, sleep proved elusive; so many thoughts swirled in my mind.

Short months ago, I was a single man with no real responsibilities outside myself. Then a new development came into my life. While it was unplanned, it was not unwelcomed. The timing of our marriage came as a surprise to both of us but we welcomed this new reality into our lives. My brain had to be reprogrammed to register that new development. We were united as one and I had to take Diana into consideration in everything that I undertook.

Early on in our marriage, a neighbour invited us over for tea and to congratulate us on our recent wedding. She had just purchased a brand new coloured television and wondered if we would be interested in taking over her old black and white set. She *said* that she wasn't certain that it even worked any more but we gladly volunteered to put it to the test. The screen was small and the picture was clear and the volume worked fine. We were left to wonder if that was our neighbour's way of *giving*. We were happy. Every Friday night around ten o'clock, *Hawaii Five-O* was on. We made ourselves available for T.V. viewing at that time.

When our landlady, discovered that Diana and I were happy *Five-O* addicts, she invited us upstairs to her living room to watch the program with her and the family on their coloured television. She further spoiled us by serving us tea along with dessert. It became a weekly ritual. We so enjoyed the pampering and the conversation (and the television).

Once more I looked in on Diana and the baby. Trevor was tightly wrapped in blankets contentedly sleeping. This most recent development, having a baby, and becoming a father, gave me a completely new identity and focus. A profound feeling of intimacy and completeness seized me. My thoughts turned to my own father, my Pa. Overwhelming emotion seized me as I saw the face of my own father reflected in the countenance of my son. My father, so long departed... how I wished he were alive still, to have seen his grandson. He would have been so proud.

I wondered what my father's thoughts were when I was born. Was he overjoyed, as I was? When did the joy of childbirth turn to frustration and defeat? How long after we were born did he become overwhelmed with responsibility? I know so very little of my father and his innermost thoughts. That is something that I now regret; I wished that I had not been so absorbed in my own thoughts growing up and had taken time to really know him. I was but twenty when Pa passed on; perhaps I thought that there would be time in the future. There was no such time. From somewhere deep within, a realization struggled to find a voice.

I looked at Trevor once more. He was still fast asleep. I imagined my father's sentiments and allowed them to flow through me.

Trevor, Welcome.

84

A Caribbean First?

By mid-summer I had to face the fact that gaining a teaching position for the upcoming school year was not in my immediate future. I put all my energy into the job at hand: driving taxi. I accepted every shift that was offered. As a consequence, I did not see much of Diana and Trevor. I tried to compensate for my long hours away by dropping by the apartment whenever I had occasion to be in the neighbourhood. Occasionally, when my work took me to the local supermarket, I managed to pick up a grocery item or two. When I would drop them off at the apartment I would be afforded a brief glimpse of my family.

As yet uncertain of my next life step, I remained absorbed driving taxi. (Earlier on in the year, I had forwarded an application to the University of Ottawa. Since I had no firm teaching job offer, it was my intention to complete a Masters Programme in Education. I had not yet received a reply.)

Early one afternoon I was craving Chinese food for lunch. Knowing that there was a take-out place on River Road, I stopped in to place my order. Not wanting to miss any calls from dispatch, I waited outside in my vehicle while the order was being prepared. I parked the taxi so that it faced out toward the street; ready to go in either direction should a call come in from the office. From my vantage point I commanded a view of the traffic flowing in both north and south. Highway traffic also had a clear view of me.

I noticed a station wagon headed toward County Fair Plaza. Suddenly the vehicle was no longer travelling in a northerly direction. The driver rushed a u-turn and quickly headed my way. I remember thinking that perhaps this was a tourist in need of direction. I rolled down my window in anticipation of a request. Brakes screeched and stones scattered as the car squealed to an abrupt halt. The driver veritably flew out of his vehicle and rushed toward the taxi.

I became anxious for him; his need must be of the utmost urgency, so intent was his expression. From within my vehicle, I turned to face him, hoping that I could provide assistance. I noted that he was not alone. His wife and children were also in the vehicle and appeared to be in no small measure of distress. From inside the station wagon I could hear the plaintive urging of a woman's voice.

Before I could offer a word of greeting, my face reeled back as the "tourist" applied a fierce blow to my head. Then, while I was yet in shock, the man opened my door leaving me to fall victim to an explosion of fists from the hysterical man. My face and head received the brunt of the battery. As he struck me over and over again, he yelled, "You son of a b****! I'm going to kill you!"

Somehow I managed to grab the radio connecting me to dispatch. I pressed the button repeatedly hoping to raise the alarm. I could feel blood gush from my nose and trickle down my face. I lapsed in and out of consciousness. I could hear yelling and screaming but I no longer knew from where the sounds came. Some appeared close, others eerily distant. I knew only that I was still breathing.

Two other Roach's taxis, having been alerted by dispatch that I was in some sort of distress, pulled up beside me. They radioed for an ambulance and I was rushed to the hospital, treated for my injuries, and released.

Shaken by the experience, I took a few days off work; I needed time to think. Shortly before the incident I had received word of acceptance from Ottawa University. One assault was just one too many; I craved the sanctuary of university life; I decided to return to school.

When I returned to the office some days later to collect my final pay, there was a small gathering. By now, word had spread that I was leaving the Lakehead to pursue a master's degree and several of the drivers had made a point of being around when I came in to say good-bye. The guys had always joked that I was getting a better education driving taxi than could be afforded by any institution.

To my utter surprise, Jordy was on hand to make a presentation. "Frank, we know you have already graduated as a teacher. Getting that degree was a piece of cake." This statement was immediately rewarded by a ripple of laughter.

He continued, "The harder test by far was becoming a taxi driver. That proved to be no easy task. But, Frank, you worked hard and we are pleased to inform you that you passed with honours."

That having been said, Jordy then presented me with a special card, inside of which was crafted a certificate attesting to the fact that I now had a *Bachelor of Honours in Taxi Driving* from Roach's Taxi. I could not hide my happiness, nor did I want to, at being accorded this honour. The staff went out of their way to pay tribute to this simple Trinidadian, who, at that time, had the unenviable distinction of being the first foreign cab driver from the *Caribbean* to be beaten up.

As I was about to leave, Howie teased, "So Frank, when you get to Ottawa, don't go putting the moves on another man's wife. We won't be there to rescue you."

Everyone but me laughed; I did not understand the humour. By way of explanation Howie offered, "Don't be so serious, Frank. It was supposed to be funny. Frank, we know you. Relax."

It was only then that I understood that they were merely teasing. Later, when I was recounting the story to Diana, she pointed out a curious fact to me. She told me that a number of times while on campus, she had almost mistaken another man on campus for me. She said that we bore a striking resemblance to one another and in our early days, she had mistaken him for me on several occasions. She further explained that this young man had a bit of a reputation as a *playboy* both on and off campus.

The full reality of what had happened to me in my cab the day I was beaten came to me then. Finally, I understood why I had been attacked. I could now understand the reason for the man's extreme rage.

My mind drifted to Ottawa.

PART V

Navigating the So Very ...

85

For Want of Fifteen Hundred Dollars

In August, 1972, Diana, Trevor and I took up residence in Ottawa. The top level of a three-storey home that had been turned into an apartment became our new home. We spent our first weekend in the apartment scraping away the evidence that others had once shared these same quarters. We had to ensure that it was baby friendly. Our apartment was located on a beautiful street, just minutes from the Rideau Canal. While only slightly larger than our previous basement apartment in Current River, it demanded double the rent.

At the beginning of the work-week, I hurried to the university to complete making arrangements regarding my finances. While still in Port Arthur, I had sent in a modest deposit along with my registration in order to secure my place in the Master's of Education Program at the University of Ottawa. I now needed to advance a more substantial sum before I could begin taking classes. While concerned, I was not worried. Previous discussions with the university revealed that students undertaking post graduate work at a Master's Degree level received a special fifteen hundred dollar grant from the university. The promise that this grant held gave me the courage to uproot our little family and relocate to Ottawa some fifteen hundred kilometres away. The fifteen hundred dollar grant would just about cover a year's rent in our new apartment. I cannot adequately describe how utterly relieved and grateful I was knowing that that money was available.

Hurriedly, I made my way to the registration office. I had an appointment; a Mr. Dupuis was expecting me. As I was ushered into his spacious office, he was going over my file. He spent some minutes reviewing it before acknowledging me. He looked up over the top of his glasses as he ventured, "Ah, Mr. Maraj, our accounts indicate that you have indeed made a deposit—a very small deposit." He hesitated a moment before continuing, ensuring that he had my full attention. "I am afraid, Mr. Maraj, that that amount is insufficient to qualify you for registration."

Old familiar feelings of discomfort began to resurface in the presence of this man. I felt his lack of regard for me as a person. Trying to ignore his implied disrespect, I directed, "Mr. Dupuis, perhaps there has been some mistake. There should be some indication regarding a fifteen hundred dollar grant that I have coming to me, recorded in your files. Surely that is more than sufficient to cover my registration."

Unwilling to acknowledge or even entertain the possibility that a mistake may have been made, Mr. Dupuis countered in his most authoritative and condescending tone, "Mr. Maraj, this office has an established reputation; such mistakes are extremely rare. You do *not* have any grant for fifteen hundred dollars." He made sure to emphasize the word *not* so that there would be no doubt about what he had said.

"But, Mr. Dupuis," I began, "when I spoke to the Registrar, he assured me that…"

Having no interest in allowing me to finish, he interrupted, "Then take your case to the Registrar."

Temporarily stunned, my reason failed me. I could muster a stutter only, "But, but…"

"Mr. Maraj, there are no buts. With respect to you, your case is really quite simple. Your account is outstanding. Do you have in your possession right now the means to secure the remaining amount due?"

"No, Mr. Dupuis, I do not."

"Then, Mr. Maraj, I'm afraid that you are cut off for the present. No classes until the fees are paid. Good-day."

With those words he effectively dismissed me from his office; feeling both diminished and pathetic, I was at a loss. Not knowing where to turn, I proceeded to the office of the Registrar.

Because I had no appointment, I waited... and waited. After several hours' wait, I was granted an audience. He wasted no time in pointing out, "Mr.Maraj, the grant that you were expecting... that fifteen hundred dollars... never materialized. The government has effectively ceased issuing grants for students pursuing a Master's Programme. It is not the fault of this university." And then, almost dismissingly added, "That's government for you!" As a further afterthought so as not to appear totally insensitive to my plight he ventured, "Now, is there some other..."

"Sir, when we last spoke, when I called you from Thunder Bay, you assured me that regardless of what the situation was, you would certainly "assist" me...

"Mr. Maraj, I made no promises to you, did I?"

"No, Sir. Yet, I was led to believe..."

"Mr. Maraj, I will make a recommendation for a small loan to get you started. I will speak to Mr. Dupuis on that account. Sorry, you'll have to excuse me now; I have... "

I don't remember what other business to which he had to attend. I walked out of that office feeling so pedestrian. So far, in Ottawa, neither my person nor my name was of any real worth. The human qualities of understanding and consideration seemed to have no cache in this highly mechanized and robotic institution. Having been tossed out like so much garbage, I questioned myself and wondered how I could have misinterpreted the earlier more optimistic words of the registrar.

The registrar himself had told me that the government was threatening to stop the funding to the program. But, he also assured, "Mr. Maraj, don't worry. The government makes this threat all the time. And even if they were to withdraw the grant, we will not. We will take care of you. So come on. We look forward to having you here with us."

Given his position as registrar, I had no reason to doubt his word. His words, his optimism, his sentiments are what brought me to uproot my family and move to Ottawa. I was left to wonder why the spirit of our previous conversation was not only disregarded but dishonoured and denied. Was this a common practice in larger centres?

I had to put aside my negativity; I made an appointment to see my student advisor, Dr. McNeil.

86

My Student Advisor

I had barely finished knocking on the door of Dr. McNeil's office when he opened it, and, offering a welcoming smile, invited, "You are Frank Maraj?"

"Yes, Sir."

"Do come in. Please have a seat. Mr. Maraj, welcome to Ottawa."

His manner was most impressive and professional. Being friendly took nothing away from his professionalism; it served, however, to enhance his humanity.

While his suit and tie marked him as a professional, his genuine smile and warmth distinguished his real persona.

Having dispensed with the pleasantries, I came directly to the point of my visit. I informed Dr. Mc Neil of my desire to complete the Master's Program in a twelve month period rather than the usual two year academic period.

"Frank, why are you in such a rush? Why not take the full two years..."

"Dr. McNeil, I am married and we have a baby. I am a family man and I need your help."

Dr. McNeil had grave concerns regarding the feasibility of my intentions and advised,

"Frank, you may very well be digging a deep hole for yourself. Really, the program demands a full two years and even at that..."

I could not allow Dr. McNeil to continue speaking in that particular vein. Feeling the need to redirect his focus, I countered, "Dr. McNeil, I have a proposal. Please let me explain it to you."

"Go ahead, Frank. I'm listening."

"I wish to take some of the additional courses during the current year."

"That will make for a heavy load. I really don't think it's an advisable course of action to pursue, Frank."

"Dr. McNeil, I am focused; I am a hard worker. I can do this," I assured him. "With your permission, of course, I have been thinking that I may wish to tailor certain courses to address the particular needs in Trinidad."

"Trinidad?"

"Yes, Sir. It is my intention to return to Trinidad. I am hoping that you can assist me in selecting courses that will be of value in Trinidad."

"Frank, you are getting too far ahead of yourself. Let's take it one step at a time. Let's say that I allow you to take two additional courses for now; we'll monitor your progress and as the semester progresses, we'll revisit your proposal. Are you okay with my recommendations?"

"Absolutely, Dr. McNeil. Thank you."

"I did nothing. I simply made a recommendation."

"No, Dr. McNeil, you did far more than just make a recommendation."

Indeed, my first impression of this professor had proven to be correct. I felt the promise of brighter days.

I began to like Ottawa again.

87

The Rambler... Like No Other

While we were yet in Thunder Bay, I bought my first used car in Canada. This was not just *any* used car. It was a car that, when I lived in Trinidad, was considered to be among one of the most prestigious vehicles that one could own. It was a Rambler.

Considering my constant financial difficulties, one might wonder how I came to be the proud owner of such a treasure.

Diana and I had been married for nearly a year when we had our first baby. During that time we were both still students and ran daily to catch the bus to the university. After Trevor was born, life changed. Freedom fled. No longer could we run after buses and hitch rides with friends. We always had another consideration—baby Trevs. Someone always had to be home with him. We could not go out together as we once did and accomplish all our tasks. We had to divide up our responsibilities so that someone, usually Diana, was home with the baby. Having the baby, changed our lives; having a baby and not having a car, restricted our movements.

Within three weeks of Trevor's birth, our landlady approached me with a proposal.

She explained that an older lady friend of hers owned a Rambler, and that she was selling it at a quite reasonable price. She had already asked her friend to hold off about officially advertising that the car was for sale until we were told about it. Knowing that my present financial state would not allow me to purchase the car outright, she went so far as to advocate on my behalf for monthly payments.

Telling me about it she implored, "Frank, the car would be perfect for you. Think of Diana and the baby. Think of what it would mean to them."

For whatever reason, I did not say no to my landlady.

The reasons I said yes have become blurred. I know that I wanted to make Diana and Trevor's lives more comfortable but I think that my motives may have contained some element of selfishness. I am sure that a part of me jumped at the chance to be the proud owner of this car that had proven to be a most coveted car on my island.

At first glance, I was hooked. The shining chrome provided a wonderful contrast to the rich burgundy exterior colour. The plush burgundy of the interior was irresistibly alluring. I agreed to the purchase price of five hundred dollars.

After consulting with Carl Roach, my boss at Roach's Taxi, he agreed to accommodate me with any extra shifts at the job. That summer, Diana saw very little of me as Carl accommodated me quite generously and I was able to manage our extra expenses.

I felt very fortunate indeed to have a family, a job *and* a car.

And, it was that very car that brought Diana, Trevor and me and all of our possessions to Ottawa.

Memories of that first trip still linger. Gas was forty-nine cents a *gallon*. Milkshakes and hamburgers were just a quarter each at Mc Donald's.

The music of Daniel Boone singing "Hi, hi, hi, beautiful Sunday," spilled out of our eight track stereo player as we rambled through the countryside. We felt like we were in heaven—music at our fingertips and the world just a road away.

Taking that first road trip to Ottawa—Canadian roads all the way—I began to comprehend the vastness that was Canada, (not to mention the vastness of its bug population).

I remember too my anxiety to wash that car upon our arrival in Ottawa and to restore it to its previous grandeur; how dare such a colony of bugs commit suicide on my beautiful car?

88
A Trial of Rambler Ills

Barely two weeks after arriving in Ottawa, one of the most important members of our family, began showing signs of illness. At the first sign of distress I took her for her first check-up. Strange sounds were emanating from her underbelly and I was worried. Our Rambler was our ticket to the outside world—to sanity—and she needed to be in tip top shape.

Someone referred me to a garage near the University of Ottawa.

The attending mechanic quickly came up with a diagnosis: acute muffler failure. The remedy was readily available—a complete muffler transplant. The operation was successful and the patient made a full recovery; I paid the bill.

All seemed well… for three weeks.

This time the cause of the ailment was less obvious and infinitely more critical. It seemed that the life blood of the car had ceased to flow and the car would not start. The critical care team was sent out in advance to carry the patient directly to the operating room.

I did not much care for the rough manner in which they hoisted up my beloved Rambler. I asked that they be gentle with her. Since we acquired her, she had never been away from us. I worried that home-sickness might set in.

Once safely settled in the garage, a new team of specialists was dispatched to test the circulatory system. Fortunately no emergency had to be declared. No one had to be dispatched to seek out unconventional parts. Again, the necessary and critical organ was on hand. A simple battery transplant was performed requiring only a short stay away from those who loved her. The operation was a huge success. I paid the bill.

A few weeks after the transplant, the car groaned in pain. All was not well in Ramblerville. Again an emergency team was dispatched to carry the patient to hospital. Further examination revealed that a faulty starter was responsible for the most recent ailment. A brand new one was ordered and implanted. The patient responded immediately. Another bill was dispatched... and paid.

After each new diagnosis and treatment came hope for a full recovery. With each new diagnosis also came a bill. My resources, while limited, managed to cover each charge. My faith was still in my Rambler.

All went well for another few weeks. Suddenly, without warning, she went into cardiac arrest after collapsing suddenly en route to the university. The cause of this most recent illness was not easily diagnosed. After yet another tow to the garage and many expensive tests later, it was determined that the car was suffering from a rare form of alternator failure. It would appear that this vintage car was about to succumb to this latest disease. Nevertheless, a team was dispatched to find a cure. Death was not to be the victor yet. A miracle was determined to have happened when a match for this exceedingly rare starter was unearthed. The new life-restoring alternator was implanted. All was well with the Rambler. Not so my pocket book.

Over the past few weeks I had been pouring money into my car. Each repair promised to be the last. Sadly, that was not the case. Now I was really in trouble. I could not afford to fix the car again. I swore that if it suffered one more attack, I would not commit to taking it for any more check-ups; I would rather commit it to its grave. Having thus resolved the situation in my mind, I commenced preparing the obituary:

Here lies my once coveted life companion—my Rambler
It served me faithfully... for three months.
After valiantly battling a series of afflictions,
She suddenly expired.

May my pocketbook now find peace.

******

Peace... Short-lived

For a series of weeks after that, the Rambler seemed to be enjoying the best of health, and we along with it. It appeared that all that could go wrong had already gone wrong and my wallet and I enjoyed some much needed down time. It was pure joy to get in that beautiful car and drive from the apartment to the university and back.

I spent long hours at the university; Diana spent even longer hours alone at the apartment with Trevor.

One day I returned home earlier than expected and suggested to Diana that we go for a drive. I was amazed at how quickly she was packed and ready! Later on she told me that she kept a bag, packed and ready for just such an occasion. She did not want to waste one precious moment of our family together time searching for things and getting ready.

What sheer pleasure it was for us to discover Ottawa together. For Diana these little excursions became highlights—moments in time when the isolation brought on by her new role as mother, was temporarily suspended. Only a few months ago, Diana had been so vitally connected to the world of education. She had graduated with a Bachelor of Arts degree barely three weeks before Trevor was born. Trevor's arrival had completely transformed her world. She never complained; the only thing she ever asked for was for me to never take her directly home after one of our drives; she always wanted just one more trip around the block. I understood and always obliged. The highlight of our week invariably occurred when we discovered Mc Donald's and its twenty-five cent milkshakes and hamburgers. She beamed.

The Rambler figured prominently in our happiness. It allowed us to enjoy Ottawa to the fullest while also allowing us to indulge in the occasional mini-excursion and picnic outside the city limits.

All too soon our life of rambling ended; life was once again reduced to *Rambler ailings.*

By early spring, the car was once again showing signs of distress; the watery vessel within had erupted. The radiator needed urgent attention.

Distress and unease accompanied me once again as she was towed to the garage. I was asked to remain in the waiting area while the car underwent a complete inspection. I checked my pocket for my wallet. It was thin: so too my hopes of the car's survival. I waited as one waits for Death.

At long last, the chief mechanic, Martin, approached. His look was ominous. Death seemed imminent.

"Frank, I have some really good news… and, I have some really bad news."

"Hold nothing back, Martin; tell me everything."

"Frank, the good news is that I *can* fix the leak; it will, however last for only a very short time. You need a new radiator; to get and install a new radiator in this car will be very expensive. But, that is the least of your problems."

The *good news* thus far was still bad enough to render me silent.

He continued, "Maybe you had better sit down to hear this next part, Frank. It's really bad."

I did not want to sit. "Just continue."

Continue, he did. "Frank, you need to get rid of this car. Sell it if you can. It has a very serious problem."

"What do you mean? What could be so wrong? We've practically replaced every moving part. It should be good. No?"

"Frank, take my advice, and don't ask me any more questions—"

"Sell it while you are still in a state of ignorance."

"You must tell me."

"Alright, alright. Just remember, you asked for it. Frank, you have a knock in your engine."

"A knock? What is that? Can it be fixed?"

"You cannot *fix* this engine—you have to *replace* this engine."

Gradually the news began to sink in. I took advantage of the aforementioned chair. The problem was really serious.

While I tried to process the news, Martin grabbed each of us a cup of coffee. Even with sugar, nothing could have been more bitter than that last piece of information. The cost of replacing the engine would far exceed the current value of the car itself. *Was it worth replacing?*

My only consolation throughout all these deliberations was the fact that my particular car was a cut above the ordinary. I still felt that I owned a classy automobile. *Was I wrong?*

Martin must have read my mind. The force with which he delivered his next statement erased what little hope I still had.

Between sips, he looked me straight in the eye and declared, "Frank, your Rambler is a lemon!"

The look of incredulity that spread over my face was answer enough.

Martin continued, "Frank, Ramblers are a dime a dozen here in Canada; nobody wants to buy a lemon. I'm afraid you're going to have a hard time selling your car."

Eventually, the news sank in. How could things be so different here in Canada? How is it that this same type of vehicle, in Trinidad, would be courted by members of the upper class, but, here in Canada, it had no class.

Sensing somewhat the tremendous toll this news was taking on me, Martin attempted to soften the blow when he said, "Frank, I have to tell you. This car is so beautiful… what a bloody shame."

His words were little comfort.

He patched the radiator.

I paid the bill.

But only, just barely.

Leaving the garage I tried to come to terms with my situation. I guess all along I knew that this was inevitable. I just did not want to admit it. *Had not the car itself given me ample warning? Why had I been so slow to respond?*

Well, there was very little room to manoeuvre now. Martin had laid everything out very plainly. Indeed this car was a lemon. The thought itself left a sour taste in my mouth.

Over the course of the next week, I must have checked out a dozen different used car lots covertly. One day a salesman approached me. Soon we were actively engaged in conversation about good used cars. When I intimated that I might be in the market for a used vehicle he loudly proclaimed, "Do I have a deal for you!"

Quickly he ushered me over to a most attractive four-cylinder car. He went so far as to approach his supervisor to "get me a real deal."

When he returned, he asked if I had a trade-in vehicle. I indicated that I owned the Rambler parked in the front of the lot.

To say that he was unwilling to negotiate a trade-in would be an understatement. His response left no room for doubt, "Look, buy this car and I personally will give you fifty bucks to get rid of that piece of junk."

I had no answer for him.

Discouraged, I walked away.

A similar fate awaited me as I tried to negotiate for another vehicle at yet another dealership.

By now the knock in the engine was most audible. And, if that was not sufficiently grave, the transmission started to give me problems.

I could not take it to another garage. I could not begin to consider incurring another huge repair bill.

I took the car to an isolated area to consider my options. The car was near death. It was time to put both it and me out of our respective miseries. We both needed closure. I came across a box of matches in the glove compartment! A fiery ending would be quick, I reasoned. I imagined life without her—no more ailments, no more emergency visits to garages, and, best of all, no more bills. I knew what I had to do.

Just as I was about to take action, Diana's face appeared in my mind. I saw her. I saw her holding Baby Trev. She was smiling and talking to the baby. "Don't worry, Baby. Daddy will be home soon to take us both out for a drive. Say, 'Thanks, Daddy.'"

And an exchange of a million kisses bound us all to that car.

I could not take away their happiness. I needed a better resolution.

Within minutes both the Rambler and I were back at the apartment.

Was it just my imagination or was the car really sounding a little less rattled?

89

Intervention: A Lemon Upgrade

And what happened to that car?

Eventually, I did deal with the problem of my lemon Rambler. But I did not accomplish this on my own for I really loved my Rambler and could not bear to part with it. I'm not quite sure how the situation would have been resolved had it not been for a friend's timely intervention.

One day I just happened to be driving this friend to a car dealership where his car was being repaired. As we drove, he remarked on the very noisy rattle coming from the engine in my car. He volunteered to have his contact at the dealership "look over" my vehicle.

At the time, I still was not actively searching for a vehicle since I had no real resources with which to purchase one. I reasoned that the least I could do was to hear him out. *Listening doesn't cost anything.*

My greatest worry was that this man might insult my car; an insult to my car was tantamount to an assault on my personal dignity. *And that*, I wished to avoid.

Much to my surprise however, this salesman confided that he knew someone who would appreciate my car, especially in the condition it was. That was almost a compliment! He further explained that the man enjoyed the challenge of fixing up cars like mine.

This salesman won my heart. He gave me hope.

Then he took me over to have a look at a beautiful and shiny bright red Plymouth Cricket. As I drew nearer to the vehicle, I swear I heard her call me closer. The car had a distinct appeal; furthermore, it was just one year old.

It seemed to be calling out to me, "Buy me, I'll be real good to you!" (In retrospect, I believe the voice truly belonged to the salesman, himself.)

My heart responded with some caution, "But, I don't know you. I don't know if I can trust you."

Again the car seemed to promise, "You will have no regrets…"
I believed.

Within hours, I became the proud owner of this one year old Plymouth Cricket.

One might wonder, *how does a university student in graduate school, without a job, without any tangible collateral, come to own a one year old car?*

The answer should be no surprise… *only in Canada.*

More importantly perhaps is the question, how could I go from owning a Rambler—a car known to be a *lemon* in Canada, to owning a Plymouth Cricket, a car which was quickly developing its own reputation for being a fruit from the same vine as the Rambler.

I have nothing to say in my own defence. I guess I had to learn the hard way.

But for now, all I knew was that this Cricket was no lemon. In my mind, she was a real peach.

90

Wanted, Just a Little Something

The snow that fell in the Lakehead during my first few years in Canada paled in comparison to the snow that engulfed Ottawa the winter of 1972. While winter seemed to come later in Ottawa, when it arrived, there was no doubt but that the snow was here to stay.

And, since I owned a vehicle, I too had to do my fair share of shovelling. While in the Lakehead, I often volunteered to do some shovelling. Because I was a volunteer, I found the experience to be exhilarating. Now, suddenly being required to shovel, the task became less novel and infinitely more tedious. The exhilaration and enchantment of snow evaporated rather quickly after a few shovelling sessions.

This having been said, I do have to admit that watching the first few snowfalls each year brings its own enchantment. In Ottawa, the falling snow was a thing of beauty and added considerably to our enjoyment of the city.

Diana, Trevor and I often ventured out in our Rambler to take in the coloured lights heralding the Christmas season. Outside our apartment there were plenty of indicators that Christmas was just days away and the streets bordering the Rideau Canal were especially beautiful. Inside the apartment, however, there was little to signify that Christmas was nigh; there were none of the usual indicators: no tree, no lights, and no presents. This simple fact did nothing to destroy the spirit within. Diana baked her special Christmas Nanaimo Bars and I always seemed to find a station that was playing Christmas music. Neither of us complained. We had each other and we had Baby Trevs. We accepted that that was how life was to be... for now.

I did however, feel the lack of a little Christmas *something* to brighten our apartment; and by Christmas Eve day, guilt was creeping its way into my psyche.

Just after lunch I left the apartment—alone. I did not know where I was going or why. I drove the streets mindlessly when I spotted a simple everyday hardware store. I do not know what force directed me to the store; I have even fewer ideas about what caused me to enter the store. What was I hoping to find? After entering the store, a flight of stairs directed my way to the basement. Once there, I noticed a modest toy section. My heart leapt a little when I saw a little teddy bear. Trevor did not have one. In fact, Trevor had very few toys. We purchased mostly books. Trevor played with the lids from the pots and pans and seemed most happy with the noise he could make with them. But, I wanted to know that I could buy something for my son's first Christmas. This teddy bear would be perfect. The price, however, was not perfect. I walked on.

Further on I noticed a tiny Christmas tree, completely decorated, sitting in the middle of a table. It was beautiful. The lights flashed on and off and I was transfixed. At that moment, an announcement came over the loudspeaker indicating that the store would be closing in five minutes.

I remained immobile wishing and hoping that somehow I could make it mine.

Then when a clerk came by and unplugged the tree lights, I exclaimed quite outright, "I love that Christmas tree!"

Uncertainly, the clerk turned to me, "Sorry. Were you speaking to me? Did I hear you say that you love this tree?"

"Yes."

"It's marked down to three dollars."

I said nothing.

She looked once more toward me and ventured, "I'll make you a deal. Have you got one dollar?"

"Oh, yes. I think that I have two."

"The tree is yours for one dollar. Is there anything else that I can help you with?"

While she was marking down the price of the Christmas tree, I brought her this little blue toy telephone. She marked it down to one dollar also. Happily, I handed over my two dollars.

Christmas really was going to be special.

I was overwhelmed with gratitude to the clerk. I struggled to thank her for her gift of understanding.

Awkwardly I began with words, "Ma'am, thank you so much; I really appreciate... "

Not allowing me to finish, she reached out and touched my hand, saying, "Merry Christmas and the very best to you and yours."

And then she was gone.

I'll never forget how Diana's face lit up when I showed her the tree. She could not believe that the tree came complete with its own set of decorations. She set it in one corner of the living room on a box that she covered with a piece of red cloth. Once the lights were lit, we turned off all other lights and welcomed Christmas.

I was excited; we even had a present for Baby Trev. It was just what we needed for our first Christmas together with our baby.

Late into the night, I sat, alone in the darkness marvelling at the peace that came into my spirit as I took in the image of Christmas through the symbol represented by that tiny tree.

91

Delirious

In January, the three of us became very sick with some sort of flu bug. Trevor seemed the sickest but was the easiest to pacify. I remember Diana and I each taking to a couch in the living room. At any given moment, one of us would have Trevor snuggled on our chest. Whenever he awoke, we would have just enough energy to pat him on the back. He would fall asleep immediately.

The illness took its toll on all of us. Diana however, seemed to be particularly hard hit. I believed that it was something more than just the flu. She was sad; but not just sad, sad. She was the kind of sad one gets when one is pining for home.

I had taken this girl over one thousand miles away from any kind of support system—a thousand miles away from all her family and friends. She had been happy to come with me. But, the stress of being a new mother coupled with the stress of being home alone all day with the baby, may have triggered the beginning of a deep sadness.

Seeing the sadness in her face, I knew that I needed to do something.

I said nothing to her about what I had observed.

That afternoon, before going to the university, I went to a branch of the Royal Bank. After asking to see the manager, the receptionist told me that I had to make an appointment. I tried to impress upon her that it was imperative that I see him as soon as possible. She accommodated my request and soon I was in the office of the manager, Mr. Davis.

His greeting was business-like but nonetheless, cordial, "Mr. Maraj, I am Donald Davis. Please have a seat. Now, tell me what I can do for you. My assistant said that your situation was urgent. Well, you have my attention. The floor is yours."

Mr. Davis struck me as a man who appreciated forthrightness. I decided that my best option was to get to the point right away.

"Mr. Davis, I must be perfectly candid with you. I need your assistance. I am asking for a loan in order that I might purchase two return airfares from Ottawa to Thunder Bay."

When I began speaking, he appeared pensive; by the time I finished, he was merely puzzled, "A most unusual request... one I have not heard before. But tell me Mr. Maraj, wherein lies the urgency accompanying your request? Has someone died? Do you need to return home for a funeral?"

He looked to me to justify my request. There had been no death—not in the normal sense—just a death of spirit. Nothing I could say would make sense from a purely business perspective.

When next I spoke, I acknowledged that my request probably made no sense to him. "Mr. Davis, I do not deny that I am acting on impulse. Let me explain. My young bride and I have recently moved to Ottawa from Thunder Bay so that I can attend graduate school. While I am at school all day and half the evening, she is home alone with our young son. Cut off from family and friends she is very much alone."

I paused. Dare I tell him about her sadness and my pain at seeing her sadness? To make such a personal disclosure and have it summarily rejected would cause injury to my spirit. I began to think that perhaps I ought not to have come. Perhaps I was wrong to even think of pursuing this cause. Reluctant to continue, I waited.

It was Mr. Davis himself who encouraged me to speak again when he urged, "Mr. Maraj, I sense that the reason you are here is very personal. I understand that you wish a loan to purchase two return tickets. Tell me why it is so important; I am listening."

Yes, Mr. Davis was listening. His tone had changed; he was not just a money manager. He showed a sense of compassion when he invited me to speak.

I spoke openly; I told him about coming home and finding Diana looking so sad. I told him about her pining for home and family. I told him about my scarce finances.

When I could no longer continue speaking, we sat in silence.

After some moments, Mr. Davis broke the silence, "Mr. Maraj, you really are asking for a loan so that you can purchase two plane tickets because your wife is missing home?"

"Yes, Mr. Davis, that is exactly what I am asking."

"Then that is exactly what has to be done. Now, go and find out the final details regarding the cost of the air fares; when you come back, we will have the necessary paperwork ready."

"But, Mr. Davis, what about collateral? You never asked."

"Mr. Maraj, you're right. In this business we need guarantees and collateral. It makes business sense. But, there are rare occasions when we exercise "gut instinct." This is one such occasion.

"Mr. Davis, thank you, Sir."

I left the bank knowing that I had just encountered a rare businessman—a gentleman who recognized that a man's true collateral is his family.

With renewed optimism, I went home to mine.

92

Haunting Reflections

I had arranged for our trip to the Lakehead to coincide with my university's study week. While we awaited Diana's parents' arrival, I took some time to revisit the university.

After taking the bus to the campus I felt irresistibly drawn to the library and in particular, to the third floor. During my five years attending this university, I had spent countless hours on this floor. I soon located the carrel at which I used to sit, and it felt like home. Looking out to the sky brightened my spirits and triggered a soft explosion of memories of my time spent in this city.

I recalled how good the Lakehead had been to me. Not just my professors and the friends I made through school, but also, the people who interacted in our lives in small ways every day. In particular, I recall a certain bus driver who came to know Diana and me quite well because we commuted on his route quite regularly. I was quite sick this one evening and could not ride the bus with Diana to her stop. I remember asking the driver to "take care of her." He took the words quite literally. Later, Diana told me that he stopped the bus at the end of her street and waited with the doors of the bus wide open so that he could see that she had made it safely to her door (which just happened to be some five houses in from the street).

That was not the only driver that was very obliging and accommodating. We used to transfer buses at the Prince Arthur Hotel. Recently married, Diana and I were very tired returning home from a long day at school. We both loved our Kentucky Fried Chicken. The franchise was located several blocks away down Cumberland Street. Not having time to go there and order directly and still manage to catch the bus to our Current River home, I took the liberty of phoning ahead and placing an order for a bucket of chicken. I hoped that the order would be ready by the time the bus passed by the store. When we boarded the bus at the hotel, I explained to the driver what I had done and hoped that he would not mind stopping to allow me to pick up the order.

At first, he just gave me that look—that look that said *are you crazy*.

I wasn't quite sure what was going to happen when I pulled the string to get off at the KFC until he hollered after me, "Hurry, I can't wait all day."

I had my money out and ready. The chicken was bagged and ready too. The transaction time was less than a minute and I was once again back on the bus. Needless to say, we shared our chicken with the driver. I had never tasted better chicken.

Just then, I heard a voice call me out of my reverie. It was one of my most distinguished English professors, Dr. R.

I acknowledged him with a simple, *Sir*.

He nodded and walked on.

I doubted that anyone would forget the famous Dr. R. When I attended his class, there was a group of nuns also in attendance. This group of nuns, however, had good reason for wanting to forget this professor and his infamous dissertation on two of the Romantic poets.

It was a during my second year at Lakehead University that I took a course on the Romantic Era in English literature from this particular professor. He had a voice that commanded attention. One was not just invited to listen to his lectures, one felt compelled to listen. There were no *sleepers* in his English class. He spoke with such clarity of tone and distinction of diction, that it was pure pleasure to hear him read the poetry of the great Romantic writers. One day, while delivering a lecture on the Romantic Poets, Wordsworth and Coleridge, he addressed the theme "Strange Love" found in their writings. When boldly he read the line: "*... for we too were one in spirit,*" he paused, then declared, "This is proof, hard proof, that Coleridge and Wordsworth were lovers."

Then, while removing his glasses, he looked directly at the six nuns seated in the front row, and declared, "If anyone wishes to refute this statement, do so now, or forever hold your tongue."

The group of nuns, still dressed in the traditional black and white head coverings and long flowing gowns, rose as one unit and left the classroom in protest.

Seemingly unperturbed by their action Dr. R looked at the class and asked, "Anyone else?"

No one else moved a muscle.

No one else seemed to be affected. *Was I the lone dissenter remaining? Were others equally shocked by this professor's blatant disregard for the presence of the nuns? Had he been merely baiting them or was he really that insensitive?* In the late sixties and early seventies no one in my circle of friends was openly discussing homosexuality. The topic was still taboo and I had such difficulties reconciling the idea of homosexuality with everything I felt I knew about God and religion; in my world it was still such an alien concept. I had studied the works of Wordsworth and Coleridge and found their writings evocative, and, at times, compelling. In particular, their notion that man was not merely mechanical, that inbred within him, was the soul; and that soul was not isolated, for the soul was connected in some inexplicable way to nature. Such a notion fuelled my imagination to aspire to the highest areas of the soul. However, when Dr. R intimated that Wordsworth and Coleridge were much more than friends and indeed lovers, I felt betrayed—betrayed by my teacher and the Romantic poets. *Was I being naïve in my expectations regarding this professor and this university?* Perhaps. I know that professors have a right (and perhaps even an obligation) to put forth their own interpretation of published works. This has never been an issue. What was an issue however, was his method; *that* I did question. I questioned whether he had to be so dismissing in word and action. I questioned whether he could have found a less abrasive way of presenting his findings. I questioned why he did not simply lead us through a process of discovery and allow us to come up with our own conclusions. Finally, I questioned his decision to be so blatantly didactic. This professor had a real gift for oratory. His delivery was smooth and effortless. I admired him so much... up until that day. And, I might still be an avid admirer and supporter of his today had he adopted a more subtle approach with the nuns and the exceedingly sensitive nature of the topic of his lecture.

Seeing him today brought back the sadness of my loss.

93

Strange Irony

After leaving the library, I decided to follow the path which led from the university proper to the Faculty of Education. I had no real agenda; I merely wanted to revisit. Upon reaching the entrance I stood still. I had a choice—right or left. I chose right and began walking.

Just ahead of me I recognized the distinct figure of Mr. Mc C, my former Language Arts instructor. (He was the professor who had given me a zero the poetry section of an exam.) When Mr. Mc C saw me he stopped dead in his tracks; there was an initial awkwardness as our eyes met and our minds went to our own separate reflections of remembrance.

He came towards me.

I wanted to walk away.

Knowing that such an action would be considered impolite, I stood still.

Mr. McC recalled my name as if no time at all had passed since our last meeting.

"Mr. Maraj, may I speak with you?"

"Of course, Sir," I obliged taking care to disguise any hint of reluctance I may have felt in my heart.

"Please, Mr. Maraj, let's go to my office."

In spite of our past differences, I recognized the sincerity inherent in this man's character. Because of that, it was easy to follow his lead.

He did not go behind his desk to sit in his comfortable office chair. Instead, he sat in one of the regular chairs in front of his desk. He motioned for me to sit beside him in the other chair.

After a moment of silence he found his voice. His face was growing increasingly red and his voice trailed as he spoke,

"Frank, I am so sorry, I was wrong; you were right."

I could not believe what I was hearing. As far back as I could remember in my lifetime, no teacher had ever apologized to a student before.

He continued, "Can you ever forgive me? You did not deserve the mark I gave you."

Not only had he apologized, he was now asking forgiveness! *Was this real?*

Genuine anguish accompanied his earnest apology.

A new respect for this man was born within me. Any residual feelings of hurt or resentment vanished. Before I could respond he continued, "And the tragedy is I cannot change your mark. I wish..."

"Sir, it is okay. Don't worry."

"But I do worry. Your mark as recorded is not what you have earned. You should have..."

I interrupted, "Mr. Mc C, thank you for your gift."

"What gift?"

"Mr. Mc C, when I received that mark of zero I was sad and hurt. Because of your action today, that mark stands a testament to your dignity. At the time, you did what you thought was right. The fact that you have taken time not only to reflect on our conversation but to change your position, honours both of us. So again I say thank you, Sir. From the depth of my heart, I thank you."

When we parted, I was on a high as never before.

What a strange irony.

After leaving his office I eventually made my way upstairs and found myself outside the office door bearing the name Mr. Femar. He was the English professor with whom I had had a serious difference of opinion regarding one of his favourite authors. My legs would not carry me away from that door. I found my hand knocking softly. Surprisingly, a voice returned, "Come in."

As I opened the door and stepped inside I noticed that Mr. Femar was standing with his back to me staring out the window. In one hand, he clutched a copy of the once familiar text. As he turned around, I could see instant recognition in his eyes. Without a moment's hesitation he came directly to me. An expression of nervous excitement accompanied his voice, "Frank Maraj, I was just thinking of you at this very moment. How relieved I am to see you."

"Sir?"

"I am about to begin my next unit. My mind went directly to you as I reread the particular work that you chose to critique. I now realize that

I was blind, Frank Maraj; I did not see your argument. Worse, I did not *want* to see your point of view. How wrong was I? How could have I been so wrong about you?"

"Sir?"

"Yes, Frank."

"Know that I always respected you and admired you greatly. Today, Sir, I salute you."

"Salute me? After what I have done to you? I don't understand. I gave you a grade that is not fair. I wish..."

"Mr. Femar, I salute you most willingly." For as long as I can remember I had been relegated to dwell in the pit of the unintelligent and the stupid. I was just beginning to climb out of that pit when his evaluation of my paper catapulted me once again into the cave of the perpetually unlearned. But today all that changed. Today, Mr. Femar's remarks rescued me from the darkness and transported me into the light. "Sir, what I feel right now is indescribable."

"Frank, I have injured you. You, my student, have taught me a life lesson—to encourage thinking. All these years I thought that I was a person who..."

"Sir, you are a most inspiring instructor. Today, you are my professor still; today you have set before me an example that I shall never forget: that you, a person of such renown can apologize to me, a mere student is..."

"Frank, you are not a mere student. You are, young man, a student with an intuitive mind...a good mind. Never lose nor abandon your mind. It is your greatest asset."

This was too much of a compliment.

"Mr. Femar, I am likely Sir, to learn from your book of life. I have already taken a few pages to add to mine. Sir, you rate prominently in my book."

What were the chances that I would have such an encounter with one, let alone *both* of these incredible teachers? Never again have I had occasion to meet either of these esteemed professors. From each I have gained deep insight regarding both myself and the world of education. What an incredible day of affirmation this has been for me—a day never to be forgotten.

94

A French Connection

Both Diana and I returned to Ottawa with renewed energy. The visit home seemed to have lifted the veil over Diana's spirit and once again the sparkle returned to her eyes. My attentions were now able to be focused fully on my university studies.

Mr. Piché was my psychology professor. There were very few students in his class, perhaps no more than fifteen. Because of our small numbers, we came to know one another very well and would often meet to discuss the various issues generated in the class.

One of Mr. Piche's lectures centred on the teachings of Sigmund Freud. He began by introducing the laws of nature and by noting that man has several needs: the need for air, the need for water and the need for food. It is incontestable that one could not exist without any one of these factors. They are the necessities of life.

He paused for a moment to ask if there were any questions regarding that premise.

When there were no questions he continued. Nothing that he had said previously prepared us for the bomb which followed.

"According to Sigmund Freud, the human being cannot exist without sex."

The room was absolutely still as this bomb fell on our ears. It shattered our thoughts and exploded our minds detonating fragmented conversation in the room.

One student yelled above the din, "Yes, that is obvious."

And another affirmed, "It is the most natural reality."

This discourse that had been generated by Freud's statement was of such a lively nature that I seriously doubted Mr. Piche's ability to regain control of his class. He seemed, however, to be thoroughly enjoying the chaos that he created. He allowed the animated conversations to continue for a while before asking once again, "Are there any questions?"

Again, there were no questions, but there were more comments.

One student applauded the notion that studies at this level were indeed liberating and refreshing. Mr. Piché was pleased by this response and once more encouraged, "Before I conclude, any questions?"

My hand responded to the question before the rational side of my brain could prevent it. A part of me did not want to ask a question, but another, perhaps stronger part of me, did. Before I knew it, I was the object of a mass stare. I wanted to retract my hand, but the damage had been done; I (and my hand) had been noticed. *If ever a question had to be posed*, I rationalized, *let that question be asked in Mr. Piché's class*; for in his class, one was relatively safe from ridicule.

Noticing my raised hand, Mr. Piché focused his attention on me, "Frank, you have a question?"

It still wasn't clear in my mind if I wanted to speak up so my statement was posed as a question, "Sir, I think I do?"

"Well, Frank... continue. Let's hear it."

"Sir, I am not sure how to frame the question, without appearing..."

"Stupid, Frank?"

"Well, the word I was thinking of using was more like *insensible*, Sir, but *stupid* will suffice if that is more to your liking."

Mild laughter followed the gentle banter. Then Kent, a class associate urged, "Frank, ask away, what the heck, man?"

I summoned my courage, and asked, "Mr. Piché, are you saying that it is Freud who actually made that statement, or is it a general understanding?"

For a moment Mr.Piché was pensive. He did not respond immediately.

Kent filled the void with teasing, "Frank, are you Presbyterian? This is the seventies; come out of the Dark Ages—Liberation is here, yeah!"

His remark triggered ripples of laughter.

When the laughter subsided, Mr. Piché responded, "Frank, you ask a legitimate question. Let me check up on that. I'll get back to you tomorrow."

Since there were no more questions, Mr. Piche smiled and concluded the lesson.

As we all headed out of the class, I was, as I expected, the natural target of many comments. None, however, were barbs intended to wound. Everything that was said, was said in the spirit of good fun and camaraderie.

Kent could not contain his excitement, "Can't wait until tomorrow. It's going to be a blast."

I too was excited for tomorrow. But not in the way Kent was. My excitement was tainted with a little anxiety and much trepidation. How was it that this very conservative individual, namely me, would speak up about such a private subject? I did not know how it happened, but it did happen and I was stuck with the consequences of my action whatever they may be.

My only comfort in all of this was that the students, who were in the class with me, while they enjoyed a relative freedom of expression, always maintained an air of respect both for the teacher and for one another.

The very next day, as promised, Mr. Piche had a response. Much to Kent's dismay, it came at the end of the class, "Frank, I would like to thank you again for your question from yesterday. I did some research, and this is what I have discovered."

The class was focused; everyone became serious.

"Upon investigation, and in answer to Frank's question, I have made this determination. Indeed, Freud did say that sex is a necessary attribute, but he made this statement regarding a group of people whose intellect, shall we say, was challenged."

There was a hush; the disappointment was palpable. The students had been looking forward to Freud for confirmation regarding their own newly liberated views. And now, that confirmation had been denied.

Mr. Piche resumed, "So, students as much as you would like to elevate this concept to Maslow's Hierarchy of Needs, I am afraid that it would not be a legitimate claim. So, that's it for the day. And once again, Frank, thank you for your question."

Kent converted the disappointment in the room when he jokingly hollered, "Boo, Frank!"

His comment brought a momentary return to the past where I had been constantly booed and denigrated. The memory however, was fleeting; although it dredged up the past, it was not a repeat of the past. There was no hurt intended in this *boo*.

This boo meant that I belonged.

95

Boosted

As I was about to leave class that day, Mr. Piché asked me to stay back for a moment, "Frank, may I ask why you raised the question about Freud and sex? No one else questioned it."

Although I knew why I asked it, I was not sure that I wished to disclose my reason.

My hesitation must have given him pause for second thoughts. Before I could make my decision he countered, "Frank, it must be a personal matter; I do not wish to intrude. Yet, I do wish that you would tell me. Whatever you decide; I trust your judgement."

"Sir?"

"Respectfully, I ask, why did you raise this question? What was in your mind?"

"Sir, if Sigmund Freud were right, then my mother should have died years ago."

"Then your mother is a widow?"

"I lost my father more than a decade ago. My mother never remarried. I know my Ma. I just sensed that when you first made the declaration that according to Freud, that sex was as vital as air, that there must have been a mistake... or some misunderstanding. That's all, Sir."

"I know you want to be a teacher. Stay the course."

After that, we went our separate ways. Now more than ever I yearned to return to Trinidad to teach. The university was providing me with the necessary skills and knowledge to be a teacher; men like Mr. Piche were giving me the necessary confidence to return.

I was inspired to continue.

******

Some days later, Kent and I met at the lounge. Immediately, he asked, "Frank, when I called you a Presbyterian back in class, did I offend you?"

"Not at all."

"I think that I would have been offended had someone called me that. And yet you say that you were not offended. Why not?"

"Kent, I sensed that your words came from a heart that was without malice toward me. Knowing that, how could I take offence?"

"Well, Frank, I must say that I now am glad that you spoke up. Even though we kidded you about it, it was good that you spoke up."

"Thanks. I know that now."

"What you don't know Frank and what you need to know is that you helped me—you helped us—to rethink our comments. Thanks, Frank. Good to know you, man."

Nothing more was said. Nothing more needed to be said.

When he left, I was left with the very best feeling.

I embraced it.

96

Ma Comes to Ottawa

Ma was planning on coming to Ottawa in early April of nineteen seventy-three.

We were ecstatic at the prospect of having her all to ourselves for three weeks.

The reality of the eternal cloud of pennilessness threatened to revisit. I was not about to let my lack of funds spoil her visit. Of all the people on this earth my mother is the last person that I would forsake.

My problem was not that unusual. I needed money.

How was I to get it?

My exceedingly heavy course load occupied me for long hours at the university. I barely saw Diana and the baby as it was. But, I reasoned that I just needed a little extra cash to get me through the period of Ma's visit. Diana and I were good at pinching pennies. I thanked God many times that I had married a woman who was quietly content with whatever I could provide. The occasional twenty-five cent burger and shake at McDonald's always lifted our spirits.

I already had private loans from the Royal Bank, and from the University. *How was I to get over this next hurdle?*

I knew however, what I could not, and would not do. I would not ask family for assistance; that had never been an option in the past and it was not a present option.

I reflected on the matter, searching for a way out of my troubles. At school, I was unable to focus on my studies. All I could think about was *Ma is coming and I am ill prepared*. I began losing sleep.

I became obsessed with my own thoughts.

Then, one day, as I was on my way to the university, I stopped by at my regular garage and spoke with the owner. An idea had come to me just as I left home and I acted on it immediately. I explained to him that my

Ma was coming for a visit and I needed to earn just a little extra cash to see me through the next few weeks. I asked if he could use me for a couple of hours a day as a driver or in any capacity he thought that I could best be of service.

Martin's curt and quick answer surprised me but not as much as his subsequent action, "No, Frank. You are not going out of your classes to work. You need to attend classes."

I protested, "But Martin, I thought you would understand and help me."

"Frank, I am helping you," and then he reached around into his back pocket and pulled out his wallet. "Here, this is from me to you for your mother."

I was speechless.

"Frank, if you don't mind, I have to get back to work."

"Martin, this is a loan, right?"

Martin, did not hear me. He was back at work, under the hood of a car tending to the engine.

I had to slap myself to prove that I had not just been dreaming.

The university could wait.

I had cupboards to fill.

****

When Ma arrived our cupboards were no longer bare; Diana gladly relinquished control of the kitchen to her. The days were filled with cooking and eating. Midnight fry-bake marathons were the rule. Ma cooked all my favourites. I think that I gained ten pounds during the course of her three week visit. Ma was overjoyed with the praise being lavished on her and her creations. I was having the time of my life. Having Ma there in our home made me feel like I was back in Trinidad.

Ma and Diana talked late into the night—every night. I lost my wife to my mother but it was okay; they were bonding. Ma bonded with Trevor too as she shared with Diana the way mothers of her generation cared for a baby. She ran through the routine of oiling and exercising each limb of the baby after his morning bath.

Ma loved her grandson beyond measure. One evening, when I came from University, I walked in on a very special ceremony. Ma was burning incense and was conducting a special ceremony in Hindi for Trevor. She chanted softly as she placed a *tilak* on Trevor's forehead, at the point where the spiritual eye is believed to be. She then brought forth her gift of jewellery—a gold bracelet and a gold ring for the baby. Ma ended the ritual with a silent prayer. Once again this proved to be a defining moment in my life, a moment when Ma was free to do and say what she needed to do and say to us… and we bowed respectfully to her wisdom and insight.

Following the blessing of the baby, Ma proceeded to bless our home and yes, even our car.

When Ma wasn't cooking or cleaning, she was out walking with Diana and the baby. They explored all the walking paths in and around our apartment. Sometimes they would pack a lunch and be out all day. Ma loved Ottawa. She loved its beauty but she especially loved it for its cleanliness. She was hard pressed to find any dwelling that even remotely resembled the shattered remains of burnt out buildings that once were apartments in the poorest parts of Brooklyn, New York.

When we went for drives, she invariably commented, "How clean this place is!"

One day I followed up her comment by teasing, "You want to move to Ottawa, Ma?"

To which she responded simply, "I like Ottawa, Frank. My home is in New York."

That is when I knew that she had accepted that her new life was in New York. As usual, Ma was right. Once again I marvelled at her wisdom.

All too soon it was time for Ma to leave. We said our goodbyes in the airport lounge and Ma headed off to the departure area. I stood there waving until she turned around and started to come back. Upon reaching me, she grabbed hold of my hand, and placed a folded bill in my fingers. She rushed away before I could take stock of what had just happened. I looked over at Diana holding Trevor. Her eyes were misty with tears. Ma had left her mark upon all of us. When I unfolded my fingers, I regarded Ma's gift; in my hand she had left an unbelievable and completely unaffordable twenty dollar bill. That was Ma. She always had something tucked away to share with others.

How fortunate was I to have in my life two such women as Ma and Diana. I loved them both… differently, yet completely.

Few are afforded such a blessing.

97

The Grimmest of Realities

It was hard to see Ma leave us, in more ways than one. Her presence masked for a time the grim reality that awaited us upon her departure. While Ma was with us, it appeared as if we did not have a care in the world. All of our needs were being met and we were more than content with one another and our simple life. When Ma left, I was literally flat broke and my spirit was near the breaking point. I kept the direness of our financial reality to myself.

By the end of April, I had completed my first set of courses and I determined that the most prudent course of action would be to find a job... immediately. I approached every fast food outlet and every cab company looking for any kind of work; the answer was always the same: *sorry but we don't require any help at the moment.*

I had known financial hardship before but never had I felt so defeated and hopeless. As a single person, I always knew that I could make it somehow. There was always something that I could do without. But now, things were different; not only was I married, I had a baby to support. I could not ask the same sacrifices of them as I did of myself.

The reality of the next step that I had to pursue hit me full in the face while I was driving to class. A man was trying to flag me down for a ride. Initially I was not inclined to stop, but the exaggerated effort he employed to attract my attention worked and I relented.

As he climbed into the car he was already uttering his profuse thanks, "Thank you, thank you. You are a real life-saver. I have to get to the Welfare Office. I am afraid that I am going to be late and those people... you know what they are like when you are late. They..."

"Hold on. I will take you there, okay? Don't worry. It will be alright."

My deliberate attempt to calm him had the opposite effect and he yelled, "No, it will not be okay. They warned me not to be late. If I'm late, and they call my name... man, they will cut me off."

"I understand. Look, I'll speed up a bit. You direct me to the address."

In almost no time we arrived at the office and he hurried off to his appointment.

I was left standing outside the Department of Welfare. A strange feeling invaded my legs and propelled me into the building. At that moment, the need to get help for my family took precedence over whatever remaining pride I had left in me.

Immediately I was ushered into a huge waiting room. Many others were there before me. I looked at the people and wondered what circumstances had conspired against them to bring them to this juncture in their lives; they needed help and were asking for a hand. Could I do likewise?

I started to make my way to the information desk; I turned back before reaching it. I headed out of the building but was soon stopped by an inner voice, "Frank, in a few days, you will have to pay your rent. What will you do? You have no money. You also have an innocent baby who needs care—forget your foolish, stubborn pride and ask for help."

I heeded that inner voice and returned to the information desk. The clerk did not lift her eyes from her paperwork as she inquired, "You here to apply for welfare?"

Hearing her say the word *welfare* out loud caused me to temporarily lose my voice. Such was my mortal embarrassment upon hearing the word, I could not utter the simple *yes* in affirmation.

Taking my silence for acquiescence, she then directed, "Take this form, fill it out and take it to the office marked *Applications*."

This event marked not just the hardest of times, but also the saddest of times. Filling out that form I realized that courage comes to us in many ways; it was indeed courage that I needed now to take the next steps along life's path. Against a will that was firmly planted in a soil that grew independence, I now succumbed to a need that was greater than my need for independence—survival. After filling out the application form, I dutifully approached the next office in the chain—*Applications*.

The office was filled with so many applicants that my immediate instinct was once again to leave; reason once again prevailed and I patiently awaited my turn. When my turn finally came I was directed to an adjoining room for a private interview. The interview and the interviewer while thorough were purely mechanical. All the bases were covered: married, small infant, student. Each of these factors registered points in my favour. As I was in dire need of rent, I was told that I would be contacted in a couple of days.

The whole experience left me cold. I felt reduced in spirit, diminished in stature and dehumanized in nature.

Had *I* now become a beggar?

*****

Within two days the call came asking me to report to the office. I did so immediately. Once inside the office I was directed to the Cashier. Taking my place in line again I waited. Finally, it was my turn.

"Your name?"

Something prevented me from giving it. I knew not what.

The next time she spoke she raised her eyes and directed, a little more forcefully, "Your name?"

I still would not, could not, give it.

Impatient to be finished with me, she raised her voice and shouted, "I don't have all day! Give me your name, so I can give you your cheque!"

It was then that I screamed, "I don't want your cheque! I want a job!"

I don't know from where that voice came. It was far louder and bolder than I had intended. Suddenly the whole place was silent. All I could hear was the pounding of my own heart. My outburst had silenced the clerk. She looked at me dumb-founded; then she left her office. In a moment she returned with her supervisor. He asked that I follow him to his office.

Once inside, he spoke, "Mr. Maraj, we have a cheque for you. You qualified for assistance yet you refused the cheque? I don't understand."

"Sir, I meant no disrespect. I merely reacted. I don't want your money. I want a job. I need it, badly."

"I understand, but until you have a job, you need some relief... just for a while. Now, here is your cheque."

"Thank you, but, no! Thank you, Sir, for your kindness. If you want to help me, you must find me a job."

Then, shaking and trembling, I walked out wondering why I reacted so violently when presented with the cheque.

On my way home I passed by a cinema that specialized in showing only old films. The admission price was one quarter: a bargain even back then. I purchased a ticket and for three hours, I was lost in the charm of two John Wayne movies. For three hours I had no problems; for three hours I was entertained.

****

The very next day, the supervisor himself, Mr. Warren, asked that I come to his office. He gave no indication of why he wanted to see me. Once inside, my curiosity was further piqued when he reached out, shook my hand, and said, "Mr. Maraj, I hope you believe in miracles, because a miracle of sorts just happened."

"Mr. Warren, a miracle? I don't understand."

"Well, we have found you a job. Last night, the driver for a certain company lost his licence when he was caught driving under the influence. He was involved in a terrible accident, and was liable. Do you drink, Mr. Maraj?"

"Only socially, Mr. Warren."

"Great. Well, here is the name of the manager and the address. You are to report to that office immediately."

I could hardly believe my good fortune, "Mr. Warren, how can I thank you, Sir, for helping me to find a job? Nothing you could have said could make me any happier than I am at this very moment."

"You could do something that would also make me feel happy."

"What could I possibly do for you?"

Then Mr. Warren handed me the cheque that I had refused earlier. I studied the lines on his face and knew that I was looking into the face of a man, not some mechanical automaton. There was no judgement in his face—only honesty and compassion. I cannot believe that I reached out, smiled, and said, "Mr. Warren, I am grateful. Thank you kindly."

Mr. Warren returned my smile.

I am forever grateful to Canada for extending her arms to me.
I am forever indebted to Mr. Warren for restoring to me my dignity.

98
Dr. Mc Neil

Now that I had the offer of a job, I could turn my attention to other things. The next most pressing need that I had to focus on was to arrange for the summer courses I needed to take in order to complete my Master's Degree. To that end, I arranged to meet with Dr. McNeil.

Seeing him heightened my joy. But, I must admit, that I was feeling slightly anxious about what I was about to ask.

After exchanging cordialities, I came right to the point, "Dr. Mc Neil, I have a proposal regarding my studies that means a great deal to me. I would like to share this proposal with you. I also ask that you consider my proposal."

"A proposal, Frank? Sounds intriguing. Tell me what you have in mind."

It felt so good to finally have found a place in education where one's thoughts and opinions can be considered. Dr. Mc Neil's office was one such place. He might not accept my proposal but I was assured that I would have the distinct pleasure of being heard.

And so, I began, "Dr. Mc Neil, I believe that you are aware that I do intend to return to Trinidad and seek a position in education there."

"Yes, Frank, I am well aware. You speak about it all the time. I know how important it is to you to go back to your home."

"Sir, the courses that I have studied so far reflect Western outlook. Western ideology is infused in all the courses. Now, Trinidad too is certainly guided in its educational methods and philosophy by Western practices. In particular, Trinidad's own educational system is modelled after the British system. This seems quite natural considering our past history with Britain."

When I cast a glance at Dr. Mc Neil, I could see that he was indeed listening; I was encouraged to continue.

"Dr. Mc Neil, Trinidad boasts an East Indian population equal to its Negro population, yet the philosophy and ideology of Eastern culture is not represented sufficiently in the overall curriculum of Trinidad."

"And you, Frank Maraj, are suggesting that one of your courses should revolve around Eastern thought. How am I doing?"

"You have hit the nail dead on!"

"I welcome your initiative, Frank, and I assure you that I will look into the matter. Meanwhile, you still have to select other courses. Let's do that now."

We agreed on a program.

I deliberately chose courses that began after five o'clock. That choice allowed me to accept the job I had been offered. I did not let administration know that I was accepting a full-time day job. I knew that they would try to dissuade me from adopting such a path for they already thought that trying to do my degree in one full year was challenging in and of itself. The courses threatened to be very time consuming but I felt that I was up to the challenge.

99

A Nebulous Mr. Blubber

Mr. Warren had provided me with the address of the warehouse to which I was to report for my new job. While it was located in the city of Ottawa, it was close to the bridge that led to Hull, Quebec.

I went inside and made my way directly to the office where I had been instructed to meet with the manager, Mr. Clarence Blubber. Our first meeting was devoid of formality. For the first few moments he merely stared at me. When he spoke, there were no introductions, only a question.

"Do you speak French?"

"No, but I understand a little."

"I suppose you took a course at a university..."

He went on to mumble incoherently about something or other but I could not understand one word of his utterances.

He took a slight pause from his ramblings to emphasize, "You will need to understand some French. We have clients that are French. But, never mind about that now. You do have your driver's licence?"

I nodded.

I felt no real connection between this man and myself. Not only did I not feel a connection, worse, I felt a distinct distance between us. At the very least, he was *unwelcoming*. But that is not what troubled me. What did trouble me was the way he stared at me. His stare was the stare of one disappointed or disgusted.

He did dress well, however, and he gained a certain regard because of that one condition only. It did not dawn on me until much later how inconsistent his manner of dress was given the nature of his job in a dust filled warehouse. Eventually, I came to understand his choices.

When he took me on a tour of the warehouse he took a moment to explain the nature of the business. "We are a Good Will agency. We pick up household items from people who no longer have a use for them and store them here until they are needed by someone else. When we get a request for a certain item from someone in need, we then deliver it."

There were fridges, stoves, washing machines, dryers, couches, beds, chairs etc. scattered everywhere. I wondered how anybody found anything in the confusion.

He must have anticipated my question for his next comment was, "The warehouse needs proper organization. Certain items need to go to the dump. Decisions have to be made. I expect that you will act responsibly. We do understand each other?"

"Yes, Sir."

"Very well. Follow me. I will introduce you to the other two workers. Now, I expect production."

I was introduced to two other young men, Andre and Danny. I liked them right away. Before leaving, Mr. Blubber said, "Frank, if you need anything, speak to Andre. He will know. He is experienced. Now, we need to make some trips to the dump. We have to make space. We have too many useless items here."

Still mumbling, Mr. Blubber left.

I looked at Andre and Danny. We smiled knowingly at one other as if we shared a secret. I was left to think that these two young men had also been subject to *the look* from Mr. Blubber. In that sense, we shared a common bond.

Andre took the lead in initiating Operation Clean Up. I was a happy follower.

******

I am… I am?

When I arrived at work on my fourth day, Mr. Blubber was there—waiting for me. Without so much as a good-morning, he called me into his office. Neither of us sat down. I did not sit because I had not been invited to do so; Mr. Blubber did not sit because he found that he could yell louder from a standing position. As he yanked out the log book, he pointed to the previous two days' entries and yelled, "Frank, your production rate is unacceptable… in fact, your delivery record is most unprofessional. It is just as I suspected. You are the wrong person for the job. I have to…"

I had to speak up; I did not know what he was talking about. "What's wrong, Mr. Blubber?"

He jabbed his finger repeatedly in the log book yelling, "Look, look at this. See for yourself. Unacceptable. Unprofessional."

The book to which he was referring recorded where trips were being made and the time it took to accomplish each trip. In the last three days, the crew had made several trips to the dump transporting unnecessary items from the warehouse. We had made only a few actual deliveries.

I could not understand why I was bearing the brunt of his anger when I was the newest hire and the least experienced in the ways of the warehouse.

He grabbed the book with both hands and almost shoved it in my face shouting, "Frank, you are wasting a lot of time making trips to the dump! Your number of deliveries should be double what is recorded here. These numbers just confirm my initial impression. I never ever thought that you were up to the task. This record proves it. I need to..."

Sensing that I was about to be fired, I took a chance and interrupted him before he could actually complete his thought, "Mr. Blubber, should you not be talking to Andre? After all, he is in charge."

"What are you talking about? Andre's not in charge."

"But you told me to talk to Andre if I had any questions..."

"Frank, you have what used to be Andre's job. When he lost his licence he no longer drives. He is no longer in charge."

"Then, Mr. Blubber, who is in charge?"

"Who is the driver of the truck?"

"I am."

"Then, you are in charge."

"I am?"

Mr. Blubber then began mumbling something about university students being stupid.

I chose to ignore his remarks. After all, I just learned that I was in charge.

In my mind, not only had I escaped being fired, I had been promoted.

Things were about to change.

*****

The previous evening, the three of us, Andre, Danny and I, had prepared a load for the dump. It was already loaded on one of the trucks and was ready to go.

Andre met me as I was leaving the office. Evidently he knew that I was being reprimanded by Mr. Blubber and he had words of consolation ready for me. "I guess the boss is uptight. Frankie, he is always complaining. Don't pay him any mind."

The three of us climbed into the truck and headed for the dump to unload the items that were designated as being unusable. Some of the things that we, as an agency, were throwing out bothered me. I felt that some of the items, especially the furniture items, were salvageable. Some pieces were better than the furniture items we had at our apartment. There was a temptation to *rescue* a few of the pieces; but, I resisted. I resisted, not on any moral code, for, truth be told, I felt it was immoral to throw away items which still had value. No, my motives were purely self-preserving—I wished to keep my job. I did not wish to attract Mr. Blubber's attention any more than I already had.

Over the past few days, a trip to the dump was routinely followed by a trip to the coffee shop—a reward for a job well done according to Andre. Today, however, when we had finished unloading at the dump, I took a different route.

Andre was quick to point out my *mistake,* "Frankie, you're going the wrong way. It's time for our coffee break. This is not the way to the coffee shop."

I ignored him and kept on driving. I took us directly back to the warehouse. We prepared another load and again headed for the dump. Once that cargo was despatched, I accommodated Andre's request and headed to the coffee shop.

Danny and Andre loved to sit and check out all the young ladies who were also having their breaks at the same shop. While they were thus engaged, I went into the truck to get the log book. While I chose not to sit with Danny and Andre, I sat near enough so that we could easily communicate. I did not want to impede their harmless pleasure; I did, however, want to impress upon them the importance of upping both our work ethic and our productivity.

"Andre, and Danny, you need to know something. Mr. Blubber is ready to fire me. I feel it."

"Frankie, he is just barking. Don't pay attention to him"

"Andre, my job is on the line. Production is off— we have to do a better job. So, boys—no more extended breaks and we have to do twice the number of loads."

Andre objected, "But Frankie, we need our coffee breaks. Come on, you can't cut us off. Right, Danny?"

Then, Danny spoke up, "Frankie, you and Andre each have someone in your lives, right?"

"Yes?"

"Well, I don't have anybody in mine. This is a dump job. Why, if I didn't have the coffee breaks at this spot, I would have nothing to look forward to. You can't cut off the coffee breaks—man, I need it. Things are different for you and Andre."

"Danny, are you prepared to do the work? We have to produce more and show Mr. Blubber that we are not wasting time."

Andre proposed, "Give us our coffee breaks, and we'll give you production. How about it, Boss?"

Andre had called me *Boss*. How could I refuse?

Over the next few days, production was way up—*a testament to the power of coffee.*

100
What a Turn Around

By the middle of the summer of seventy-three, life was beginning to sort itself out. I worked during the day and attended classes in the evening. I was beginning to find balance. During the day, however, I continued to walk a fine line between the expectations of my co-workers and the high expectations of my boss. At every opportunity, Mr. Blubber had his nose in the log book. I was left to assume that my production was satisfactory since I had not been summoned again to his office. There is not a single doubt in my mind that had I not increased production and maintained that increase, not only would I have been severely chastised, I would have been fired. The threat of being fired remained omnipresent and for that reason I always pushed myself to work harder and do more both in and around the warehouse. I hoped that my actions would inspire Danny and Andre to do the same. Imagine my surprise when I learned that it was having an opposite effect.

One day when neither of them could hold in their disappointment with me, they spoke up. Andre was the first to address the issue, "Boss, we don't understand you. You're always punishing us. You keep us so busy all the time. We always have so many deliveries and when we get back here to the warehouse you are always doing something."

This inspired Danny to inject his thoughts, "Boss, why are you working so hard on the floor? You never relax and take a break."

And then he dropped the bomb, "Are you trying to show us up?"

I could not believe how little of me they understood after all this time together. I had to set the record straight. "Guys, you've got me all wrong. I'm not trying to do anything but keep my job. Mr. Blubber has his eyes on me all the time. I'm always worried that he could fire me at any time. So, I am trying my best to hold on any way that I can. I don't understand why Mr. Blubber seems so against me."

Then, Andre cut in. He spoke plainly, "Why are you calling old Blubberhead, *Mister* Blubber? He ain't no master to us. He wears those fancy suits as though he really owns them. The only thing he really owns is that old Cadillac that he drives."

Then, Danny added, "He thinks he is some hotshot. He wants everyone to think he is high class; he is really a snake, a low class snake. He is probably afraid of you."

"Danny, I don't get it. Why would Mr. Blubber be afraid of me?"

"Because, you are going to university. He feels threatened by university students. He is always complaining about them. He is forever on their case."

Then, Andre interjected with this telling remark, "He thinks people like us are low class. He feels that he is higher than we are... snake that he is."

After the boys had discharged their minds sufficiently, I understood their outrage. Immediately I felt their sense of low esteem. *Had I not walked in their shoes? Had I not been demoralized at work by a supervisor?*

Once again, the person in a position of authority, the person who had every advantage, the person who could easily reach out to extend the branch of civility, chose instead to chop out the root of humanity.

Their outcry demanded at the very least, validation. I had to be careful not to fuel their outrage further while seeking to validate their feelings. Furthermore, I knew how important it was that I attempt to restore to them some measure of dignity.

"Boys, hold on. You have good reason to speak as you do. I see now that Mr. Blubber's opinions and actions have caused you much pain. I am so sorry for your hurt."

Then, Andre lashed out, "You don't have to apologize. You did nothing wrong. You are such a decent boss. Old Blubberhead is the rat that should be apologizing to us—he treats us like sewer rats when he is the biggest sewer rat of all."

"Andre, why do you speak like that?"

I felt like I was losing them. Their anger at the man ran far deeper than I first suspected.

Andre continued to defend his words, "You don't know anything about Blubberhead— the *real* blubberhead."

I had to distract them from their negative preoccupation with Mr. Blubber. I really needed them to be working *for* something not just reacting against Mr. Blubber.

After a moment's hesitation, I knew what I must do. The affectionate way in which they called me *Boss* was very affirming. The very first day that we met I felt that connection; it had merely grown over the following weeks, and now that the air was clear between us I felt that I could trust my decision to ask them for their help.

"Andre, Danny, I need your help."

The forthrightness of my appeal caught them both off guard.

"You need our help? How so?"

"I need you both to help me keep my job. I really need this job, and I really like working with you guys..."

As if he could read my mind, Andre smiled and said, "Boss, I think I know what you are getting at; you want us to work hard with you. Then we can all look good."

"Yes, nothing would make me happier. We'd be a real team."

"Deal! You've got it, Boss!"

When Andre spoke those words, I knew that I had found a true friend, for it was Andre who had lost his licence which in turn triggered an opening for me in the organization. He had good reason to resent me for I had taken over his job as driver and all the little advantages that were attached to that position. The fact that he was willing to help me showed me what depth of character he truly possessed. I am grateful to have met such a man as he.

101

The Duplicitous Mr. Blubber

Several days later, I received a very personal and direct order from Mr. Blubber himself. No work order was presented; just an address and a time recorded on a scrap piece of paper. Mr. Blubber, however, attached one additional verbal request to the order. It was a reminder that we were to make sure that we were *decent* because he did not want to be embarrassed.

I wondered silently about Mr. Blubber's remark; he had never before made such a stipulation and I was puzzled.

Ottawa is a city of dignitaries, diplomats, and politicians. It was to the house of one such dignitary that we were sent.

I had never before been to a house such as that before and I looked forward to this brand new experience. I was later to discover that the experience itself was not all that new.

Andre, Danny, and I arrived at the address at the appointed time. A caretaker at the locked gate announced our arrival. Mr. Blubber and the lady of the house came out to us. Mr. Blubber brought us into the living room; it was filled with articles that separated the merely rich from the decadent opulence of the really rich. The three of us simply stared, lost in the lavishness of these new surroundings. (If we did not have drop jaw syndrome, we should have.)

Noting our inactivity, Mr. Blubber shouted, "Idiots, don't just stand there! Get over here, and start working."

The note that Mr. Blubber had provided us with indicated a time and a place only. There had been no indication of what our responsibilities were beyond showing up on time. *Now, Mr. Blubber was yelling at us and calling us idiots?* I was incensed at the tone of his voice and the insult itself. Not just for myself, but also for my co-workers. I swallowed the insult however, because I needed the job. We went right to work.

Then the lady of the house, and I use the term *lady* loosely, informed us that she had changed her mind about the number of items that she wanted to be cleared from the room when she announced, "Clarence, I have changed my mind. I thought that I wanted to donate the furniture only. But I see that I'll have to change everything about the room so you might as well have them take everything. Take everything from the dining room and the living room."

"Beema, what do you mean, *everything*?"

"Everything means every single thing. Tell them I want to see the floors empty and the walls bare. Tell them it must be done right away."

While I may not have known this woman personally, I was all too familiar with her type. I knew that tone; that haughty sense of superiority was unmistakable. Her words were meant to hurt, meant to demean. And Mr. Clarence Blubber was an all too willing accomplice.

While the circumstance of birth may have denied him access to the socially elite, he never stopped trying to gain access. He used his position as manager to elevate himself, at least, in his own eyes.

I could not wrap my mind around the fact that the woman no longer wanted any of those perfectly beautiful pieces of furniture; all were to be condemned to the warehouse. While Danny and Andre had already begun to comply, her request had rendered me both speechless and immobile.

Perturbed by my lack of action, Beema sneered, "That one standing there! Does he not comprehend English?"

Again I held my tongue. Before I could move, Blubber barked, "Frank Maraj, don't just stand there like an idiot. MOVE!"

As long as Clarence and Beema were within earshot, no one said anything. We channelled all of our energies into our work. Soon, we had loaded everything onto the truck.

By now, Clarence and Beema were outside on the patio sipping tea. Andre made the mistake of deigning to enter into their presence... *uninvited*. His innocence was rewarded with a royal reprimand and dismissal, "You are not supposed to be *here*. Get out and wait for me by the truck. I will see you there shortly."

Clarence and Beema, bonded by their assumed superiority, shared a knowing look. As if to emphasize his elevated status, he derided us further by saying, "See the type that I have to put up with? That's what the government of Canada provides—Undesirables!"

Then Queen Beema mocked, "In my country, we have, how shall I say it, *better* hired help."

They both found humour in her belittling comment and laughed.

When he came to the truck, Mr. Blubber handed Andre a note which he quickly read and then put in his pocket. We left the residence and started the drive back to the warehouse. No one spoke a single word, but I could sense the discontent simmering in the truck. It was a good ten minutes before Andre found his voice. He was seething; his language reflected the depth of his anger. "Frank, we are not going to the f...ing warehouse. We are going to f...ing Blubber's house."

I did not know why this made him so mad. All I could do was listen and drive.

Then, just before we arrived at Mr. Blubber's house, I offered, "Coffee, anyone? My treat."

Andre smiled.

There was nothing unique about Clarence Blubber's house. It was in all respects just an average grey and white house in an average middle class neighbourhood. Attached to the side of this very average house was an average single car garage.

The disdain with which he treated his employees led me to believe that he lived in more austere surroundings. He certainly tried to manufacture an air of superiority by the way he chose to dress. He always managed to be wearing clothing which bore the mark of the exclusively rich. Because of that, I had expected that Clarence Blubber's house to have been slightly more distinguished.

When Andre directed all of us to get out of the truck, I asked, "Andre, why are we stopping here?"

"Well Boss, you are about to find out. Come on, Danny, let's show him."

When they opened the garage it was like any other garage. It had just enough space for the Cadillac. But, they did not stop there; they did not even pause. They continued walking through the garage until they came to another huge door. When Andre opened this door I felt my mouth open and my jaw drop. I could not help it; such was my shock.

I was looking at a self-enclosed mini-warehouse; there were no windows or doors. Inside, neatly arranged, was a collection of fridges, stoves, washers and dryers and a host of furniture—all new or almost new. We unloaded our truck. I noticed that both Andre and Danny helped themselves to some small articles of interest to them. Then, we headed back to the warehouse.

On our way back, Danny asked, "So Frank, you get the picture now? You see how that snake operates. Every time we get a call for "Operation Removal" that rat is the first one on the scene. He steals the best, then he sells it on the side."

Then, Andre added, "That's how he gets all his fancy clothes—they were *donated* to the cause. He always takes the first pick. I wouldn't be surprised if he got his show-off Cadillac that way. Anyway, he makes plenty of money off all his loot. That's why he can well afford his stupid Cadillac. And you call him **Mister** Blubber? Do you now understand why we have no respect for this f…ing snake? He is vermin. He is lower than the low."

I listened, just listened, for they had so much to say. It was a most unflattering portrait that they painted of Mr. Blubber. Mr. Clarence Blubber was no Robin Hood; at the very least, he was a common crook. There was nothing in his conduct that I could find worth defending; I therefore maintained a sad silence.

102

Our Common Humanity

It was no longer a pleasure to go to work.

I was not able to dismiss what I had seen at the second warehouse and this new knowledge coloured my perception of Clarence Blubber. I could no longer make excuses for this man's ill treatment of his employees. Each new act of disrespect distressed my spirit and I found myself with respect for neither the man nor his position.

One day, I found a way to ease the pain.

It was the day Blubber sent us to make a delivery to a woman he frequently referred to as an old hag. Her name was Queenie. He explained, "Queenie has been on my case again. The old hag wants a washing machine. Well, she wants one, and by god I'll give her one."

He walked over to where the washing machines were assembled and chose the oldest, most decrepit machine. It was not even an automatic washer; it was the old style ringer washer. As he made the selection, he gave a victory cry; I wondered just what battle he thought that he had won.

We loaded up the machine and headed to the address. Queenie lived on the third floor of a four storey building. The front entrance was locked; we went around to the back. There we discovered a set of steel stairs on the outside of the building that went all the way from the ground up to the fourth floor. Andre quickly scaled the stairs to the third floor. Then, he motioned for us to bring the washing machine to those stairs.

After a laborious climb, we reached the third level with the ancient machine. We gained entrance through a back door. A small landing area was connected to the stairs. After securing the machine on the landing we stopped to catch our breath as Andre knocked on Queenie's door.

The door was opened by a tiny, frail body.

Andre said, "We are here to deliver your washing machine."

Noting that we had come up by way of the fire escape, Queenie was most apologetic for the inconvenience. "Oh, thank you, thank you. What trouble I have caused; you have had to bring it up through the back. I am so sorry."

When she looked at the machine a smile spread across her face. "Oh, it will be a big help. I have pain…in my hips…in my arms. It is so hard to do everything in the sink. This machine will help me out so much. Oh, I forgot my manners. Please, come in. I have tea…"

Then I interrupted, "Ma'am, I am so sorry. I must apologize. I just noticed that we have brought you the wrong machine."

I looked to Andre and Danny for confirmation. They understood immediately and they too apologized for the mistake.

She looked surprised and a little disappointed.

I assured her, "Don't worry, we will be back within the hour. We are so sorry for our mistake. Would you excuse us?"

Still somewhat taken aback, she nodded and added, "I'll be here waiting. I'll have tea and cookies waiting for you when you get back." She closed the door.

Left alone on the stairs with the machine we conferred. "Boss, I don't know how we are going to get that machine down those stairs. It's hardly worth the trouble," complained Danny.

"I fear that this machine may have a serious accident in the near future," I predicted.

Andre nodded in agreement.

Danny ran down the stairs ahead of us and stood below on the open grass. Andre and I lifted the machine to the top of the railing taking care to balance it perfectly. Danny looked around to make sure the area was clear and then he yelled, "Let her rip!"

Death came quickly to that heap of junk. Quickly we gathered up all the pieces and returned to the warehouse. Covertly, we selected the best washing machine and hastily made our way back to the apartment without being detected. This time, I went up ahead of the others to tell Queenie that we were back. Andre and Danny brought up the newer machine by way of the regular stairs.

When Queenie saw it her eyes lit up like stars, "Why, this is a new washing machine. Are you sure that this one is for me?"

The three of us blurted out an affirming, "Yes!" in unison.

Her delight could not be contained, "Oh, please come in and sit awhile. You have worked so hard for me today. You must stay. I have tea… and cookies too. Everyone calls me Queenie."

Queenie's sincere appreciation moved each of us. We never discussed what it was about her that touched us so deeply and caused us to do what we did.

We left Queenie's apartment feeling good about the day's events. The four of us were bound together by something that no one could every take away. That day we were reminded of our common humanity.

We had Queenie to thank for that.

(Unknown to us, however, in her haste to show the depth of her appreciation, Queenie called ahead to the warehouse and personally thanked the Blubber himself.)

103
Trouble with their Imperial Majesties

Impatient and highly agitated, Clarence Blubber awaited our return.

The truck had barely stopped when he yelled, "Frank Maraj, to my office, now!"

I wondered why he was so irritated. He could not possibly have known about the exchanged washing machines.

I followed him into his office. To my great astonishment, Beema was there also. Never in a million years would I have expected to see her royal highness condescend to visit such a common establishment. Yet, there she was, resplendently regal in attire and royally haughty in attitude.

Blubber spoke first, "Frank Maraj, you acted like a common thief. You stole my washing machine and gave it to that old…"

I interrupted. Before he could use the word *hag* I said, "Lady?"

"I have it in mind to deduct the cost of that machine from your pay. You had no authority to conduct such business. You acted irresponsibly. So, you thought you could get away with it. That stupid woman phoned to thank me. Imagine, that old hag, thanking me for sending her an almost new washing machine. I bet you never counted on her doing that."

I was livid; not because I had been *found out*… I could live with what I did. There was no shame in that. No, I was incensed that this blubbering fool insulted Queenie. Oh, how I wish I could have re-arranged his brain cells. Yet, I bore his knavish insult without any outward protest.

His majesty's diatribe was not yet over. He continued to berate me for my action, "You deliberately disobeyed my instructions. How dare you remove property from this warehouse? That is like stealing. Now, what do you have to say for yourself?"

For a moment I could not respond; my mind revisited the time when as a child I had been called a thief for taking a tin of cocoa that had been tossed in the garbage. I was accused by a man who was himself a thief. I was struck by the similarity of these two events. As a child, I was baffled by the man's lack of integrity. Once again I am baffled by the lack of personal integrity of my *superior*. How quick he was to judge and condemn. As a child it came as a shock to me that an adult could knowingly misrepresent the truth; as a grown man, more than thirty years in age, it still shocked my system that men in positions of authority would often fail to do that which is decent. I now found myself facing a situation where someone who had authority over me was ready to toss me into the pit of infamy. Have I not crawled out from such a pit on numerous occasions before today? Once again I summoned my rational mind to guide me in my response.

As much as I wanted to unload my mind and tell him off, common sense prevailed. The reality of my responsibilities to my wife and child took precedence over any selfish desire for revenge that I may have entertained. The everyday needs of being able to provide food and rent had to take priority. Thus, I re-examined my desire to present a defence and pleaded guilty.

"Mr. Blubber, I am guilty as charged. I acted without your expressed authority. I should not have done so. For that, I am sorry."

Before Blubber could respond to my apology, that woman, Beema, scoffed, "Oh, my my, Clarence. He speaks... and quite well. Whatever shall we do with him? His kind cannot be trusted. Fire him, Clarence."

Neither Blubber nor I responded to her inflammatory remarks immediately.

After a moment's consideration, Blubber decided to deride me some more.

"Come here!" he commanded.

I obliged. As long as he was still talking, I felt I had a chance.

"Frank Maraj, you are an example—very typical example—of why I do not approve of university students. They think they know. They know zilch. They don't know how to receive and follow orders. You are bold but I will give you this. You are not rude. You know your place."

I swallowed his remarks.

Then, he barked, "Get back to work... now!"

"Yes, Sir."

I felt that I had won. Until...

Beema fired, "Clarence, you should have gotten rid of him! Why didn't you?"

Although I was infuriated by her depraved disregard for my person I did not engage in any further discussion.

I had to content myself with speaking my mind *in* my mind only, "Madam, I do speak. I understand only too well your contempt of my person. It is obvious that your claim to an elevated class is both baseless and hollow. You lack the hallmarks of civility: courtesy and tolerance and manners; these are traits that are foreign to your understanding. Moreover, your presumed arrogance is rivalled only by your often offensive and condescending tone. Madame... how ill bred you are, is apparent even to the most blind among us. I would appreciate it if you would please refrain from commenting about my person. You are not qualified to speak on such matters."

Such an exercise proved most satisfactory; I felt a sense of vindication.

I had not been defeated.

Then I heard Blubber thunder, "Idiot! Frank Maraj, get to work."

Happily, I complied.

104

Blubber, Unveiled

Some time later, as Andre, Danny and I were headed to the dump, Andre asked me to make a quick detour to his place. I consented.

Once at his place, Danny and Andre began unloading a few items from the truck. I remained quiet.

Right after the unloading was accomplished, Andre asked me if we might go for coffee directly. I was considering his request when he said, "Frank, we have something to talk about. It is important."

I drove straight to the coffee shop.

After ordering, Andre led the way to a private area in the back of the shop. This, in and of itself, was highly unusual; Andre and Danny always opted for a spot in the front and near a window where they could take in all the *scenery*. Andre really must have something serious on his mind.

Once seated, Andre questioned, "Frank, why did you let old Blubberhead insult you the way he did? We heard him yelling at you."

"Andre, I did not want to get fired. I was afraid..."

"Afraid! Man, he could never fire you."

"Really?"

Then, Danny interjected, "Frank, you saw with your own eyes what he has at his personal warehouse. Andre and I both know about how he steals. No one else was supposed to find out. But, since Andre and I have both lost our licences, we had no choice but to let you drive there. And he knows it!"

Andre, who had been quietly seething, yelled, "That f...ing b.... Beema, she wanted you fired. Only old Blubberhead could not fire you. That ugly fake of woman is so low class. She pretends to be high class. Those two belong together. They are nothing but high class frauds. They are nothing but crooks. Frank, do you know why that b.... paid Blubberhead a visit? Any guesses?"

"No, Andre. I don't have a clue. I thought that her being at the warehouse was strange. Do you know why she was there?"

"Buddy, she was there to collect. Do you really think she *gave* all those things as an act of goodwill? Do you want to know the ugly truth? Everything she donated will be replaced, but not from her pocket. Some government has to pay for that. She gave that stuff to our agency, yes, but she gave it to Old Blubberhead in particular. He sells those things on the side. That is why he has a private warehouse. He makes money and she makes money too. The whole operation is nothing but a huge bloody scam; everyone is out to get a piece of the action. The whole world is full of scams. And Blubberhead thinks he has the right to ride shotgun over us. Frank, that is the dirty truth, buddy. You can bank on it."

This outpouring of information left me somewhat overwhelmed. What Andre divulged was true but it was not *the truth*. I felt so helpless.

But, before I could say anything, Danny too discharged his mind, "Frank, don't take any offence. When you leave here every day, you go home to the good life. You know that you have a better life to shoot for. You come from another country and your folks must be swimming in a river of cash. We don't swim in that river. We are in a cesspool. This job for you is mere pocket change, right?"

What do I say to that? Again I had been misread. How do I begin to correct this misinterpretation of my status?

In my mind, Andre and Danny were very much like my two brothers, Clive and Boysie; they, like my Pa before them, were desperately working to eke out a living in an unreliable and inconsistent world; and I, Frank Maraj, was part of that same equation... no better, no worse. I was still my father's son, and like him I too sought to claim my small portion of the dignity that this life had to offer. So often it was denied him... just as it had often been denied these two struggling young men...

Danny's words brought me back from my melancholy, "Frank, are you angry at me? You're not saying anything, did I offend you?"

Quickly I assured him, "Danny, in no way did you offend me. It is just that you are..."

Andre encouraged, "You can tell us; we will not be offended. We trust you."

Trusting their words, I completed my thought.

"Guys, you are mistaken about me."

They waited for me to continue.

"You see, when I leave you here at the end of the day, I do go home, that is true. But that is not the end of it. There is no time for relaxation and fun. I go home quickly and grab a bite to eat and see my family. Then I am off to school. I am still attending classes at the university. I still do my studies and research for my essays. This job does not provide pocket change; that is where you are most mistaken. This job is necessary. If I did not have it, I really don't know what would happen to me or my family."

Then I turned to Andre and asked, "Have you an idea how I came to get your job as the driver?"

"All I heard, from Blubberhead, was that he had to accept some dumb university student. Then, you showed up."

"Yes, I am that dumb student. I don't know if you could guess what government agency helped me get this job?"

My question left them somewhat puzzled.

My answer stunned them, "The Welfare Agency."

I let that piece of information sink in before I continued, "You see boys, when I was a child, I had a simple dream. I wished to go to high school."

Danny could not understand how going to high school could be considered a dream and asked, "Frank, of all things to dream about, why would you dream of going to high school? That makes no sense."

"Danny, you forget. I am not from Canada. I come from a country and from a time when not every child was guaranteed an education. Our family of ten lived in a two bedroom house. There was no hydro, no indoor water. My Pa was a common labourer; he owned a mule and a cart. He did not always get work. You see, because I was not selected to go to the free government high school, even if my father wished to, he could not afford to send me to a private high school."

"But, Frank, you're here at university, so you must have made it through high school. How did you do that? Who paid for you?"

My answer may have struck them as a little melodramatic but, nonetheless, it served to demonstrate the point. I got out of my chair, rolled up the legs of my pants and pointed to my feet.

Andre was confused, but Danny got it, "Andre, Frank is standing on his two feet. He is telling us that he made it to high school on his own two feet. Right, Frank?"

Relieved that I did not have to spell it out any further, I responded with a simple, "Yes."

Their imaginations completed the story. Then, Danny spoke from a state of quiet reflection, "Frank, here we are, complaining. You are standing up for yourself and are trying to make a better life for yourself. Man, hats off to you, Frank."

Then, Andre left and went out to the truck. He returned with a small box and gave it to me.

"Frank, this is from Danny and me to you. Go ahead, open it."

For a moment, I hesitated to accept the box. I wondered about it. Did they help themselves to this present from the warehouse? That may very well be so. But, at this moment that was a secondary consideration. It seemed so right to just accept their gift and to accept it graciously. In a way, that gift symbolized their acceptance of me. Through that acceptance, Andre, Danny and I were connected. I opened the box. Inside was a collection of LP records—The Reader's Digest Treasury of Timeless Classics.

*****

There is a corollary to the subject of these LP's which occurred near the end of my time with the agency.

My confession seemed to have bonded us in a way that nothing else could have. We continued to work together, even harder. One day as we were cleaning up the warehouse, Blubber made an appearance and thundered, "Boys—into my office—now! March!"

Not knowing what could have precipitated such an outburst, we looked questioningly at one another as we complied with his order.

Blubber wasted no time in revealing the source of his most recent discontent, "I had a precious box of LP records. It was a one of a kind classic collection. I can't find it anywhere. I know that one of you three took it. Which one of you was it?"

Without a moment's hesitation, Andre quickly responded, "I think we accidentally threw it out with the other garbage."

"No way, I don't believe that for one second. One of you has it; now..."

"Mr. Blubber, that box is in my possession," I advised.

"Are you admitting that you stole my collection?"

I sensed that Andre and Danny wanted to intervene. I motioned for them to say nothing.

Then Blubber dismissed them and told them to go back to work. He instructed me to stay, saying, "We have unfinished business."

Reluctantly, they left.

I was relieved that they were not with me for what was about to transpire. Their honour and my honour were at stake.

Blubber began by threatening me, "Frank Maraj, you *are* a thief. I knew I never should have agreed to hire a university student. You're all just a bunch of thieves. I should call the police."

"Go ahead, call the police. It is true that I have that collection in my possession. I will confess to it. Are you ready to confess about all those things that you have in your possession in your private warehouse? Who is the thief?"

His face first turned red, then purple, then red again.

He was rendered speechless.

I walked out.

I might have been seen to indulge in a slight smile.

Danny and Andre were waiting for me outside the office.

Concern was written on their faces. Quickly, I put them at ease, "All is well."

Andre commented, "I suppose you'll be glad to be finally rid of this cesspool…"

"No, Andre; that is not true. You see, I began looking forward to coming to work, despite Blubber."

"Really, Frank? Why?"

"Because of you two. I am happy to have met both of you. This is a part of my life that I will remember. You guys are such good people, and you put yourselves down. That is so sad. You don't recognize your own true worth. That saddens me."

Danny offered me his hand and said, "Frank, I could learn from you a thing or two."

I reached out and shook his hand; then Andre placed his hands over ours and teased, "The Three Musketeers!"

My heart silently affirmed, "Yes, yes."

Thus, my time at the Goodwill Agency concluded on a positive note.

Never again did I see Andre and Danny, but I remember them often.

A storm of another nature was brewing on the shores of my academic life.

105

Accused

"Mr. Maraj,"
"Yes, Sir."
"I am so disappointed."
"Disappointed, Sir?"
"Your essay, I cannot believe it."

Then, Dr. R, the professor in charge of overseeing my work on Eastern Education was silent. He quickly flipped through the pages. I had no idea why he expressed such disappointment regarding my work. His comments made me uneasy.

He continued, "Mr. Maraj, you have plagiarized parts of this essay. This is a serious offence. I have no choice but to assign you a grade of zero."

While such a statement should have crushed me, it did not.

I simply stood still.

Dr. R was still speaking, but I heard him not.

My mind took flight; into the distant past I floated.

As I descended from the clouds of recollections I landed on the sturdy shore of this memory.

The memory took me back to my second year of high school. I had gone to visit a relative who lived in San Juan, in Trinidad. Although we were about the same age we attended different schools. As I arrived at his home, I saw Jeevan, stretched out in a hammock. The hammock was visible as I approached the home for it was strung between two columns in the open area of the main floor. The house itself had an upstairs which sprawled the length of the property. He was oblivious of my presence as I approached for he was completely absorbed in a book. I called out to him quietly; he did not respond. When I got closer I greeted, "Jeevan, how are you?"

I startled him.

I felt guilty for having disturbed him, but when he saw me he was not annoyed; I was relieved.

"Frank, it is you. Man, I am happy to see you. In fact, I was just thinking about you."

"Look, Jeevan, I am so sorry that I disturbed you. You were so absorbed in that book."

"Frankie, this is why I was thinking about you. It is this book. You have to read this book. Here, take it."

I held the book in my hand. It was rather old, and I had to be careful as the binding was weak. I opened the book and there was an inscription,

If by chance your eyes
Were to behold
Then may you become
Illuminated.

Jeevan saw me staring at the inscription and explained, "This book is a treasure to be passed on. I don't know who wrote those words. When I first read them, I became interested, and you, Frankie? What do you think? Are you interested?"

"Jeevan, there is something about this book. I have to read it."

"Then you can have it now; I am finished Frankie. I know you have been reading the British Classics: Dickens, Bronte, and so forth. Now, read a classic about your own culture, your own roots."

"Say no more. I will read this book."

I noted the author's name: Rabindranath Tagore. I wondered, *Who was this author*? Little did I know that the work of this particular author was to become inextricably woven into the very fabric of my life at a much later date at university. Tagore, along with his dear friend, Mahatma Gandhi, would become pillars of thought in my life. However, at the time, my main interest was in the poetry and the philosophy of Tagore. The name itself, Rabindranath Tagore, became a source of intrigue and interest from the time I was sixteen.

How well I remember that meeting between Jeevan and me. I remember so little about anything else. There is something so compelling about someone who asks, desires and insists that you do something that he recommends—something that he sees with visionary eyes. My friend had indeed been right about Tagore. I read this book and was mesmerized by the writing. The views of Tagore were captivating; his style was lucid and his imagery was riveting. Tagore, from the very first word, was compelling and

I laboured to discover other works without much success. Then, I became absorbed with my own demanding realities and Rabindranath Tagore slipped into my unconscious to be re-awakened in my later university life.

Which was now, here in Ottawa, under the critical eye of Dr. R. He] was not just East Indian; he was the pre-eminent expert in Asian studies. In particular, he was a renowned authority on Tagore.

During my studies, I had examined several works by Tagore, and was in complete admiration of this legendary and celebrated author, who had received the Nobel Prize for Literature. Tagore's style was simple yet powerful. His poetry captured the essence of India's spiritual heritage. His philosophy reflected the voice of the universal man. In particular, I was captivated by his use of vivid imagery. I was not conscious that I had adopted a style that emulated Tagore's. I do not mean to imply that I possessed a style similar to Tagore's! No, that would be too presumptuous. In my innocence, I might have had traces of the Master in my papers; I so worshipped Tagore.

For this reason, Dr. R ruled that I had plagiarized.

I did not re-act to this accusation.

I was not confused by this accusation.

It was as though a compliment had been offered; unfortunately the compliment was wrapped in a most disconcerting indictment. The unintended compliment, however, resonated with my spirit more than the accusation.

Perhaps, I was in disbelief and shock, that I, Frank Maraj, could possible write in any manner that suggested a mere glimpse of the master Tagore himself. The verdict had been declared and I offered no resistance.

I was guilty without being guilty;

I was innocent, without innocence.

Through it all, I maintained a quiet dignity. Knowing that I was not guilty of the crime of which I was accused, I accepted the guilt. I knew not why.

Dr. R's voice returned me to the awkwardness of the present. He cautioned, "Mr. Maraj, I will have to report you to the Dean. This action will undoubtedly affect your..."

"Dr. R, you say I have plagiarized part of my essay."

"You certainly did, Mr. Maraj."

"Then, Sir, do what you must."

I turned to leave. He continued, "Your conduct is highly confusing, Mr. Maraj. I would expect at the very least that you would show remorse."

"Remorse, Sir?"

"Yes."

"Sir, respectfully, I cannot do that."

"And why not, Mr. Maraj? Your attitude is strange, unusual. You should be contrite..."

"Dr. R, with all due respect, I know that in the courtroom of your mind, I stand guilty. I cannot defend myself against a mind that appears to be closed. In the courtroom of honour, however, two souls know that I am innocent; two souls know that I did not plagiarize. Who are these two souls? I am one such soul, Sir."

"And who is the other soul?"

"I leave you to your musings. Good-day, Sir."

106

Surprisingly, Vindication

The time had come for the oral examination; it was the final step in the completion of my Master's Degree in Education at Ottawa University. A group of ten gathered in the conference room to conduct this important final assessment.

Presiding over the examination was Dr. M, our Dean. Among the distinguished professors were Dr. R and Dr. Mc Neil.

Dr. M began by formally addressing the group, "Gentlemen, we are gathered here to conduct the Oral Comprehensive Examination in Mr. Maraj's quest to complete his Master's Degree in Education. Shall we begin?"

She then addressed me, "Mr. Maraj, our questions are aimed to discover what you know and understand that relates to academics. Equally important and at times, more important is the subject of maturation. In short, have you, through your academic pursuits, gained in maturity. That, therefore, will be the focus of this examination. Do you have any questions regarding what I have explained to you?"

"Not yet, Dr. M."

"Then let us begin. The floor is now open for dialogue."

Thus, each professor took a turn at posing a question. There were times when I would be in the process of answering a specific question from one professor, when another question would be posed by another. At times, it seemed as if I was under attack. It was all designed to determine the degree to which I could compose myself and my answers while under fire.

I felt that I was holding my own for most of the process. But, Dr. R. had not yet spoken. When he took the floor, my nervousness increased tenfold. In his hand, he held a list of the names of books that he deemed mandatory; he studied the list pensively. All were quiet as he framed his question, "Mr. Maraj, with regard to this book—a most important text which you would have read undoubtedly. Therefore, will you give us a brief analysis of the author's views as contained in this particular text?"

He spoke with such confidence and self-assurance.

My nervousness had been justified. My spirit threatened to leave my body. I had not read the text. If it was his intention to catch me and reveal me as unprepared, he was well on his way. *What was I to do? Dare I attempt to bluff my way out?*

I replied, "Dr. R, while that is a text that I possess, I have not as yet read it. I am sorry."

"Mr. Maraj, you have not read such an important text. I am afraid..."

Before he could berate me further, I interrupted, "Sir, I have read other texts by the same author. May I be permitted to frame an answer from the other readings?"

Annoyed, Dr. R protested, "Certainly not! This clearly shows..."

Dr. M then interceded, "Dr. R, perhaps we can be generous. Shall we allow Mr. Maraj to respond to your question from his other readings of the same author?"

Dr. Mc Neil affirmed that it was a *viable* option and looked to Dr. R for confirmation.

Reluctantly, Dr. R nodded. He then folded his arms in such a way as to indicate that he really had no longer any interest in the proceedings. In spite of the withdrawal of Dr. R, I proceeded with my answer. It seemed that my response was quite acceptable for no one interrupted with additional questions.

Finally, Dr. M rose from her chair and declared, "For all purposes, this examination is concluded. Mr. Maraj, after our deliberations we shall acquaint you with our findings."

"Thank you, Dr. M, and thank you, panel."

I left hopeful. Yet, at the back of my mind was the worrisome thought that I had disappointed Dr. R.

A few days later, I ran into Dr. M. She smiled as she shared, "Frank, congratulations on your oral examination."

"Dr. M, does this mean that I passed?"

"Of course you passed, and quite well, I might add. The panel was impressed. I must be going."

At that moment, my feet were no longer in contact with the ground.

107
Glad to be Wrong

Days later as I visited with my advisor, Dr. Mc Neil, I was most restless. He asked, "Frank, why are you so nervous? Relax."

"How can I, Sir? I wish I knew how I did on the rest of my courses. I wish..."

"Is that what's been bothering you? Wait here."

Within minutes he returned with my marks.

"Do you want to see your marks?"

"Do I?"

I grabbed the paper from him.

I scanned down the paper until I reached Dr. R's course. His was the course about which I was the most worried. Beside the course code was the letter 'A'. I smiled. I had hoped for a pass; I did not expect an 'A'. Had I misjudged this professor?

******

A Step Closer to my Dream

"Frank, stop for a moment. I have to talk to you. You have time..."

"Dr. Mc Neil, I have to just..."

"Whatever you are about to do can wait. What I have to show you cannot wait."

"Yes, Sir. Lead on."

Excitedly, Dr. Mc Neil led the way to his office. He showed me an ad he had circled in a newspaper.

"Frank, your dream is about to come true. Here, take a look for yourself."

He was beaming. After looking at the advertisement I became very excited also.

The University of the West Indies, Trinidad Campus, had placed an advertisement for several teaching positions. One ad in particular stood out; it suggested that the successful applicant needed to be qualified both in the areas of literature and philosophy. This matched perfectly my Honour's Degree in which I had a double major: English and Philosophy. Furthermore, the ad specified that the university was searching for a candidate who had a Master's Degree in Education; this qualification too, I now possessed. Finally, the ad indicated that it would be an added asset if such a candidate was also a citizen of the Caribbean. I felt that the advertisement was designed especially for me. Overjoyed, I blurted out, "Dr. Mc Neil, I can't believe it, can you? Imagine a position as a lecturer at the Department of Education in Trinidad. This is just too good to be true."

"Frank, it is all you ever talked about—your desire to return to Trinidad as an educator. This is it; here is your chance. This job is practically yours."

"Dr. Mc Neil, what do you mean by *practically yours*? Do you know something that I do not?"

"Frank, when I saw the ad, I made some inquiries. The job is real; it is open. Thus far, there have been some applications, but no applicant has a Master's Degree in literature and philosophy. You do. Seems Fate is on your side."

"Sir, can this really be happening? Am I dreaming? It is so good. Is it real? Could my luck be changing?"

I looked at this beloved professor, so confident and smiling. I should not have been surprised when he divulged, "I have already started to prepare a recommendation on your behalf. I have already approached two other professors. They have happily consented to advocate for you. Now, Mr. Maraj, go and do your part and complete this application form for *lecturer*!"

"Yes, Sir! At once, Sir."

He smiled, then he quipped, "And, Mr. Maraj, you don't get off that easily. All this comes with a price."

"A price, Sir?"

"Of course! As soon as you settle in your new position, let me know. I will be your first visitor. I look forward to visiting your paradise."

"That would be my pleasure, Dr. Mc Neil. I would be thrilled to have you."

I left his office and headed directly to the library to complete the application.

One portion required that I forward copies of all degrees and the accompanying grades. I carried all that information with me in my briefcase. I took a moment to briefly review them. As I scanned the grades from my first degree, my Bachelor of Arts, I recognized that to others they would not be impressive. To me, however, the grade was only a small part of my achievement. I knew what they represented to me. The marks from the following years reflected progress and improvement. My most recent transcript represented my greatest achievement. I certainly had come a long way. In fact, I felt that I had finally arrived. I uttered a silent prayer of gratitude.

Happy, was I to be in Canada; happier was I at the prospect of returning to Trinidad.

108

Trinidad Bound at Last

So optimistic was I about my prospects in Trinidad, that I purchased a one-way ticket only from Winnipeg to Port-of-Spain. While it was exceedingly delightful to finally be on an Air Canada flight en route to Trinidad, the trip seemed endless and I could contain neither my anxiety nor my impatience. Then the flight attendant announced, "Ladies and gentlemen, we are approaching Port-of-Spain, Trinidad, please return to your seats and…" I know that I heard every word that she uttered, but the three syllables that really meant anything to me belonged to the name of my island—Trinidad. The flight attendant was standing at the top of the stairs to greet of us as we exited the plane. As I passed by, she graced me with a warm smile and inquired, "Holidaying, Sir?"

Not hesitating for a moment, I responded instinctively, "Permanently!"

I stood alone on the tarmac drinking in the majesty of the Northern Range. So many wonderful memories came to mind when I beheld that familiar site. It truly was good to be home.

I proceeded to Immigration. The immigration officer examined my passport and after noticing that my ticket was for one way only, commented, "Mr. Maraj, you have but a one-way ticket. Are you here to stay?"

"Yes, ma'am."

"Welcome back, Mr. Maraj. Happy to have you. Returning from university I take it?"

"Yes, ma'am."

"And hopefully you have a job prospect?"

"Yes, I do," I smiled broadly as I passed through inspection.

My brother, Boysie, beamed when he saw me. He alone had come to pick me up from the airport and his greeting was so welcoming and full of pride. I was touched. We were both so much at peace. Proudly, he proclaimed, "Congratulations, and welcome home, Brother."

When I arose the next morning I prepared to take my shower. It felt so good to step out onto the familiar terrain and make my way to the outside shower stall. I was delighted to see both Boysie and Clive waiting to greet me as I began my first day. Everything about it felt right. I luxuriated in the familiar. Even the mango tree delighted my senses. I was home.

The news of my arrival had reached the ears of all our neighbours and soon our yard was full of eager well-wishers.

"Frankie, how long yo here for?"

Clive, unable to contain his enthusiasm, answered for me.

"Frankie is home for good. He is now a *professional*."

I looked over at Boysie. He too was just beaming. My success at school meant so much to both of my brothers and I knew that they were both proud of me and proud for me. In no small measure, my success was their success. That was just the reality of families.

As they approached, the neighbours extended their congratulations. I could feel their pride pulsating and I drank in the elixir of acceptance. The discomfort and misunderstandings that had marred our earlier years had completely dissipated. The future was indeed promising.

Later that day I walked to the University of the West Indies; it was a mere two miles from our home. I was primarily interested in checking out the Department of Education and the houses that surrounded the university. There was a modest grouping of houses clustered at the rear of the university. Beginning lecturers lived in those dwellings on a temporary basis until they became established lecturers and found their own permanent quarters. It was comforting to know that I would have access to decent living accommodations when I was hired. I liked everything about the campus; I had goose bumps just thinking about working there and living there as a professional.

As I followed the railroad tracks and headed for home, I passed by the savannah and open fields that had once been my playground. Everything was so familiar; everything felt so right. I was excited to be home finally.

Early the following day I drove to the Ministry of Education near the outskirts of Port-of-Spain.

As I entered the office I was struck by the large number of clerical staff. I did not know where to begin; I could see no sign signalling an information or reception centre. I approached the worker who was the closest to me. She directed me to the *Inquiry* station which was a bit set off from the rest of the office which explained why I did not see it immediately upon my arrival. At Inquiry, I related that I needed to see the Administrator. The clerk directed me to the secretary to the administrator. After waiting several minutes to see her, I described the nature of my visit. She explained however, that I would first have to see Mrs. DeSousa, the assistant to the Administrator.

Finally, I approached the desk of Mrs. DeSousa.

Mrs. DeSousa, failed to acknowledge me. Perhaps she had not seen me. I moved in closer; her typing continued unabated.

Thus I ventured, "Hello."

Still no response. *Perhaps she did not hear me*, I reasoned. I raised my voice a little, "Hello."

That second hello elicited a reaction. She looked up; only her eyes moved as she peered over her enormous spectacles.

She offered no word of greeting—merely an instruction.

"Take a seat there. I will be with you *in a while*."

The sign on her desk boldly proclaimed that this was the desk of *Mrs. DeSousa Administrative Assistant*.

Obediently I sat where she had indicated on a small wooden bench on the far side of the office. From there I waited and waited; and then waited some more. Two hours elapsed and I was still waiting.

Finally I caught her eye. She removed her glasses and motioned for me to approach.

"And why are you here?" she asked.

It was her tone more than her question that threw me off. It contained no hint of friendliness, no token affability. It is as if I were a bother and an inconvenience to her.

Ignoring her tone, I replied, "I am here to inquire as to the status of an application for a teaching position at the Department of Education. I forwarded the application to this office from Canada."

"And your name?"

"Frank Maraj."

"Did you say Frank Maharaja?"

"No, Mrs. DeSousa, my name is just Frank Maraj."

I could not help but feel mocked. Being an islander herself, she should have recognized the difference between Maraj and Maharaja. This apparent slight made me uncomfortable. First she had kept me waiting; now she seemed to be deliberately mispronouncing my name. I did not think that I was over-reacting. The prospect of getting this job however, overshadowed everything and I chose to overlook this minor irritation.

Without further communication, she left. Even though there was additional seating at her desk, I returned to my designated bench; I had not been invited to sit elsewhere. After nearly an hour's absence, she returned; once again she motioned for me to approach. Hoping that finally I was to be accorded some modicum of respect and be invited to sit, proved futile. Mrs. DeSousa haughtily informed, "Mr. Winchester has advised that he is otherwise engaged. If you still wish to see him you must wait. Understood?"

Once again she pointed to the bench; once again I had been dismissed as if I were little more than a school boy. Not knowing what else to do, I sat down and waited; I waited for the rest of the afternoon.

Throughout the entirety of the afternoon, Mrs. DeSousa offered not one further word of acknowledgement. I was no longer just uncomfortable. My discomfort had nothing whatsoever to do with the bench.

I returned the next day and once again assumed my position on the bench. Half way through the morning, Mrs. DeSousa motioned to me and advised, "Mr. Winchester is utterly occupied. You may have to wait a long time. It might be wise for you to give us a phone number and let *us* contact *you* when he is free."

Not deterred in the least by this most recent ploy to extricate me from her space, I countered, "Thank you for your courtesy. As I am here, I will wait. Let us hope that Mr. Winchester can see me soon." Again I returned to my station and waited. At the conclusion of that second day, I was still waiting. Even though my spirit felt assaulted by her breach of civility, I tried my best to conceal my pain. I remembered that here, in Trinidad, things often took a long time to conclude.

While thus engaged in my mind, Mrs. DeSousa approached and commanded, "Follow me!" Surprised, I happily followed her up a flight of stairs to Mr. Winchester's office. His name was boldly engraved on the door; there was no mistaking his importance.

After knocking lightly, Mrs. DeSousa opened the door and ushered me inside. Mr. Winchester appeared to be totally engrossed in paper work. Mrs. DeSousa left without offering a word of introduction or explanation; I was left standing most conspicuously and uncomfortably just inside the door. If I had expected an invitation to sit, I would have been sorely disappointed. Mr. Winchester made no attempt to acknowledge me; the papers on his desk claimed his full attention. It was only when I boldly stepped into the room and sat down near his desk that he deigned to respond to my presence.

"Who are you?"

Who am I? Why is he asking me such a question? Did not Mrs. DeSousa already approach him and inform him as to the nature of my visit?

Taking great pains to ensure that my tone was in no way offensive, I began my explanation slowly, "Mr. Winchester, I am Frank Maraj. I came to see you regarding an application for a teaching position..."

He interrupted, "Just a minute... let me get it."

He left to retrieve my application. I could not understand why he did not have it on hand right there in his office. I was confused. *What was happening?*

Again I waited. Finally, he returned bearing an envelope. As he pulled my application from the envelope and hastily scanned it, he said, "Ah, yes. Here it is."

"Mr. Winchester, there should be two applications. You have mine. There should be another from Diana Maraj."

"There is nothing from a Diana Maraj. Let's deal with yours."

"But Mr. Winchester, I submitted both applications together to the office of the ambassador in Ottawa, and . . ."

"Well, I can assure you that there is no application here from any Diana Maraj. Shall we now deal with you, or do you prefer..."

"Mr. Winchester, let us proceed as you recommend."

"Exactly. But before we go any further, there is an urgent matter that needs attention immediately."

"An urgent matter, Mr. Winchester?"

"Yes—most urgent. It deals with your so-called qualifications."

"I don't understand, Sir."

His whole demeanour changed. He took great pleasure in announcing, "Yo will soon understand. Listen up, now. Yo see yo people go abroad and purchase your degrees and yo come back and claim yo qualified."

"We *people* purchase our degrees?"

"Exactly. And don't play innocent with me. We know about you imposters. You people go to Canada and purchase your degrees. No doubt about it."

I could not believe my ears. *He just accused me of purchasing my degree!* Each word pierced my soul with the force of a bullet. My legs threatened to give out beneath me and I had to sit down. He was not yet finished with me. He reloaded and fired one more round. "We have to assemble a special committee to examine your qualifications—your *so-called* qualifications. Yo in my hands now. We will judge yo... "

The rest of his words floated around me in a foggy haze. I heard only sounds, not words. I did not need to. It was painfully obvious that I had been targeted from the outset. Now, suddenly everything made sense. Mrs. DeSousa and her antics were designed to frustrate and discourage me from pursuing my goals. The *waiting game* that she played with me over the last two days was a deliberate attempt on her part to undermine me and to shake my confidence. What a shock it must have been to them to have me withstand their little ploy. Previously, I had heard rumours about this type of treatment being meted out to discourage those of our Indian heritage from aspiring to government positions. I did not *want* to believe the rumours, but here I was being faced with the reality in my own life.

The words, *Yo people purchase your degrees*, played over and over in my mind. I had to ask myself some serious questions: *Was I now a lowly doormat? Was I going to allow a man like Mr. Winchester to walk all over me?* Something inside me snapped and I railed against the forces that would have me so diminished. In my mind I vowed, *I would be no one's doormat.*

Gathering up every ounce of residual strength remaining in my body, I stood face to face with the man who had so misjudged me and queried, "And, Mr. Winchester, pray tell, *who* exactly will constitute that committee?"

"Well, I, of course, will chair the committee. Mrs. DeSousa will be there, and the other members will come—"

"Tell me, *Sir*, will you invite any members from the University? Perhaps someone from the Department of Education?"

"No way. We don't need no teacher to conduct any such investigation. We have our own people. We will make up our own panel. We are most capable and I assure you . . ."

"Mr. Winchester, are you telling me, Sir, that *you* and other members of *this office*—and *not one member* of any *teaching* staff—will attempt to investigate and evaluate my credentials?"

"That is exactly right. And . . ."

"How *dare* you, Sir, *presume* that you can evaluate my credentials! Tell me, Sir, have you or any member of your panel distinguished yourselves by the acquisition of any university degrees? Let me put it in simpler terms... do you have any degrees whatsoever, Mr. Winchester?"

I believe that my last comment raised his ire and caused his face to turn black. In a feeble effort to protest, he huffed, "How dare you stand there and question me—you little... "

"I take it that you and the members of your panel have distinguished yourselves simply by being loyal to the bureaucracy that saw fit to hire you in spite of the fact that you have no real qualifications... no real degrees of your own. I now understand your quick distrust and dismissal of any one whom you have judged as being beneath you and who claims to have credentials. My question to you then, Sir, with all due respect, is this, how can you, who have not even attended university, dare presume to sit in judgment of someone who has? Not only do you insult me, you insult the dignity of the office that you represent. Your stupidity is exceeded only by your arrogance, Sir."

Nothing but silence filled the room.

His massive six-foot, six-inch frame threatened to overwhelm me. Also, he was a good ninety pounds heavier than I. Nevertheless, I was not to be deterred. I would have my say. For too long I had been the victim of similar knavish assaults; and always I had to navigate around them ever so carefully. Well, not today. Today nothing could keep me from speaking my mind. No amount of flailing arms and garbled speech could deflect me from my course. His cheap attempt to emasculate me had to be challenged and I was more than ready to meet the challenge. Thus, I continued, "Mr. Winchester, your long-standing affiliation with the present government has obviously advanced you well—consider, you are the Administrator—I recognize that distinction, Sir, but for you to presume to be able to evaluate me is not only inappropriate and hollow but also is highly suggestive of intimidation. You, Sir, are nothing but an over-paid and under-qualified bully."

The man was now without coherence. He reached for my application. Frantically, he grabbed hold of a stamp and pad from his desk. With the greatest of effort he first stamped the pad, gathering up as much red ink as he could, and pounded its redness onto my application all the while shouting, "*Rejected*! You are now officially *Denied*! We don't need *your kind* in Trinidad. The more we deny and reject you and your people, the more you will disappear. *Now disappear!*"

I could not believe that Mr. Winchester openly declared his prejudice. His true colours had surfaced. His flagrantly racist diatribe cut me to the core. Still wanting to defend myself against his invectives, I hesitated. A part of me advised against saying anything further. I was prepared to walk away...

That is, until the man reloaded his mouth—this time with deadlier and more caustic threats.

"See here Maraj, or Maharaj, or Maharaja—whatever your name is, whatever kind of Indian you are! You no longer exist. You will never ever get a government job in Trinidad. I just buried you!"

He was writing something in a black notebook. Instinctively, I took a step closer; I wanted to see for myself what he was writing. He was putting my name in his personal black book. Essentially, I was being black-listed, or should I say *brown*-listed. Seized by a further boldness, I declared, "Mr. Winchester Sir, be sure you spell my name correctly. You do not wish to ostracize the wrong person. My name is Frank Maraj, and Maraj is spelled M-A-R-A-J. Got it?"

He exploded; this time, language from the gutter spewed forth from his mouth as he debased both my person and my heritage with the ultimate insult: "You *mirasmee*! You Indian! You Coolie! Get out or—"

He moved toward me; it appeared that he was about to strike. I headed for the door in order to avoid his blow. He stopped in mid attack. I opened the door but did not leave.

I turned and thus we two stared at one another. A calmness had entered my body and I remained rooted to my spot. He, however, possessed no such calm; his breath was coming in short gasps and he was holding his chest. The encounter was not yet over. A thousand years of humiliation long buried cried out for relief.

"Mr. Winchester, thank you Sir, for reminding me that I am a coolie; I will strive to be a civilized coolie and not call you or address you by any name that will denigrate your person or your people or your race. You see, Mr. Winchester, I—a coolie as you dubbed me—ventured abroad and earned my degrees. I did not purchase them. Furthermore, I desperately looked forward to returning to my island, my home, Trinidad. You made it abundantly clear that we Indians are not valued. We, for the most part, are rejected and devalued. Sir, you have the power of a bully. Indeed, you have become the consummate bully in the way you wield your power. That power has allowed you a false sense of entitlement; you have the power to deny any Indian a position in government. This seems to give you great pleasure. Well Sir, this is one Indian—one coolie—you will not subjugate."

He hurried towards me; hands extended. *Did I need to protect myself? Would more words of self-righteousness and indignation have any impact on this man's soul? Would anything that I had to say be received?*

Then it dawned on me; the vile disease of bigotry possessed his mind and the pestilence of racism inhabited his soul. Rampant contamination of the blood of fair-play oozed from his pores. Once again I regarded this man's face and wondered, *Had the brown people been in government, would a black man be recounting this very story of rejection?* I am sorry to say that the answer to that question is not *'No'* but rather, *'Perhaps'*.

Already my mind was elsewhere as I exited the building.

******

The Return

Within days of this dreadful encounter, I was once again on board an Air Canada flight bound for Winnipeg. Somehow, I managed to secure a one-way ticket back to Winnipeg. I cannot begin to quantify the depth of negativity of soul infused in that solitary action: purchasing a one-way ticket. So deep was my hurt that I could not bear to contemplate the mere idea of ever returning to my homeland. I had been rejected and cast aside.

As the plane became airborne, the stark reality of my situation settled in my soul. I had been forced into making a choice that went against everything that I believed in or thought that I believed in. Politics and bigotry had dictated my actions. I was most uneasy with the only option left open to me. Never had I considered a life that did not include my native land. Never had I considered making another land my home. True, I had married a Canadian, but Diana was prepared to make her life with me in Trinidad. That had been our shared dream.

Now, however, filled with disillusionment, I had to bid an emotional farewell to Trinidad and to everything that I had loved about it: its winding roads and bustling thoroughfares, its multiple cinemas and beaches, its colour and confusion...

As the lights inside the plane dimmed, I closed my eyes and my mind drifted back to more pleasant times. The first memory was a recent one that had happened just days ago when I was at the park at Macoya Road. Some young teenage boys were engaged in a game of football (soccer). At one point, the ball was kicked out of bounds and landed near me. Happily, I retrieved the ball and executed some dribbling moves before finally kicking it to the player who came forward to claim it. I was so surprised when he politely encouraged,

"Uncle, yo still have the moves.
Come join us.
We are short a player.
Come Uncle, the game is on."

How typical this was of a Trinidadian invitation to play. "Come Uncle, join us." I delighted in hearing those words—*the game is on*—I so wanted to join in. But, for the moment, I could not accept. I was not wearing the proper clothing or footwear. Yet, I did not mind missing out on that game for I anticipated that I would have ample time and opportunity to indulge in many games very soon. *After all, I was about to permanently relocate to Trinidad, was I not?*

And then, once more I remembered the painful encounter with Mr. Winchester. That fleeting joyous spirit that encompassed my spirit a moment ago was now replaced by the visage of this man: my ultimate nightmare. I fought to banish the memory once more. Desperately, I tried to erase this man from my memory. I was in a locked position; escape was not possible. I resigned myself to reliving the ordeal. I went over everything with a microscope. *Had I not been patient? Had I not exercised extreme forbearance in the face of each obstacle?* My mind could not comprehend the reason why I was denied even the smallest courtesy. *What criminal act had I committed to be so utterly dismissed and denigrated? What had I done to be deemed unworthy of the slightest trace of civility?* As I pondered these questions a perspective dawned; it was a perspective that I wanted desperately to dismiss as being unworthy of anyone in the field of education. But, the thought would not leave my mind. There was no other explanation for my treatment. The heinous offence of which I was guilty was that I was 'brown'. There was no way around it. I was not 'black'; I did not share the pigmentation of the 'preferred colour' at that time in Trinidad's history. The ability to lay claim to a black ancestry also allowed one to lay claim to the finest government jobs. It would naturally follow, therefore, that being 'brown' and of Asian ancestry, was grounds for Denial and Rejection.

I was troubled as to the reason why my counterpart, Mr. Winchester, had adopted such a one-sided view. *Did not both black and brown, share a common history?*

Frank Maraj

> *Did not History teach that*
> *Decades ago in a distant land,*
> *The black man was snatched from the cradle of his precious Soil*
> *By the Long arm of Inhumanity*
> *And transported to a foreign land and enslaved,*
> *Shorn of everything familiar?*

And History wept....

> *And did not History also teach that*
> *Decades ago, in another distant land,*
> *The brown man was also snatched*
> *From the cradle of poverty*
> *And transported to the new land,*
> *As indentured labourers?*

And History rejoiced that the two,
Tilled the land together.

Decades later the people of the island became splintered. They broke down into factions that fell along the line of colour. The Whites were regarded as interlopers and were strongly "encouraged" to leave their positions of power and leadership within the business community. The prevailing Black government quickly rushed in to fill the roles vacated by the Whites with members bearing a consistency in both their political views and their *pigmental* hues. It seemed that there was little room in their politics for the Brown. Decisions were made to exclude him from the political mainstream. These decisions were not always subtle. The plan worked. Little by little, those who were able sought alternative opportunities abroad. Now, I, too, had joined the ranks of the disillusioned and the disenfranchised.

History wept for her forgotten children and the child called Discrimination was born. In time, this child evolved and married full-fledged Racism. Together they flourished on the island, spawning many offspring.

And history's dream was shattered.

So, too, were my dreams shattered by the child spawned by Discrimination and Racism. *But, how could that be? Was I not born a native Trinidadian?* All my life I had held on to a dream. And my thoughts returned to the moment in time when that dream became my all. I can see it clearly as if it had only just occurred.

Ma and I were walking the cows across the savannah at the back of our property bordering the railroad tracks. I must have watched this scene play itself out a thousand times or more: a train stopped on the tracks; students waiting to disembark; students on their way to St. Charles Boys' School or St. Charles Girls' School. I so admired the boys and their uniforms; I was in awe of their blue shirts and striped ties, their khaki shorts, and their white socks and black shoes. I so wanted to be one of them. It became my dream.

That day, a tremendous sadness gripped me as I stood riveted to my spot. I had been unable to write the exam that would have allowed me to attend a free government sponsored school had I passed. Even though the chance of passing was slim, the *possibility* of passing existed. Now, however, I felt doomed; the only alternative to the free government sponsored school was a private school... and this private option was not free—hence, my sadness.

Watching those students in their school uniforms brought my dream back to life. I wanted to go to high school. I needed to go to high school. It was really that simple. In my little-boy mind, it was all so clear. That simple desire translated itself into a vision that became implanted firmly in my soul. I wanted to wear that uniform: blue shirt, striped tie, khaki pants, and socks and shoes. My mind was consumed with that sole purpose; going to high school became my obsessive dream.

Soon the train was gone and we were free to cross the tracks; none of this registered in my mind. I was in another world. Ma reached out to me with her voice, "Frankie, where is yo mind? What yo thinking?"

When I failed to answer, she teased, "Sometimes, yo act crazy. Come on, we don't have all day."

My body may have moved in unison with Ma and the cows as we crossed the tracks, but my mind was far removed from that present reality.

I was immersed in a very distant world, a world of high school and education, a world of uniforms and ties and socks and shoes. That is how I saw myself in my mind: that is the snapshot of the dream I kept hidden and locked away in my heart. I told no one.

Once again, I dusted off that picture in my mind. Knowing that I had achieved that dream and had gone far beyond my childhood imaginings brought me such joy. Then I made new dreams: dreams of high school and university and of an eventual return to my homeland where *all* could be one... dreams that had been effectively erased by the very real nightmare bearing the name *Winchester*. Once more I heard the corrosive accusation, "You people purchase your degrees."

Had I not stayed the course? Had I not remained true to my childhood dream? Had I not proven my worth with dogged determination and sacrifice? It was painful to consider even for a moment that anyone would think that I did not *earn* my degrees. In my mind, that indictment was the ultimate mockery and my preoccupation with it invited madness.

Again, I fought to alter my mindset. In thinking about what *might* have been I saw the face of my professor, Dr. McNeil; in *his* confidence was born *my* optimism for Trinidad.

For a mere moment, I held paradise in the palm of my hand; for a mere moment, I dared to believe that my dream to teach at the University of the West Indies could come true; for a mere moment I dared to hope that Tunapuna might again be my home. The dream was so close to becoming a reality; I could taste it.

How easily was this dream snatched away!

Then a voice broke the silence snapping me out of my reverie: "Ladies and gentlemen, we are about to land in Winnipeg, Canada." Suddenly, the clouds of despair parted, and a ray of sunshine shone through the clouds.

In my mind's eye, I beheld Diana holding Trevor and whispering, "Trevs, Daddy is coming home; yes, Daddy is coming home."

That picture—that image of Diana holding Trevor was the defining "snapshot."

That picture represented the sum total of my life; suddenly, it was all so clear. I knew what I had to do; I had to create a new dream—a dream that represented my new reality... in Canada.

Our family "snapshot" was already being transformed. Trevor was soon to have a new playmate; that reality was just months away.

Just days ago I was forced to navigate the raging waters of racism.
I was tossed into the dismal sea of discrimination.
Returning to Canada, I hoped for calmer waters.

The picture was developing.
It was becoming clearer.

My heart was making room for Canada.
Would Canada make room in its heart for me?
The question that remained was this:

Canada, wilt thou have me once again?

******

Also by Frank Maraj

SNAPSHOTS
   A LIFE
      REVISITED

Published by: Trafford (2008)
ISBN: 9781426903861

A reflection on a young Trinidadian's life - full of heartache, regret, and hope. By chronicling Snapshots of his life, Maraj allows readers to gain some understanding of a very different culture - growing up poor in Trinidad. He struggles with balancing his responsibilities to the family after his father's premature death, with his compelling desire to go abroad to study.